Mafia Organizations

How do mafias work? How do they recruit people, control members, conduct legal and illegal business, and use violence? Why do they establish such a complex mix of rituals, rules, and codes of conduct? And how do they differ? Why do some mafias commit many more murders than others? This book makes sense of mafias as *organizations*, via a collative analysis of historical accounts, official data, investigative sources, and interviews. Catino presents a comparative study of seven mafias around the world, from three Italian mafias to the American Cosa Nostra, Japanese Yakuza, Chinese Triads, and Russian Mafia. He identifies the organizational architecture that characterizes these criminal groups, and relates different organizational models to the use of violence. Furthermore, he advances a theory on the specific functionality of mafia rules and discusses the major *organizational dilemmas* that mafias face. This book shows that understanding the organizational logic of mafias is an indispensable step in confronting them.

MAURIZIO CATINO is Professor of Sociology of Organizations at the University of Milan – Bicocca, and Visiting Scholar in the Department of Sociology at New York University. His writing has been published in *Organization Studies*, *European Journal of Sociology*, *Scandinavian Journal of Management*, and *Cognition Technology and Work*, among others. His most recent book is *Organizational Myopia* (Cambridge, 2013).

T0349192

Mafia Organizations

The Visible Hand of Criminal Enterprise

Maurizio Catino

Professor of Sociology of Organizations at the University of Milan – Bicocca, and Visiting Scholar in the Department of Sociology at New York University

CAMBRIDGE
UNIVERSITY PRESS

University Printing House, Cambridge CB2 8BS, United Kingdom

One Liberty Plaza, 20th Floor, New York, NY 10006, USA

477 Williamstown Road, Port Melbourne, VIC 3207, Australia

314–321, 3rd Floor, Plot 3, Splendor Forum, Jasola District Centre, New Delhi – 110025, India

79 Anson Road, #06–04/06, Singapore 079906

Cambridge University Press is part of the University of Cambridge.

It furthers the University's mission by disseminating knowledge in the pursuit of education, learning, and research at the highest international levels of excellence.

www.cambridge.org
Information on this title: www.cambridge.org/9781108476119
DOI: 10.1017/9781108567183

© Maurizio Catino 2019

This publication is in copyright. Subject to statutory exception and to the provisions of relevant collective licensing agreements, no reproduction of any part may take place without the written permission of Cambridge University Press.

First published 2019

Printed in the United Kingdom by TJ International Ltd. Padstow Cornwall

A catalogue record for this publication is available from the British Library.

Library of Congress Cataloging-in-Publication Data
Names: Catino, Maurizio, author.
Title: Mafia organizations : the visible hand of criminal enterprise / Maurizio Catino.
Description: New York : Cambridge University Press, [2018] | Includes bibliographical references and index.
Identifiers: LCCN 2018035537| ISBN 9781108476119 (hardback) | ISBN 9781108466967 (pbk.)
Subjects: LCSH: Mafia. | Organized crime. | Organizational sociology.
Classification: LCC HV6441 .C384 2018 | DDC 364.106–dc23
LC record available at https://lccn.loc.gov/2018035537

ISBN 978-1-108-47611-9 Hardback
ISBN 978-1-108-46696-7 Paperback

Cambridge University Press has no responsibility for the persistence or accuracy of URLs for external or third-party internet websites referred to in this publication and does not guarantee that any content on such websites is, or will remain, accurate or appropriate.

To my parents and my brothers.
To Delia, Martina, and Anna.

Contents

Figures

Tables

Acknowledgments

A great many people gave generously of their time and knowledge in discussing the ideas in this book. I would like to thank Delia Baldassarri, Francesco Calderoni, Paolo Campana, Gino Cattani, Francesco Curcio, Nando Dalla Chiesa, Marco Del Gaudio, Itena Dhrami, Diego Gambetta, Giuseppe Gennari, Alex Hortis, Jim Jacobs, Sharon Ingrid Kwok, Kent Lee, Frederick Martens, Monica Massari, Francesco Moro, Antonio Mutti, Victor Nee, Salvo Palazzolo, Valeria Pizzini-Gambetta, Michele Prestipino, Selwyn Raab, Ernesto Savona, Salvatore Sberna, Anna Sergi, Louise Shelley, Elisa Superchi, Paolo Storari, Federico Varese, and Peng Wang.

I benefited greatly from comments and suggestions I have received at invited lectures and conferences. In particular, I presented at the American Sociological Association Annual Conference (August 2013), the Puck Seminar of the Department of Sociology at New York University (May 2014), the European Consortium for Political Research General Conference (Prague, September 2016), the Department of Sociology at Cornell University (November 2016), and the American Society of Criminology General Conference (November 2016 and 2017).

I am grateful to the Department of Sociology at New York University for hosting me as a visiting scholar in the past few years. Parts of this project were carried out in this context. Chapters 4 and 5 build on, revise, and update the content of two previously published journal articles: namely, "How Do Mafias Organize? Conflict and Violence in Three Mafia Organizations" (Catino 2014), and "Mafia Rules: The Role of Criminal Codes in Mafia Organizations" (Catino 2015). All translations into English of quotations from sources in other languages are my own.

Introduction

Observing the actions of various mafias, certain questions arise: Why do they establish and follow such a complex mix of rituals, rules, and codes of conduct? How and why do they enter legal businesses? How do they reconcile the requirements of secrecy with those of visibility? Why do some commit many more murders than others? Why do some target high-profile people far more often? How, in the recruitment processes, do they handle the trade-off between admitting family members and attracting the most promising and skillful foot soldiers?

These are just some of the questions that this book will attempt to answer.

Many books have been written about mafias. This book, however, approaches the topic from a new and different perspective, with the aim of making sense of mafias as organizations. Mafias must be considered as organizations because they possess all the distinctive aspects of the latter: a coordinated collective action; a division of labor with roles that are varied and defined; careers and systems of reward and punishment; a system of control and command with related communication channels, rules, and codes of conduct; a clear distinction between members and nonmembers; and formalized recruiting systems with initiation rituals for novices. In addition, they must be seen as organizations because as such they are able to carry out criminal activities at levels that no individual or group, without mechanisms of coordination, could possibly attain. Organizational analysis should therefore precede any other perspective in the study of mafias. Yet, public and scientific discussion lacks a clear understanding of the organizational side of these extralegal organizations. This book, through the perspective of organization theory, aims to understand the behavior of these particular organizations.

To consider and analyze mafias as formal organizations makes it possible to provide answers to our questions, starting with the main assumption that the type of organization makes a difference. To understand the behavior of people who are members of a group, it is fundamental to know how the group is organized. Therefore, to understand the *mafioso* criminal behavior, how mafias work, how they do business, and how they use violence, we must first understand how mafias are organized.

Examining the different kinds of mafia organization, it can clearly be seen that not all forms of organization are equal. In this book, I intend to explain how different modes of organizing determine the behavior, the conflicts, and the use of violence in mafias. The purpose is not to offer a theory of the origins of the mafias, but a theory about, or more accurately, a perspective on, the behavior of mafias as types of formal organization. Of course, mafias are hardly comparable, even remotely, to the Weberian ideal type of bureaucracy (Weber 1922), with written rules and rigid administrative procedures.

Mafias are a specific type of formal organization. They are organizations, not corporations. Organizations and corporations are not the same. All corporations are organizations, but not all organizations, of course, are corporations. Mafias do not have offices, addresses (except the Yakuza), opening and closing hours, etc., and they tend to leave few signs and traces of their presence, except when they intentionally want to signal something.

Mafia organizations are highly adaptive and long-lived, far more so than many legitimate firms. Despite working in extremely hostile environments, violating laws, committing crimes, and being subject to intense prosecution by law enforcement agencies, they are among the most resilient ever known. For instance, the Sicilian Cosa Nostra has its roots in the mid-nineteenth century, the American Cosa Nostra in the early years of the twentieth century, while the Yakuza and Triads go back to some centuries before.

Mafias are not mere criminal organizations: they would otherwise probably have vanished a long time ago. They are economic organizations that derive their strength from the fact that they sell protection and services (often forcibly imposed) that someone buys. Above all, however, they are deeply embedded in the economy, in politics, and in society. No criminal organization has ever infiltrated legitimated institutions in society in the way that mafias have proved capable of doing. Mafia physiology shows how relevant interrelationships with the "legal" world are, in order for them to carry out their activities. Without the ability to operate in this world – without, in other words, the complicity of many legal actors – the mafia would be very small beer indeed.

Mafias have been studied by various academic and research communities – criminologists, sociologists, economists, historians, political scientists, and legal scholars. Nevertheless, organization studies have conspicuously neglected mafias – despite the fact that organized crime, and mafias in particular, controls large and remunerative illegal markets.

Moreover, they also operate in legal markets, affecting the economic development of entire regions. Finally, they have longer lives than many legal organizations. With some exceptions, organization studies have preferred to study legal and transparent organizations, developing most of their theories and management models on the legitimate business organization (the corporation) and the bureaucratic form of organization.

Why did this happen? Shadowy organizations such as mafias are not easy to decipher. One of the main reasons why mafias are understudied as organizations may be that they are almost inaccessible to scientific study: reliable data are hard to come by and standard data collection methods are severely limited. Excluding interceptions (telephone and environmental) and ex-mobster statements (which always require very careful consideration), most sources and documents are *about* the mafias, not *from* the mafias – not, that is, actually produced by them, given that they are organizations that carefully avoid the production of written documents. This is not true only for mafias, but also for most hidden and clandestine organizations such as terrorist groups. Analyzing how they are managed requires more than studying the sensational aspects of group actions, such as strange rituals and heinous homicides.

If the study of criminal organizations is generally difficult, the study of mafias is further hindered by four main factors, clearly spelled out in Gambetta (1994). First of all, the subject is highly *emotional*: mafias' cruelties and their impact on society make it difficult for scholars to maintain an objective perspective. Second, there is a lack of *empirical evidence*: only in the last few decades have law enforcement agencies and judicial bodies specifically focused on the mafias, distinguishing them from other criminal organizations. Third, *mass media* – especially books, movies, and TV series – have contributed to the diffusion of a romanticized and overly exciting representation of mafia life. Finally, there is a *no shared theoretical framework*; as a result, scholars have adopted different, and sometimes opposing, perspectives.

The result is that, despite having a theoretical and conceptual apparatus more than adequate to study a socially and organizationally relevant phenomenon, organization studies on the mafias are rather few. It certainly does not mean that the main studies on the phenomenon do not consider the organizational aspects of the mafias. There is a specialist literature on organized crime and mafias. By and large, these literatures constitute separate fields, and none systematically uses an organization science perspective. Simply put, investigation by those – the organizational scholars – who would be equipped to carry it out is scarce. This book bridges two areas of research, organization studies and mafia studies, that have much to say to one another, but have rarely been integrated.

Analyzed from within, mafias appear less organized than they might seem to an outside observer. Constant tension exists in these organizations: competition, disloyalty, communication breakdowns, arguments, quarrels, and other forms of disorganization are the order of the day. The history of these organizations is also a story of fierce internal struggles for power. All mafias are conflicting groups, where conflicts may be latent or manifest, and although the degree of conflict is variable, generally there are very few mafia heads who die of old age. In some especially conflicting mafias, characterized by a "horizontal organizational order" (which we will call *clan-based*), longevity is really very low, and the average life span of a member is closer to that of a man at the dawn of the industrial age than to that of an individual in the twenty-first century. Nevertheless, the fact that problems and tension exist within mafias does not exclude them from being described as organizations. No organization is, in fact, free from conflict and tension – not law enforcement agencies, not universities, not business firms, not even the church. Hardly surprising, then, that this is also a feature of mafias. What is certainly different, however, is the way in which conflicts are handled, with the frequent use of violence.

If mafias are organizations – something that many, though not all, scholars agree upon – what type of organization are they? Are they an organizational phenomenon sui generis, or are there similarities to other kinds of organizations, such as legitimate economic organizations? Some observers have defined mafias as a model of management,[1] urging the managers of legitimate organizations to learn from the example of criminal organizations. Of course, they did not – we hope – mean that legitimate organizations should engage in illegal activities: rather that the low number of management levels, capacity for adaptation, flexibility in managing business, and control over subordinates were considered an effective model for American corporate executives.

To understand mafias, two commonplace ideas have to be set aside. The first is that if it is stated that a mafia is organized (such as the Sicilian Cosa Nostra), it means that it is also hierarchical, like a Hobbesian pyramid culminating in a Leviathan boss of bosses. The second is that if, instead, higher-level bodies of coordination are lacking, as in the case of many Camorra clans, then this means that there is no organization. Aspects relating to organizational order and coordination are central to the understanding of organizational functioning. An organization, as

---

[1] M. Goodman (2011), What business can learn from organized crime, *Harvard Business Review*, November, 27–30; "Mafia Management", *The Economist* ("Schumpeter" section), August 27, 2016, 51.

Wilson noted, "is not simply, or even principally, a set of boxes, lines, and titles on an organizational chart ... The most important thing to know is how that coordination is accomplished" (1989, 24).

Mafias have been described both as hypercentralized, according to a "bureaucratic-corporate model" (Cressey 1969), and as "patron–client networks," in terms of culture, kinship, and patron–client relationships (Albini 1971; Ianni and Reuss-Ianni 1972). As we will see, both of these conceptions prove to be reductive and inappropriate. Mafias cannot be categorized either as having the corporate bureaucratic form typical of a multinational firm, or as having a centerless network form. Nor are they reducible to a typical Southern Italian cultural phenomenon, as has long been claimed by some scholars, in particular in Italy: how, otherwise, is it possible to explain the existence of such organizations in culturally very different countries, such as Japan, China, Russia and the United States? From an organizational point of view, mafias are not based on a mechanistic model, such as Max Weber's ideal type of legal-rational bureaucracy (Weber 1922), but on an organic model (Burns and Stalker 1961). They are economic organizations characterized by a mix of clan organizational form and feudal hierarchy, with the presence, in almost all cases, of higher-level bodies of coordination.

In studying mafias as organizations, it is important not to be limited to an in-depth analysis of one single organization: it is necessary to consider a larger number of cases, in order to highlight, by comparison, similarities and differences. This book looks at various mafia organizations in different countries: in particular, the three Italian mafias (the Sicilian Cosa Nostra, the Camorra, and the 'Ndrangheta), the American Cosa Nostra, the Japanese Yakuza, the Hong Kong Triads, and the Russian Mafia (*Vor-v-zakone*, thief-in-law). The interesting fact is that, despite originating in different historical contexts and in places very distant one from another, the various mafias are characterized by common organizational features. These similarities seem to derive, not from a process of mutual understanding and learning (possible only for the Italian mafias and the American Cosa Nostra), but rather from the common problems that the different organizations have had to face over time. In other words, rather than isomorphism, it has been a matter of a common evolutionary and adaptive response to common problems and needs by different organizations.

Turning to the content, there are four main themes in this book. In Chapter 1, mafias are analyzed as a particular type of secret society and, following Gambetta (1993), as a particular form of organized crime that produces and sells private protection. In so doing, it dispenses with three main misunderstandings concerning the nature of mafias: namely,

(1) that mafias are a bureaucratic-corporate organization; (2) that mafias are not a formal organization, but a cultural phenomenon, or a particular *forma mentis*; and (3) that mafias are nothing more than a loose criminal network. Contrary to these conceptions, the chapter argues that mafias are a specific type of illegal economic organization.

Chapter 2 examines basic features of the organizational architecture of mafias. In particular, it considers the recruitment mechanisms and complex rituals that characterize organizational life, its specific learning and accounting systems, the management of internal transaction costs, as well as the mafia as a particular form of clan organization. Finally, the chapter delineates the mafia organizational structures, distinguishing between two different levels that are frequently confused with each other: (1) the level of the basic organizational unit – called *family*, *clan*, *'ndrina*, *ikka*, *brigade*, etc. – and (2) the metaorganizational level.

The basic organizational unit comprises the basic organizational level common to all the mafias and is composed of individuals who perform specific organizational roles. It is always characterized by a hierarchical form of structure, with an authoritative center represented by a leader. The metaorganizational level instead includes the higher-level bodies of coordination (HLBC) that certain mafias develop over time to regulate specific aspects of organizational life. The combination of these two levels, organizational and metaorganizational (where present), constitutes the overall mafia organization. The variety of combinations of these two levels gives rise to two different forms of government: clan-based and clan-based federation.

The *clan-based* system is based on a plurality of organizational decision makers who can act and make strategic decisions independently of each other and without having to account to higher-level bodies of coordination. In a *clan-based federation* system, on the other hand, there is a partial cession of sovereignty on the part of the basic organizational units in favor of higher-level bodies of coordination, but only with respect to certain aspects of collective organizational life. While these aspects may be quite significant, they do not relate to the business methods of the organization's individual components. In a federal system, HLBC are involved in resolving any disputes that may arise by minimizing the negative externalities arising from conflicts and excessive violence, in developing strategies of collective interest, in identifying and eliminating potential enemies of the organization, and in establishing and enforcing the rules.

Clan-based and *clan-based federation* forms are not immutable. The organizational history of the mafias shows how these patterns vary over time, moving from one system to another in the course of organizational life, as a result of endogenous factors (the degree of cohesion or conflict between clans, organizational leadership, etc.) and exogenous factors – above all, repression on the part of law enforcement agencies.

Chapter 3 analyzes in detail the main features of mafia organizational structures. Through the description of organizational structures, we will see how the mafias have different organizational configurations and how they impact organizational behavior. Organizational forms of the *clan-based federation* type, characterized by collusion between the various business components, and thanks to the higher-level bodies of coordination, seem to be more effective in curbing violence, compared to the *clan-based* organizational type. The latter, instead, is characterized by competition and greater conflict between clans for the acquisition of resources. Using data about the Italian mafias (the Sicilian Cosa Nostra, the 'Ndrangheta, and the Camorra), in Chapter 4 we see how the mafias characterized by a vertical organizational form tend to commit fewer overall homicides but a greater number of high-profile murders, such as those of magistrates, journalists, trade unionists, politicians, and members of law enforcement agencies.

This is because the presence of higher-level bodies of coordination enables mafias to resolve internal conflicts by reducing intraorganizational violence and developing strategy. They can identify the enemy outside the organization – those figures who, through public or private action, can undermine the security and economic interests of the organization. In contrast, mafias characterized by a horizontal organizational structure, with no higher-level bodies of coordination, seem incapable of effectively settling internal disputes and controlling violence. While they therefore tend to commit many more homicides, high-profile murders are almost wholly absent or at least significantly lower compared to other mafias: for these mafias, the main enemy is the rival clan, rather than the law enforcement agencies.

As illegal organizations, mafias cannot turn to third-party actors to resolve disputes and enforce agreements. Therefore, the mafias themselves have to carry out this function, through various methods such as the definition of internal rules and the use of violence, if necessary, to punish noncompliance. This absence of third-party recourse raises an important question. How can criminal organizations that lack legal mechanisms of dispute resolution, and are unable to establish binding contracts, work efficiently? As we see in Chapter 5, they establish and enforce organizational rules. Rules are an essential aspect in the life of any organization. Paradoxically, organizational rules are especially important for criminal organizations, such as mafias, for two main reasons. First, they cannot rely on law and government to enforce norms and settle disputes. Second, they need to cooperate among themselves in order to preserve their economic interests. They do not live in anarchy; they are subjected to the law of the outlaw. Even if the context of criminal organizations is radically different from the context of legitimate organizations, mafias use organizational rules for the same reason that legitimate organizations do: (1) to ensure organization, coordination, and cooperation among their members and their organizational units. In addition to this function, however, mafias need rules (2) to settle conflicts and to contain violence that, otherwise, could be destructive for the organization; and (3) to maintain secrecy and conceal information regarding their illegal activities from the outside. Legitimate organizations, on the other hand, do not need rules to settle disputes, given that they can rely on government and courts, and require secrecy only in relation to a limited number of activities (usually concerning patents, innovation, etc.). Of course, as indeed happens in many organizations, rules can be violated or employed for personal ends. But the violation of the rule only serves to confirm the existence of the rule, just as the violation of a law does not mean that the law does not exist.

Finally, in Chapter 6, we see how, far from being all-powerful organizations, as they are often portrayed, mafias suffer from multiple problems and are forced to deal with diverse and complex *organizational dilemmas* that are not easily solved. For example, if they grow in size, they increase economies of scale but reduce security and privacy. If, on the other hand, these latter aspects are given priority, then the coordination necessary to achieve objectives is penalized. Another organizational dilemma is represented by the use of violence: this is an important resource for mafias, a required means to solve many problems and to maintain their reputation. However, making frequent use of violence, mafias increase their visibility and attract the interest of law enforcement agencies. Another organizational decision regards the recruitment system: based on blood ties, it can allow greater secrecy and trust, but can result in scarcity of resources or operational skills. In this final chapter I show that these dilemmas have no single, definitive solution, but require adequate management capable of handling the continuing tensions between opposite needs. Analyzing mafia organizational action in terms of fundamental dilemmas that are always present makes it possible to escape both a rigid environmental determinism and a rigid organizational subjectivism, according to which mafias are all-powerful and can do whatever they want.

As regards the sources used, we will refer in particular to investigative and judicial sources including eavesdropping and wiretapping, statements from collaborators with justice, administrative data on murder and other mafia crimes, reports by parliamentary committees and other political institutions, historical accounts, secondary sources from various disciplines (mainly sociology, economics, political science, and criminology), and interviews and discussions with key witnesses such as magistrates and representatives of the law enforcement agencies.

Understanding mafias as organizations is important not only from a scientific, but also from a more practical point of view. Understanding the physiology and organizational logic of mafias is an indispensible step in order to combat them. An awareness of their dilemmas and organizational characteristics can offer law enforcement agencies, political actors, and civil society useful guidance on how to direct laws, public policies, and law enforcement actions more effectively to the activities of the mafias.

In conclusion, a word regarding the subtitle, *The Visible Hand of Criminal Enterprise*. Adam Smith, with the idea of the "invisible hand," and Friedrich von Hayek (1973), with the "beauty of the market" theory, emphasized the spontaneous origins of the market, and autonomous adaptation of a spontaneous kind. Organization theory, however, on the one hand, has moved to the fore the active role of organizations in "constructing" markets, and, on the other, with Chester Barnard (1938), the role of, not spontaneous cooperation, but induced cooperation, of an intentional kind determined by formal organizations: the "visible hand" of organizing. The visible hand of mafia organizations may suppress the invisible hand of the market. In other words, in the legal, as in the criminal, world, organization makes a difference.

The English jurist Frederic William Maitland, referring to history books, stated that "a book should make you hungry," in the sense of a hunger to learn, a hunger to search. If, in some way, this book arouses such a "hunger," then it will have achieved its purpose.

1   What Type of Organization Are Mafias?

Despite their social and economic relevance, mafias have been conspicuously neglected by organization studies.[1] With some exceptions, organization studies have preferred to study legal and transparent organizations, developing most of their theories and management models on the legitimate business organization (the corporation) and the bureaucratic form of organization.[2] The result is that, despite having a useful set of tools, categories, and concepts to study criminal organizations, organization studies have said almost nothing about this phenomenon.[3]

Mafias and criminal organizations evade the different taxonomies and typologies developed over time by organization scholars (Parsons 1956; Burns and Stalker 1961; Etzioni 1961; Blau and Scott 1962; Emery and Trist 1965; Woodward 1965; Thompson 1967; Perrow 1986, etc.). While many concepts developed by organization studies are suitable for the understanding of mafia organizations, management theory developed to deal with legal companies operating in legal circles does not always work as well for understanding criminal enterprises. For example, a legal company may decide to reduce the level of intermediation that separates

---

[1] For example, many of the most important manuals, reference texts, and edited volumes in the discipline do not address the case of mafia organizations; nor are there empirical references to this type of organization (i.e., Blau and Scott 1962; Hall 1977; Perrow 1986; Handel 2003; Baum 2005; Clegg et al. 2006; Scott and Davis 2007).

[2] See Feldman 1988; Bok 1989; Potter 1994; Anand and Rosen 2008; Grey 2013; Costas and Grey 2014; Sergi 2016.

[3] This problem not only concerns the study of mafias but also other types of organization. As Renate Mayntz notes: "From the large diversity of organizations covered in the path-breaking early texts (Etzioni 1961; Blau and Scott 1962; Hall 1977), organization studies have come to concentrate increasingly on one specific type: economic organizations, or firms" (2004, 5). Moreover, step by step, other kinds of organization have also disappeared from the field called organization studies, such as voluntary associations, hospitals, research institutes, and even the agencies of public administration. In some cases these have become the focus of separate and independent research fields. In general, organizational studies have taken little note of the "secrecy" aspect, and, when they have, have analyzed it mainly within the context of legal organizations (Costas and Grey 2014; 2016) and only rarely in illegal ones.

the supplier from the customer, thus increasing profits previously dispersed throughout the distribution chain. A criminal enterprise, on the other hand, in order to reduce risks and safeguard secrecy, may increase these levels of intermediation, so as to add extra levels of insulation between the company and the controllers. In other words, the logic of internalization or the outsourcing of activities is not only related to criteria of cost or efficiency, but must also take into account criteria of security and privacy.

This also applies to terrorist organizations. For example, certain groups of terrorists have chosen to strengthen their formal organization (Shapiro 2013, 16) when security conditions allowed them: from the mid-1990s until the end of 2001, Al-Qaeda pursued a highly coordinated and verticalized model. From 2002 to 2003, due to the intense repression that followed the 9/11 attack, the organization's weakening position favored a more decentralized model, based on the creation of franchise affiliates (Mendelsohn 2016). The choice between the two models was, however, dictated more by reasons of security and privacy, rather than the criterion of effectiveness of one solution with respect to the other.

Mafias present several features common to other types of clandestine organizations (Stohl and Stohl 2011), such as *underground organizations* (Varon 2004), *covert networks* (Carley 2006), *dark networks* (Arquilla and Ronfeldt 2001), *illicit networks* (Eilstrup-Sangiovanni and Jones 2008), *secret societies* (Simmel 1906), *enclaves* (Squires 2002), and *shadow states* (Reno 1995).

Like other hidden organizations, mafias are characterized by the fact that (1) members mutually agree upon keeping their own and other affiliations secret (for at least some period); (2) internal activities and collective governance structures operate furtively, outside the public realm; (3) external traces of the existence of the organization eventually become known (or at least rumored) outside the membership, although the organization may be completely unknown outside its own membership for long periods (Stohl and Stohl 2011, 1199).

According to Smith (1980; 1994) there are fundamental similarities between criminal organizations and legitimate businesses. One fundamental difference between mafias (and other criminal organizations) and legal organizations is that the former cannot use the law to resolve disputes. As is known, contract law serves as the ultimate appeal, delimiting threat positions.[4] The lack of third parties to resolve disputes and the

---

[4] As Karl Llewellyn wrote: "The major importance of legal contract is to provide a framework for well-nigh every type of group organization and for well-nigh every type

impossibility of resorting to the law represent distinctive elements of these organizations and help to explain organizational dynamics.

1.1   Different Conceptions and Some Misunderstandings

Three main conceptions characterize the debate concerning mafia organizations: (1) a mafia is like a bureaucratic-corporate organization; (2) a mafia is not a formal organization; it is a cultural phenomenon, a particular *forma mentis*; (3) a mafia is a kind of a criminal network.[5]

(1) The first perspective, the *bureaucratic-corporate model*, conceives the mafia as a hypercentralized organization, pyramidal and top-down, like an octopus with a head and a host of tentacles. There are a top level that makes all the decisions and a base that faithfully carries out these decisions. According to this view, mafia organizations are similar to multinational firms, with a CEO, many specialized different business units, and a division of work intentionally designed to achieve specific goals. The origin of this conception can be traced to an erroneous and oversimplified understanding of Donald Cressey's work (1967; 1969).[6]

of passing or permanent relation between individuals and groups ... a framework highly adjustable, a framework which almost never accurately indicates real working relations, but which affords a rough indication around which such relations vary, an occasional guide in cases of doubt, and a norm of ultimate appeal when relations cease in fact to work" (1931, 736–7).

[5] It should be pointed out that to start with the debate mainly involved two mafias in particular, the Sicilian and American Cosa Nostra, and gradually expanded to other mafias. It follows that the different perspectives refer in particular to these two mafias, although these considerations are largely extensible to other mafias. The debate has also widened considerably over the decades, and for further details readers are referred to Abadinsky 2013; Lombardo 2013. The United Nations Office on Drugs and Crime (UNODC) conducted a survey of forty organized crime groups in many countries around the world. The results were published in 2002 in a report that presents a typology of five different organizational models: *standard hierarchy*, *regional hierarchy*, *clustered hierarchy*, *core group*, and *criminal network*. Some of these models are basically superimposable (standard and regional hierarchy); others do not directly regard mafia organizations but other types of criminal groups. On the problem of "recognizing" the mafias, and on their ontology, see Santoro 2015.

[6] Cressey, a sociologist who served as consultant to the 1967 President's Commission Task Force on Organized Crime, was the first scholar to explain mafia behavior (in particular American Cosa Nostra) through an organizational approach, introducing a new paradigm. Cressey described the American Cosa Nostra, an organization whose members had Italian-American origins, as the most advanced and resilient form of organized crime. This criminal organization provided illegal goods and services and resorted to extortion and the corruption of public officials. They killed competitors, witnesses, alleged informants, as well as innocent people (see Martens 2017 for a historical account). Of course, Cressey's analysis was limited by the information available at the time, and he thus overestimated the level of coordination and centralization of the American mafia syndicate. Although the organizational model that

(2) The second perspective argues that the mafia is not an organization, nor a cohesive unit or a corporate group: rather, it is a cultural phenomenon (Hess 1973), a collective attitude (Hobsbawm 1959), or a method (Albini and MacIllwain 2012). The mafia is considered a cultural attitude, a *forma mentis*, and a form of power with no corporate dimension (Arlacchi 1986). "The *mafioso* exists, but not the mafia," stated Lestingi (1880, 292). The mafia is neither a sect nor an association; it has neither regulations nor statutes, claimed Pitrè (1889). The mafia was characterized then as a "*mafioso* spirit," a social practice, a behavior and a power, and not as a formal, secret organization (Blok 1974; Ianni 1976; Schneider and Schneider 1976).

(3) The third perspective affirms that mafias, like other types of organized crime, can be understood in terms of networks. Networks can be defined as a set of nodes (e.g., persons, organizations) linked by a set of social relations (e.g., friendship, transfer of funds, overlapping membership) of a specific type. Previous research suggests that social relations, kinship and *patron–client relationships* are the basis of criminal organizations (Albini 1971; Ianni and Reuss-Ianni 1972). Mafias are not formal organizations like business corporations; instead "they are responsive to culture and are patterned by tradition" (Ianni and Reuss-Ianni 1972, 153). Mafias are traditional social systems based on kinship networks, and "members (and their associates) are involved in independent legal and illegal activities that are their own and from which they derive income" (Haller 1992, 2).

The three perspectives briefly presented here have some limitations. The first overestimates the degree of articulation and organizational formalization; the second perspective does not take this into account at all; while the third confuses, at least in part, a method of analyzing relations with an organizational model. All three suffer from (1) an erroneous conception of what an organization is, while (2) the third is based on an erroneous conception of what a network is.

(1) *An erroneous conception of what an organization is*: The three different perspectives suffer from an inadequate understanding of what an organization is, as well as of the developments in organization theory. They

---

he described was quite rigid, static, and monolithic, his contribution was fundamental for the study of mafia organizations. Subsequently, many scholars criticized his work (Albini 1971; Albini and MacIllwain 2012) as a sort of "mafia mystique" (Smith 1975), often without a full understanding of his main argument. As von Lampe puts it, "tragically, his [Cressey's] importance lies not so much in the breadth and depth of his analysis but in serving as a sort of 'punching bag' for an entire generation of scholars who gave contour to their findings by seeking to contradict Cressey" (2016, 41).

commit a double error: (a) on the one hand, they refer to a totally unsuitable model of organization, such as the big corporation; (b) on the other, they confuse the characteristics of criminal markets – disorganized, in that they are often not monopolistic – with those organizations operating in that area, which must therefore be disorganized. Let's look at this in more detail.

(a) The reference model is inadequate because the three conceptions reduce the concept of organization to the model of the hierarchical and bureaucratic organization, taking as empirical references only some of the many models and types of organization, such as the ideal type of Weberian organization (Weber 1922), or big corporations, with their structure reducible to an organigram. This happens both in the perspective of the bureaucratic-corporate model, which considers mafias as formal organizations, and in the perspective that considers them as a cultural phenomenon, which distances itself from the formal approach, and criticizes it radically, in the case of the patron–client network model.

(b) Organizations can, in fact, assume a number of forms, more or less hierarchical, more or less horizontal. The debate, however, seems focused on the simplistic idea that if there is hierarchy, then there is organization: some scholars believe that the mafia is organized because it is hierarchical, others that it is disorganized because it lacks or is deficient in hierarchy. Hierarchy is, certainly, an important element in organizations, but the presence of a hierarchy is not enough in itself to define an aggregation of individuals as an organization. Similarly, the absence of a hierarchy is not sufficient in terms of not categorizing an organization as such. For example, The Orpheus Chamber Orchestra, founded in 1972, is a classical music orchestra that operates in the absence of a conductor, but this does not mean that it is not an organization. A second interpretative misconception derives from superimposing market characteristics on those of the organization that work in that market. So, if the market is disorganized – without, in other words, a collective entity capable of coordinating actions – then the organization working in that market is also disorganized. Studying certain illegal markets in New York (illicit bookmaking, loan-sharking, and dealing in drugs such as heroin), Reuter (1983) shows that there is no single organization able to control them, no central management that can direct and coordinate the multitude of actors and organizational units present. Instead, while the organizational units that carry out different activities are in fact organized hierarchically, and in some cases very powerful, like the mafias, there is no single center able to manage and coordinate the entire underworld – something that Cressey's thesis (1969) deems to exist. Illegal markets of this kind are, therefore, fragmented, without any kind of centralized direction and, to a certain extent, indeed, disorganized. Rather than talking about organized crime, then, Reuter says that it is necessary to speak of *disorganized crime*. Here, however, lurks the misunderstanding mentioned earlier: Reuter says that there is disorganized crime because it lacks a single entity capable of coordinating other actors and able to manage all criminal activities hierarchically. But he refers to the characteristics of the market, not the internal organizational structures of the criminal enterprises that operate there. In particular, his intention is to refute the theory put forward by Cressey that there was a kind of underworld monopoly in the hands of the mafia. Some readers have instead understood that the organizations were disorganized, not the market. The absence of an entity able to control the entire criminal market does not imply that the companies operating there are disorganized, and a careless reading is likely to confuse the absence of monopolistic control with the absence of organization. But in many industrial areas – for example, the automobile sector – there is no body that can control the entire market (fortunately for the consumer): this does not mean that the companies active in that area can be considered disorganized.

(2) *An erroneous conception of what a network is*: The first problem is that the third perspective, analyzing mafias in terms of networks, at times uses the concept of network as an alternative to that of organization. But the concept of an organizational network includes all the forms of relationship that are contained within an organization, which may be either horizontal (flat) or vertical (hierarchical). Mafias, like any other organization, evolve out of and are transcended by networks (von Lampe 2009): indeed, mafias heavily rely on the relationships among their members. According to scholars who follow this perspective, in organizations (understood in terms of the "big corporation" model), relationships between people are *tight*, while in mafias they are instead *loose*: the problem is that *loose* relationships are not considered as a degree of possible interaction, but rather as an indicator of the absence, or near-absence, of organization.

A certain amount of confusion arises, therefore, in proposing the concepts of organizational structure and those of networks as mutual alternatives. Moreover, relationships within mafias are anything but loose, as evidenced by the fact that it is (almost) impossible to get out (alive) from these organizations, and what can happen if certain rules are violated. They are more similar to "total institutions" (Goffman 1961) than to loosely coupled organizations, even though there are no physical barriers to the outside. As we will see in more detail in the next section, mafias are organizations in that there are coordinated collective action; division of labor with different and defined organizational positions and roles; a leadership system, a system of control and command with related channels and methods of communication; a system of rules, for the most part unwritten; a clear distinction between members and nonmembers; and formalized recruiting systems, with initiation rituals for novices. Mafias are not unified and rigidly hierarchical bureaucratic firms; nor are they reducible to patron–client relationships, because the network is, if anything, between stable positions and not only between people. People can go away (to be killed or arrested), but the positions remain, and so, in fact, does the organization.

Rather than being assimilable to one of the three perspectives outlined previously, mafias appear to be organizational hybrids, combining the main elements of reference of the three perspectives in the way that they function: hierarchy, strong social and blood ties, and networks.

1.2   Mafias as Organizations

Mafias are organizations with modules and models that differ one from the other, and so must be studied as organizational phenomena, albeit of a particular type. Before proceeding, it would be appropriate briefly to clarify some concepts that will be used in our analysis of mafias, by specifying what is meant by *organization*.

Organizations are man-made: they are social artifacts. They enable an organized form of collective action that single individuals, by definition, cannot obtain. They are intentional systems (Parsons 1956), in the sense that the characteristic that defines them, distinguishing from other types of social systems, is the primacy of orientation toward the achievement of specific objectives,[7] even if they are at times recalcitrant with respect to the ends for which they were designed (Perrow 2007), and this may produce unintended and unwanted consequences. To conceive the organization as a unitary actor would be rather controversial, a *fiction*, an overreaching that would lead to an anthropomorphic representation, simplifying reality and taking the observer in the wrong direction. To consider the organization as a unitary subject has some usefulness only in

---

[7] Objectives can be multiple and, sometimes, contradictory. In any case, in organizations, people's behavior is in some way finalized, and this makes activity with an organization different from simple sociable interaction between people.

terms of sketching a general picture of the relationships between organizations and serving the purpose of a preliminary investigation, before going on to analyzing the *interna corporis* of the organizations and how these internal dynamics affect relations with the external environment. According to teaching deriving from the Weberian tradition of organization studies, we can say that organizations can be understood better if they are considered as contexts within which conflicting interests act. The organization is seen, therefore, as a political arena, with actors who have divergent interests and aims, and enter into relationships of alliance and/or conflict with one other (Cyert and March 1963; Crozier and Friedberg 1977). The winning coalition becomes the dominant coalition that governs the organization, but always in an unstable and tendentially temporary way, as shown by the events of the *scalata dei Corleonesi* (the Corleonesi takeover)[8] in the Sicilian Cosa Nostra, which we will look at more closely in Section 4.2.

Organizations have boundaries, in the sense that there is a distinction between members and nonmembers, with the latter excluded from participation in organizational life. On that basis, we can define organizations as (1) social entities, (2) understood as a process of actions and decisions, (3) that pursue a goal or set of goals, (4) based on processes of differentiation and integration (5) with distinct roles assigned to participants and (6) with a system of authority recognized and accepted by the members as a decision maker, (7) in dynamic interaction with the external environment.

Let's have a closer look at this definition.

(1) Organizations distinguish between those who belong to the organization (called "made members" in some mafias) and those who do not belong. They are *social entities*, composed of people that contribute to the achievement of organizational activities in exchange for various types of incentives.

(2) Organizations are a *process of actions* endowed with intentional meaning and *decisions*, characterized by bounded rationality, oriented to realize the (3) *specific objectives* that distinguish each organization. The objectives are to be understood, not as the desires of a reified organization, nor even as the sum of the objectives of the participants, but as

---

[8] The Corleonesi clan is a faction within the Sicilian Cosa Nostra formed in the 1970s, so called because its most important leaders was from Corleone (a town in the province of Palermo, Sicily): Luciano Liggio, Salvatore (Totò) Riina, Bernardo Provenzano, and Leoluca Bagarella. Other clans from other territories outside Corleone then allied themselves with this faction.

future fields of action primarily defined by the ruling coalition, or by those who govern and control the organization.[9]

Each organization (4) tends to differentiate the activities necessary to achieve its objectives, allocating responsibilities and tasks to different organizational units (as is the case in the production process of a car, divided into subprocesses carried out by different units, or in a hospital, where activities are differentiated in various departments). The process of differentiation constitutes a functional requirement of the organization and determines the need for the integration processes that ensure coordination between the different units.

People in the organization cover (5) *specific roles*, involving the implementation of certain activities relating to the defined objectives. The roles are independent of the people assigned to them and are in some way independent of single individuals, even though each person can give a particular shape to the role he performs. The more a mafia group resembles a corporate organizational chart, the more stable it is, and the better able to handle a leader's death. It makes the organization stable: if one element is removed, the rest of the organizational machine can still function. Mafias are organizations, independent of the people who perform specific roles. When a person is arrested or dies, another is ready to take his place.

All organizations have a hierarchy, a (6) *system of formal authority* that is recognized as legitimate by the participants and made evident by the configuration of the organizational structure. Finally, each organization works (7) in an *environment*, in the sense of that which is external to the organization.

The environment constitutes the main source of uncertainty for an organization: it is made up of other organizations and can be divided into two levels: (a) the *task environment* (Dill 1958), which includes factors and elements that have a *direct* and *significant* impact on the organization in achieving its objectives (for example, where a company is concerned, competitors, suppliers, the labor market, consumers, trade unions, and financial institutions); (b) the *general environment*, which includes factors and forces that, while not having a direct impact on an organization's activities, may *indirectly* influence its behavior (such as government policies, sociocultural factors, technological innovation, and the economic conditions affecting the specific environment of the organization).

---

[9] The dominant coalition is to be understood more as a dynamic, changing process than as a static entity (Thompson 1967). Objectives can change over time, sometimes even contrary to the original objectives for which the organization was created, as has been highlighted in research by Michels (1911) and Selznick (1948).

These are the elements that define and constitute organizations; the lack of certain of these means that a social grouping cannot be defined as an organization, or as a *real* formal organization.[10] From the operational point of view, therefore, mafias are certainly organizations, though they are characterized by organizational models very different from those normally adopted to describe business organizations or public administrations. Studying one of the 24 families of the American Cosa Nostra, Anderson notes that the *family* does not function as a business firm and the boss is not the chief executive officer of a business empire: "The criminal firm operating in an illegal market is in a very different position from a legitimate business firm. Ownership of the firm is not legally recognized and thus cannot be legally transferred" (1979, 44). Rather than businesses, says Anderson, mafias are quasi-government structures: internalizing the cost of violence, distinguishing when this can, and cannot, be used legitimately; controlling the behavior of members so that there is no violence within the organization; and protecting the property rights of members are all functions, says Anderson, of a government rather than a business. This is because the actual provision of these services requires that "the exercise of authority and power in making and carrying out these decisions be viewed by the members as legitimate" (1979, 45). Anderson is right in saying that a mafia family is not assimilable to a business, but this does not mean, of course, that it is not an organization – although, as we have seen, of a particular kind.

Mafia organizations are involved in and provide protection through a variety of activities, both in illegal and criminal markets and in legal ones. In the underworld, mafias are active in many areas, such as extortion, drug trafficking, weapon trafficking, usury, cigarette smuggling, robbery, illegal gambling, and illegal immigration trafficking. In the upperworld (the world of legitimate business), mafias are active in many sectors, including construction, earthworks, catering, commerce, transportation, and many others. In these sectors, they can operate both "legally," in the sense of not necessarily violating the laws in force and merely managing

---

[10] For example, train passengers are not an organization, though they use trains as a means of transport, while the company that manages the service is. The public at a football match are not an organization, while the soccer team is. Spectators become an organization when they create a *fan club*, equipping themselves with the tools to support a team in sports events (stadium chants, banners, souvenirs, etc.). Sometimes the distinction between an organization and a nonorganization is not so obvious, as in the case of collective movements; however, the proposed definition makes it possible to identify most organizational phenomena. *Partial organizations*, too, which lack at least some elements of formal organizations, are examples of organizations (Ahrne and Brunsson 2011).

economic activities, and illegally, using their own personal brand to limit competition, corrupt public officials, and procure work and customers in illegal ways.[11] These activities can be controlled (1) directly by the mafia organization; (2) through subcontracting groups and criminal cells that are not an organic part of the mafia organization, which benefit from a percentage of the earnings (e.g., drug dealing);[12] or (3) in copartnership with other criminal groups and/or other mafia organizations. However, the core business of mafia organizations is providing protection and "market governance," the monopolistic control of every relevant illegal economic activity. Other criminals must ask their permission and pay for a specific task to be carried out. However, particularly in areas where mafias are newly present, certain of them tend to limit themselves to trading activities, rather than becoming involved in the protection business (Campana 2011). As we will see in Section 2.8.2, there are certain legal areas that are particularly porous in terms of mafia penetration.

According to some scholars (Abadinsky 2013; Hortis 2014), the organizational model most similar to that of certain mafias, such as the American Cosa Nostra, is represented by franchise companies (like the chains of hotels, restaurants, or clothing stores). With this model, the franchise companies allow the use of their trademark to franchisees in exchange for a percentage of the profits. The franchise company controls the minimum standards, assigns the territories for the activities, and resolves any eventual disputes. The franchisees are autonomous and economically independent, and make use of the brand to carry out their business. Similarly, the mafias (in this case the American Cosa Nostra) do not pay salaries, but allow their members and associates to operate using the trademark of the organization of reference, making money in both the underworld and the upperworld. The strength of the trademark lies in the reputation acquired over decades of activity and threats. This analogy certainly captures many aspects of the functioning of the mafias, especially the American Cosa Nostra. However, other mafias cannot be immediately related to such an organizational model, as we will see later.

---

[11] In a classic study, Annelise Anderson (1979) highlighted the various reasons mafias have for legitimate investment: 1) establishing a tax cover, 2) support for illegal market enterprises, 3) provision of services to members of the group, 4) diversification for reducing the risk of prosecution and conviction for illegal activities, 5) profits independent of illegal activities.

[12] For example, in the early years of the twenty-first century, the boss of the Camorra, Paolo di Lauro, organized narcotics traffic and distribution by giving the drug-selling areas over to various *capizona*, local bosses, "in concession." The beneficiary had to pay a percentage of his earnings, and in return, in addition to the use of the particular area, received protection from the clan, so that his business could be carried out without interference from other criminals (Di Fiore 2016, 307).

1.2.1   Mafia as a Type of Organized Crime

There are two fundamental elements that distinguish mafia[13] organizations from other forms of criminal organizations: (1) the government of illegal markets and the control of the territory in which they operate; (2) protection.

(1) With regard to the first point, many scholars have argued that mafias are criminal groups that aim at controlling entire markets and territories. Schelling points out that *organized crime* is substantially different from *crime that is organized* (1971, 72). Both operate in the world of illegal markets, but the former includes crime that involves functional role division, planning, and cooperation. The latter actually attempts to govern them, by seeking to achieve a monopolistic control on illegal economic activity.[14] Each mafia group exercises (or tries to exercise) control over all the licit and illicit activities taking place within its territorial jurisdiction. For example, with reference to the drug market, while a mafia organization can be involved in the production of drugs and their commercial distribution, what really distinguishes these organizations from other criminal structures is the desire to attain government over the markets and control over the territory. No one can consider carrying out a criminal activity of any importance without the prior approval of the relevant *family*, without risking the imposition of sanctions (OSPA Stajano 2010). Even licit activities, construction companies in particular, submit to the control of the family. According to the collaborator with justice of the Sicilian Cosa Nostra Salvatore Contorno, it is an easy matter, given the location of a building, to trace the family that protects the builder of the building itself (OSPA Stajano 2010, 112). This rule of rigid respect for family territory exists also, and above all, among the mafia members themselves, who cannot perform any activity without the approval of the relevant family. Homicides follow the same requirements: no one can be killed in a territory without the consent of the head of the

---

[13] The name "mafia" first appeared in 1863. Its most likely origins are from a play called *I Mafiusi di la Vicaria* (The Mobs of Vicaria). It initially indicated the Sicilian criminal organization, which later took on the name "Cosa Nostra" (Our Thing), and it is now used to indicate a specific type of organized crime. The play was about a group of criminals in the Palermo jail. In this drama, the "mafiuso" is the man of honor, the individual who adheres to a code of brotherhood and who displays courage and a sense of superiority. In a classified document of April 1865, signed by the then-Prefect of Palermo, Filippo Antonio Gualterio, the first reference is made to the mafia as a criminal association.

[14] There are, however, markets that cannot be monopolized, as they are too big, such as drugs or arms traffic, but this does not stop mafia organizations from operating in such markets.

family of that particular territory. Collaborator with justice of the Sicilian Cosa Nostra Vincenzo Marsala said that in order to carry out a homicide, "when it comes to local issues, the consent of the representative should always be sought; then, if the murder is to take place outside the territory of the family involved, then the consent of the representative of that other territory is required, and that of the district boss (*capomandamento*)."[15]

(2) *Protection.* In Schelling's view (1971), mafias do not supply a real service: the real business of organized crime is extortion from illegitimate and legitimate entrepreneurs. Organized crime forces protection on illegitimate operators, and goods and services on legitimate businesses under extortionate conditions. However, an increasing number of scholars claim that mafias are a form of governance that specializes in supplying a variety of services to business operators, and in particular, different forms of "private protection" (Gambetta 1993; Chu 2000; Varese 2001; 2014; Frye 2002; Hill 2003a; Campana 2011; Shortland and Varese 2014). This point of view was put forward in the nineteenth and the early twentieth century by Leopoldo Franchetti in 1876 and John Landesco in 1929 (Varese 2014).

Diego Gambetta argued that the essential characteristic of the Sicilian mafia is that it is "a specific economic enterprise, an industry which produces, promotes, and sells private protection" (1993, 1). He developed a "property rights theory of mafia emergence," according to which the Sicilian mafia can be understood as a response to the lack of trust in the state specifically affecting Southern Italy; as a response to a late and rapid transition to the market economy in the early nineteenth century, in the presence of a state unable to protect the newly granted property rights, and the supply of unemployed people with tendencies toward violence. Under such conditions, the mafia emerged to meet a high potential demand for private protection. As with the birth of the feudal system, a bottom-up process that took place because of the demand for power structures that would fill the void left by the imperial monarchy, so different mafias originated in order to fulfill a request for protection, arising from the weak power of the state and from the offer of protection from people in a position to employ violence.

Following this theory, mafia organizations are not only illegal entrepreneurs involved in the supply of illegal goods and service to the public. They are a set of firms specializing in the supply of private protection (Gambetta 1993): for example, protection against extortion, theft, police

---

[15] OSPA 1985, *Ordinanza Sentenza della Corte di Assise di Palermo contro Abbate Giovanni +706*, Palermo, November 8, vol. V, 904.

harassment, and competitors, as well as protection of property rights, and debt collection. They also provide protection by settling a wide range of conflicts and disputes, and intimidating customers, workers, and trade unionists for the benefit of employers. The mafia is a set of firms active in the protection industry under a recognizable feature: the word "mafia" has become a trademark in the protection market, a sort of brand – a trademark – of a severely violent reputation (Gambetta 1993, 155). In this context, violence is used to build up and maintain a protector's reputation as a credible protector.

In line with this argument, Varese (2010; 2014) identifies mafia groups as a subset of organized crime groups (OCGs), which specialize in protection. Mafias aspire "to govern transactions in the underworld by providing services of dispute settlement, cartel enforcement and more generally governance of illegal transactions" (Varese 2011, 12).

The term "mafia" can be used not only for the Sicilian mafia, but also as a general term for such OCGs that share the same core characteristics as the Sicilian mafia: the American Cosa Nostra (Reuter 1983; Gambetta and Reuter 1995), the Russian Mafia (Varese 2001), the Hong Kong Triads (Chu 2000), the Camorra (Campana 2011), and the Yakuza (Hill 2003a). This last, in particular, is very active in resolving disputes concerning civil affairs, by making use of its reputation for violence in order to obtain economic benefits. For example, in cases of traffic accidents involving a high level of contestation, given that the legal process is slow and expensive, the parties concerned find it convenient to turn to the Yakuza to negotiate an agreement outside the legal process. The agreement, however, rather than allow the victory of right and reason for the parties involved, reflects the interests of those who have recourse to mafia protection. And in cases where this includes both the parties involved, preference is always given to the one who has the stronger protector (Hill 2004). It should be noted, however, that this is not an activity intended to apply impartial justice to the situation and indeed is based on an asymmetrical power relationship that, frequently, benefits one party at the expense of the other.[16]

---

[16] Forms of protection are also present in the animal kingdom, for example, between two different species of bees, the *Nomada marshamella*, which is a parasite on another bee, the *Andrena sabulosa*. The former enters the nest of the latter without encountering particular resistance and lays its eggs alongside those of the parasitized bee. Even though recognizing them as such, the parasitized bee feeds the parasitic bee pupae, probably thanks to an exchange between the two species: unlike the parasitized bee, the parasitic bee is endowed with a stinger at the end of her abdomen. Remaining near the nest, she thus provides protection against any predators and "the host accepts the damage done by this one parasite and acquires in exchange a partner who protects her against others" (Zahavi and Zahavi 1997, 190).

Mafia protection, states the collaborator with justice of the Sicilian Cosa Nostra Vincenzo Marsala:

is enforced by the threat of damage, preceded by some advice or a phone call; in some cases, the person involved will appeal to the representative (the head of the family) or another family member spontaneously. One of the forms of protection is also the imposition of a guard, in the sense that hiring an affiliate to the family as guardian means that the business is able to avoid any concern or damage.[17]

To summarize, we can affirm that (1) there are mafias that develop as a result of the inability of the state to afford protection as a public good within the geographical area over which it claims jurisdiction (e.g., Sicily, Russia, Japan). This is the "property rights theory of mafia emergence;" (2) there are mafias that come into existence because of the existence of illegal markets, and therefore transactions in these markets lie outside the jurisdiction of the state (e.g., Prohibition era in the United States); (3) there are mafias that can also emerge within "functioning market economies and for reasons to ensure protection of property rights or lack of trust. A sudden boom in a local market that is not governed by the state can lead to a demand for criminal protection, even in countries where property rights are clearly defined, trust is high, and courts work relatively well at settling legitimate disputes among market actors" (Varese 2014, 349).

1.2.2   Mafia as a Type of Secret Society

Secrecy is endemic within organizations and not just mafias and criminal organizations in general. All organizations operating in highly competitive environments require some degree of secrecy in relation to their activities, for example, to protect the "technical core" from the outside world (Thompson 1967), the patents and discoveries that are being worked on, advertising campaigns for a new product, marketing strategies, innovations, etc. Although many firms might gain efficiency from the internal disclosure of information, there are a risk and constant concern that the staff might reveal some information to rival firms (Baccara and Bar-Isaac 2008). Secrets and the safeguarding of secrets are therefore essential to the protection of knowledge and information from competitors, to organizational survival and competitiveness (Dufresne and Offstein 2008; Costas and Grey 2016).

---

[17] OSPA 1985, *Ordinanza Sentenza della Corte di Assise di Palermo contro Abbate Giovanni +706*, Palermo, November 8, vol. V, 895.

Not only private companies but also public authorities have to ensure some form of secrecy in their activities: the "official secret," said Weber (1922), is one of the distinctive features of bureaucracy. If the secret "intentionally conceals knowledge, information, and/or behavior from view of others" (Bok 1989, 5–6), organizational secrecy consists in "the ongoing formal and informal social processes of intentional concealment of information from actors by actors in organizations" (Costas and Grey 2014, 4). Secrecy in organizations can assume a variety of forms.[18] If it is true that secrecy is important to all organizations, it is equally true that for some organizations – such as secret societies – this requirement is a vital building block. These organizations represent the institutionalization of secrecy (Erickson 1981).[19]

Secrecy and secret societies have been studied since the origins of sociology as a discipline (Weber 1904; Simmel 1906). Despite the theoretical and empirical relevance of the phenomenon, however, it has not been studied a great deal over the years (e.g., Goffman 1959; Bok 1989; Zerubavel 2006). Organizational studies have also seldom systematically analyzed the phenomenon, with some exceptions (Feldman 1988; Anand and Rosen 2008; Jones 2008; Parker 2012; 2016; Grey 2013; Costas and Grey 2014), assuming, moreover, the substantial transparency of decision-making and communication processes in organizations (Taylor and Robichaud 2004). As we will see, organizational structures and systems are relevant in order to understand the possibilities and methods of secrecy.

The literature on the phenomenon (Hutin 1955; MacKenzie 1967; Davis 1977) shows a strong resemblance between the different types of historically existing secret societies, including mafias, and the presence of

---

[18] In this regard, Goffman (1959) distinguishes three types of secret: 1) *dark secrets*, which a certain group possesses and hides, since, if others become aware of them, they would damage the image that the group tries to maintain (for example, secrets related to facts that contradict that which an organization claims to do and to be); 2) *strategic secrets*, which are kept hidden from the public to prevent the latter from reacting effectively to what the group is planning (e.g., the secrets of an action by military forces, a terrorist, or a criminal group, or secrets related to the launching of a new product for a company); 3) *inside secrets*, possession of which defines an individual as a member of a group, contributing to making him feel part of that group and at the same time different from the others who have no knowledge of them (e.g., secrets relating to the initiation and promotion rites of a criminal group).

[19] Depending on the modulation of the level of secrecy, different kinds of organizations can be distinguished (Mackenzie 1967): an *open* organization, which has no need to keep its activities secret; a *limited* organization, which selects entry of its members but does not prevent external disclosure of its activities; a *private* organization which establishes strict rules for recruiting, does not publicize its activities, and keeps some of them secret (e.g., private companies, some public bodies); and finally, a *secret* organization, which adopts highly selective recruitment rules and maintains external, and, in part, internal, secrecy regarding its own activities. This last type includes clandestine organizations such as mafias.

a certain similarity in operating patterns (Massari 2013): for example, a symbolic-ritual heritage of reference, rigid selection mechanisms for members, the presence – though very variable – of hierarchical articulation, the importance of maintaining silence with regard to community life, and other aspects. Studying secret societies in China, Davis (1977) identifies a number of common characteristics, in terms of both objectives and concrete forms of activity, with the brotherhoods of northern Germany (Weber 1922), such as (a) mutual aid in case of personal injury or threat, (b) financial assistance in cases of need, (c) the settlement of disputes, (d) the physical preservation of the money of members of the sect, (e) fraternization and social parties, (f) funerals and the participation of members at funeral ceremonies, and (g) the representation of common economic interests. Many of these features of secret societies are present in various ways in mafias.[20]

The *omertà* (the code of silence) and the silence that characterize mafias, more than specific cultural codes, tend to be crucial requirements for the lives of illegal secret organizations, as well as for other secret organizations (Hutin 1955; Davis 1977; Massari 2013). The problem of secrecy management in the mafias regards both *external* privacy – when the members of an organization attempt to keep certain information secret from those who are external to the organization – and *internal* secrecy – when the members of an organization seek to keep information secret from other members of the organization (Fine and Holyfield 1996). This makes intraorganizational communication in mafias, between different members and between different organizational units, very complex and difficult (as we will see in Section 2.2).

Communication is an essential tool for the coordination of an organization, but for the mafias it constitutes an element of potential vulnerability. A large volume of communication, not only toward the external world but also within organizations, between people and/or organizational units, constitutes an equally large number of possibilities of being discovered. Knowing how to remain silent is a typical ability in secret

---

[20] According to some historians, the secret political movements of the mid-nineteenth century had a significant influence on the symbolic and organizational structures of mafia associations, in particular, the Carboneria (a secret Italian revolutionary society founded in the then-Kingdom of Naples during the early nineteenth century on the basis of patriotic and liberal values) and Freemasonry (Pezzino 1990). Mafia and political associations were probably able to communicate during periods of imprisonment, especially in the prisons on the islands of Favignana and Ustica, off the coast of Sicily. The members of the revolutionary secret societies made use of initiation rites and swore respect for common values such as brotherhood, the secrecy of their activities, mutual help and respect for the wives of other members, and so on. Such elements are, in part, still present in some Italian mafias.

societies (Simmel 1906). The mafia organization is frequently associated with the term *omertà* to indicate a specific kind of behavior involving informational reticence. In its current use, this concept denotes a particular sort of behavior regarding secrecy and the ability to maintain silence, above all in terms of refusing to cooperate with state bodies and especially as regards the investigations of criminal acts. For a mafia organization, managing secrecy means first managing information, both by restricting the diffusion of what is known (silence) and in the active search for new information (espionage). Information is a strategic asset for these organizations and, rather than constituting cultural codes, silence and espionage are two sides of the same coin, necessary requirements for the marketing of protection (Gambetta 1993). Silence constitutes a policy of total honesty and loyalty of the members of the Sicilian Cosa Nostra toward one another, but not toward people external to the mafia organization.

The collection of information is essential in order to carry out mafia activities. To be taken seriously as guarantors of transactions, it is necessary for the mafias to know many things regarding their protected (the victims/beneficiaries of protection), including financial information and facts about their private activities (Gambetta 1993). The ability to obtain information is, therefore, a cornerstone of the mafias' reputation, and continuous control of the territory ensures that the mafias know exactly everything relevant that is happening from an economic and social point of view. The collection of information is essential also to counter possible threats, both internal (from other clans in competition with them) and external. As the facts are not always clear and unambiguous, the ability to read information and its symbolic content is a fundamental skill in mafia behavior: "the interpretation of signs, of gestures, of messages and silence is one of the principal activities of the man of honour" (Falcone and Padovani 1992, 31), as well as of those who fight these criminal organizations. Knowing the "pragmatics" of mafia communication, the ability to read the signs and signals used by mafias, is essential for those who want to combat them effectively.

Information management is, therefore, a serious problem for the *mafiosi*. In illegal markets, states Gambetta, "the problems of managing effective signaling codes – spreading the knowledge, overcoming variations in meaning, avoiding the difficulties of memorization or ambiguity – are compounded by the need for secrecy" (2009, 171). Silence and obedience are strict rules. Just as the knightly orders require members to maintain confidentiality in all circumstances, the men and women of the mafia must keep everything within. "What you talk about with me, you must not talk about anywhere else," said a businessman, suspected of links with the Calabrian clans in Lombardy, to his daughter. "You have to close it up in your stomach." The less a person knows, the fewer problems there can be: "The less one knows, the less there is one needs to be trusted about" (Gambetta 2009, 51).

Through the rule of silence and the obligation to tell the truth (see Section 5.2.2), the Sicilian Cosa Nostra ensures that the flow of information is limited to the essential and, at the same time, that the news reported is true. This code, which regulates the circulation of news within the Sicilian Cosa Nostra, explains why only a few words are required, or even merely a gesture, for men of honor to understand each other perfectly: "So, for example, if two men of honor are stopped by police in a vehicle in which a weapon is found, all that's necessary is an imperceptible nod of understanding between the two in order for one of them to take responsibility for ownership of the weapon, and all the consequences of this, saving the other" (OSPA Stajano 2010, 77).

2 Organizational Architecture

In this chapter, we will look at some of the main organizational aspects and issues that mafias have to come up against and deal with. As we will see, these are issues and problems that are typical of any organization, whether public or private, legal or illegal. All organizations, for example, have to deal with recruitment problems, coordination, learning management, accounting, transaction costs management, etc. However, while the issues they face are common to the various types of organization, for mafias the methods of implementation and management are different. For example, every organization must address the problem of informational asymmetry in recruitment, but the methods developed by the mafia, as well as other secret and criminal organizations, are different: these organizations cannot use the same tools and the same implementation practices typical of legitimate firms. In all mafia organizational and business management activities, there is a particular requirement that must be guaranteed, and that is secrecy – with the consequent severe constraints on communication, together with a number of organizational dilemmas that have to be faced and dealt with, as we will see in Chapter 6.

2.1   Recruitment and the Problem of Informational Asymmetry

How to recruit people and how to make sure that they do what they have to do (the "problem of incentives") are two conundrums of particular importance in any organization. It is well known that a firm's most valuable asset is its people, and this awareness is even more true for mafias. The management of these organizations is particularly complex because their human capital is a highly distinctive element: mafias cannot go to court to resolve problems with suppliers or staff. The quality of their novices is a fundamental point for mafias, who, operating in conditions of uncertainty (with regard to the future and the most appropriate action to be taken), not being able to provide detailed job descriptions about the tasks to be carried out and requiring high levels of commitment, flexibility and secrecy, have to be extremely selective in choosing their membership. Recruitment is a process of exchange between an organization (or a group of persons) and individuals. This process depends, on the one hand, on the availability of people with the skills necessary for the organization and, on the other, on the demand for such skills. A multinational company such as Google or Apple can choose their staff by selecting those who best suit their needs from out of thousands of candidates with a high level of education and training. They can check behavior through interviews and can interrupt the relationship at any point if things do not go well for one or for both parties. Moreover, the confidence in the enforcement of the state's norms in cases of new recruits' inappropriate behaviors leads to an increased trust in strangers (Nee, Opper, and Holm 2018).

For mafias, however, as for many clandestine organizations, employee recruitment works in a different way, due to a serious informational problem. Since low-quality recruits could be very dangerous for the organization, mafia recruiters require more, and more reliable, information with regard to their potential candidates than recruiters for legal organizations do. A mistake in this process could in fact have very serious consequences for the organization, particularly in terms of security.

The leadership of an organization exercises control over organizational boundaries – in other words, it has the ability to expand or decrease the size of the organization, acting on recruitment criteria (Aldrich 1979). During the leadership of Raffaele Cutolo (1975–83), for instance, the Camorra opened its doors to new organization members, lowering threshold requirements and standard constraints. Other mafias, however, have maintained the selection criteria for recruiting over time, in order both to avoid imbalances in the relationships between different families and to reduce the risk of infiltration by undercover agents. The first strategy, to become more open, has the advantage of expanding the organization's links with the environment, augmenting social consensus, but has the disadvantage of increasing the costs of integration, coordination, and internal control: allowing entry to people who are not fully socialized with the specific characteristics of the mafia organization can intensify internal conflict, as well as constituting a greater danger to organizational secrecy.

From the point of view of people management, one serious problem for mafias is to identify potential members of the organization with the right background. In organizations, an effective recruitment process and an equally effective socialization process make control less necessary, and therefore less expensive (Simon 1947).

Recruitment, called "opening the book" by the American Cosa Nostra, is, however, an extremely risky activity. Every new member is a potential threat to organization security. Given the high costs of entry and exit from the organization, the risks of making wrong choices, and the associated problems of trust, this is a process that requires great care and caution. In 1957, in order to control the number of family members, the American Cosa Nostra decided to "close the book" and not to admit any new members until 1976 (Abadinsky 1983). This decision meant "keeping their hands tied" a little, so that one family could not outgrow another one in size by too great an extent and thus jeopardize the balance. Therefore, a limited number of members in a family of the American Cosa Nostra, on the one hand, improved the quality of membership through a more targeted selection, and, on the other, guaranteed a certain balance in terms of size and power, or at least a nonexcessive imbalance, which would ensure a deterrent effect with respect to possible expansion strategies and the resulting conflicts (Raab 2016).

The case is different with the Hong Kong Triad societies, which make no attempt to control the number of members. In fact, triad office bearers often engage in selling membership for financial gain. In addition, a triad office bearer today may set up his own unit without asking permission from his original organization (Chu 2000, 136).

Mafia recruitment presents two trust problems (Gambetta 2009). The first is to verify whether a particular individual is trustworthy. The second is to verify whether the signals of trustworthiness displayed by the initiand are true or false, as in the case of undercover agents pretending to be what they are not. For mafias, as for other organizations,[1] the different ways of dealing with the problem of *ex ante* trust are reflected in the different ways that recruitment is carried out.

To reduce the problems of information asymmetry and adverse selection (Akerlof 1970, Spence 1974) in recruiting a new member, the families cannot resort to classical control tools such as wages linked to results, test periods, and educational qualifications. Mafias must be certain that new recruits possess the appropriate criminal skills in terms of toughness, reliability, and secrecy.

Therefore, as is the case with other clandestine organizations, they resort to certain strategies, such as (1) selected area of recruitment; (2) screening and gathering information; (3) costly and severe initiation, with proofs and tests; (4) vouching (see Table 2.1).

---

[1] For similar aspects with reference to gangs, see Densley 2012.

Table 2.1 *Recruiting strategies to reduce information asymmetry*

Strategy	Method
(1) Selected area of recruitment	Recruiting people in the territory in which the organization operates (street/family/prison, etc.)
(2) Screening and gathering information	Collecting signals of commitment and toughness; long periods of observation of criminal behavior; information on the candidate's biography and family of origin
(3) Costly and severe initiation	Establishing disincentives to entry as proof of real interest to join the group; e.g., associate donations of earnings that exceed profit realized from the donations
	Proofs and tests of criminal skills; homicide as an entrance test
(4) Vouching	Resorting to guarantors of the recruit

(1) The first strategy to reduce information asymmetry is that of the *selected area of recruitment* to provide new membership for the organization. For example, one way to reduce information asymmetry and avoid dangerous recruitment errors is to recruit people in the territory in which the organization operates (Pizzini-Gambetta and Hamill 2011), in order to have as much information and knowledge as possible about the candidate and his history. Not being able to resort to the typical methods of legal firms, both public and private, but sharing the same problem with regard to candidate reliability, mafias mainly seek their recruits in three ways: in the street, in prison, and in the family (in particular the 'Ndrangheta).

In all three modes, the field of reference is either ethnic or regional (in Italian mafias). Cases of organization membership of members who belong to the ethnic group of another are extremely rare.[2] This also occurs in other criminal organizations such as Albanian organized crime groups (Arsovska 2015), and in many gangs, such as La Nuestra Familia (California), the Mexican Mafia, and the Aryan Brotherhood, which select their members on grounds of race.[3] Here, mafia behavior is very different from that of public and private legal firms, which, on the one hand, cannot (easily) discriminate by race because it is prohibited by law

[2] There are some cases of members of the Camorra affiliated to the Sicilian Cosa Nostra and cases of members not of Italian origin in the American Cosa Nostra, but these are exceptions.

[3] A different case is constituted by cartels of Nigerian traffickers who mainly recruit among their fellow Nigerians. However, for the heroin trade from Europe to the United States they make an exception and tend to make use of white women as mules, since in general they are stopped less frequently for airport checks (Naìm 2005).

in many states, with the risk of serious sanctions, and, on the other hand, have strong incentives to select personnel by fostering diversity, given that this is related to improved organizational outcomes.[4]

In order to maintain secrecy, the selection of members is a key factor. One of the mafia's great strengths is its highly selective, closed recruitment system: "One reason why the mafia has had a relatively strong, self-reproducing organization is that it recruits from real families. Lower-class gangs, in contrast, often recruit from broken families, and are unable to use family ties much as a basis of organization" (Collins 2008, 491).[5] Prison is an important selected area of recruitment as it provides useful and reliable screening devices (Gambetta 2009). The simple fact of being a prisoner is a sign of criminal inclination, a "badge" for a person's criminal career.

The American Cosa Nostra requires new male members (there are no women in the organization) to be of Italian ancestry (Pistone 2004, 77). According to Jerry Capeci[6] there are procedures and rules that govern the induction of new members:

- New members can be "made" only as replacements for mobsters who have died, although each family is allowed to add two new members at Christmastime.
- Names of proposed members, and the deceased members they replace, must be circulated to the other families, who have two weeks to lodge an objection – for example, the candidate is an informer or the candidate is an associate of another family.
- Families may not replace a defector who cooperates with the government, until he dies.
- Families may never replace a member the family has killed.
- Both parents of an inductee must be of Italian heritage, a change in previous policy requiring that only the father's lineage be Italian.

Recent evidence seems, however, to indicate a significant change in the recruitment of the American Cosa Nostra, with the admission of people of non-Italian origin as organization members, and so with a non-Italian

---

[4] There is a long list of managerial publications that highlight the benefits of diversity in organizations (e.g., Roosevelt 1991; Gentile 1994; Thomas and Ely 1996; Bell 2011. See also G. Llopis, "Diversity Management Is the Key to Growth: Make It Authentic", *Forbes*, June 13, 2011).

[5] As Paoli (2003) noted, entering a mafia clan, a novice underwrites a "status contract" not a "purposive contract." The first involves a change of the legal and social status of the novice; the second is typical of market organizations.

[6] J. Capeci, "The Life, By the Numbers", *New York Magazine*, January 17, 2005, http://nymag.com/nymetro/news/crimelaw/features/10871/ (last accessed on April 5, 2018).

surname. This amounts to a radical innovation, one probably deriving from the difficulty in recruiting persons of Italian origin who are reliable and of course willing to be part of the organization.

The 'Ndrangheta constitutes a special case. Sons of men of honor, stated the collaborator with justice Antonio Zagari (1992), are directly considered young men of honor from birth. The child is "half in and half out" of the organization (Ciconte 1996), a potential 'Ndrangheta member who must then formalize his entry into the organization. The age of entry into the 'Ndrangheta can be very low, with cases of affiliation as low as the age of fourteen, while in the other mafias this is generally higher.

In the Japanese Yakuza, suitable people to recruit are found among those who have already embarked upon a career of deviancy (Hill 2003a, 82), from the *bosōzoku* (hot-rodder) youth motorcycle gangs, to two groups who have suffered relentless discrimination in modern Japan: the ethnic Koreans living in Japan and the *burakumin*, members of Japan's ancestral untouchable class. These three groups are attracted to the Yakuza because of (Gragert 2010, 167) (1) the offering of a surrogate family; (2) the provision of a vehicle for upward social mobility; (3) the sense of belonging to a group, which is all-important in Japan. There are also numerous cases, especially in Tokyo, of members who are boxers and martial artists. From the numerical point of view, there has been a significant decline in membership: from 184,000 in the 1960s to about 39,100 members (17,470 of which are made members) at the end of 2016 (NPA, National Police Agency, 2017). To tackle falls in "subscriptions," the Yamaguchi clan started a brand washing operation through the web with an antidrug campaign aimed at creating a more positive image of the organization.[7]

The problem of reliable recruitment is a very serious one for mafias. It is always difficult to recruit people who simultaneously possess the ethnic requirement (sourced from specific geographical areas of origin, etc.) and that of criminal ability (and/or economic capacity). The recruiting problem is particularly important when mafias are expanding into non-traditional areas. For example, over the last thirty years, the 'Ndrangheta has greatly expanded in northern Italy (Varese 2011; Sciarrone 2014; Dalla Chiesa 2016; Moro and Catino 2016). This expansion has influenced the recruiting process. Moving into new territory, this becomes even more complex. A survey by the Milan Police, in Italy, has shown

---

[7] While the income deriving from drug trafficking represents if not the main, certainly one of the main sources of income, and 50 percent of those arrested for such trafficking belong to one of the Yakuza clans.

Table 2.2 *Territorial origins of persons investigated for mafia association ('Ndrangheta)*

	Total	Born in Nontraditional Areas
Associates	99	34 (34%)
Made members	300	72 (24%)
Total	399	106 (27%)

that the 'Ndrangheta, expanding in northern Italy, has "softened" some rules regarding the selection of novices, even allowing persons not originally from its home territory, Calabria, to be affiliated to various groups in Lombardy. This greater openness also became necessary after numerous arrests as a result of the investigations of law enforcement agencies (more than 300 arrests in a single operation, the Crimine Infinito (Infinite Crime) investigation in July 2010.[8]

From the analysis of 24 investigations[9] that represent the major operations carried out in Lombardy after 2005 (and in part of preceding events) regarding mafia expansion in the north, in particular the 'Ndrangheta, it is revealed that out of 399 persons investigated for mafia association, 106 (26.6 percent) were born in nontraditional areas – in other words, in regions that were not the typical home of the Italian mafias (Calabria, Campania, Puglia, and Sicily; see Table 2.2). Of the 106, 72 are made members, and thus directly affiliated with the organization (boss or society head, vice, organizer, partner).

(2) The second recruiting strategy aimed at reducing information asymmetry consists in *screening and gathering information* about novices leading to selection. This collects signals of commitment and toughness in the candidate and is achieved through a long observation period of the potential member's behavior, in order to assess his criminal capacity and to acquire the greatest amount of information possible about his past and his family.[10] The decision to recruit a new member also depends on the assurance from other organization members regarding the criminal credentials and trustworthiness of the subject to be recruited. The recruiting

---

[8] C. Giuzzi, "Delusa dai politici, la 'Ndrangheta candida gli affiliati", *Il Corriere della Sera*, October 5, 2014, 16.

[9] *Ordinanze Custodia Cautelare* (pretrial court orders for remanding the suspects in custody): Bad Boys, Bagliore, Benfante, Black Hawk, Blue Call, Briantenopea, Cerberus, Clan Valle, Dionisio, Fidanzati, Infinito, Insubria, Isola, Lampada, Liati, Metallica, Metastasi, Parco Sud, Pensabene, Platino, Porto, Redux Caposaldo, Stellittano, Tenacia.

[10] Signaling theory predicts that mobs will look for signs that are too costly for mimics to fake, but affordable for the genuinely trustworthy (Gambetta 2009).

process in the American Cosa Nostra can take a long time: a member can expect to wait eight to fifteen years "to be made," and in some cases even twenty years, as in the case of Tony Accetturo, former captain of the New Jersey family, who became a made member in 1976 (Raab 2016). Even in the Sicilian Cosa Nostra the observation period to identify potential new members can last many years; for example, Gaspare Spatuzza became a member of the organization in all respects, with the rite of initiation, in 1995, after about twenty years of participation.

However, the process can also be shorter, with exceptions for meritorious service (Abadinsky 1983). In the American Cosa Nostra, to minimize tension, the bosses of the five families of New York decided from 1931 on to share the names of their candidates for new members, in order to prevent creating made members who were in conflict with other families (Capeci 2004, 20).

In the 'Ndrangheta, says collaborator with justice Antonino Belnome, references from guarantors and ancestry are not enough in themselves: a prospective member is put to the test to assess his criminal capacity with a series of low-profile activities, such as shooting at the window of a bar or a shop, or at a car, or setting fire to a store. Subsequently, the person moves on to more important criminal acts. Talent, intelligence, and detachment are the most important skills for an organizational career (in Barbacetto and Milosa 2011, 426–7).

The mobster Domenico Bidognetti stated that becoming a member of the Camorra and being admitted to the initiation rite required presentation from persons of trust after a long period of "apprenticeship, and proof of criminal ability on a number of occasions and in various situations, also including homicide."[11]

Other clandestine organizations also resort to this strategy. For example, the Brigate Rosse (Red Brigades, Italian left-wing terrorist group) allowed entry to the organization only after testing and verification throughout long-term militancy in the movement (Moretti 1994).

(3) The third strategy – *costly and severe initiation* – consists in making entry to the organization even more difficult, in order to test the criminal skills of the candidate, and whether the aspiring member is truly interested in joining. Before entering most mafia organizations on a stable and permanent basis, the recruit must spend a certain amount of time, which can be very long, as an associate, facing a series of trials and tests. This involves an operational, executive role, carried out in close contact with

---

[11] Tribunale di Santa Maria Capua Vetere 2013, *Prima sezione penale collegio A, Processo a carico di Antonucci Esterino+altri*, March 22.

an organization soldier, and, more than one designed to bring rewards, can be an expensive business, with the obligation to give a large part of his earnings to the soldier he is partnered with.

From a psychological point of view, a practice of severe initiation performs the function of inspiring the new member with a greater sense of commitment to the mafia organization, making him accept all the activities required to become a made member in all respects. This method is widely practiced in other illegal organizations, such as ETA (Clark 1983), as well as in some legal organizations (such as the steel industry, Haas 1972). "Making your bones" is a sort of euphemism used by American Cosa Nostra for passing the entrance test. Mafia tests employ a crescendo of difficulty that can culminate in homicide. Murder as an entrance test (*blood in*) is often found in mafias, in the American Cosa Nostra in particular, and is required both as proof of the candidate's criminal courage and as a guarantee that the initiand is not an undercover agent (Pistone 2004). As the American Cosa Nostra underboss Sammy Gravano stated:

Committing a murder – making your bones – was not a prerequisite for induction into Cosa Nostra. But more often than not, it would happen. Murder was the true linchpin of Cosa Nostra – for control, for discipline, to achieve and maintain power. For made members and associates, it was an everyday, accepted fact of life. The code that could trigger a hit was very clear. If someone broke the rules, he would be whacked. Murder was the means to bring some semblance of order to what otherwise would be a chaos. (in Maas 1997, 46)

Several families require that the new member be involved in a homicide. Ex-member of the Philadelphia mob and collaborator with justice Nick Caramandi stated that

no one could make it into the Scarfo organization without "doing some work." This was the euphemism mob members used to describe taking part in a murder. Killing someone was the final rite of passage. You couldn't be made until you had helped take a life. (in Anastasia 1991, 143)

The Sicilian Cosa Nostra mob member Leonardo Vitale affirmed that to become a made member he had to show his value by killing a man guilty of having acquired the tax payment without permission (OSPA Stajano 2010). As emerged during the Maxiprocesso[12] (Great trial) against the Sicilian Cosa Nostra:

---

[12] The trial began in Palermo in 1985 and was called "maxi" since it involved 475 defendants.

Prestige within the mafia family is achieved above all through the carrying out of a homicide, in the sense that this is the test in which the man of honor truly demonstrates his worth. In this case, it is said that this is a person who is "worth something." And the more important the murder is, the more the prestige of the *mafioso* increases... In other words, an essential feature of a *mafioso* is ruthlessness and decisiveness. (OSPA Stajano 2010, 111)

The FBI official James Nelson stated that

at one time it was mandatory that a member of La Cosa Nostra participate in a murder. Today it is generally true that they require participation in a murder. However, we know of examples where people have been brought in, for whatever reason, who have not yet participated in a murder. Participation in a murder serves two main purposes: To show, in their terms, the willingness to do the dirtiest of deeds and, second, to enjoin them in a conspiratorial activity of a murder and hopefully, according to them, insure that he abides by the rules of the mafia or La Cosa Nostra. (in Abadinsky 1983, 118)

Murder as a kind of entrance test helps to indicate trustworthiness: "There was a rule that to be made you had to go out on a hit, at least as a witness" (Pistone and Brandt 2007, 71). On the one hand, it is an act that indicates the ability of the new member, and, on the other, it is a way to create "skeletons in the closet" (Gambetta 2009). In fact, criminals who commit deviant actions reinforce internal loyalty by exchanging evidence of their actions. This is an act that commits them to silence and increases the cost of informing. If a member is willing to betray the organization and become an informer, he will always end up incriminating himself for at least one murder, the one required by the entrance test.

Particularly violent entrance tests also exist in other clandestine organizations, such as rebel recruitment (Hegghammer 2012) and gangs (Decker and van Winkle 1996), with activities such as beating someone up, or even shooting him, in order to discourage those who are less determined and less able. In the Red Brigades, for example, the rule existed that anyone who asked to join the organization had to commit a crime, such as robbery. On the one hand, it was a kind of initiation rite through which some social barriers and conventions were thrown down, and, on the other, it was designed to reduce the likelihood of the police infiltrating someone into the organization, since he would never be allowed to commit a crime (Fasanella and Franceschini 2004).

Tests of courage of this kind are not required in mafias for those figures who represent, to use the effective expression of the Sicilian Cosa Nostra collaborator with justice Salvatore Contorno, the "clean face" of the mafia – namely, professionals, public administrators, and entrepreneurs, who are not employed in violent criminal operations, but provide a useful work of support and cover in apparently licit activities (OSPA Stajano

2010). Some mafias, such as the Yakuza, are increasing their percentage of recruitment of such white-collar figures, given the increasing number of activities in which they are involved: thus, for example, computer and financial experts are especially welcome in the Yakuza (Hill 2003a, 84).

The commitment of particularly heinous acts seems to be a *condicio sine qua non* in order to reach the top positions. Joseph Pistone says that the best way to make a career in the American Cosa Nostra is to participate in a homicide – which also happens, of course, if only figuratively, in big corporations:

> You climb the ladder by eliminating somebody. When self-appointed Bonanno boss Carmine Galante got whacked with a cigar clenched between his teeth in the backyard dining area of Joe and Mary's Restaurant in Ridgewood, Brooklyn, in 1979, both Sonny Black and Big Joe Massino instantly went from soldier to capo, and Rusty Rastelli, although in jail, moved back in as boss. (Pistone and Brandt 2007, 22)

In any case, many bosses of the five families of the New York American Cosa Nostra were promoted by gunfire. In the Gambino family, after John Gotti and Philip Rastelli, Joey Massino became family boss in 1991 after a rapid climb to the top, which saw the killing of three captains (at the time, 1981, the position also held by Massino), an important step in his promotion to future leader of the family (Crittle 2006). Career progression in the 'Ndrangheta is gradual, degree by degree. As mobsters Fortunato Gallo and Mercuri explained to member Pasquale Ambesi: "the granting of *doti* (ranks) takes place step by step, but, in his case, an exception was made thanks to his merits and age." In fact, Ambesi had received the highest benefit provided by the Società minore (the lower level of the organization), becoming *sgarrista* (or *camorrista di sgarro*) and thus jumping three intermediate levels (*picciotto liscio, picciotto di sgarro,* and *camorrista di sangue*). Skipping career steps is quite rare, and usually just one at a time at the very most, but in this case an astonishing total of three were jumped.[13]

Mobs are experts both in their use of violence and in their use of social relationships, and their aptitude for business, legal and otherwise. A balance among these different skills is required in order to make a career and to hold on to the positions acquired. A high level of ability in the use of violence that is not balanced by a high level of ability in business could keep the person in secondary roles for a long time. At

---

[13] Tribunale di Milano, DDA (*Direzione Distrettuale Antimafia,* District Anti-Mafia Directorate) 2014, *Operazione Insubria, Ordinanza di applicazione di misura coercitiva con mandato di cattura,* Ufficio del giudice per le indagini preliminari, 12053/11 R.G.N.R.

the same time, a boss with a great ability to generate profits that is not balanced by sufficient toughness, on the one hand, gratifies the group in terms of the economic opportunities created, but, on the other, leaves him exposed to possible internal climbing. This is what happened to Gambino family boss Paul Castellano, who was killed by John Gotti so that the latter could take his place.

Trials and tests are common in the recruitment processes of many clandestine organizations, although they can be realized in different ways. For example, in the Italian Red Brigades, the strategy had a strong cognitive dimension, given the ideological nature of the terrorist organization. Once the potential candidates had been identified, the members of the organization gave him a series of the organization's political documents to read, to gauge his reaction and test his degree of adherence to the armed struggle (Petrillo 2013). On the basis of reactions and real interest expressed by the candidates, they proceeded with documents and speeches that were increasingly explicit with regard to the operating methods and aims of the organization, until, once the actual level of motivation had been verified, the proposal of gradual membership was made.

(4) The fourth strategy to reduce information asymmetry in the recruiting process consists of a mechanism called *vouching*. Studying rebel organizations, Weinstein showed how the organization

> instead of looking to actors outside of the movement to authenticate the pledges of new recruits, it relies on the credibility and commitment of current members ... Potential members must be invited to join by current rebel soldiers. And in the process of becoming a rebel, the current soldier must vouch for the honesty and commitment of the new member. If a new recruit fails to live up to his or her pledge, both the recruit and the current soldier bear the costs of his failure. (2005, 606)

In mafias, as well as in many secret organizations, the initiand must be introduced by one or more members of the organization, who act as guarantors of his criminal qualities, and of the fact that he is not an infiltrator. For the five New York Cosa Nostra families the candidate had to be sponsored by the *capo* he would work for (Raab 2016). It is, in practice, a kind of recommendation system based on the wisdom of experts. But it is not a method that can always avoid possibility of infiltration, as was seen with the case of undercover FBI agent Joseph Pistone (aka Donnie Brasco), who, for six years, managed to infiltrate the Bonanno family of the American Cosa Nostra in New York. But the punishment for those who made this possible, those, in other words, who were not aware of his real role, was the severest of all: death.

Subsequently, and as a result of the infiltration by agent Pistone, rules for the presentation of new members were changed. Two *mafiosi* and not simply one had to vouch for the new recruit and one of them had to have known him for at least fifteen years (Pistone and Brandt 2007, 70). In addition, every new member had to have a verifiable history of at least fifteen years.

Recruiting strategies make it possible to increase the reliability of the candidate, minimizing security risks. However, these strategies result in a particularly complex organizational dilemma, as we will see in Section 6.6: a dilemma that involves selection based on merit compared to selection based on kinship.

2.2   Coordination and Communication Problems

Coordination is the essence of organization (Barnard 1938): it involves the organizing of individuals so that their actions are aligned toward a defined outcome. In some ways, coordination and organizing are synonymous. Organizing, indeed, "tries to ensure that different things are where we expect them to be" (Gabriel 2008). In complex organizations, coordination is a complex process to realize, as it requires the coordination of a collective set of interdependent tasks involving a number of actors with potentially diverging interests and under conditions of environmental uncertainty and instability (Okhuysen and Bechky 2009). If coordination is very difficult to achieve in legal organizations,[14] it is even more so in those that are secret and illegal, given the limits on communication and exchange of information, such as mafias. Whereas greater information diffusion among criminal members might improve efficiency, this may increase organizational vulnerability to external threats, for instance, law enforcement agencies (Baccara and Bar-Isaac 2008). The minimal organizational units that are the components of the larger system of a mafia are substantially independent of each other within the

---

[14] There are several factors common to all organizations that can hinder coordination (Heath and Staudenmayer 2000): (1) *partition focus*, which relates to the tendency of people to overlook coordination because they focus more on division of labor than integration; (2) *component focus*, which relates instead to the tendency of people to focus on the tasks they are responsible for more than interaction with other parts of the process, involving the neglect of interrelationships and interactions between components; (3) *inadequate communications*, which worsen the situation of coordination neglect. Communications tend to be inadequate because of multiple psychological processes that make it difficult for an individual to consider the perspective of other individuals in communicating; (4) finally, the existence of *specific languages and specialist knowledge*, making communication problematic within complex organizations and between organizations, favoring processes of "structural secrecy" (Vaughan 1996).

environment of the territories of reference. The situation is thus one that Thompson (1967) defines as "pooled interdependence." This is the case, at least, in peacetime or in the absence of shared business. When, however, the situation is one of war, of conflict between clans, or a business situation created together by multiple clans, interdependence becomes reciprocal.

Where the realization of the product is visible, as in manufacturing operations, coordination is easier, since the progress of activities and achievement of objectives can be monitored more easily. In service activities, on the other hand, coordination is less easy, and top-down planning of activities is less feasible if the carrying out of the service is complex. Since mafia activity consists of the realization of a complex service (protection), and not a product, coordination is more difficult, also because, in such situations, communication, highly problematic as it is for an illegal and secret organization, is essential for the coordination of activities. As Diego Gambetta argued:

Criminals face severe constraints on communication imposed by the action of the law, and, unlike the rest of us, cannot easily develop institutions aimed at circumventing them ... and if failures of communication in the world of regular business can lead to a loss of business, in the underworld they can result in years behind bars, or worse. (Gambetta 2009, x, xi)

In addition to the uncertainty of the external environment, coordination in the mafia is influenced by the characteristics and requirements of internal activities. As secret organizations, the gangs have limited, and often encrypted, communications, with extensive use of codes, the omission of specific points in communications, the use of allusion and nicknames, absence of detail, and the limited use of communication technology (mobile phones). In addition to such limitations, constraints exist on the realization of meetings, with a limited number of physical locations for encounters and the absence of formal working premises (with the exception of the Yakuza). All this makes exchanging information and communications problematic.

Abadinsky reports a conversation between Carlo Gambino (the boss of the Gambino family), and one of his captains (*caporegime*), as an example of a typical conversation in the American Cosa Nostra:

CAPTAIN: You know that guy we talked about in Newark?
GAMBINO: Yeah.
CAPTAIN: Well, everything is okay; he's falling into line.
GAMBINO: What's with that guy from Newark?
CAPTAIN: He ain't doin' what he's supposed to.
GAMBINO: I'll take care of it. (1983, 6–7)

It is extremely difficult to understand the actual content of this kind of communication. Mobsters avoid mentioning names, places, specific dates, events, and any other information that could be used by the police. At the same time, "organized crime *etiquette* prohibits asking questions about conversations to which one has been privy but are not of direct concern. Only a naive undercover agent would violate this rule" (Abadinsky 1983, 7). Collaborator with justice Anna Carrino, wife of the Casalesi clan boss Francesco Bidognetti (Camorra), explains the mode of communication, through conventional gestures and signals, adopted to receive messages from her husband in prison during conversations there:

To indicate Luigi Guida (a Camorra boss) and in particular that I had to say something to his wife, Bidognetti would touch his right hand and the ring finger of his left hand or at least make a gesture with his left hand, because I had been godmother to Guida's daughter and then the *compare di anello* (a role similar to maid of honor) to Nunzia Casanova. To indicate that I had to deliver a message to Giuseppina Nappa, Bidognetti touched his chin to indicate a beard, since Nappa is the wife of Schiavone (known as Sandokan) who is famous for his beard. To indicate Alessandro Cirillo, he touched his shoulder to indicate the uniform rank of a sergeant. To indicate Francesco di Maio, he made the gesture to indicate a tall person, since Di Maio is very tall. Guida was also referred to as "O 'Curt" (short guy), making the gesture to indicate a short person.[15] (from an interrogation used in the trials, in Ardituro 2015, 21)

An example of coded communication to talk serious business is this phone call on May 5, 1982, between two members of the Sicilian Cosa Nostra, Gaspare Mutolo and Mimmo Condorelli:

CONDORELLI: Listen, about that thing with your brother, for that car that you need, at the moment we don't have any of these cars; could be quite a few days, I don't know how many.
MUTOLO: If you get the chance, you let me know and I'll come up, or you and the others can come down here.
CONDORELLI: No problems about that. For that car you told me about, I'll give you an answer in a few days. What kind of price would we be talking about here, anyway?
MUTOLO: I don't know, we can talk about that later. Look, like I told you ten days ago, with the car, I had an accident in Foggia, that's why I needed a car. All right?
CONDORELLI: Sure, sure, but it isn't so easy... At best, I can let you have a 127 (a car produced by Fiat).
MUTOLO: OK, Mimmo, anyway, say hello to everyone for me; best to all of you, ciao. (OSPA Stajano 2010, 227)

---

[15] The use of nicknames based on the physical or behavioral characteristics of a *mafioso* is widespread in the mafia.

The two are discussing a criminal activity, and the word "car" refers to drugs, heroin in particular. Given the dangerous nature of the topic of conversation, Mutolo at a certain point introduces an invented item, the traffic accident in Foggia, to indicate the dangerous situation to Condorelli, in case of interception, and Condorelli, having understood the message, responds by saying that it will be possible to give him a Fiat 127. The "car" turns up again a few days later, in a subsequent phone call on May 9 between Mutolo and a drug trafficker from Singapore, Koh Bak Kin:

MUTOLO: ... Look, big problem:
KIN: Eh?
MUTOLO: Big problem. Yeah, because the car isn't the one you usually give me. Look, you've got to get down here, can you come here to Palermo? (OSPA Stajano 2010, 228)

Koh Bak Kin has never worked in the car trade, being a drug dealer, especially heroin. So, the "big problem" arising from the delivery of a car that was different from usual means that the consignment of heroin provided by Kin was of poor quality.

Judicial investigations are full of interceptions of this type, with allusive phrases, words denoting objects that are different from their actual meaning, etc. The 2014 investigation *Mafia Capitale*, the so-called Roman mafia, highlighted the different communication techniques used by members of the organization to maintain secrecy and avoid detection by law enforcement agencies. These include the use of specific telephone devices, with periodic changes of mobile phones and phone cards, made out to persons who are completely unrelated to their relational circuit; the frequent use of public pay phones or devices pertaining to public services deemed to be secure; telephone conversations often immediately prior to appointments in person, in places agreed upon or indicated through allusive references; the limitation imposed on members in terms of having direct contact with Massimo Carminati, the undisputed head of the association, and the order never to mention him on the phone; the use of systems aimed at avoiding being intercepted at meeting places and the frequent measures taken to detect and remove listening devices from places and vehicles.[16]

The security of communications is more important than efficiency and may result in the preparation of complex modes of communication

---

[16] Tribunale di Roma 2015, *Operazione Mondo di Mezzo, Ordinanza di applicazione di misure cautelari di Carminati Massimo+38*, Ufficio del giudice per le indagini preliminari, Flavia Costantini, November 28. See also La Spina (2016).

exchange. A survey by law enforcement agencies carried out on the Sicilian Cosa Nostra[17] in August 2015 highlighted the careful arrangements that went into the communication methods employed by Matteo Messina Denaro, the *capomandamento* – district head – of Castelvetrano, and representative of the province of Trapani, one of the most important bosses in the organization. A fugitive since 1993, he communicated with members of the organization using "pizzini,"[18] small pieces of paper containing his orders, thus avoiding use of the telephone and other means of communication with a high risk of interception and traceability. This system, however, besides being rather slow, requires an ad hoc organization with a large number of people to transmit communications. The apical role in the message chain was carried out by Vito Gondola, the *capomandamento* of Mazara del Vallo, who had the task of managing the time and delivery method of Messina Denaro's correspondence. Gondola collected the *pizzini* from the boss and hid them under a rock outside the city. To communicate confidentially with other mafia bosses, persons of proven reliability were used as go-betweens. The transmission of correspondence took place on a quarterly basis, the method dictated by the boss: the *pizzini* had to be destroyed after reading and the answer had to reach the boss within fifteen days. The message was written in code, to make it even more difficult to decipher. This mode of communication, certainly very reliable and safe, was very challenging from an organizational point of view, and hardly prompt. However, it was adopted by several mobsters, including Bernardo Provenzano, one of the most important bosses in the Sicilian Cosa Nostra (Palazzolo and Prestipino 2007).[19]

Moreover, given the constraints of secrecy, even recognition is complicated. Collaborator with justice Antonio Zagari (former member of the 'Ndrangheta) says:

---

[17] *Operazione Ermes*, August 2015, carried out by the Public Prosecutor of the Republic of Palermo, the Palermo police, the Trapani police, and the Carabinieri.

[18] *Pizzino* is an Italian word derived from Sicilian, now widely used to refer to the messages that the Sicilian mafia uses for high-level communications.

[19] In the late nineteenth and early twentieth centuries, the families of the American Cosa Nostra communicated by mail. The mobsters carried "letters of recommendation" from their leaders when traveling to new cities. This system involved a number of risks. The United States Secret Services seized letters from the Morello family, using them as judicial material against family members. In the United States, the use of wiretaps as evidence for trial was forbidden by the Federal Communications Act of 1934 and until 1968. Therefore, in that thirty-year period, mobsters were safely able to use this communication tool to organize their affairs and coordinate people and activities, thus consolidating the organization (Hortis 2014, 64–5).

It is not always easy to know the rank and special duties of members of the 'Ndrangheta, especially if they occupy high positions and levels in the organization, because the rule is that people at a higher grade are not required to disclose their position to inferiors. Indeed, lower grade members are absolutely forbidden from asking anyone questions concerning the hierarchical position of elders and superiors. If a more than plausible reason does not exist, the member cannot be forced to reveal rank and affiliation, unless this is imposed by members with a higher, or at least equal, rank. You can recognize a member and also their position by means of a specific jargon through which you can come to understand the position and title of the member without them revealing this openly. By means of such jargon it is possible to know the rank of equal and lower-level members, but it is practically impossible for the opposite to occur.[20]

The development and maintenance of a communications system constitute the first directive function in an organization, and the interview is the most universal form of human cooperation, and perhaps also the most complex (Barnard 1938). It consists of a physical event (energy, sound waves), a biological act produced by living things, and a social act. Despite the various ways of communicating through codes and *pizzini*, it is still important for mafia organizations to organize actual talks, face-to-face meetings, even with a large number of members, thus risking the possibility of being identified and arrested by the forces of law and order.

For the Yakuza, this is not a significant problem because, given the organization's legal status (which will be looked at in more detail in Chapter 3), members can meet without problems in their headquarters, a known and visible premises recognizable by signs at the entrance. The leaders of the different gangs meet monthly and on that occasion the decisions of top executives are announced together with other information relevant to community life, while routine day-to-day decision-making is decentralized. In addition, there are numerous ceremonies, such as weddings, funerals, office openings, ceremonies of succession, initiation rites, and celebrations of jail release, in which members must participate, despite the expenditure of time and money. In fact, such events serve to demonstrate gang cohesion, prestige, power, and the importance of network and hierarchy (Hill 2014, 238). However, as a result of increased police repression, these occasions have assumed a low profile.

For mafia members, meeting up represents a problem. Meeting places are often public places (restaurants, social clubs, etc.): for example, the former bakery J&S Cake, at 58–23 58th Road in Maspeth, Queens, was the main meeting place for Bonanno family captains and boss Joey

---

[20] Tribunale di Reggio Calabria, DDA (*Direzione Distrettuale Antimafia*, District Anti-Mafia Directorate) 2010, *Operazione Crimine*, vol. I, 451.

Massino[21] (Crittle 2006). According to 'Ndrangheta collaborator with justice Antonino Belnome, the clan normally held a meeting once a month, unless urgent business came up (in Barbacetto and Milosa 2011, 426). The Infinito investigation[22] identified two types of summit involving 'Ndrangheta members in the Lombardy region:

The real summit, planned by members of the "Lombardia" (the district of the region) and the members of each individual *locale* (the main local organizational unit), with the aim of conferring *doti* (ranks), to address and resolve problems that have arisen within the individual *locale* or between the latter. Social occasions: weddings and funerals of senior members of the 'Ndrangheta, or their relatives, are not only opportunities to share moments of joy and grief, but are also opportunities to meet to discuss issues regarding the 'Ndrangheta's community life. These meetings are governed by precise rules of mafia etiquette.[23]

With regard to summits at the Lombardy level, fourteen were documented between February 2008 and October 2009 through observations of the police, video recordings, interceptions, etc. The meetings took place in public places (restaurants, in most cases, but also warehouses), since in theory these guarantee greater safety, even though the investigation demonstrates the opposite. The topics of the meetings ranged over the balance among the various organizational groupings, conflict management, the conferring of ranks, etc. The participants included high-level figures, such as bosses of different *locali* (together with the *'ndrine*, the clans of the 'Ndrangheta) in Lombardy, and while some meetings were limited to small groups, others involved the participation of large numbers of people (even more than sixty members, when positions and ranks were conferred).[24]

Other types of meeting take place within the individual *locale* to address matters of organization management and are held in public places, mainly restaurants and bars.

In addition to formal meetings, the so-called summits, there are many events organized on the occasion of funerals and weddings. During these events, alliances are discussed, as well as positions and problems relating to the mafia organization. One important event, for example, was the "Hollywood-style wedding"[25] of the children of two mafia families and with the same surname (Elisa Pelle and Giuseppe Pelle). The marriage

---

[21] M. Howe, "U.S. Gambling Raid Seizes 2 Social Clubs and 200 Pet Birds", *The New York Times*, July 20, 1988.

[22] Tribunale di Milano, DDA 2010, *Richiesta per l'applicazione di misure cautelari*, 43733/06 R.G.N.R.

[23] Ibid., 87.

[24] Tribunale di Reggio Calabria, DDA 2010, *Operazione Crimine*, vol. I, 182.

[25] Tribunale di Milano, DDA 2010, *Richiesta per l'applicazione di misure cautelari*, 43733/06 R.G.N.R., 111.

took place on August 19, 2009, in two places that, for the 'Ndrangheta, are important from a symbolic point of view: the church of San Luca and the municipality of Platì. During this event, attended by some of the organization's leading exponents, the new "crime boss" – the highest office in the 'Ndrangheta – was identified, Domenico Oppedisano.

In conclusion, for mafias, coordination is not only very expensive; it also requires constant communication and interaction among people, thus exposing the organization to security issues. Coordination also becomes more problematic as the number of persons involved increases, thus developing into a trade-off to be managed, maintaining limitations on the size of the organization while forming small groups within it. We will return to this issue in Chapter 6, by analyzing certain organizational dilemmas that mafias have to deal with, such as the need for security, on the one hand, and the need to coordinate and communicate, on the other.

2.3   Learning

One little-explored aspect in studies on mafias regards learning processes, in particular organizational learning,[26] understood as the process of creating, retaining, and transferring knowledge within an organization. With organizational learning, members of an organization develop new knowledge regarding their actions and outcomes, share knowledge throughout the organization, incorporate that knowledge into organizational routines, and possess an organizational memory. Organizational learning includes processes that occur at individual, group, organizational, and interorganizational levels (Levitt and March 1988; Crossan et al. 1999; Easterby-Smith et al. 2000; Boh et al. 2007; Easterby-Smith and Lyles 2010). Organizational learning is not simply the sum of individual learning. In order to become organizational, individual cognitions and actions must be shared with others and incorporated into operating rules and routines, so as to become independent of any single individual (Argyris and Schön 1996; Berends et al. 2003).

Thus individual *mafiosi* learn, and the organization learns. The organization learns from interaction with the external environment, and in particular interaction with the subjects with which it is in competition, such as other criminal groups, and those with which it is in opposition, such as law enforcement agencies.

---

[26] The issue of learning has been addressed, albeit sporadically, in the study of terrorism and drug trafficking (Forest 2006; Kenney 2007).

Obstacles in the learning processes of mafias are linked to two reasons. One is the secrecy of the organizations, which requires compartmentalized organizational structures and thus allows a limited flow of information. The circulation of information, together with communication, is, however, an essential precondition for the learning process, both individual and organizational. The second reason relates to the limited presence of explicit, formalized knowledge, which is a typical feature of legal businesses.

Notwithstanding these limitations, mafias learn in an adaptive way, modifying their methods of action, taking past events and failures into account. According to many scholars, in fact, learning is primarily driven by failure (Wong and Weiner 1981; March 1994; Lipshitz and Barak 1995; Argyris and Schön 1996; Zakay et al. 1998; Ron et al. 2006; Catino and Patriotta 2013). The general premise for learning is that the organization can differentiate between success and failure (Luhmann 2000), that it is capable of solving known problems, of analyzing and reflecting on the sources of failure and error and of making inferences of cause and effect (Mahler 2009). Argyris and Schön (1996) argue that organizational learning, like that of humans, has first of all to do with the detection and the subsequent correction of error. According to the two scholars, learning occurs when error – in the sense of a misalignment between intention and consequence – is recognized, corrected, and removed. This is what happens, for example, when a mafia organization decides to change certain trade routes as a result of the successful activity of law enforcement agencies. The identification of an error constitutes, therefore, the first step in the learning process. In this regard, Argyris and Schön identify two forms of learning: (1) single-loop learning (*incremental*), which involves altering routine following the detection of error and its correction, while leaving the existing organizational norms that generated it unchanged and (2) double-loop learning (*transformational*), which implies a more radical change in the organization, through the modification of existing assumptions, norms, and strategies that were held responsible for the generation of erroneous behavior. This change, altering the underlying assumptions relating to behavior and trying to reduce the repetition of error, interrupts the course of present routine and fosters organizational learning. In this way, a criminal group reconsiders what activities require modification and what strategies and organizational models need to be adopted. This is the case in particular when a severe misalignment between the organization and the external environment is evident.

Single-loop learning is very common and has for example to do with the continuous changing of meeting venues, the alteration of communication codes, the continual replacement of communication tools, etc. An example of double-loop learning is provided by the new rules for mafia membership after the resounding "error" that allowed the infiltration of FBI agent Joseph Pistone into the Bonanno family of the American Cosa Nostra in New York. After this event, the American Cosa Nostra not only physically eliminated those who had not realized that Pistone was an undercover agent (single-loop learning), but modified the rules of membership, so that in the future at least two members must present an initiand as a new candidate, and each candidate must possess a verifiable history of at least fifteen years.

Another example of double-loop learning is provided by the decision of the Bonanno family boss, Joey Massino, after Pistone's infiltration, to increase the degree of compartmentation in the organization, in order to minimize damage from informants or undercover investigations. Massino introduced a clandestine cell system for his crews, forbidding them to contact one another and to meet their *capi*, and created a new committee that would relay his orders to the crews (Crittle 2006, 164–5). This new regime made the family more impenetrable, isolating the position of the boss. In addition, to reduce exposure to the outside, in contrast to his contemporaries, particularly the publicity-friendly Gotti, Massino adopted a relatively low public profile.

In the Sicilian Cosa Nostra, the mass killing strategy promoted in the 1990s from the top, and primarily by the boss Totò Riina, led to severe repression by the state, with hundreds of arrests and highly restrictive prison sentences. It was a strategy that did not yield significant benefits for the organization, proving to be a serious error of judgment. The organization leaders then opted for a different organizational policy, characterized by a lower level of conflict with the police and the judicial system, a strategy of lesser visibility. This encouraged victimless crimes that were less problematic for public opinion and the media and consequently also for the law enforcement agencies.

It is conceivable that the methods and magnitude of learning depend on the mafia organizational structure. In situations where mafias have higher-level bodies of coordination, it can be assumed that double-loop and systemic learning are more frequent. The discussion of adverse events is in fact carried out within higher-level bodies that, by virtue of their role, benefit from the possibility to communicate and exchange information regarding risks and solutions. At the same time, positive solutions can become new rules that are valid for all the organizations involved. This is much more complex for mafias that do not possess higher-level bodies of coordination.

As Kenney noted (2007), while for legitimate businesses organizational learning is often linked to greater efficiency, in the case of illegal, clandestine business, it is paradoxically the opposite that may occur. By operating in hostile environments and having to avoid law enforcement agencies, security and reliability become more important than efficiency. Therefore, in conditions of high risk and low security, an illegal organization may decide to reduce its activities temporarily.

It is worth pointing out, and this dilemma will be discussed in detail in Chapter 6, that learning processes are hampered by the compartmentalization process. While, on the one hand, this prevents damage in case of any eventual infiltration, and limits it in case of a member's collaboration with law enforcement agencies, on the other, it makes it very difficult to exchange information and knowledge, thus constituting a barrier to organizational learning.

2.3.1 Criminal Community of Practice

In many terrorist organizations (especially those pertaining to Islamic extremism) knowledge is of a very explicit kind, encoded in handbooks, novels, videos, discussion forums, training manuals, and other artifacts (Gunaratna 2002; Forest 2006; Trujillo and Jackson 2006). There also exist military-style learning programs. In addition to tapping into this explicit knowledge, terrorists learn tacitly, through socialization processes and learning by doing: building bombs and detonators, discharging rifles and handguns, etc. (Kenney 2007). Terrorists also develop their own practical experience through informal learning, on-the-job training, and combat simulations, thus integrating formal training with the personal intuition and local knowledge that come from practical experience (Kenney 2006).

In the case of mafias, however, learning is mainly tacit, not codified. There is no explicit, codified, and formalized learning path, nor a master's degree in mobster administration, nor formalized training programs. The learning process therefore takes place through socialization, without explicit, codified knowledge, mostly on the job, through a form of coaching, with the initiand observing the expert and participating in increasingly complex criminal activities. With regard to learning the work of a *mafioso*, former Sicilian Cosa Nostra mobster Gaspare Spatuzza says:

There's no kind of formal education. You follow in the footsteps of the people who introduce you into this world and then you act accordingly ... There is not an explicit and formalized apprenticeship. People adapt before you ask them to do it. (Dino 2016, 94)

Such learning processes are configurable as a learning process based on the participation of the *mafioso* as a member, at first peripheral, of a specific (criminal) "community of practice."

Communities of practice share (Jordan 1989; Lave and Wenger 1991) discourse, vocabulary, ways of speaking and of building arguments; the sense of what is a problem and what is acceptable as its solution; tools and methods with which to carry out typical practices; a social network between participants and members; a common history.

An example of how a "criminal community of practice" functions is taken from the operation of drugs trafficking enterprises. Since these organizations, like mafias, cannot resort to formal written rules, these rules "are embodied in informal intersubjective understandings among participants about the *way things are done around here*" (Kenney 2007, 37). As a former pilot for a prominent Colombian drug smuggler says:

We never said, "Be careful," or, "if you go this far, you going to be dead…" You don't have to say it. It was implicit. We knew that because of who the people were that we were working with, we had to keep a low profile. (Kenney 2007, 37)

These implicit understandings are communicated through conversations, stories, body language, and other methods that allow experts to share standards, practices, and experience with their younger colleagues. An important element of this learning process consists in so-called war stories. These are particularly significant events in the life of the organization, sometimes exaggerated by those who tell them, but emblematic of how the organization has addressed a critical event in its life. These war stories allow the initiand to learn not only how certain events took place, but how the organization dealt with them (positively or otherwise).

The community of practices of work are identified as informal groupings defined not only by their members but by the sharing of the ways in which they do things and in which they interpret events. The concept of practice refers both to the activities that are effectively implemented and to the skills possessed and deployed to achieve them. Learning is accomplished through a process of integration within a community of practice according to a path "from the periphery to the center," a path of "legitimate peripheral participation" that allows novices and experts the realization of shared *sense-making* processes (Weick 1995).

In various mafias, after recruitment, there is a training period before formal initiation. For example, in the Yakuza, the trainees live in the gang offices, where they learn a number of aspects of organizational life, including Yakuza etiquette and behavior. Trainees are expected to "see with their eyes, hear with their ears and keep their mouth shut" (Hill

2004, 108). The learning method is based, in fact, on the observation of practices more than explicit education (Hill 2014, 237). In the past, this period could last as long as three years, but has now been reduced, in some cases to just six months. This has caused some dissatisfaction among the organization's "old boys" with regard to a decline in standards, and in particular the fact that the physical and mental toughness of trainees are not sufficiently tested.

Given that there are no schools that provide training for the profession of the *mafioso*, the entrance selection requires that the candidate has already developed a number of skills during his previous life experience, especially in the street. He must have developed qualities such as toughness and courage, and the use of violence. There is plenty of empirical evidence of this in mafia biographies. Sammy Gravano, who later became the underboss of the Gambino family, proved his courage in a fight against three of his peers at the age of nine and his bravery and strength earned him the nickname of "The Bull." His talents impressed the mobsters who had observed him and from then on continued to keep him under observation until his entry into the organization (Maas 1997). Philip Leonetti, underboss of the Philadelphia family and known as "mad-dog killer," has said that he acquired his criminal training under the tutelage of his mentor, Skinny Razor DiTullio (Leonetti et al. 2012, 28). Like an artisanal apprenticeship, learning by doing and coaching are the cornerstones of mafia learning.

Other forms of learning can relate to work processes. For example, cocaine producers in Colombia have developed a way to produce up to 60 percent more cocaine from coca leaves than in the past, using new chemical precursors and new machinery, but also taking advantage of the knowledge of the farmers, who introduced a series of small improvements in the production process that made it possible to increase product output (Wainwright 2016).

2.4   Reputation

CASSIO: Reputation, reputation, reputation! O! I have lost my reputation. I have
    lost the immortal part of myself, and what remains is bestial. My reputation,
    Iago, my reputation!
IAGO: As I am an honest man, I thought you had received some bodily wound;
    there is more offence in that than in reputation. Reputation is an idle
    and most false imposition; oft got without merit, and lost without
    deserving: you have lost no reputation at all, unless you repute yourself
    such a loser.

        William Shakespeare, The Tragedy of Othello, the Moor of Venice,
                                 Act II, Scene III, 262–9

The reputation of an organization is an opinion about that entity, typically a result of social evaluation on a set of criteria, or certain positive or negative qualities. Reputation is made up out of the opinions of others, is social information, and is difficult to create: it requires time to be built and is even more difficult to maintain over time: "It takes twenty years to build a reputation and five minutes to ruin it," stated Warren Buffett (1995, 109), an American business magnate and one of the most successful investors in the world. Akerlof (1970) sees reputation as a good expedient to neutralize uncertainty with regard to quality, to stabilize future economic relations, and to ensure long-term relationships. Thompson (1967, 110) considers reputation the most affordable way to gain power.

From an organizational point of view, reputation is "a perceptual representation of a company's past actions and future prospects that describes the firm's overall appeal to all its key constituents when compared to other leading rivals" (Fombrun 1996, 72). Firms rely on both tangible and intangible resources to gain a competitive advantage against rivals (Fombrun 2005). Where positive, reputation constitutes a form of capital for an individual or organization; where negative, it constitutes a fixed cost where relationships are concerned (Mutti 2007). A good reputation encourages shareholders to invest in a company. It attracts good staff and retains customers (Markham 1972), and it is important to sustain an organization through tough times. A great deal of research shows that reputation has become increasingly important for companies and their management in recent years (Bonini et al. 2009; Scott 2013). This also applies to criminal enterprises such as mafias. As Diego Gambetta noted:

By far the most striking feature of a *mafioso*'s reputation is that it saves directly on production costs. Car manufacturers benefit from a good reputation, but they still have to produce cars. By contrast, a reputation for credible protection and protection itself tend to be one and the same thing. The more robust the reputation of a protection firm, the less the need to have recourse to the resources which support that reputation. (Gambetta 1993, 44)

As for other organizations, we can distinguish three different conceptualizations of organizational reputation in mafias: *being known*, *being known for something*, and *generalized favorability* (Lange et al. 2011).

Being known refers to the generalized awareness or visibility of the firm, the prominence of the firm in collective perception. In this view, "organizational reputation is stronger if awareness of the firm is broader and if perceivers have a more distinctive perceptual representation of the firm, irrespective of judgment or evaluation" (Lange et al. 2011, 155). The visibility of the "brand" (Gambetta 1993) and its often mythical fame are important elements in this kind of reputation, as "image and identity can be usually seen as the main components of reputation" (Chun 2005, 105). The judge Giuseppe Gennari (2013) says: "The 'Ndrangheta is a little like a brand. It is a mafia trademark of quality that groups together several confederated families" (73).

The conceptualization of organizational reputation as *being known for something* focuses on the perceived predictability of organizational outcomes and behavior relevant to specific audience interests. Reputation entails perceptions that the firm possesses specific attributes of interest and value to the perceiver: high-quality products, for example (Milgrom and Roberts 1986). In the *being known for something* perspective, "organizational reputation fills a necessary role in that limited information context, consisting of subjective perceptions held by a particular audience with respect to the likelihood of seeing desired behaviors and outputs from the firm in the future" (Lange et al. 2011, 158). Reputation in mafias relies on the capacity for carrying out protection, making violent threats, and providing reliable services. This type of reputation is a clear sign of organizational reputation based on *being known for something*.

The fact that, as we will see in Section 2.8, more and more entrepreneurs are seeking the protection of the mafia, and not vice versa, is clear evidence that the mafia organization has a powerful reputation for *being known for something*. The case of the Italian entrepreneur Angelo Siino, who turned to the Sicilian Cosa Nostra to coordinate the public tender system in Sicily, and that of Asset Development, where the company sought mafia protection to solve social and political problems, are a clear example of how the mafia organization's reputation is based on the fact of being perceived as a service agency: it is the legal business that seeks out the criminal organization to make use of its services. This is not extortion, but a reciprocally beneficial relationship of joint interest between a legal business and a mafia organization.

Generalized favorability regards perceptions or judgments of the overall organization as good, attractive, and appropriate. Managers can make strategic use of their company's reputation to signal its attractiveness (Fombrun 2005, 343). More than the ability to satisfy specific needs by providing services and products, reputation based on generalized favorability has to do with the degree of acceptance and validation of an organization by the external environment. According to this conception, reputation is a general organizational attribute that reflects the extent to which external stakeholders see the firm as "good and not bad" (Roberts and Dowling 2002, 1078), and how they admire and find attractive those organizations that appear to have "desirable character traits (i.e., trust-worthiness, reliability)" and/or that "conform to practices that are locally appropriate and culturally desirable" (Love and Kraatz 2009, 316). Reputation such as *being known* and *being known for something*, on the other hand, emphasizes comparison between organizations.

Reputation understood as *generalized favorability* is based on public awareness of the organization, on its visibility. This helps explain why mafias are actively involved in certain public events, exposing themselves to the risk of interception and arrest. In Italy, for example, the Sicilian Cosa Nostra, the 'Ndrangheta, and to a lesser extent the Camorra support a number of religious festivals[27] that feature processions involving the display of a statue of the local saint (Gratteri and Nicaso 2013b). This has also been the case for a long time with the American Cosa Nostra, who financed and organized the San Gennaro festival in Little Italy in New York.[28] In addition to financing such initiatives, the mobsters participate physically, sometimes carrying the statue themselves and making stops in front of the house of a fugitive, a boss, or an important figure in the criminal organiza-tion. Control of the festivals is exercised through (1) the management of the timing of the festivities: the procession stops, the times and places for setting off the fireworks, the times of the return of the statue (*fercolo*) to the cathedral; (2) the location of the stalls, whose revenues are determined by the location along the route of the procession; (3) the management of the cash flow, both illicit (betting) and licit (e.g., the sale of candles; orders for the fireworks; the fees of the bearers of the statues and the *candelore*, the heavy wooden candles carried by groups of six to eight men; the collection of donations; the finding of the sponsors). During the procession, there are frequent deviations from the established route and stops that have very little to do with the religious aspect of the festival.[29]

---

[27] For example, for the Sicilian Cosa Nostra, the festival of Sant'Agata in Catania; for the 'Ndrangheta, the festival of Seminara, or of the Madonna delle Grazie of Oppido Mamertina; the Madonna della Montagna in Polsi; the Addolorata dell'Affruntata in the Vibonese area; others in Reggio Calabria, etc.

[28] In the United States, the American Cosa Nostra (in particular the Genovese family, one of the five New York families) has for a long time run the San Gennaro festival, held every September since 1926 in Mulberry Street in New York's Little Italy. The criminal organization handled the huge donations and extorted money from the various sellers. Since 1997, the management of the festival has been freed from mafia control and handed over to an association, "The Children of San Gennaro." Nevertheless, it seems that the percentage of income donated to charity is very similar to the percentage given when the party was under mafia control (G.B. Smith, "Little Italy's Feast of San Gennaro donates under 5% to charity - just slightly more than when Mafia ran the festival", *Daily News*, September 19, 2014).

[29] The festival of Sant'Agata, in Catania (Sicily), has long been controlled by the Sicilian Cosa Nostra, in particular from 1999 to 2005 by the Santapaola and Mangion mafia families

Through the control over religious festivals, mafia organizations increase their criminal prestige, consolidating their reputation as city power centers. With regard to this, the deputy prosecutor of Reggio Calabria, Nicola Gratteri, states: "Mafias feed on popular consensus, to exist, they seek amongst the people, are present where there is business and popular participation, in sports, in the rites of the Church . . . for the bosses of the *'ndrine*, processions are a showcase."[30] For mobsters, maintaining a close relationship with religion and the rituals connected with it represents not only prestige, but above all authority. Taking this away from them means that the organization loses control of the territory.[31]

Similarly, the Hong Kong Triads are actively involved in traditional Chinese festivals celebrated each year (Chu 2000), such as the birthdays of the Kwun Yam (the Goddess of Mercy), To Tei (the God of the Earth), and Tin Hau (the Sea Goddess). The various Triads compete to appear more numerous than the others during these events and to occupy a place at the head of the procession. While, in the Sicilian Cosa Nostra, protection firms compete in toughness with each other to be the most credible protector in the territory,

the case of Hong Kong Triads suggests that protection firms have different strategies for establishing their reputation. An individual triad society can do it by presenting the strength of its numbers, displaying emblems and banners, or struggling for possession of the "bamboo" slip in public during the celebration of Chinese festivals. Young triad bosses may show their power by mobilising a large number of people in another triad's territory. Street gang leaders may resort to violence to enhance their notoriety in the area. Thus, violence is only one of the means used to establish the reputation of a protection firm. (Chu 2000, 137)

Chu also says that

it is claimed that violence in Triads is irrational because it is usually used for trivial things, such as for girlfriends or simply for "face." The evidence above shows that violence is used to build up and maintain a Triad's reputation as a

---

from Catania. On February 4, 2015, the Sant'Agata procession stopped below the house of a Sicilian Cosa Nostra mobster under house arrest. In Oppido Mamertino (Reggio Calabria), in July 2014, the procession deviated from its usual route to stop and pay homage in front of the house of Giuseppe Mazzagatti, an old 'Ndrangheta clan boss, 82 years old and already sentenced to life imprisonment for murder and criminal association with the mafia. The *carabinieri* abandoned the march in protest ("Processione Calabria, Cei: 'La Madonna non s'inchina ai malavitosi,'" *la Repubblica*, July 6, 2014).

[30] C. Macrì, "Processione 'commissariata'. Il paese si ribella, rito annullato", *Il Corriere della Sera*, April 20, 2014, 18.

[31] To try to prevent mafia control of religious festivals, the church has now and then resorted to measures such as the drawing of lots from a preorganized list for the statue bearers, or entrusted this activity to members of the civil protection organization. This has in some cases raised protests from the faithful.

credible protector. Since Triads have established their reputation for violence, some people are able to use this "trademark" to make profits. (2000, 39)

Ames (1981) observes that in the Yakuza: "Gangsters are very concerned with 'face' (*kao* or *mentsu*), and a gangster's power is directly related to his reputation," and a boss of one of the families has stated that "face is more powerful than money" (114). As Gambetta observed (1993), "this peculiar form of sponsorship – the sponsor is the *mafioso*, the saint his innocent beneficiary – relies, like all publicity, on contemporary beliefs and exploits both the general attributes of sanctity and those specific to each individual saint" (48). The Yakuza was very active after the great Tohoku earthquake (March 11, 2011), providing substantial aid to the victims for the first few weeks immediately after the disaster. This was a calculated public relations choice designed to live up to their carefully cultivated public image.

The reputation of a mafia organization stems from several factors: (a) the recognition granted by protected/extorted subjects – the recipients of mafia action; (b) the recognition granted by other organizations, both legal and criminal; (c) its ability to speak on behalf of the entire organization, with any nonconformist behavior contained. Bill Bonanno (1983) explains the way in which this reputation works. If someone asks "a man of honor" to recover a stolen ring, the man of honor requires connection between bandits and brigands in order to retrieve the object. He will ask the owner of the stolen ring for a sum of money as a reward and, through his network of relationships, will find the ring and pay to get it back, keeping the difference for himself for his mediation work. The reputation of these men of honor is based on the fact that they are "qualified in all aspects of life, qualified to deal with all types of people. Usually, these men use diplomacy, astuteness and friendly persuasion; sometimes, however, they resort to violence" (Bonanno 1983, 41). This example clarifies the role of the *mafioso*, who is not a mere extortionist, and certainly not a simple thief; rather, he acts as a bridge between two parties (the thief and the person robbed). The real story, however, may be rather different, in the sense that, if the thief has operated in territory controlled by a family without having been given authorization to do so, he will certainly not receive any money to return the ring and will undergo violence.

In illegal markets, reputation is a two-edged sword:

On the one hand, it serves to deter rival gangs from direct challenge. On the other hand, the economy of illegal markets is not an autonomous economy, ruled only by its own institutions. It is a part of a larger society, which may not respond to various marginal changes in those markets but is capable of effectively penalizing those gangs whose reputation give them power within the world of illegal markets. (Reuter 1985a, 29)

The cost of having the reputation of dominant gang is increasingly targeted law enforcement activity. Reputation is not, of course, only a positive thing. And a bad reputation can be used to political ends (Fine 1996; Parker 2004; Mutti 2006). For example, prior to physically eliminating his opponents, Sicilian Cosa Nostra's boss Totò Riina discredited them by circulating false information in order to isolate them, reducing their alliances and protections.

Mafia reputation is associated with violence. Studying the Russian gangs, Stephenson (2015) showed that if a member of a gang lost face publicly, this could have consequences for the gang's reputation. Even the smallest provocation can lead to a war, and an insult must be absolutely avenged, on pain of loss of reputation for the person insulted. This is the case for many criminal organizations, such as those in Albanian organized crime (Arsovska 2015), where the "eye for an eye" philosophy is at the basis of many blood feuds.

2.5 Sagas, Rituals, and Collective Events

Being part of a mafia organization is not only a matter of entering a "normal" criminal organization. Mafias are characterized by systems of norms and rules of conduct, rituals and references to organizational sagas, cultivated and supported by the leaders as well as by ordinary members of the organization. This constitutes an element of strength that allows mafias to succeed where many modern corporations fail. Contrary to certain reconstructions, the rituals are not mere folklore, the crude and anachronistic remnants of a lost world, or inoffensive indicators of the archaic nature of the mafias. Instead, they play an extremely important role in terms of organizational functioning and are still highly relevant. On August 15, 2007, in Duisburg, Germany, six people were brutally killed at the doors of an Italian restaurant. The victims, too, were Italian, from San Luca, a small town in Calabria. At least seventy shots were fired and, at the end of the slaughter, the killer fired a shot into the head of each victim, so that death was assured. The victims were close to, or members of, the 'Ndrangheta, as were the perpetrators of the massacre, which had its origins in a feud between different groups of the criminal organization. One of the victims had a *santino* – the image of a saint – in his pocket, and this card had been burned: a sign that he had recently been made a member of the organization, and that probably the rite of initiation had been performed the same evening as the massacre itself.

In the twenty-first century, rituals and myth still play a significant part in the organizational life of mafias, not only in their places of origin, but also in the areas into which they have spread and expanded.

In addition to ritual, an element of great interest that characterizes mafias is that, despite being illegal secret organizations, they make use of mythical reconstructions relating to their origins: "organizational sagas," in other words.

2.5.1 Organizational Sagas

Most mafia organizations are characterized by some form of saga, a kind of historical narrative that describes the unique exploits of a group and its leader, as a rule in epic terms. The term "saga" originally refers to a medieval Icelandic or Norse account of achievements and events in the history of a person or group. An organizational saga "is a collective understanding of a unique accomplishment in a formally established group" (Burton 1972, 178). It is based on the historical exploits of a formal organization, offering strong normative bonds within and outside the organization. Sagas provide pride and favor internal cohesion among members.

On numerous occasions, various Italian mafias, in particular the 'Ndrangheta, have made reference to the criminal organization's saga of origin: the legend of Osso (bone), Mastrosso (masterbone), and Carcagnosso (heelbone) (Ciconte et al. 2010; Dickie 2012),[32] three legendary Spanish knights who were part of the Garduña[33] of Toledo, in Spain. Sought by the authorities for killing a man who had offended the sister of one of the knights, they fled to Italy in 1412 and settled on the island of Favignana (Sicily), where they remained, according to the legend, for twenty-nine years, eleven months, and twenty-nine days. During this long period, they drew up the rules and laws pertaining to the mafia, and then journeyed, respectively, to Sicily, Calabria and Campania, where they, respectively, founded the Sicilian Cosa Nostra, the 'Ndrangheta, and the Camorra. It is certainly a legend that still has the power to fascinate the new members of criminal organizations, and is the only legend that tells of three mafia organizations.

---

[32] Of the various mafias, it is the 'Ndrangheta who have developed written versions of the codes, both to regulate different aspects of community life and to strengthen the sense of belonging to a community (Malafarina 1986; Ciconte and Macrì 2009; Trumper et al. 2014; Ciconte 2015).

[33] A legendary secret criminal organization, which probably existed from the fifteenth century until the nineteenth century.

The legend of the Beati Paoli sect, meanwhile, deals only with Palermo and relates to the origins of the Sicilian Cosa Nostra. First described in 1909 (Natoli 1971), the story tells of the adventures of an order of knights fighting to help the commoners and the poor. In 1071, in Sicily, with the introduction of the feudal system, the nobles began to exploit their advantages. At the same time, the church created an atmosphere of fear through the Inquisition. Every action committed by the poor and the commoners that could be interpreted as treason or heresy could be punished by death. The Beati Paoli were founded, according to legend, to oppose this overwhelming power in the hands of the nobles and the church. They wore black hooded coats and operated at night from their refuge in the remains of the catacombs and underground channels of Palermo. With their exploits resembling those of Robin Hood, they have been considered, in the popular imagination and mafia ideology, as a protomanifestation of the Sicilian mafia. The *mafiosi* regarded themselves as the successors to the Beati Paoli, carrying out similar deeds in a modern context. Bosses as important as Totò Riina and Gaspare Mutolo have referred to this saga under judicial interrogation. Another collaborator with justice, former mobster Antonino Calderone, said he was told when he was initiated into the Sicilian Cosa Nostra that a *mafioso* should "follow the example of the Beati Paoli" (in Gambetta 1993, 13).

Bill Bonanno, son and adviser to the boss of the New York Bonanno family of the American Cosa Nostra, traces the origin of the Cosa Nostra (Sicilian and American) to a proto-*mafiosi* group, the Avengers, who were active in the second half of the eleventh century: a group of brave and talented men fighting against the foreign rulers of the island (Bonanno and Abromovitz 2011). Of course, historical sources do not support such a claim in any way, but this is not the point. What is important to note is the search for an original purity, a founding myth that gives legitimacy to the organization. The very name Cosa Nostra itself (Our Thing) would indicate, according to Bill Bonanno, an organization based on tradition:

We understood the concept of *mafiosi* to refer to men with a shared ideology and lifestyle based on tradition, not a criminal organization ... and characterized by certain core beliefs, such as that we must aid one another, be true to our friends against all enemies, defend our dignity and that of our friends against all threats, and never let trespasses go unavenged. (Bonanno and Abromovitz 2011, 6)

After referring to other unlikely origins of the term "mafia," related to the activities of groups organized against the French invader, Bonanno returns to the myth of the Beati Paoli as a group that was a precursor to the gangs of the Sicilian Cosa Nostra and then the American Cosa

Nostra, going back to the Robin Hood origin myth. In this interpretation, the Cosa Nostra was intended not as a vehicle to break the law for its own sake, but as a way for oppressed people to band together, to favor personal connections over exploitation by a foreign power, and to ignore oppressive laws when they conflicted with local moral traditions: not a criminal organization in search of profit, but a stew of loyalty, righteousness, mutual help, and courage.

Joe Bonanno (1983), Bill's father and boss of the New York Bonanno family, mythicized his flight from Italy in terms of fleeing from the fascist police, as a form of rebellion against the domination of the regime: in Bonanno's discourse, mafia and antifascism are synonymous. The reality, however, was quite different: he fled to the United States not because of oppression from the totalitarian regime, but to avoid being arrested for numerous illegal activities. For Bonanno, the mafia is a group of men of honor, and represents a "tradition" based on respect, justice (the mafia type), and courage. Men of honor, stated Bonanno, "were essential to Sicilian society in their capacities as brokers, facilitators and arbiters. But to serve as a middleman, a 'man of respect' needed more than personal courage. ... His effectiveness depended on his network of friendships" (1983, 40). As the proto-*mafiosi* (the Beati Paoli) opposed – again, according to Bonanno – feudal power and the Inquisition, so the mafia opposed fascism and its attempt to establish control over everything, and especially its attempt to eliminate the "tradition" of the men of honor. The escape to the United States became the only chance of maintaining that tradition in a new land.

So, in Bonanno's view, the mafia was not an organization, but the practice of, and the respect for, a tradition: one may speak of a "*mafioso* way of life, a Tradition if you will, a set of ideals and customs, a mode of thinking, that is peculiar to Sicilians. This Tradition provides a code of conduct for a Sicilian to follow, regardless of the enterprise he's engaged in" (Bonanno 1983, 219). Former American Cosa Nostra mobster Vito Palermo (an alias) states: "My meaning of mafia is that there are in fact groups of people who are tightly knit by virtue of ethnic and family ties who participate in all forms of criminal activity on a highly organized basis" (in Abadinsky 1981, 118). Of course, behind this interpretation of the mafia, there are also powerful interests related to a judicial defensive strategy aimed at minimizing the role of the organizational aspect of the activity in order to avoid a more severe level of punishment.

Other mafias, such as the Triads and the Yakuza, are also given origin tales with noble motives. The Triads have produced a legend according to which they originated in China as a group of monks in the Shaolin Temple in the mid-seventeenth century whose aim was to fight the alien

Qing government and restore the native Chinese Ming dynasty – a legend designed to build a positive myth into the construction of the criminal organization (Chu 2000). The Yakuza, on the other hand, claim to be descendants of the *machi yakko* group, a self-help society formed from the victims of ill treatment by the nobles of the time and who fought against the latter as a sort of fifteenth- and sixteenth-century Japanese version of Robin Hood and His Merry Men.

It is particularly interesting to note how different criminal organizations are characterized by a common aspiration to, and need for, a sense of legitimacy in terms of the origin of the organization – an aspiration and need that go beyond those of a criminal organization. Albeit characterized by highly different sociocultural contexts, they demonstrate obvious similarities in the common search for an origin story, a founding myth that legitimates the organization in its general objectives of seeking justice and defending the weak. It is an element typical of mafias and that is not found in other forms of organized crime. There is, however, no evidence to support the existence of these ancient myths.

2.5.2 Rituals

Organizations frequently have recourse to the creation of rituals: for example corporate parties, hiring and retirement ceremonies, periodic conferences, annual assemblies, etc. These are types of event that, in addition to the explicit function, perform a latent function of reinforcing organization culture and integration, fostering a sense of belonging and commitment from members. Ritual also contributes to the simplification of control, due to people's tendency to introject, making the organization's objectives their own. Ritual is, therefore, a fundamental element of organizational cultures, seen as the glue that helps hold together the organization through the sharing of meaningful patterns (Siehl and Martin 1990). In ritual, there is maintained a "predictable and regular observance of some act or procedure, which has a symbolic element resulting in the inculcation or reinforcement of shared values and beliefs" (Coyne and Mathers 2011, 74).

As Deal and Kennedy (1982) have shown, in some corporations, such as IBM and Mary Kay (cosmetics), organizations frequently employ ritual in a strategic manner in order to create and strengthen organizational culture. In companies, management thus exercises a hegemonic control over the workers, especially those at a lower hierarchical level (Willmott 1993; Alvesson 2002). In this context, ritual is an instrument of power in the hands of management and used for largely self-serving political aims, and for channeling and repression of conflict (Lukes

1975). Kunda (1992) shows the largely instrumental use of a set of organizational rituals deployed in a high-tech corporation, such as top management presentations, training workshops, and formal group meetings. While these events seem open, informal, and participatory, they actually serve to exert cultural control over the workforce, molding it to conform to the interests of top management. As Anand (2005) pointed out, "The enactment of rituals allows for individuals to invoke and internalize collective social categories central to an organization, defining, for example, what is sanctioned and what is taboo, who is an insider and who is not" (353). In this sense, ritual contributes to organizational sense-making, helping participants to make sense of the various organization rules and values (Ritti and Funkhouser 1987). Ritual is important not only in organizations, but also in political life. An idea – even one that is difficult to understand – can be made visible through myth, symbol, and ritual, says Mosse (1974).

Collins (2004, 48–9) argues that ritual is characterized by certain ingredients and provides specific outcomes. The main ingredients are group assembly (bodily copresence), the barrier to outsiders, a mutual focus of attention, and shared mood. Ritual provides certain outcomes such as group solidarity (a feeling of membership), an emotional energy in individuals, symbols that represent the group, and standards of morality, meaning the sense of rightness in adhering to the group.

Many rituals have rational foundations, and they exist for many reasons, such as identity, signaling, and common knowledge (Coyne and Mathers 2011). If a great deal is known about ritual in both complex societies and organizations, less attention has been paid to criminal rituals, with a few exceptions (Skarbek and Wang 2015). Mafias and other criminal organizations employ ritual for the same practical reasons legitimate organizations do. According to Skarbek and Wang (2015), criminals establish ritual to enhance the effectiveness of their groups, "by creating common knowledge, reducing asymmetric information, and reducing social distance" (291). In particular:

Criminal rituals become more important (a) when the number of people involved increases, (b) when the tasks become more complicated and interdependent, and (c) when communication is more difficult; (292)

Criminal groups are more likely to use rituals when there is asymmetric information about an important, unobservable characteristic; (294)

Criminal groups are more likely to use rituals the more costly it is to monitor members' behavior. (298)

The following sections will look at some of the main rituals: *initiation*, the most articulated and complex from a symbolic point of view;

integration and aggregation, such as parties and other events; and, less well known and articulated, *degradation*.

2.5.3 Mafia Liturgies: The Initiation Rituals

Eliade (1976) groups together initiation rites into three broad categories. The first covers all the collective rituals that mark the passage from childhood or adolescence to adulthood. A second category includes membership rituals in secret societies and religious and military brother-hoods. Finally, in the third category, Eliade places all the rituals that mark the entrance to a mystical vocation, such as the shaman and medicine man in ancient times. Initiation rites are also present in many organizations. For example, the recruitment and training rites of army recruits or other military groups are rites of passage, initiation into modern organizational life. They mark the transition to the status of a soldier, and are aimed at eliminating the patterns of behavior based on bourgeois identity through the learning of new behavior patterns (Bourne 1967). Similar rites are also present in many corporations. Rohen (1973) describes the training of Japanese banking executives and the series of extremely difficult and complex rites of passage, involving a period of three months in which the new employees had to meditate and abstain from food in a Zen monastery, do exercises, perform voluntary work in the local community, go on holiday together, and take long, tiring walks. Such practices were designed as a means for the effective socialization of new recruits. Certain of these rites, in general less complex, are present in a third of medium to large Japanese corporations, with positive effects on productivity and employee commitment.

Secret organizations, too, make use of socialization processes and rituals (Simmel 1906). For mafias, one of the most well-known rituals consists of the initiation ritual. In its complexity, it constitutes a form of liturgy, a particularly important ceremony for a mafia organization.

As Erikson highlights, "Ceremonialism permits a group to behave in a symbolically ornamental way so that it seems to represent an ordered universe; each particle achieves an identity by its mere interdependency with all the others. In ceremonial stylization, the vertical and the hori-zontal met" (1958, 186).

The initiation rite is a form of ceremonialism that, for the candidates for initiation (the initiands), marks the abandonment of the world to which they belonged and the entrance into a new world, into a commu-nity and into a world of new values in the context of a new life. It is a rite of institution (Bourdieu 1982), in the sense that it institutes and sancti-fies the new order that has been established with the entrance of the initiand into the organization – the initiand is endowed with a new status. It is a sort of rite of investiture, like that of a knight. Symbolically, initiation represents a new beginning and it is therefore necessary to abolish everything that already exists and which is considered old. Finally, rituals of initiation feign boundaries between members of a group and outsiders (La Fontaine 1985).

In mafia ritual, there is a mixture of sacred and profane symbols. The *mafiosi* rituals are rituals in all respects: they are *encoded* – they follow, in other words, a precise sequence of gestures and acts; they are *reiterated* – repeated within a defined cyclic time; they are *effective* – they modify the individual who takes part. In fact, at the end of the ritual, the initiand will be another person, with a different status. As in other secret societies' "rites of passage," the initiation is intended to achieve the psychological effect in the individual of a transition from one state of being, held to be inferior, to a higher state, completing the transformation of the profane in the initiate (Hutin 1955). This ritual is sometimes called "baptism," to emphasize the entry into the mafia organization and the impossibility of leaving. The oath of the mafia member, as it is with the members of other secret organizations, makes the pact between the member and the organization explicit, and its violation is punishable by death.

The rite of initiation proves to the initiates that they are truly important for the organization:

> It marks their acceptance into a community of those who can keep secrets, and who have important secrets to keep ... Initiation rites serve group purposes of transforming individuals from indifferent outsiders to completely loyal insiders. For individuals, the rites promise access to innermost secrecy, prestige, self-transcendence, and enlightenment. (Bok 1989, 49–50)

According to Max Weber (1922), the oath is one of the most universal forms of all brotherhood contracts and involves, in addition to the performance of certain acts, the individual's becoming something qualitatively different from before. As well as this sense of otherness, there is a sense of superiority on the part of the members, the idea of belonging to an elite, by virtue of the special qualities, such as courage, that the adept has to demonstrate. Informant Antonino Calderone, former member of the Sicilian Cosa Nostra, stated that "one shouldn't forget that the mafia is an organization of people who have taken an oath" (in Arlacchi 1993, 37).

Initiation rites are present in criminal organizations such as gangs (Padilla 1992; Decker and van Winkle 1996) and in other mafias. They are also present in some of the Camorra clans, though, less so than in the past (Mastriani 1889–90). They share many similarities: for example, between the rituals of the Sicilian and the American Cosa Nostra[34] (Gambetta 1993; Critchley 2009, 63; Lupo 2011a).[35]

The Cosa Nostra ritual has many variations, but it is possible to identify a typical sequence consisting of three phases. (1) First, the initiate is brought into the presence of other members of the family that he will join; (2) A description of the organization is then given and the main rules presented; (3) Finally, the oath is taken, which states that the middle finger of the hand that the new member uses to shoot is pierced by the member officiating the ceremony, using a needle, knife, or safety pin, until the finger bleeds. The blood that emerges stains the image of a saint. This will then be set alight and the initiate must pass the image from one hand to the other while reciting the swearing-in formula (Maas 1968; Anastasia 1991; Arlacchi 1993; 1994; Fresolone and Wagman 1994; Maas 1997; OSPA Stajano 2010; Raab 2016).

As for rites of passage (van Gennep 1960), the initiation ritual has a tripartite structure, with three phases. First, there is the preliminary stage of (1) *separation* (preliminal[36] phase) in which the subject is detached from the context in which he finds himself – a stripping away of his initial state. The initiand is taken to a particular place in the presence of the leadership and the mafia hierarchy, thus symbolically abandoning his belonging to a former world. There is then phase (2) *transition* (liminal phase), in which the subject is in an ambiguous state, and passes through a symbolic step that represents the climax of the ceremony, with the rite of *pungitura* (wounding), the burned saint and the recitation of the oath. Finally, there is the phase of *integration* (postliminal phase), in which the transition is complete and the subject is reinstated to his existence with a new social status, into a new stable state, kissing those present.

The initiation rites of the Triads also share many similarities with those of the American and Sicilian Cosa Nostra. In the modern triad initiation ceremony

---

[34] The initiation ritual is the same for all American families, except the Chicago Outfit. Since the origins of the Chicago clan, including its famous leader Al Capone, were in Naples, the Chicago mobs rejected the rite, which originated in Sicily. The entrance ceremony for the organization is limited to a formal dinner during which the initiand is introduced to the other members (Capeci 2004). Even the Camorra has practiced, and in some cases still practices, the rite of initiation. But the ritual was almost completely discontinued at the start of the nineteenth century, only to be resumed a few years later. Al Capone, therefore, was probably not aware of it and continued to believe it was a custom of the Sicilian mafia.

[35] Gambetta (1993, 146, 262–70) detailed thirteen Sicilian Cosa Nostra rituals and two American Cosa Nostra rituals, concluding that they are similar.

[36] From the Latin word *limen*, which means "boundary."

the recruit, accompanied by his sponsor, is first informed of the history of the Triads and reminded that his initiation must be completely voluntary. He takes an oath before an altar which is decorated to represent the mythical triad capital of Muk Yeung. He is then warned of the fate of traitors, swears loyalty to his brothers which may include drinking a mixture of his own blood and that of other initiates, and pays a symbolic sum of lucky money as a form of joining fee. At the end of the ceremony the recruit is taught some recognition signals and triad poems so that he can recognise fellow members. Recently, the sacrificial chicken has been often replaced by an egg, and in some cases new recruits are asked to suck their own blood from their finger instead of mixing it with others. (Chu 2000, 33)

In the past, this ceremony was rather long and complex, involving a series of stages, and took place in a special space (lodge) with the physical center of the initiation ritual consisting of an altar, as a place for burning incense and bringing offerings. The ceremony took place in the presence of numerous people, with clothing typical for this sort of ceremonial occasion and a multitude of objects (such as flags, swords, umbrellas, rosaries, white papers, fans, Morgan 1960) – powerfully symbolic items that often recalled mythical figures in Chinese history (La Fontaine 1985; Ter Haar 1998). The recruit had to pass through a series of "entrances" before reaching the triad altar, where the ceremony took place. A particularly significant moment of the ritual was that of the "Heaven and Earth Circle" (Morgan 1960, 155–6), which involved a large bamboo hoop with sprigs of pine cedar, the Chinese symbols of longevity, on the sides. The recruit had to pass through this hoop, an action that carried a double significance. First, the event commemorates the legendary flight of the monks from the monastery, and, second, it symbolizes the rebirth of the recruit from his previous life into the new life of the organization. In addition, there is an oath (called "The Thirty Six Oaths of the Society") in which the recruit vows to respect a set of commandments relating to various organization commitments: to brotherhood and mutual aid, both physical and financial, toward other members of the organization; to maintaining secrecy; to never using violence against other members of the organization; to showing respect to women (wives, sisters, or daughters of members); to neither cheating nor stealing in such a way as to harm other members; to never attempting to assume organization roles falsely without authorization; and to other prohibitions and codes of conduct that a good member of the organization has to follow (Morgan 1960, 157–60). In the past, this ceremony could last for an entire day and involve the participation of many people. Today, partly for security reasons, it is much shorter (about an hour), with the presence of just a small number of people: about nine to twelve new members at a time and with only two or three minor triad officials presiding.[37] The same process of simplification of procedures, with shortening of duration and reduction in number of those present, has been noted in various mafias.

As in other mafias, blood also plays a special role in the Triads: the members mingle their blood with that of other recruits, and, after having sipped the mixture, they become blood brothers, a fact that can never be altered. And, as with the other mafias, entrance into the organization is for life, with only death terminating membership (Morgan 1960, 263).

In the past, in the Camorra, rites were very common as important moments in community life. Admissions and promotions were surrounded by rites, solemn and superstitious ceremonies, combining the mystical and the sectarian (Alongi 1890). With the beginning of the twentieth century, these rites gradually lost importance, until, during his leadership (1975–83), the boss Raffaele Cutolo reintroduced a number of procedures into the clans affiliated to him. These procedures in part derived from the rituals of the nineteenth-century Camorra, which were in turn influenced by the Spanish Garduña, and in part from the membership rite of the 'Ndrangheta. The new *picciotto* was introduced into the presence of other members, and the boss opened the session – called "baptism," "legalization," or "loyalization." The prospective member had to choose a "blood brother" who, instead of taking blood from the member's finger, made a cut in the latter's forearm in order to establish formally his entrance into the criminal organization.[38] This was followed by the oath of loyalty to the organization and the vote of approval for the new member, ending with an embrace from all those present and the recitation of rules to be respected. The interesting thing is that even the rival clans to Cutolo, the cartel called the Nuova Famiglia (New Family), reintroduced various rituals and membership formulas, borrowing procedures and patterns from the old Camorra[39] (De Gregorio 1983; Di Fiore 2016).

There were also ceremonies for career advancement in the various roles of the criminal organization, for example the role of *sgarrista*

---

[37] In the past, mass ritual initiations could involve up to 100 new members. Such events were later avoided for safety reasons, being too visible to law enforcement organizations.

[38] Taken from: "Il giuramento di Palillo" (The Oath of Palillo), the membership ceremony of Raffaele Cutolo's *Nuova Camorra Organizzata*, from the cassette impounded at the entrance to Novara prison; decree-sentence *Sentenza Abagnale-Agostino+711*; in Di Fiore 2016, 376–8.

[39] On May 8, 1981, the *carabinieri* halted two important Camorra mobs, including the boss Mario Fabbrocino, who was in possession of a notebook of sheets written in capital letters containing the rules, ordinances, and formulas of the Nuova Famiglia (De Gregorio 1983).

(lawbreaker), a higher grade than that of *camorrista* and with the power to appoint the *capizona* (area managers) responsible for specific geographical districts for the association. In this case, the procedure in the first part of the ritual coincided with those of the initiand, but differed in the matter of the cut, made in the shape of a cross on the right thumb, while the *sgarrista* recited the formula "I will give my blood for the Camorra." The rite was completed with a number of clarifications regarding the commandments, the ethics of the Camorra, and the characteristics of a member ("A *camorrista* must always reason with his brain, never with his heart"), together with references to historical myths, principles of brotherhood, equality, and social justice.

In the 'Ndrangheta, the initiation ritual (also referred to as "tail docking") includes a series of questions and answers between the person officiating the rite and the initiand. In this case, too, there follows the act of a cutting a cross, usually into the thumb or palm of the right hand of the initiand, as collaborator with justice Antonino Belnome says (in Barbacetto and Milosa 2011, 418), so that the blood moistens the image of a *santino* depicting the archangel St. Michael; the card is then burned in the hands of the initiand. In the 'Ndrangheta, the son of a member is a potential *'ndraghetista*, and the membership ritual is shorter, given that the bond of blood is a mark of loyalty and endows the oath with assurance.

Initiation ceremonies in the Russian Mafia have, instead, the distinction of being, in some cases, extremely expensive, costing from $150,000 to $1 million (Siegel 2012). At the end of the ritual, the new members are given tattoos as a sign of their new status, the process being a rather brutal and painful one. The designs include religious images, such as the crucifix, church domes, representations of the Madonna with the child, and other icons of the Orthodox religious tradition. Throughout the member's life, other tattoos are added to the body, with no part excluded, creating a kind of uniform, with ranks and decorations that indicate the criminal status achieved (Baldaev and Vasiliev 2004; 2006; 2008; Varese 2017). Anyone wishing to make use of these symbols without having actually earned the right to do so risks severe punishment, from the amputation of parts of the body to the death penalty.

In the Russian Mafia the new *vory* has the mark of his new status tattooed on his body, using a needle and a razor to apply the picture on the skin (Varese 2017). Also in other mafias, the introduction ritual can be very brutal and painful. The Yakuza amputate a part of the initiand's finger. This practice, called *yubitsume*, is also used as punishment for behavior considered to be inappropriate and for a violation of the code of conduct. There are several accounts of how the ritual is carried out; as

Morris (Bosmia et al. 2014) explains, the offender places his left hand, palm down, on a small piece of clean cloth placed on a flat surface and uses a sharp knife called *tanto* to amputate his small finger. Then, the severed portion is wrapped in the cloth and handed to the head of the offender's Yakuza family, who supervises the event.

However, this rite is becoming gradually less common, partly for reasons of security, to prevent identification.[40]

Regardless of the different forms it takes in different mafias, the crucial function of the initiation rite is to instill a deep fear in the new member regarding the consequences of its violation, in the sense of betraying the organization's rules. It also places great emphasis on the extreme importance of maintaining confidentiality with respect to the association's activities. Membership is for life: the status of a "man of honor," once acquired, ceases only with death. A *mafioso*, whatever may be the vicissitudes of his life, and wherever he resides, whether in his homeland or abroad, will always remain a *mafioso* (OSPA Stajano 2010).

Collaborator with justice Tommaso Buscetta states that "once you have sworn to be a man of honor, you remain so for life. You cannot in any way spontaneously release yourself from this oath, unless there are justified reasons … a man of honor can never give up his membership of the *family*."[41] Former Philadelphia mobster Nick Caramandi says that "once you are admitted into this mob and you take the oath, there is no way you can quit. The only way you can go out, you get killed. There is no retirement" (Anastasia 1991, 319).

Membership of mafia organizations is total, as if it is a matter of belonging to "total institutions" (Goffman 1961).[42] With regard to the Sicilian Cosa Nostra, an investigator has said: "The mobster who has been part of Cosa Nostra has woken up in the morning thinking about the Cosa Nostra and fallen asleep thinking about the Cosa Nostra. He has been in actual permanent service, not just working in a band of criminals, but in a mysterious world, a world made fascinating by the secret sect; he believed in it, experiencing it as something extraordinary" (Di Cagno and Natoli 2004, 22). An organizational world separate from the world outside: "The doubts arise when you start no longer finding a justification. As long as you're within the Cosa Nostra, what public

---

[40] In 1971, this involved up to 45 percent of the members. Since 1994, this percentage has fallen to 33 percent (Hill 2003a, 75). In some Yakuza families, the reconstruction of the finger is tolerated.

[41] Testimony of Tommaso Buscetta given to Giovanni Falcone (Investigating Judge of Palermo), et al., July–August 1984, vol. III, 23.

[42] However, it should be noted that, with regard to the Italian mafias, there have been many cases of double affiliation by a member of one mafia to another (Ciconte 1996).

opinion thinks isn't really something that interests you," said Gaspare Spatuzza, former Sicilian Cosa Nostra mobster (Dino 2016, 72).

Mafia organization membership is based on specific principles that Weber (1922) defines as "segregation" and "exclusivity." Respect and honor are only guaranteed within the organization, while the outside world is seen as a "contrast," a 'Ndrangheta term to denote the outside world. This strong sense of belonging to a group and clan has implications for the use of violence: the higher the submission to the group, the easier it will be to avoid moral qualms and guilt in committing violence and homicides.

As with other initiation rites of a religious kind, some common essential elements in the structure of the rite are also found in mafia initiation rites. The first element refers to an archetype, in the sense of a model placed at the organization's origins and considered as the initiator of the rite. References to figures that are sacred (such as the holy image burned during the ceremony in Italian mafias) or profane, or references to characters that are mythical and emblematic of the organization's origin, are an example.

A second element is the symbolism of initiatory death. Initiation means death – a symbolic one, of course – for the new member as a person and, as other ethnological evidence indicates (Ries 1986), the wound, the *pungitura* (the stab into a finger or cut made in the hand to draw blood), or the use of tattoos, as with the Russian Mafia, demonstrates this.

Finally, the third element is represented by the new birth, after the initiatory death, which means for the new member to acquire a new existence as part of the new life to which he has been introduced through the initiation ritual and the rules as a new made member of the criminal organization.

2.5.4   Integration and Aggregation Rituals

Several other particularly interesting rituals exist in mafia life. Some of these are rituals of integration and aggregation, such as parties, meetings, promotions (similar, in terms of the functions performed, to company celebrations, conferences, and the annual general meetings of corporations). Their function is to encourage and revive the common sentiments that bind the members together and ensure their commitment to the organization.

In the Yakuza, ceremonies known as *girikake* frequently occur, on occasions of events in community life, such as changes of leadership or promotions. In addition to these obvious features, and as mentioned for companies, they also carry out latent functions such as reinforcing an individual sense of belonging to the group and its history and tradition.

In the Triads, promotion may be granted after at least three years of activity in the organization, and the ceremony to celebrate it requires that the candidate be sponsored by one of the older officials in the society, with the *incense master* and the society's leaders officiating in the presence of other important figures in the organization. This ceremony too has its own special spaces, a number of instruments and verse reading, as in the initiation rite, but the entire procedure has apparently (Chu 2000) been much simplified today. The Triads also have another ritual designed to strengthen the bond between the members, known as *Burning the Yellow Paper* (Morgan 1960, 226–78): it may take place in a temple, in a private home, or in the open air, and it consists of an oath of loyalty to the organization and the exhortation always to tell the truth. During the oath, a piece of paper is burned: on it there are, written in Chinese, the names of the participants, the date, and the exhortation to tell the truth. The ashes of the paper are mixed with wine and with the blood of the participants, and then drunk by the recruits in small sips.

One of the 'Ndrangheta rituals of aggregation, on the other hand, involves the "baptism" of the *locale* (the basic organizational unit, composed of *'ndrine*). The rite is chaired by the boss of the society and consists of the purification of the *locale*. It takes place with the recitation of the following dialogue:[43]

BOSS: Good eventide, wise companions.
OTHERS: Good eventide.
BOSS: Are you prepared to baptize this Locale?
OTHERS: We are prepared.
BOSS: In the name of our ancient forbears, the three Spanish knights Osso,
    Mastrosso and Carcagnosso, I do baptize this Locale, if before it was known
    as a place that was a haunt for cops and the infamous, from now on
    I recognize it to be a holy and inviolable sacred place where this honored
    body of the society may assemble and adjourn.

Or, in a variant of a code found in Rosarno (Calabria):

I baptize this holy and inviolable sacred Locale as they baptized the three ancient Spanish knights Osso, Mastrosso and Carcagnosso, and if before it was known as a Locale of transit and passage, from now on I recognize it as a baptismal space where *picciotti*, young men of honor, and *camorristi* may be baptized.

After the *locale* has been purified through baptism, there follows the formula of the "Formation of the Company," which makes it possible

---

[43] Several variants exist of the formulas for the ritual of baptism (see Ciconte 2015).

to carry out there any of the 'Ndrangheta meetings that concern any of the local activities.

The best-known formula is as follows:

BOSS: Good eventide.
OTHERS: Good eventide.
BOSS: Are you prepared?
OTHERS: We are prepared.
BOSS: With regard to what?
OTHERS: With regard to the rules of the society.
BOSS: In the name of the Archangel Gabriel and St. Elizabeth, this circle of the society is formed. What is said in this circle in the form of a horseshoe, is said here, and here remains, whosoever speaks outside of this place is declared a *tragediatore*, a rumour-monger, responsible solely to himself and no responsibility of this society.

At the end of this second formula, those present at the meeting kiss each other's hand and then sit with folded arms, as they will sit for the entire duration of the meeting with the exception of the boss of the society. The meeting then begins.

Of particular importance to 'Ndrangheta organizational life is the collective gathering of a number of members and leaders from around the world, which takes place every year at the festival of the Madonna di Polsi in Calabria.[44] It is, in some ways, a kind of rite of pilgrimage. During this event, responsibilities are ratified, as are the career promotions of various *locali* in Italy and abroad. The structure of the criminal organization is redrawn, alliances are formed, wars are declared, and overall criminal strategy is planned.

Finally, still with reference to the 'Ndrangheta, a particularly important role is played, in terms of sealing alliances, celebrating promotions and new members, and integrating members of the organization, by the so-called *mangiate* – banquets – that typify real mafia summit meetings.[45] These events are very frequent in community life, as the act of eating together (and especially eating goat meat) has the ceremonial value of a confirmation of the values of solidarity and mutual friendship, and represents an integral part of a significant moment for the life of the organization. Also the ceremony for the promotion to a higher grade finds its necessary complement in a *mangiata*, where the man of honor

---

[44] On October 26, 1969, the police discovered a gathering of about 150 'Ndrangheta members in the Polsi area, involving a number of different levels in the organizational hierarchy (Malafarina 1986).
[45] DNA (*Direzione Nazionale Antimafia*, National Anti-Mafia Directorate) 2016, *Relazione annuale sulle attività svolte dal Procuratore nazionale e dalla Direzione nazionale antimafia e antiterrorismo*, 735.

who was beneficiary of the promotion expresses his new status for the first time.[46]

Therefore, commensality, or the ritual of eating together (the *mangiata*), is not simply a gastronomic event, but is clearly a rite of aggregation (van Gennep 1960) in which an individual is asked to join, to be a member of, a new society – the 'Ndrangheta, in this case. Rules of commensality constitute a mechanism of ethnic separation and exclusion (Weber 1993).

Collaborator with justice Antonino Belnome points out that

food, gestures, the rituality and arrangement of the diners at table are the result of strict ceremonialism and serve to emphasize the hierarchical position of the participants: "Meetings, banquets with goat or lamb (the typical meal of the *'ndrine*) with all the men sitting and myself sat at the head of the table, I looked everyone in the face and everyone could look at me, the meal could start when I gave the invitation with a *"buon appetito."* No one could eat until these decisive words were spoken, and only I could speak them, it was like being three meters above the sky … I remember the day of the ritual and celebration of my joining the 'Ndrangheta, we were on a piece of land with a cabin and for the occasion a banquet of roasted meat was organized. (in Barbacetto and Milosa 2011, 415–17)

The menu is also carefully chosen, because the dishes eaten during the *mangiate* should be typical of Aspromonte in Calabria, to help reinforce the concept of identity – which Belnome metaphorically calls the "umbilical cord" – between the Lombard *locale* and the Calabrian motherland: "When certain banquets were organized, the wine, the cheese, the bread, the salami, were all scrupulously brought up from Calabria as tradition required."

Such events follow strict rules relating to the hierarchy of the participants, and the process of endowment of the ranks, the promotion ceremony, is divided into several parts: (1) first there is agreement among those at the highest levels, with the demonstration of opinion regarding the merits and demerits of any members singled out for promotion; (2) there follows the organizational phase of the convivial event or simple meeting to celebrate the granting of the new ranks, identifying the location for the meeting and choosing the participants; (3) the event continues with the execution of the ritual in the course of the planned banquet; (4) last, the promoted person who has received the new rank organizes a *mangiata* of thanks.[47]

---

[46] Tribunale di Milano 1997, *I fiori di San Vito*, Sentence 1743/98.

[47] Tribunale di Milano, DDA (*Direzione Distrettuale Antimafia*, District Anti-Mafia Directorate) 2014, *Operazione Insubria, Ordinanza di applicazione di misura coercitiva con mandato di cattura*, Ufficio del giudice per le indagini preliminari, 12053/11 R.G.N.R.

The rites for promotions in rank are especially important for the 'Ndrangheta. In the ceremony to become *santista*, the highest position of entry into the society (see Section 3.1.2), the candidate must actually take an oath to poison: as collaborator with justice Antonino Belnome tells it, in the ritual a lozenge represents the poison that the candidate himself must take in the event of treason. According to the rules, once the rank of *santista* has been acquired, the 'Ndrangheta member cannot die at the hands of others (although there have been cases when members of this rank have died at the hands of other members of the organization, for the violations they have committed). During the ceremony, after the oath, a cross is made on the right shoulder of the *neosantista* with a knife. For a higher rank than that of *santista*, the *vangelista* (evangelist), the cross is made, again with a knife, but on the left shoulder. The higher ranks (*tre quartino*, *quartino*) are also provided with specific rituals, including related oaths of allegiance and further crosses inscribed on the shoulders, while for the rank of *padrino*, godfather, a cut is also made in the index finger of the candidate's right hand (in Barbacetto and Milosa 2011, 447–8).

2.5.5   Removal and Degradation Rituals

Not all the mafia rituals are festive and affirmative for those who participate. Apart, of course, from the funerals, there are some rituals aimed at doing harm to individuals within the organization. These are rituals of exclusion, expulsion, excommunication, and degradation.

Garfinkel defines a ceremony of status degradation as "any communicative work between persons, whereby the public identity of an actor is transformed into something looked on as lower in the local scheme of social types" (1956, 420). These rituals help to defend the boundaries of the group, redefining who belongs and who doesn't. In these rituals of degradation, certain common and recurrent stages can be identified (Garfinkel 1956; Gephart 1978; Pfeffer 1981): (1) a connection is established, not necessarily true, but plausible, between the behavior of the *degradando* (person to be disgraced) and certain organizational problems and failures; (2) the person's character is discredited, perhaps with the use of help from figures outside the organization; (3) the person is removed from office.

In mafia organizations, this sequence is somewhat different. The mafia degradation ritual begins with (1) the discrediting of the person; (2) his subsequent isolation; (3) frequently, his physical removal. Totò Riina skillfully made use of these rituals of degradation to isolate his real and potential adversaries in the Sicilian Cosa Nostra. Once they are isolated, it is easier to eliminate them without generating any particular conse-quences and dissension from within the organization.

The expulsion of a man of honor, decreed by the boss of the family or, in serious cases, by a committee, as a result of serious breaches of the Sicilian Cosa Nostra code, is the only exception to the principle of the indissolubility of the bond with the Cosa Nostra, and is often the prelude to the killing of the offender (OSPA Stajano 2010). A man of honor who has been expelled is, in the mafia lexicon of the Sicilian Cosa Nostra, said to be *posato* (shelved). American Cosa Nostra collaborator with justice Dominick Cicale says:

Shelving someone means removing all the rights and privileges to which a made member is entitled; they aren't even allowed to earn. It's basically an option to getting rid of someone other than murdering him, typically because the person egregiously broke Mafia rules. To be shelved was considered disgraceful. (Cicale and Scarpo 2014, 4)

The same is true for the 'Ndrangheta. Former mobster Antonio Zagari states in regard to this:

It is absolutely impossible for members to dissolve the oath and the associative bond; the bond can only be dissolved by the death of the member, with treason or through the decision of the bosses, in cases where the member is no longer deemed worthy and deserving of being considered a man of honor.

However, Zagari goes on:

I should point out that the hypothesis that a person expelled from the 'Ndrangheta continues to stay alive is a very remote possibility. Anyway, even if the organization decides not to kill a former member, this person would no longer be acknowledged by other members and could never again be in the company of a man of honor.[48]

Although rare, the idea of estrangement is contemplated by some mafias and is covered by certain rules. 'Ndrangheta ex-mobster Calogero Marcena described the procedure as follows:

The *mastro di giornata* (day master), receiving this information, conveys it to the boss of the society and the boss of the *locale*, who give or do not give their consent depending on the validity of the reasons given. If the person who requires the estrangement has the rank of *santista* or higher, however, the person responsible for local control must be informed, and will communicate the news to the various local bosses. The estranged person will lose any responsibility within the *locale*, but not his rank. He will not be employed in any of the activities of the *locale*, nor informed about these. During the period of estrangement, if it is motivated by

---

[48] Tribunale di Reggio Calabria, DDA 2010, *Operazione Crimine*, vol. I, 451.

health reasons or serious family situations, the estranged member continues to receive his monthly salary. There is a further and different sort of estrangement, which covers those who have voluntarily decided to leave the organization. The procedure for the authorization of the relevant *locale* is the same. For members of the rank of *santista* and above, however – those in other words at a higher level in the organization – estrangement can always be canceled at any time, depending on the needs of the organization. (in Ciconte 2015, 46–7)

Expulsion does not bring an end to the link with the community. The suspension could also be resolved with the reintegration of the man of honor. The expelled person, therefore, continues to be obliged to observe the mafia rules, even though he cannot maintain any kind of relationships with other members of the organization.

2.5.6   Conclusions

To sum up, mafia rituals perform many different functions.

> *Reinforce individual and organizational identity and group solidarity, fostering a sense of belonging and cohesion.* Social events (weddings, parties, christenings, funerals, *mangiate*, etc.) strengthen the sense of belonging to the criminal organization. From the point of view of social and organizational identity, ritual helps define the characteristics of a social group through the sharing of a common symbolic language. A person may be proud to participate in a ritual, as if belonging to the organization that celebrates it is a defining characteristic of his personal identity (Coyne and Mathers 2011).
>
> *Simplify control.* Rituals and collective events favor the creation of a shared vision or purpose, with common meanings and enahanced commitment – all essential elements in the running of the organization. As in terrorist organizations, initiation rituals are a way to reduce preference divergence, screening out less committed recruits and facilitating punishment by making it hard to leave the organization (Shapiro 2013, 54). In particular, the internalization of organizational values and objectives by the members may be a far more powerful control system compared to one based exclusively on material incentives or force, as it reduces the need for direct control over the work of the members.
>
> *Reduce uncertainty.* Rituals make "ephemeral certainty" possible in a world of great uncertainty (Gambetta 1993), in particular because they help to reduce problems relating to asymmetric or imperfect information. For example, regarding the matter

of verification of membership in criminal organizations, the presentation rules (which will be looked at more closely in Section 2.6) make it possible to understand whether a person is a made member or not, reducing the chances of undercover agents infiltrating the organization.

Reduce coordination problems and create common knowledge (Chwe 2003; Coyne and Mathers 2011; Skarbek and Wang 2015). When different people wish to achieve a common result, coordination problems may arise that, in general, can be solved through communication. But when communication is not enough, ritual can help solve such problems by creating a "common knowledge" that allows everyone involved to have the same information. For example, with regard to the organization's governance rules: by participating in rituals, a mobster not only learns rules and organizational codes, but also realizes that others know the same rules and that everyone knows that the others know. This helps solve coordination problems (Chwe 2003), particularly when communication is not always possible or effective, or when the use of written rules is not possible on grounds of secrecy. Finally, common knowledge facilitates punishment in cases of rule violation (Skarbek and Wang 2015).

Seal nonwritten contracts and justify punishment. Ritual seals agreements for which a simple handshake would be too weak a gesture, clarifying that betrayal of the pact would lead to certain death (Gambetta 1993). Ritual represents a precaution against betrayal, as if to emphasize "Remember that you signed a contract for life and if you violate it, your life is what you will lose." The violation of the rules and the oath taken in a ritual can trigger the desire for revenge of the other members, who share the sense of justice that means that those who contravene the rules must be punished.

Reduce cognitive dissonance by increasing the mythical and sacred aspect of the organization. The mafia organization is not only an economically oriented criminal business, but also an organization with a mythical and sacred aspect. Therefore, the acts committed within it are not crimes (for those, that is, who take part). This belief reduces the cognitive dissonance (Festinger 1957) generated by having to perform particularly brutal acts. Rather than transforming the external environment – something very difficult to do – or their behavior, disobeying orders, they modify their cognitive world, explaining their actions with reference to the organization's sacredness. If the organization is sacred, the acts committed in its name are not crimes, even though they may appear despicable. As Bandura (2016) argued, *sanctifying* is a "way of justifying the rightness of harmful practices. It includes not only religious justifications but also ideological, social, economic, and constitutional forms" (49).

An analysis of organizational structures and rituals shows that these tend to be more present in vertically organized mafias, with higher-level bodies of coordination (e.g., Sicilian Cosa Nostra, Yakuza, 'Ndrangheta), and less present in horizontally organized mafias, where higher-level bodies of coordination are weak or absent (such as the Camorra and American Cosa Nostra). This can be explained by the fact that, in vertically organized mafias, "brand management" is more centralized, so there is greater propensity to protect its use through ritual.

But why do mafia rituals still exist in a modern and increasingly globalized world? As Coyne and Mathers (2011) pointed out, "rituals are often 'sticky' once established due to path dependence and identity" (83). Once created, they tend to persist even if they perform no real function in an organization or social group. Rites are not folklore, but, as stated by former 'Ndrangheta mobster Gianni Cretarola: "They represent the true strength, the real glue of the 'Ndrangheta ... they help members resist years and years of prison sentences and convictions!" (in Ciconte 2015, 114).

When do rituals change, if they change? According to North (1990, 90–1), exogenous shocks can lead to discontinuous changes in existing path dependencies. For example, a strong crackdown by law enforcement agencies can lead to a review of certain ritual practices in order to maintain the secrecy of the organization, as happened with the Camorra, for example, after the Cuocolo trial[49] in the first decade of the twentieth century. In general, the process of reduction and simplification of rituals can be traced back to reasons of security rather than any real move towards secularism itself.

2.6   Accounting

Mafias engage in both legitimate and illegitimate activities to earn money. It is very difficult to measure the "turnover" of mafia organizations, and

---

[49] The trial took place in Viterbo in 1911–12 and, for the first time, members of the Neapolitan Camorra were among the accused. In the following years, the Camorra higher-level bodies of coordination were dissolved (Barbagallo 2010; Dickie 2012).

even more so the "profits," for a variety of reasons. First, being illegal organizations (except the Yakuza), they have no legal obligations to report their financial statements, and therefore only an inductive form of analysis can be used to estimate revenue. Second, since they are secret organizations, it is very difficult to get reliable information about the value of their activities, in both the legal and illegal markets. Finally, there is a methodological problem, relating to what is to be measured. If a mafia organization sells protection, the measurement of the amount of revenue must be related to this type of service being sold and should not include all the activities and earnings pertaining to the subjects who "benefit from" (in a manner of speaking, although in many cases this is actually the case) the protection provided. Otherwise, there is the risk of the synecdoche effect – in other words, confusing the part (mafia) with the whole (all protected activities, illegal and otherwise). The risk, as Gambetta efficaciously notes (1994), is to attribute to the mafia the incomes of those it protects, as if, in evaluating the revenue of an insurance company, all the turnovers of its customers were also to be included. It is precisely this error that often leads to the production of exorbitant figures, amounting to several percentage points of the GDP of a country, through a lack of clarity regarding whether the overall turnover is intended or the profits deriving from activities. This is not, also considering the difficulties mentioned, the place to assess mafia income.[50] At this stage, what we are interested in is looking more closely at an important aspect of mafia organizational life: the management of accounting and economic resources. In mafias, two main types of financial management and payment can be distinguished: (1) a *top-down* system and (2) a *bottom-up* system. The main features are illustrated in the following.

2.6.1   Top-Down

This model is based on the bottom-up collection of economic resources, which are gathered into a common fund then distributed to the members of the organization in a top-down process. The economic resources, therefore, first go from the bottom upward and then back downward again in the form of wages, typically monthly, sometimes weekly. This pattern is typical of the Italian mafias, the Sicilian Cosa Nostra, the

[50] In Italy, for example, they have a turnover for illegal activities that fluctuates between 8 and 13 billion euros, equivalent to between 0.6 and 0.86 percent of the Italian GDP (Transcrime 2013), to which we have to add earnings from legal activities. For the Yakuza, Hill (2003a, 93) refers to an income of about 1 trillion yen, equal to around $800 million.

Camorra, and the 'Ndrangheta. The members feed their earnings, the proceeds of their activities (extortion, drug sales, etc.) into this common fund[51] through accountants or higher-level roles. In return, they receive a monthly salary (called *mesata* in the Sicilian Cosa Nostra), which varies according to their role, length of service in the organization, family situation, and general condition (whether they are free, in prison, etc.). These amounts may undergo further changes as a matter of specific contingencies (e.g., need for medical care, funeral expenses, weddings, etc.). The administration of the common fund is the direct responsibility of the organization's management roles, usually the boss or an intermediate figure, who sometimes make use of specialized figures such as accountants.

The main function of the common fund is to pay salaries to members and their families (in the case of the arrest or death of the member), legal fees for those in prison, and other forms of assistance, such as family trips to visit detainees, health care, etc. In addition to these, so to speak, welfare functions, the common fund is employed for other functions relating to the organization's criminal activities, such as the provision of resources for the purchase of weapons, cell phones, and cars, or for bribery and corruption of certain key figures, etc.

In Palermo, with regard to the Sicilian Cosa Nostra, it emerged from judicial inquiries that payment flows did not derive directly from the family but from the *mandamento* (district), the higher-level body that coordinates more than one family. These resources, intended for the support of prisoners and their families, or payment to lawyers, etc.,[52] are fed from members to the strategic higher-level bodies (*reggenti* for the Camorra, *capimandamento* or *capifamiglia* for the Sicilian Cosa Nostra, *capilocale* for the 'Ndrangheta; Colletti 2016, 58), and then return in part in the form of salaries to members of the organization.[53] In the event of a reduction in resources, or an economic crisis (such as the financial crisis that began in 2007), some clans have launched an internal spending review, resulting in a reduction of salaries and expenses.[54]

In a police operation against the Brancaccio family of the Sicilian Cosa Nostra (Di Cagno and Natoli 2004) a document was found that

---

[51] This common fund can have a variety of names: *baciletta* (basin), *bacinella* (bowl), *barattolo* (jar), *calderone* (cauldron), *pentolone* (pot), etc.

[52] Tribunale di Palermo 2008, *Sentenza di rito abbreviato nei confronti di Adamo Andrea+56*, Sezione giudice per le indagini preliminari, Piergiorgio Morosini, January 21.

[53] Carabinieri Regione Campania 2003, Comando Provinciale di Caserta, Nucleo Operativo, *Informativa circa la denuncia a carico di Avenia Marcello+33*, April 11, 96/34–2002.

[54] In 2012, the ledger of the Graviano family was found by the police; it showed a strong reduction in expenditure, particularly to the detriment of the detainees, who had also suffered a halving of their salaries (S. Palazzolo, "Mafia, trovato il libro mastro del clan Graviano - Ecco la spending review varata da Cosa nostra", *la Repubblica*, November 23, 2012).

contained the accounts of the organization, with different entries for prisoners, fugitives, lawyers, etc. With regard to this, one magistrate observed that

there is a concentric core of people that revolves around the Cosa Nostra organization, which has a cost, there will be corrupt people, there will be consultants to pay, there will be various professionals ... there is all this, and that is the real strength of the Cosa Nostra... there are all these contiguous persons that keep the organization strong. These may be people who have relationships in society; so when we attack the phenomenon, we not only attack the military phenomenon, but also the whole relational phenomenon of the Cosa Nostra that seeks to build relationships with all the categories that contribute to the power system that is dominant at a certain historical moment. (in Di Cagno and Natoli 2004, 66)

This network of figures is of particular importance to the vitality of the organization. They are highly professional people, and the cost to replace them may be extremely high: an accountant, a doctor, or a compliant lawyer might be more difficult to replace than a "soldier." Former 'Ndrangheta mobster and collaborator with justice Giacomo Ubaldo Lauro explained the reasons for having a common fund operating in the organization:

Each clan, in fact, has men who do not always have their own work and therefore require a "salary" because otherwise they would not be able to support themselves. This need becomes especially required, for the men, when typical turns of events lead to going on the run or to legal problems or to going to prison. It is obvious that the organization must ensure, above all, the maintenance of prisoners, because even though there are limits to their situation the fugitive on the run can still do some form of work. For the little that a prisoner costs, if he has a wife and two children, he will receive a monthly payment of a minimum of at least 1,000,000–1,500,000 (lire, which corresponds to about € 500/750, author's note). This money will be delivered to the family by people specifically in charge of "salary payments." It is also necessary to efficiently maintain a network of protection and assistance consisting of a series of links that involves the procurement of supplies, medical care, and everything required to help someone who is on the run or in prison. It is also evident that this protection network is only active during a period of war or in the presence of great tension between the various clans. It is evident that for the disbursement of these funds and for the relative "accounting entries," each clan relies on an "accountant" – that is, a serious, elderly person, and obviously someone very close to the organization. It does not matter if this figure has been previously arrested by the law or not. Above all, he handles the cash that is the result of extortion, drug trafficking and other activities.[55]

---

[55] Tribunale di Reggio Calabria 1999, Corte di Assise, *Sentenza contro Condello Pasquale +282*, January 19, 46/93, 18/96 RG Assise, 351.

Table 2.3 *Average remuneration in two Camorra clans*

Role	Schiavone Clan	Belforte Clan
Member	€ 1,300	€ 1,900
Capozona	€ 1,900	€ 2,500
Reggente–cashier	€ 2,000	€ 5,000
Capogruppo	€ 2,400	n.a.
Boss	€ 4,000	€ 5,000

Source: Colletti 2016, 105.

As regards the Sicilian Cosa Nostra:

It is well-known that the internal rules of the organization mentioned include the provision of a monthly sum of money to members, to the maintenance of the families of detainees or to their defense expenses. The material performance of this task proves the existence of a stable associative relationship between the suspects. As reflected by the trial results, the realization of this form of assistance in the Cosa Nostra is provided by the *mandamento*, not the individual mafia family. Every *mandamento*, therefore, has its own cash fund, entrusted to a specific subject who manages it in line with the directives of the *capomandamento* and for the attainment of the objectives for which the cash fund is designed.[56]

The analysis of the payment system of two Camorra clans (Belforte and Schiavone) has highlighted some operating methods (Colletti 2016). The Schiavone clan pays members less than the Belforte clan, even though the former has a much larger number of members (about 120) than the latter (about 46) (see Table 2.3).

Thus, the stronger clan pays less. These differences are explained by various reasons, and above all by the main criminal activities. The Belforte clan is heavily involved in drug trafficking, which, while it increases organization income, also increases both the risks involved in the operations and sanctions in case of arrest. In fact, the Belforte clan has a higher average number of convictions compared to the Schiavone clan. Another reason may be related to different reputations. The Schiavone clan owns one of the most important brands in the Camorra criminal system, and therefore simply being a part of it constitutes an intangible reward with a high value in itself.

In another important Camorra clan, the Di Lauro, the data regarding compensation to various nonmember organization collaborators ranged from € 1,000 to 4,000. Drug dealers earned € 2,000 a month, the

---

[56] Tribunale di Palermo 2008, *Sentenza di rito abbreviato nei confronti di Adamo Andrea+56*, Sezione giudice per le indagini preliminari, Piergiorgio Morosini, January 21, 261.

sentinels who controlled various areas of the territory earned € 1,500, while the thugs who collected protection money received € 1,200. Income was higher for those who housed fugitives from justice, from € 2,000 to € 4,000. Killers, on the other hand, earned € 2,500 for each murder (Barbagallo 2010, 222).

Again in the Camorra, the Secondigliano clan (from Naples) rewarded organization members depending on the complexity of the task. Promoters of retail sales and *delegati* dealing with clients earned up to € 7,000 per month. Individual sellers made € 2,000, while the sentinels (young people on motorbikes cruising around to check that there is no police presence) received € 1,500 per month. Killers were paid € 2,500 for murder, while other young associates could earn € 250 per week for various activities, or € 200 at a time for urgent tasks such as looking after weapons. Finally, € 300 per month was paid to the thugs who had to enforce the payment of protection money (Scanni and Oliva 2006, 45). Salaries were not very different in one of the most violent clans of the city of Naples, Buonerba, where drug dealers and bodyguards earned between € 300 and € 400 per week, with € 150–200 per week for sentinels and up to about € 10,000 per month for the boss. The rest went into a common fund for investment in drugs, for legal fees, and for lawyers.[57]

As we have seen, as well as to pay salaries, the common fund is mainly used to pay for assistance and legal advice, the "tools of the trade" (weapons, cars, phones, etc.), any health and housing emergencies members might face, and investment in legal and illegal markets. This leads to an important consideration regarding the organizational functions of the common fund. Beyond the economic aspect, the common fund carries out an important welfare function within the organization, which reinforces the sense of belonging and sense of loyalty and helps to reduce the possibility of informing in the event of arrest (if the prisoner does not cooperate with law enforcement, he will always receive the salary from the clan, expenses for the family, legal assistance, etc.).

As magistrate Ardituro observes:

This is the true sense of the clan's strength: to guarantee a welfare system, work and assistance that is never affected by crisis and ensure regular payments; this is the deepest sense of the individual bond of membership of the organization, which is based on the guarantee of a sure way to support themselves and their families. While the boss thinks of power and wealth and is guided by the frenzy of command, members are often nothing more than piecework labor. (Ardituro 2015, 99)

---

[57] From an interception of the eponymous clan boss Genny Buonerba, in E. Fittipaldi, "Sparanapoli: In città comandiamo noi", *L'Espresso*, March 17, 2016.

In this way, the payment of wages to detainees is not the price of their suffering, but the price of silence, of *omertà*.[58] If the prisoner does not cooperate with law enforcement agencies, his family will continue to have a monthly salary, and in addition he ensures his own opportunity to resume activities once his prison time is over.

Any impediment in the functioning of this system threatens organizational cohesion and delegitimizes management and can therefore work toward the organization's dissolution, through scissions, internal power struggles, and collaborations with justice. More than being "brotherhood societies" (Paoli 2003), mafias are economically oriented companies, and if this economic aspect suffers a crisis then the whole edifice is likely to come down with it.

It should be noted that the common fund handles only a part of the organization's resources, mainly those deriving from extortion activities and drug trafficking. Other resources that result from other activities (for example, activities in legal markets) do not end up in the common fund of the organization but are managed by the strategic top management in other ways. Other clans, particularly those dedicated principally to drug trafficking, have payment models related to the daily amount of the proceeds from drug sales, depending on seniority and time served with the organization (e.g., the Belforte clan). Generally, earnings are higher, given the greater risk involved in this type of activity. In addition, salary is only one part of the possible earnings of a member, which can increase on the basis of his criminal and entrepreneurial skills. The salary, says Colletti (2016), is sometimes simply a basic minimum income.

It is important to notice that, in the economic management of the organization, as in legal enterprises misconduct can occur, also in mafias there may be certain "holdbacks" in the flow of resources from the bottom upward. Since it is very difficult to maintain a clear analytical accounting of the various operations and as there are many overpricing margins in certain activities (e.g., in producing doses of drugs, reducing the amount in the units sold), the more cunning can create extra *off the book* income in addition to salary, along with other possible forms of integration. Such "illegal" activities are tolerated by the organization if they remain limited in extent, but there may be serious penalties – including death – if they are discovered or if the amount becomes significant in size.

---

[58] A detainee in a hard prison regime ("41 bis" as it is called) costs more than a prisoner in a normal prison regime, since his silence becomes more expensive.

Moreover, the management team that manages the common fund may handle certain expenses in a personalistic manner, without having to account to the rest of the organization. The Graviano family, for example, a powerful family in the Sicilian Cosa Nostra, had two funds: one for the management of clan activities and another for personal expenditure and investment. Collaborator with justice and former Sicilian Cosa Nostra mobster Gaspare Spatuzza says:

> The *reggente*, the cashier, may also invest as he wishes part of the money deriving from lawful and unlawful activities. No one controls what the *capomandamento* (a district boss; the coordinator of three families working in neighboring territories) or the boss does, unless problems arise. But even in this case it is very difficult to prove that the fund has been badly managed. (Dino 2016, 81)

In some cases, the boss may try to falsify the accounts in his favor, but if caught, or only suspected of this, the consequences he risks are lethal, as happened in 1983 to the Sicilian Cosa Nostra boss Filippo Marchese, who was "killed – among other reasons – because he was accused of embezzling organization money. In this case, too, it was difficult to prove this misappropriation. The ledger existed and in some ways was correct. The boss was skillful enough to keep all the accounts formally in order" (Dino 2016, 81).

2.6.2   Bottom-Up

In the bottom-up model of the flow of resources, the lowest levels of the organizational hierarchy transmit a part of their earnings to higher levels, up until the boss, keeping back a part as their own income. In this case, there is no following step of transmitting money back downward from above.

In the American Cosa Nostra: "In the world of the wiseguy, all the money flows up" (Pistone 2004, 35). In an American Cosa Nostra family, a person does not receive "a salary simply because you're someone's brother or cousin; you have to earn your own money" (Bonanno 1983, 188). A member must pass a large percentage of his earnings to his soldier of reference, who in turn will pass a substantial proportion to the captain. The money that everyone earns does not belong entirely to him, and a part must always be transferred on to a higher level. The percentage varies from person to person, in some cases amounting to 50 percent of the earnings. The captains must hand over a bag containing the money every week to the family boss, without exception. This is a bottom-up model with no return: "No mafia boss is out there earning money and distributing it downward to his loyal subordinates. The grunts are the ones who have to sweat it out and send it up" (Pistone 2004, 36).

It is a model opposed to bureaucratic organizations, in which "the money goes only in one direction – upward" (Abadinsky 2013, 92). As Ronald Goldstock, former director of the New York State Organized Task Force, has said, the model of the American Cosa Nostra is less similar to that of a corporation and more similar to government: "In the Mob, the people at the bottom are the entrepreneurs. They pass a percentage of their income upward as taxes in return for government-type services: resolution of disputes, allocation of territories, enforcement and corruption services" (in Abadinsky 2013, 94).

Of course there arises the problem of trust, with the fact that the subject retains only the agreed percentage and no more. It should be noted that the ability to produce money is an indicator of the professional "ability" of an organization member and an element to be taken into consideration with regard to his career. A captain may lose his status if he fails to deliver a sufficient amount of money to his boss.

In the Yakuza, the subordinate roles (executives and soldiers) give a percentage of their earnings to the union they are members of, partly to meet the costs of those who are in prison. As has become increasingly common, the percentage has been replaced by a determined fixed amount, since many gangs were underreporting their incomes.[59]

A variant of this model is constituted by the economic management system of the Triads for illegal businesses. In this case, the activity conducted by members does not take the form of a business society but rather that of a private investment (Chu 2011). The profits that derive from such activities, then, remain with those who have produced them and are not passed on to the upper levels of the hierarchy.

2.7   Environment and Organizational Ecosystems

No organizations are self-directed and autonomous. They need resources such as materials, personnel, money, information, etc. To obtain these, they must interact with other organizations that own or control these resources. To understand the behavior of organizations it is necessary, therefore, to understand the environment in which they

---

[59] It is interesting to note how this system of a fixed amount to be given to the boss is similar to certain tax systems, such as the Italian one (with the so-called sector studies), developed for some economic categories. Given the difficulty and cost of verifying the actual amounts earned and easy opportunities to cheat with regard to earnings, the state has decided that these economic categories (professionals, self-employers, businesses, etc.) must give, on the basis of a series of defined parameters (such as business size, number of employees, where the activity is carried out, etc.), a fixed amount of their earnings. If the amount paid is less, this definitely increases the possibility of a tax audit.

operate and the interdependent relationships that come to be established with other actors and organizations. These relationships give rise to an organizational ecosystem, a system formed by the interactions of a community of organizations and their respective environments (Moore 1993; 1996). As Pfeffer and Salancick said, "To understand the behavior of an organization you must understand the context of that behavior – that is, the ecology of organization" (1978, 1). An organization, as Wilson stated, "is like a fish in a coral reef. To survive, it needs to find a supportive ecological niche" (1989, 188).

To understand mafias' behavior, it is fundamental to understand the ecosystem in which they operate, the organizational field (DiMaggio and Powell 1983), the strategic action fields embedded in the broader environment (Fligstein and McAdam 2012).[60] Like legal organizations, mafias are not, and do not operate as, closed systems, separate from their external environment. Their existence depends on the flow of resources, of different kinds, from the outside. According to this perspective, the relationship between an organization and its task environment is essentially a trade relationship: the organization will not receive the necessary input for its survival if those who are in contact with it do not evaluate it as capable of offering something desirable (Thompson 1967, 103). This leads to the concept of effectiveness. While efficiency is an internal standard of organizational performance, effectiveness is an external standard applied to the output or activities of an organization. Effectiveness concerns how well an organization is meeting the demands of the various organizations and groups that are affected by its activities. The acceptability of an organization and its activities and output is judged by those outside the organization. The organization, however, is not at the mercy of external forces: it can manipulate, influence, and promote acceptability for itself and for its activities. It follows that if a mafia organization is present in an area, its services and its activities in some way gain some degree of acceptability to the members of the environment in which it operates, and its work, therefore, is in some way effective. The organization could not survive if it were not responsive

---

[60] DiMaggio and Powell define an organizational field as "those organizations that, in the aggregate, constitute a recognized area of institutional life: key suppliers, resource and product consumers, regulatory agencies, and other organizations that produce similar services or products" (1983, 143). Fligstein and McAdam identify a strategic action field as "the fundamental units of collective action in society. A strategic action field is a constructed mesolevel social order in which actors (who can be individual or collective) are attuned to and interact with one another on the basis of shared (which is not to say consensual) understandings about the purposes of the field, relationships to others in the field (including who has power and why), and the rules governing legitimate action in the field" (2012, 9).

to demand from the environment – an unstable environment with a high level of uncertainty, given the high number of various external elements subject to continuous and unpredictable change. To this must be added the fact that the organization must operate in secret, hiding many activities and communications, with no third-party actors to fall back on should problems and disputes arise. This also explains why mafias, given their environmental contingencies, adopt organizational models of an organic, and not mechanical, kind (Burns and Stalker 1961).

In general, a business ecosystem is an economic community formed by interacting organizations and individuals. This economic community produces goods and services of value to customers who are themselves members of the ecosystem (Moore 1996, 26–7). Members of the ecosystem are also market intermediaries (e.g., selling complementary products and services), suppliers, competitors, stakeholders, government agencies, and regulators.

With specific regard to mafia organizations, there are four main forces that constitute the organizational ecosystem: (1) customers; (2) suppliers; (3) competitors; (4) regulators, governmental organizations, and law enforcement agencies. We can distinguish two types of task environment: the environment of a minimal organizational unit and the environment of higher-level bodies of coordination, which is also the overall environment of the organization. The minimal organizational unit environment is composed not only of the four elements listed previously but also of other minimal organizational units.

As far as customers and suppliers are concerned, in many cases these tend to overlap. *Customers* can be defined as all those persons or organizational units that, in exchange for a fee, benefit from the protection services (see Section 1.2.1), while the *suppliers* in turn receive a fee in exchange for a service. There is a large number of customers who receive protection (Gambetta 1993).

There is a spectrum of customers, and at least four main categories:

The customer who has legitimate needs that are met legally, the customer with legitimate needs for whom the legal market is, for some reason, unresponsive, the customer with illicit needs who cannot risk dealing with the legitimate entrepreneur (who would keep business records that could subsequently be subpoenaed by an enforcement agency), and, at the end of the spectrum, the extortionist or pirate, who is intent simply upon exploiting the domains of other entrepreneurs. (Smith 1980, 379)

Customers also include politicians, at both local and national levels, and the main resource exchanged here is the vote. Mafia organizations are able to ensure the necessary votes for electoral success: each clan, depending on its size, can produce a sizable number of votes, receiving appropriate benefits in exchange, either from the candidates or others in their political party. Such benefits might include the opportunity to take part in public works at a local level, and, at a national level, legislative opposition and inertia. This link between criminal organizations and political actors has been typical of mafias since these organizations first came into being.[61]

Customers and suppliers are essential resources for the operation of the mafia: the organization is dependent on them and could not operate and survive without them. For example, mafias have serious problems in terms of knowledge and expertise – while mobsters have skills in the use of violence and abilities to develop social relationships, they lack expert knowledge in the fields of realizing and developing business. They are therefore forced to resort to a broad set of knowledge workers, professional suppliers of services and knowledge on which they depend for the realization of various activities. The suppliers thus constitute a category of growing interest characterized by a spectrum that is very wide, and over time increasingly extensive, including professional figures such as doctors, required for examinations and treatment of fugitives and can "steer" their evaluations according to the mafias' purposes; lawyers who go beyond merely professional relationships; notaries to record changes of ownership or for the creation of fictitious companies registered in the name of front men, etc.; accountants to manage the accounting and conceal funds; financial experts for investment; magistrates and law enforcement agency personnel[62] to transmit and receive relevant information; architects and engineers to construct buildings and bunkers; journalists; officials in public administration to falsify tenders and competitions; and many others.

A third element in the mafia task environment is represented by *competitors* – in other words, other criminal or mafia organizations operating in competition, even though, as a rule, mafias do not tolerate competitors of any kind in the territories where they operate. Finally, the task environment also includes *regulators and law enforcement agencies,*

---

[61] There has been a great deal of judicial evidence since the nineteenth century involving Italian mafia organizations and the relationship between the mafia and the world of politics and electoral deals.

[62] Numerous investigations highlight the important role played by members of the law enforcement agencies in Italy: judges known for their antimafia work who pass information to the mafia concerning investigations in progress (V. Iurillo, "Pizzini anonimi, dossier e intercettazioni. I veleni della Guardia di finanza," *Il Fatto Quotidiano*, September 21, 2016) and *carabinieri*, policemen, and even a general in the finance police (F. Bufi and F. Sarzanini, "Prima una soffiata poi la lettera al legale" I pm: così il generale svelò l'indagine al clan," *Corriere della Sera*, September 16, 2016, 20).

the state and other institutional actors, relevant in terms of their ability to define policies – oppositional or otherwise – in relation to mafia organizations.

The external environment, populated by a variety of organizations, significantly influences organizational structure, tasks, and strategies. This is also the case with mafias, where three sets of factors are relevant to understanding the environment: (1) the *extraorganizational* clan: the network of relationships between mafia clan members and external organizations; (2) *aspects of the legal and social system*: the system of regulations and degree of repression by law enforcement agencies, the degree of consensus and social legitimacy; (3) *contextual factors*: the morphology of the territory, the economic context, and the production system, among other things, influence the life of the organization.

(1) The *extraorganizational clan* is the network of extraorganizational relationships deriving from past and ongoing relationships between an enterprise and its members with the external social environment (Litz and Stewart 2000). Given the necessary recruitment constraints, the mafia organization does not possess internally all the expertise and skills required to fulfill its economic activity and must therefore turn to the aforementioned professionals, people external to the criminal organization who, however, represent an important extraorganizational clan without which the organization itself could not develop and move forward. When mafias move out from their home areas to venture into new areas, more by necessity (*push*) rather than the presence of new opportunities to be seized (*pull*) (Varese 2011), they are forced to recreate these essential bonds, and this is something that may take a long time. It clearly emerges that mafias are not only more or less formalized criminal groups. Their strength comes from their capacity to operate by connecting the criminal world with the legal one. Without the ability to operate in the latter, and thus without the active cooperation in many cases of legal actors, the mafia would amount to very little.

Mafia organizations are, in at least some important respects, a political and economic phenomenon. They cannot be fully defeated without addressing their political and economic roots, including whatever local support they enjoy in the ecosystem in which they operate.

(2) With regard to the *aspects of the legal and social system*, the level of consolidation of a mafia organization depends primarily on the level of repression of the regulatory system. The *hostility* (Potter 1994) of the environment constitutes an important factor that influences the structure and behavior of criminal organizations. Such environmental hostility

refers both to the intensity of the activities carried out by law enforcement agencies and to the extent to which the local communities support their efforts. Generally, the introduction and application of stricter regulations force mafia organizations to adopt greater levels of secrecy, thus hindering their activities. Criminals can establish and develop more complex structures in a tolerant or supportive environment (Bouchard and Ouellet 2011), while large organizations seem unable to survive in a hostile environment (Potter 1994).

Second, an important element is *legitimacy* and the consequent degree of *social consensus* present in the environment in which the organization operates. Parsons (1956) stated that legitimacy was an important concept and a useful criterion to understand organizations and their relationship with their social environments. The strength of the mafias lies in the fact that they are, to some extent, in some areas and by some subjects (social, economic, and political), considered legitimate. They are organizations that are to be lived with and, if possible, used to a person's own advantage: a sort of "pragmatic legitimacy," based on the self-interested calculations of an organization's most immediate audiences (Suchman 1995, 578).

The concept of legality is juridical in nature. An organization is, or is not, legal if its purpose and its behavior conform, or do not conform, to a specific law with respect to the specific context and environment in which the organization operates. The concept of legitimacy, on the other hand, is sociological. Legitmacy can be defined as "a generalized perception or assumption that the actions of an entity are desirable, proper, or appropriate within some socially constructed system of norms, values, beliefs, and definitions" (Suchman 1995, 574). Therefore, an organization may be legal but considered by many illegitimate because of the output it produces (e.g., the sex industry). Or, an organization may be illegal, being criminal, but legitimate for certain social subjects. This is the case of certain mafias in various territories. The legitimacy of an organization, therefore, involves opportunities and constraints arising from the external environment. It follows that the degree of social legitimacy is a key indicator of a mafia's strength in a specific environment. Of course, legitimacy is not acquired once and for all – it is not stable over time. It can be brought into question and eventually disappear if civil society and the various political, social, and economic actors change their attitudes toward these organizations. It will be important to look more closely at whether specific environmental conditions are particularly congenial to particular kinds of positive legitimacy for the mafias.

In the case of the Yakuza, the organization is legitimate, and social consensus is high partly because of the fact that – as we will see in Section

3.1.6 – the organization is legal, unlike all the other mafias (while the criminal activities committed by the organization are, of course, not legal).[63] Bosses are not fugitives from the law, and the addresses and telephone numbers of the major gang headquarters are publicly available. In 1960, when U.S. president Dwight Eisenhower planned to visit Japan, the government invited the Yakuza to provide his bodyguard in order to guarantee the guest's safety (Ino 1993, in Rankin 2012a). A very similar event occurred in Naples in June 1860, when the then– Bourbon prefect of police, Liborio Romano, entered into an agreement with Salvatore (Tore) De Crescenzo, the *capintesta*, head of the Neapolitan Camorra, to have the support of the criminal organization in order to control the popular masses and avoid protests and riots when Giuseppe Garibaldi passed through the city (Romano 1873; Perrone 2009).

It is, therefore, not always entirely clear whether the relationship between the police and the mafia organization is one of control and repression, or rather symbiotic, as in many cases that have occurred in the mafia's complex history. As Rankin observes (2012b), again with regard to the Yakuza, the prevalence of bribery and protection agreements, and other forms of collusion, between police and the Yakuza is a complicating factor: police officers may expect or demand free drinks and services in bars and clubs within the territory of a gang, or the gang may offer them free. In return, police officers ignore minor legal violations, or raid another gang's territory. There is also a long tradition of plea bargaining, known in Yakuza slang as *chinkoro*, where gang members give the police information in exchange for leniency.

These forms of relationship are, however, definitely changing for the Yakuza as well. Two factors are slowly altering the relationship between the mafia organization and the social and legal systems: the first concerns the tightening of the regulatory system in order to hinder Yakuza criminal activity. In 1991, the Japanese government introduced the Anti-Yakuza Law (Bōtaihō), which reduced the areas of action available to the Yakuza, and then promulgated other regulatory measures[64] aimed at reducing Yakuza profits by suppressing financial fraud, money laundering, and transnational underworld banking. In addition, investigative measures were bolstered and penalties increased for those collaborating

---

[63] In 2010, 25,681 gangsters were arrested, about a third of the Yakuza population (Rankin 2012b).
[64] Anti-Drug Provisions Law, 1992; Organized Crime Punishment Law, 2000; Transfer of Criminal Proceeds Prevention Law, 2007.

with the Yakuza.[65] These new laws have made life for the organization very complicated compared to the past: for example, a Yakuza member cannot open a bank account, get a cell phone, or rent an apartment (Murphy 2016), all things that were possible in the past and that today the Yakuza members can only do by resorting to front men, as indeed happens for other mafias. The second factor of change in the relationship between the mafia organization and the social and legal systems is the change in society's perception of the organization, which was increasingly associated with the activity of extortion rather than that of protection. Thanks also to the economic crisis, as well as the applied regulations, many members of the organization have suffered impoverishment, and are increasingly relying on activities that earn high social disapproval, such as theft. All this lowers social consensus and increases protest, with several civic anti-Yakuza campaigns and even with public demonstrations in front of the gathering places of the Yakuza clans.

The changes in the regulatory system do not necessarily entail a reduction in the activities of the organization – or at least, not alone. The crackdown by law enforcement agencies produces changes and adaptations in the system, in terms of exploitation and exploration.

As we will see in Section 2.8, March (1991) contrasts two types of adaptive processes in organizations: exploitation and exploration. To survive in an environment, an organization must be able to exploit the existing configurations of resources and skills in order to achieve efficiency and sustain its own competitive advantage. In this context, it is a matter of *exploitation* – it involves taking advantage of what one already knows. At the same time, organizations need to know how to create new configurations of resources and skills in order to adapt to market demand and renew existing sources of competitive advantage. In this context, it is a matter of *exploration* – it involves a search for new knowledge and skills, and learning new ways of thinking and working. While the organizational change of *exploitation* is based on the exploitation of existing possibilities, within an existing operation model, that of *exploration* is broader and more innovative: it involves exploring new and unknown possibilities, different from those hitherto practiced.[66]

---

[65] Respectively, with the Criminal Investigations Wiretapping Law of 2000, and the Yakuza Exclusion Ordinances, implemented at prefectural level across Japan between 2009 and 2011.

[66] Both exploitation and exploration are essential for organizations, but they follow different kinds of logic and compete for scarce resources. Each strategy has its trade-offs. The advantages of exploration lie in variability and the ability to generate improved structures in the long run. Among the disadvantages are high costs and the slow feedback

The success of repression by law enforcement agencies "forces" mafia organizations to consider exploration, fostering innovation and change. For example, following a forceful police crackdown on gambling, the Yakuza modified its portfolio of assets, developing new sources of income, particularly the production of amphetamine (Hill 2004) together with other criminal activities. The 'Ndrangheta carried out kidnappings in the 1970s, particularly in northern Italy, but following a law that blocked the use of the current accounts of the hostages' families,[67] this activity was first curtailed and then completely eliminated.[68] There was, instead, a move into new markets, both legal, such as the construction industry, and illegal, such as building up the drug trafficking sector. In other words, repression and the intensification of regulations are important factors of change in criminal organizations, an unintentional cause of innovation in the organizational system. Of course, the type of organizational response to such external perturbations depends on specific organizational contingencies and is not immediately deducible *ex ante*. We will come back later on to the issue of the unintended consequences of repressive action.

(3) Regarding *contextual factors,* the Camorra, for example, is characterized by different organizational and logical models of action, depending on whether it is operating in an urban or extraurban context. This is because the systems of territorial control change according to the different distances that have to be covered (Ardituro 2015): while the city of Naples develops "vertically," with narrow streets and alleys,

---

on what is happening. The exploration strategy runs two major risks: to consume all available resources only to find out that the organizational structure is irretrievable and to reduce further the ability to change structure, should this become necessary. Exploitation strategy, on the other hand, has advantages such as greater reliability, lower costs, and faster feedback on ongoing initiatives. Disadvantages include the tendency to reproduce and reinforce suboptimal institutional structures, with a lower rate of innovation. This strategy also presents risks, such as the elimination of resources that might still be utilized, or the excessive use of resources for a solution that then turns out to be unstable, requiring further research and, therefore, additional cost.

[67] This was law 82/91, *Nuove norme in materia di sequestri di persona a scopo di estorsione* (New regulations regarding kidnappings for reasons of extortion) of March 15, 1991. The law required the mandatory freezing of the assets of the kidnap victims, their spouse, and their relatives. The freezing of assets could, at the discretion of the judge, be extended to cover other persons, if the fear existed that they could help the family get around the law.

[68] In the period 1969–90, 632 kidnappings took place. In the period 1991–7, with the new law on asset freezing in force, 40 kidnappings took place, thus registering a significant decrease (CPA, *Commissione Parlamentare Antimafia,* Italian parliamentary anti-mafia commission, *Relazione sui sequestri di persona a scopo di estorsione, Relatore Senatore Pardini,* October 7, 1998).

extraurban areas are characterized by large spaces, with long distances between one clan and another. Controlling urban territory means that the Camorra makes use of motorcycles and fast scooters, while the same functions of control in extraurban territory require cars and skilled drivers (Ardituro 2015).

Given these morphological differences and the resulting methods of control, there are various modes of action and of pursuing profit. In Naples city center there are shops, bars, and small artisanal activities that are not able to pay a particularly high level of *pizzo* (protection money); otherwise they would be forced to close down, with the loss of social consensus for the clan that controls that territory. So, the collection of *pizzo* is one item in the clan's economic revenue, but it is not the most important. The Camorra must necessarily look elsewhere – to cigarette smuggling, to drugs, to illegal betting, to the production of counterfeit products.

The drug business is now the most lucrative market for criminal organizations (Reuter 2014). It is a business characterized by a high level of violence: in Naples, the control of the so-called *piazze di spaccio* (drug market areas), the prevailing method for retail drugs sales, has fueled wars between clans, resulting in a large number of murders. Therefore, the configuration that involves tight spaces, with clear boundaries between one clan and another, and a certain level of territorial economy, heavily influences the modes of action and conflict and the economic activities of the city clans.

In extraurban areas, however, the clans have to control an area of hundreds of square miles, which contains a number of industrial enterprises and major food industries. To exert control, it takes many men and a more complex clan organizational structure, with greater division of labor and roles. The relationship between the geography of the territory and criminal presence and behavior is an issue that deserves further investigation and analysis.

In conclusion, then, mafias are not organizational monads, but live and develop within complex organizational ecosystems. In order to operate in these environments, the mafia management requires special skills. In particular, the ability to network and to establish collaborative social relationships with other organizations is fundamental to ensure the resources and development of the organization. Of course, there is always the possibility of resorting to violence to facilitate these relationships with recalcitrant suppliers or customers. In addition to dealing with intra-organizational relationships, managers of these organizations must be equally adept at handling interorganizational relations.

It should also be remembered that organizations are not simply determined by their environments: management can certainly promote innovations in structure or strategy, for example, but only to the extent that such innovations are acceptable to those who work within the organization and to those who, externally, have meaningful relationships with it.

2.8   Mafia Transaction Cost Economics

Observing mafia organizations and their overall structure, certain questions arise. Some involve the choice made by mafias in terms of organizational form and the use of the market to develop their own activities. For example, why do *mafiosi* create organizations that are in some cases extremely complex, which require time and resources to manage and involve issues related to the need for secrecy and the risk of sanctions by law enforcement agencies? Couldn't mobsters carry out their activities operating at an individual level, making use of market trade, or buying the services that are needed?

Others concern the real impact of mafia action on the activities of the legal firms with whom they come into contact, such as companies in the fields of construction, trade, catering, transport, etc. For such firms, does the mafia only constitute a cost, a tax imposed, or does it bring them benefits? Does it provide them with "services," and if so, what kind?

These issues lead to a fundamental question in organization theory: why do organizations exist? "Why are there organizations at all?" asked Coase (1937). It is a question that gave rise to *transaction cost economics* (TCE), developed by Oliver Williamson (1975; 1985; 1996). Given the importance of this theory for understanding certain aspects of mafia organizations, there follows a brief summary of the most important elements.

2.8.1   Transaction Cost Economics

TCE poses a fundamental question: why do organizations draw their boundaries where they do? The explanation is that firms establish their boundaries by seeking to minimize their transaction costs, deriving from the sum of production plus organization costs, when choosing their scope of activities. TCE tries to explain why organizations externalize certain transactions, relying on the market to manage exchange relationships, and internalize others, relying on hierarchical control to manage exchanges. Theoretically, a production unit may obtain the necessary resources by having recourse to the market, buying the parts necessary to achieve a given product from other units, and then asking other units to carry out the required activities, thus obtaining the final product.

Under what conditions, then, do the different units combine to form a single organization, rather than just continue to act according to market conditions? Williamson's answer is that it depends on transaction costs (Williamson 1975; 1985; 1996; Tadelis and Williamson 2013). Economic organizations will internalize transactions until the marginal cost of doing so exceeds the marginal revenue. Beyond that point they will prefer to trade externally through markets.

Transaction costs are affected by two characteristics of human nature. The first is *bounded rationality*: that is, the fact that people actually make decisions in a way that is only partially rational (Simon 1957). This is because the contexts in which people operate render their decisions imperfect, since they involve physiological, contextual limits, a matter of time or relating to the availability of information or the ability to process it. The second characteristic, *propensity toward opportunism*, is the inclination to take advantage of exchange partners when possible, by misrepresentation, extortion, and so forth. Opportunism concerns behavior that is unfair, fraudulent, illegal, or false that actors can adopt in order to achieve an advantage: for example, taking on responsibilities that they already know they cannot respect, or omitting important information, or supplying information that is intentionally incomplete or incorrect. Opportunism is favored by situations with small numbers, where only a few people are involved in the exchange. As the number increases, opportunistic situations tend to diminish, thanks to competition and the increase in circulating information.

Bounded rationality and opportunistic behavior favor conditions of *asymmetric information*, where significant elements for the making of a decision are available to only a few individuals, and others can only discover these elements through incurring a cost. This asymmetric information may occur *ex ante*, during negotiations between the actors, or *ex post*, during the execution of a contract. In the former case, an actor might hide relevant information from the others, who are forced to make their decisions in conditions of limited or inaccurate information (adverse selection). In the second case, an actor might behave in an opportunistic manner, using information in a misleading way, violating contractual terms, or indulging in behavior that reduces costs but has a negative impact on quality of service and/or the product. Theoretically, in conditions of perfect rationality and absence of expediency, contracts could contain all possible contingencies and variations, with the certainty of the respect of the parties involved (trust).

The two characteristics, bounded rationality and opportunism, create problems for market exchanges in relation to four basic elements of the transaction: uncertainty, frequency, asset specificity, and incomplete contracts. (1) *Uncertainty* regards the reliability with which a necessary good or service is available when required, or at risk of opportunistic behavior. (2) *Frequency* is the degree to which a given producer regularly needs access to a good or service from an exchange partner in order to carry out its activities. (3) *Asset specificity* concerns the degree to which goods or services are specialized in relation to a specific transaction. Asset specificity is the most critical aspect of a transaction, and is high if a seller produces a commodity that can only be bought by a single buyer or, from the buyer's point of view, if there is only one seller for the goods requested. It is low, on the other hand, if there are many sellers and buyers available for that transaction. In particular, *human asset specificity* is a form of specificity for which individuals have particular knowledge or skills that are valuable only for a particular exchange relationship. (4) Finally, *incomplete contracts* regard the fact that contracts, especially long-term ones, are incomplete, in that completeness would require extremely high costs or would be very complicated to realize.[69]

The transaction is the basic unit of analysis, and a company is set up as a structure of *governance* of the transactions, in order to minimize costs. Arrow (1974, 33) argued that "organizations are a means of achieving the benefits of collective action in situations in which the price system fails," thus including not only business firms but also consortia, unions, legislatures, agencies, schools, churches, social movements, and beyond. This is the central problem of economic organization, and firm and market are "alternative methods of coordinating production" (Coase 1937, 388). In the market-mediated exchange, a supplier provides goods and services and a buyer gives fixed payment. Both parts can renegotiate the agreements and, where disputes occur, can rely on courts. In the hierarchy-mediated exchange, a supplier provides goods and services and a buyer settles up. There is an interface coordinator that provides coordination adaptation and settles disputes.

There are costs associated with transactions that take place within organizational boundaries defined as *governance costs*: administration and coordination, hiring people, supervising production, handling personnel issues, keeping records, etc. These costs, when goods and services are bought on the market, are borne by other organizations. In conditions of uncertainty of the transaction and high frequency, market costs tend to rise and it becomes preferable to resort to the hierarchy (vertical

---

[69] Contracts are subject to disturbances (or contingencies) during the implementation phase, to problems of cooperation between the contracting parties, and to the inability of courts to settle disputes in a fixed and reasonable period (Tadelis and Williamson 2013).

integration), which Williamson posited as the internal governance of transaction. But the element that significantly shifts the decisional pendulum is the high specificity of resources. In conditions of uncertainty, frequency, and high specificity in relation to the transaction, the hierarchical solution is the best choice to govern transactions in terms of a logic of economizing.

In conclusion, only when transaction costs (those of market-based exchanges) exceed governance costs (those of organizationally based exchanges) will organizations internalize exchanges. Otherwise, they will rely on the market to manage market relations. This is the *make-or-buy* decision – or, in other words, internalization involves a "make" decision, whereas externalization involves a "buy" decision (Tolbert and Hall 2009, 174).

2.8.2 Transaction Cost Economics in Mafias

If we take the *family* or *clan* as an organizational unit frame of reference, the theory of transaction costs helps us to understand two important aspects regarding mafia organizations mentioned earlier in this chapter. (a) The first concerns the *methods* of internal organization (*make/hierarchy* vs. *buy/markets*) and the relationships with the external world: other mafia families, higher-level bodies of coordination, competitors, and other public and private actors. (b) The second relates to the *possible* "*benefits,*" in addition to the costs, for legal businesses to have services offered by mafia protection.

(a) With regard to the first aspect, the *methods*, is it cheaper for the mafia to integrate, carrying out certain activities within the organization, or rather to outsource activities and functions through resorting to the market? According to Simmel (1906), all secret societies are characterized by hierarchical structures. In contrast, Erickson argues that, for security reasons, it is preferable to decentralize:

> Secret societies under risk must be differentiated from others; that societies under risk have a wide range of structural forms; and that the major sources of structure are found in preexisting social structures rather than in psychological factors. Risk enforces recruitment along lines of trust, thus through preexisting networks of relationships, which set the limits of the secret society's structure. Structure can still vary considerably, depending primarily on the centralization of control of recruitment, in turn dependent on the control of key resources. (188) ... It is not clear that a more rigidly hierarchical structure is the best answer to security problems. In risky situations, members and hence the links they are part of, may be frequently deleted: they may be informed on, they may loose courage and leave, they may be removed at random by a hostile

regime ... Without much link redundancy, the secret society would be in continual danger of being cut to pieces. (Erickson 1981, 203)

Reuter says that in illegal markets there are factors that push in both directions. There are some indications to integrate:

Illegal markets are frequently characterized by high search costs; it may be time-consuming to acquire an alternative supplier for a particular service if the existing relationship is interrupted. It is also difficult to determine whether the price offered by the current supplier is competitive or whether there is a lower cost source. The loyalty of the supplier is uncertain, since he may be able to obtain relief from police interventions by providing the names of a few of his customers. Making the supplier an employee raises the certainty of provision of the input, increases his loyalty, and has relatively small cost in terms of loss of information about the market price of the service. (Reuter 1985a, 11)

At the same time, there are a number of factors working in the opposite direction:

The employee, if apprehended, has only one enterprise which he can put at risk in return for continued freedom, namely, his employer's, and his regular contact with the entrepreneur will increase the amount of information he can supply. Finally, he may form factions with other employees to supplant the entrepreneur. (Reuter 1985a, 12)

According to Smith (1994), illegal businesses emerge when the bene-fits of the organization exceed the costs of the organization – when, that is, the organization finds it convenient to carry out certain activities internally (make) rather than turn to the market (buy). Dick (1995) says that "transaction costs, rather than monopoly power, primarily deter-mine the activities of organized criminal firms" (26). In organized crime activity, a "firm chooses between supplying illegal inputs internally and purchasing them in the market to minimize its costs of criminal transac-tions" (39). According to Williamson, "TCE assumes that the criminals (or their handlers, such as the mafia) can, upon looking ahead, take *ex ante* actions to alter the payoffs by introducing private ordering penalties to deter defections. This latter is a governance move, variants of which can be introduced into many other bad games" (2007, 24).

In addition to the transaction costs typical of legal business, other costs exist in mafia organizations: those that are required to keep secret their illegal activities; coordination costs, rendered difficult by the impossibility of freely making use of communication technologies; internal control costs in order to prevent infiltration by undercover agents and the action of the law enforcement agencies; the costs of both intraorganizational (within families) and interorganizational (between families) conflict, without the benefits of a legitimate government that defines property rights, settles disputes, and has the power to enforce its decisions.

For mafia protection, the characteristics of the transaction costs are high *uncertainty*, given the instability typical of criminal markets; constant pressure from law enforcement agencies and competitors; and the fact that the *contracts*, complex and not always complete in the upperworld, are by definition incomplete in criminal circles with no possibility to appeal to third, legal, actors, for enforcement agreements. The transactions have a high degree of *asset specificity*, since the skills to carry out protection require special knowledge that is not easily found on the market, both criminal and otherwise.

Unlike legitimate businesses, mafias must take into account an additional factor in the choice between *make* or *buy*: *secrecy*. For a criminal enterprise, it could make sense in economic and efficiency terms, for example, to outsource a particular activity. However, risks related to the management of secrecy may instead lead to the decision to opt for the internal management of this particular activity, even though it is economically more debilitating.

Given these special conditions, therefore, of uncertainty, incomplete contracts, asset specificity, and secrecy, mafias tend to internalize (*make*) human resources for the provision of protection. However, they keep operational size within certain limitations, since the costs of internal organization and coordination would otherwise be excessively high, especially when the aspects relating to secrecy and the restricted possibility of resorting to communication technologies are taken into consideration. It is, on the other hand, convenient for the mafia organization to resort to the market for many other activities and establish contractual relations, whether sporadic or ongoing, with those professional figures (lawyers, consultants, financial experts, etc.) essential for the performance and development of economic activities – even those with a high degree of asset specificity, but that are available on the market. The latter, working externally for the criminal organization, have little incentive to betray it: on the one hand, because they have a share in the "skeletons in the closet" and so any denunciation would involve accusing themselves; and, on the other, because the risks they would run in betraying the organization are only all too clear.

Outsourcing presents serious problems in situations of incomplete contracts and asset specificity. Drug traffickers have recourse to outsourcing for drug transport, given that the asset specificity of this activity is low, but also for reasons of security and secrecy. Some drug trafficking organizations, in fact, prefer to entrust transport activities to a network of casual freelance workers, none of whom knows very much about the others (Wainwright 2016). Rather than hire people on the payroll as employees of the organization (*make*), some drug traffickers benefit from the *buy* model, organizing the work sequentially, in a series of stages. They pay people for the specific activities that they carry out, entrusting single individuals or small groups (the courier who transports the drugs from the production site to the area of consumption, drivers, those who make payments, etc.) with the performance of specific pieces of work and paying them for what they do, without these people being members of the organization. This organizational choice guarantees the effectiveness and efficiency of the activities, while ensuring safety. On the one hand, the people involved are given a great deal of responsibility for the specific phase of the process chain with which they are entrusted, and, on the other, should they be arrested, they will not be able to give very much away regarding the criminal organization itself, being at the most familiar with the phases that precede and follow on from their own activity. This organizational choice highlights how vertical integration, interpreted as the combination of several productive stages into a single organization, while convenient from an economic point of view, could be dangerous for the organization in terms of security and secrecy.

Thompson wrote that "organizations under norms of rationality seek to place their boundaries around those activities which if left to the task environment would be crucial contingencies" (1967, 39). It follows that organizational choice, for criminal organizations, must always prioritize the aspects regarding the protection of secrecy, even at the expense of the obvious economic benefits deriving from the various *make* or *buy* solutions. Such are the costs of security and secrecy.

With regard to the external transaction costs of a mafia organization, in particular in relation to the other families and components of the criminal system, these costs operate according to the prevailing system of relationships: whether it is a matter of collusion or competition. In the former case, collusion, it is a matter of the costs of coordination between the higher-level bodies of coordination. In the second case, competition, it is a matter of the costs of competition, which can also involve violence in the defense of property and territorial rights.

(b) The second aspect that TCE helps us to understand regards the *possible "benefits"* that legitimate businesses can enjoy thanks to mafia protection services offered in exchange for a "fee."

Mafias do not operate in all legal markets: they find certain markets more easily penetrable (Arlacchi 1986; Reuter 1985b; 1987; Goldstock et al. 1990; Block 1991; Dick 1995; Gambetta and Reuter 1995; Arlacchi 1998; Moro and Catino 2016). These markets can be characterized by

(1) a high number of small and medium-sized independent companies that provide products and services to the final consumer; (2) an oligopolistic sector occupied by a limited number of firms working for other companies; (3) a low level of technological development; (4) poor product differentiation; (5) unskilled labor; (6) inelastic demand;[70] (7) downstream suppliers of relatively simple, standardized goods and services rather than complex items; and (8) a decentralized industrial system.

As Gambetta and Reuter argue (1995), in "these economic situations, the barriers to entry are low, and to avoid competition, mafia organizations are invited by entrepreneurs to keep out new entrants and enforce the agreements among cartel members" (128).

The possibility of penetration by a mafia organization depends on the opportunities and incentives provided by the characteristics of the economic sector of activity. Goldstock et al. introduce the concept of "racketeering susceptibility." Racketeering susceptibility focuses on the vulnerability of an industry to racketeering exploitation and "reflects the degree to which an industry's structure and organization (1) create incentives for industry participants to engage in racketeering or (2) provide the means and opportunity for racketeers both inside and outside the industry to control or influence critical industry components" (1990, 45).

The construction industry is one of the sectors most infiltrated by mafias: the sector is characterized by a high level of racketeering susceptibility, in particular because it is very difficult for operators to defend themselves against damage to machinery. The sector is particularly vulnerable by virtue of certain of its characteristics (Goldstock et al. 1990): the labor market, the collective bargaining structure, the competitive business environment, the high costs of delay, and the fragility of the construction process. It is thus easy for the *mafiosi* to "propose" their protection against damage, especially in territorial contexts where there is no wide-ranging control by law enforcement agencies. Another area with a similar level of criticality is outdoor filming, which has had a high number of cases of triad involvement (Chu 2000).

As will be seen, however, this is only one part of the story. In many cases, the mafia organization presents itself as a real "security agency with extra-legal services," offering a number of advantages to the legal

---

[70] Demand is *inelastic* when consumers keep buying more or less the same amount as before, even in the face of big price rises. On the contrary, demand is *elastic* when it drops following even a small increase in price. For example, an increase in the price of a drug does not influence its consumption, reducing the amount of the substance purchased and consumed in a way that is hardly significant.

Table 2.4 *Mafia services offered in legal markets*

Forms of Mafia Protection	Services (Examples)
Business development	Access to markets
	New business opportunities
	Provision of services and manual labor
Limitation of competition	Creation of cartels
	Reduction of prices and costs
Enforcement	Protection from external threats
	Dispute handling
	Control of manual labor
	Credit recovery

entrepreneur. From the point of view of the activities carried out, mafias are "specialist" organizations, given the type of services (protection) provided. However, the services are provided in different markets, both legal and illegal.[71]

On the basis of decades of empirical and judicial evidence, it is possible to illustrate, from an analytical point of view, mafia protection in certain lines of activity of particular interest to legal businesses. These activities can in turn be divided into specific "services" (Moro and Catino 2016) – services that are analytically distinct, even though they are also often in fact connected: (1) *business development* of an entrepreneur client, (2) *limitation of competition* for the benefit of some business owners, (3) *enforcement* of contracts and regulations and dispute handling (see Table 2.4).

It is evident that mafia protection activities are not reducible only to protection from external threats, even though such activities are certainly present and requested. And these external threats are frequently created, in some cases with great professional skill, by the mafia organization itself. This is not to deny that there are cases, many cases indeed, of entrepreneurs who are only harassed by mafia extortion, with no benefits being received in return. It is, however, at the same time, worth pointing

---

[71] According to the theory of the *population ecology of organizations* (Hannan and Freeman 1977; 1984; 1989; Baum and Amburgey 2002; Aldrich and Ruef 2006), business organizational models can be divided into *generalist* or *specialist*, depending on the strategies they adopt in their struggle for survival. *Generalist* organizations are characterized by a wide-ranging niche or sphere, offering a large selection of products or services or serving a large market. In contrast, *specialist* organizations offer a more limited range of goods or services or serve a smaller market. For one of the few studies of the mafia based on a population ecology approach, see Sergi 2015.

out that mafia protection in legal markets involves a set of services of particular interest to certain entrepreneurs, so that the mafia organization may come to be regarded as a potential "business partner" of the legal company.

2.8.3 Business Development

The first macroquestion concerns the ability of mafia groups to provide opportunities of *exploitation* and *exploration* (March 1991) of the markets. The mafia organization enables collusive companies (1) to exploit existing configurations of resources and skills in order to achieve efficiency and sustain their competitive advantage (*exploitation*) – for example, by reducing costs of labor and of other services useful to the enterprise; (2) to create new configurations of resources and skills in order to adapt to market demands and renovate existing sources of competitive advantage (*exploration*), accessing new business opportunities previously precluded by the company. One way to create business opportunities is related to the ability of mafia groups and their business associates – such as figures employed in the public administration – to manipulate the bidding for tenders. In the judgment of the first instance concerning the Infinito investigation,[72] the figure of Carlo Chiriaco moves to the fore: medical director of the Pavia (Italy) ASL – the *Azienda sanitaria locale*, or local health care service – and identified as a boss of the 'Ndrangheta in the same city, he was known for his ability to carry out operations of different types, including the talent for "targeting" tenders in areas that went far beyond the health sector. He had, for example, guaranteed the possibility of handling the reallocation of certain areas of public housing construction in the municipality of Borgarello, in the Pavia area. One of Chiriaco's partners, Salvatore Paolillo, explained how the tenders were organized:

To take part in the tender, two envelopes were prepared containing two different offers ... and the initiative was of the three partners in the transaction [Chiriaco, Paolillo, and another partner named Introini, director of the branch of a bank] ... , the envelopes were both delivered to the Municipality on January 14 and only one was registered, but Chiriaco had said that, should the submission of offers be made by other competitors, the envelope containing the lower amount would be replaced with the other, but following the same protocol.[73]

---

[72] Tribunale di Milano 2013, *Sentenza del 6 dicembre 2012*, Ufficio del giudice per le indagini preliminari, 13255/12.
[73] Ibid., 349.

This service is clearly connected with the ability to limit competition. The fact that association with the 'Ndrangheta can bring substantial economic benefits is obvious to many entrepreneurs. The Quadrifoglio investigation[74] showed how a real estate entrepreneur sought out the cooperation of the Galati family (and in particular of Antonio, the family boss) for its ability to organize lucrative speculative operations in the construction sector in Rho, in the Milan area. From an interception, it seems clear that the possibility of resorting to violence is an important tool to ensure the success of the operation for the parties involved. As noted by the investigators, "If the deal had not been successful," Galati suggested taking the recalcitrant business partner "and removing him by force to the grounds of his property . . . and to have a 38 caliber pistol at the ready."[75]

The mafia organization plays a particularly important and highly useful role for legal businesses through the search for economic opportunities and the solving of problems.

An interesting case that demonstrates the complexity and variety of areas of action in the protection sector is the following, which also involves enforcement work. In the mid-1990s, the Sicilian Cosa Nostra decided to build an enormous multipurpose center, the second largest in Europe, in Villabate, near Palermo, in Sicily. The company charged with constructing the center, Asset Development, based in Rome, found itself faced with two problems, one administrative and one "social." The administrative problem involved the town hall and municipal council of Villabate, since it was necessary to change the legal status with regard to the intended use of the area where the center was going to be built. The "social" problem was even more complex, given that the land chosen for construction was owned by around 150 small owners, and it was necessary to get them all to sell their land in a short period. The refusal of just one owner meant that the deal could not go through. The construction company recognized "the mafia family of the territory as a real service agency, to be addressed with the aim of resolving the two issues" (Di Matteo and Palazzolo 2015, 54). The judicial investigation of the affair showed that the Roman firm had

established a true interactive relationship with the mafia family of Villabate . . . which went on stably and continuously for years and was modulated according to the typical paradigm of the reciprocal exchange of performance, utility, and benefits. The defendants exploited the strength, power, and ability of the Cosa

---

[74] Tribunale di Milano, DDA (*Direzione Distrettuale Antimafia*, District Anti-Mafia Directorate) 2014, *Richiesta di applicazione di misura cautelare*, 46647/12 R.G.N.R.
[75] Ibid.

Nostra to impose its will on the territory and the local civil administration in order to obtain access to the location where the huge and prestigious center was going to be built, to ensure the monopoly of the entrepreneurial initiative in the area and to organize the process of commercial urban planning in strict accordance with the interests of the aformentioned company. (Di Matteo and Palazzolo 2015, 55)

This was, in other words, a real trade pact between the company and the mafia family – one that would give rise to a number of economic benefits, enabling them to work on the construction of the center with their own companies and providing employment for hundreds of persons designated by the mafia organization, thus increasing social consensus in the territory involved. In addition, with the work completed, there would also be the benefits derived from the allocation of commercial space, thus providing further employment for more people. This case is of particular interest because of the complexity of the actors involved, and the practical political, administrative and social problems that the mafia organization had to solve, and the fact that it was the economic organization from Rome that requested the services of the mafia and set up the relationship, in a pact of mutual interest.

Another case of particular interest, again from Italy, regards the Perego company[76] (Gennari 2013). This is probably the first major company controlled by a mafia organization such as the 'Ndrangheta in Italy, with a turnover of about 100 million euros. In the past, in the building and construction sector, small mafia-run businesses were imposed upon the companies managing the work on the building site. With the Perego case, there was a dramatic shift in strategy, with the mafia organization acquiring control over the company overtime. The Perego company, run by the Perego brothers, was founded in the early 1990s in Lecco, in Lombardy, and quickly made a name for itself in the demolition, excavation, and construction sectors. Like many other companies, Perego too had to endure the presence of mafia companies requesting subcontract work: these remained external to the firm, however, without undermining the company's control. In 2008, in a period of difficulty partly due to the economic crisis, the Perego business found an important partner in the mafia organization. The 'Ndrangheta's entrance into the enterprise was encouraged by one of the brothers Perego, Ivano, who had already committed entrepreneurial activities that were at the limits of legality, and Andrea Pavone, a friend of a 'Ndrangheta boss and the skilled creator of engineering businesses and companies. Through a series of

---

[76] Tribunale di Milano 2010, *Ordinanza di applicazione di misura coercitiva con mandato di cattura*, Ufficio del giudice per le indagini preliminari, 47816/08 R.G.N.R. mod. 21.

modifications to the company structure, the company came under the control of two trustees who acted as a screen for the real owners, Salvatore Strangio and Rocco Cristello, two important 'Ndrangheta bosses.

Synergy with the 'Ndrangheta made it possible for the company to acquire orders thanks to mafia methods, and the presence of the mafia in the corporate structure appeared to yield tangible expansion of the business. As reported in the interceptions that are part of the Tenacia investigation, Strangio makes explicit reference to that ability to create relationships and develop business: "You want to know? The first work for the Expo, ninety-nine percent of that will go to Perego."[77] Mafia activities were not, however, confined to the stage of business development: the Perego companies redistributed work through subcontracting it to families in the criminal organization. As noted in the ordinance for preventive detention issued by the judge for preliminary investigations in Milan:

Normally – if one can speak of normality in the face of phenomena of this kind – the entrepreneur, under the force of intimidation from the mafia presence, grants contracts according to the provisions that are given. Here, with Strangio, the 'Ndrangheta is directly inside the business, and thus it is a representative of the organization itself to personally manage the work. With the agreement of the official entrepreneur, Perego – who explicitly turned over all his decision-making powers to Pavone and Strangio – the company substantially became a contracting station for the benefit of the 'Ndrangheta. This is the reason why the Calabrians have no need of acts of intimidation to obtain work; it is they themselves who are providing it. Obviously, a situation of this kind represents a qualitative step which should arouse considerable alarm, in that it registers a successful symbiosis between business and the mafia; a result often feared as a futuristic perspective to be prevented turns out to be a reality that is already fully up and running.[78]

The *provision of various services and manual labor* is a set of activities of particular interest and benefit to the entrepreneur. In several areas (waste management, construction, etc.) the mafia organization provides the human resources needed to implement the activities and ensures control over them. One of the mafia's access areas into the legal economy in Italy is represented by construction and earthmoving. This is because large legal companies can outsource work to small companies (including mafia-run ones) without requiring the antimafia certificate, the document that allows a company to work with the public administration in Italy. But above all, says Varese (2011), it is a matter of economic rationality: the bulldozer is a critical tool in building and earthwork operations, but it is expensive to own and difficult to protect. In terms

---

[77] Ibid., 207, in Gennari 2013.   [78] Ibid., 156.

of transaction costs, a large national construction company, operating in different parts of the country, finds it easier to pay for (*buy*) earthmoving services rather than own (*make*) the bulldozers needed in all areas where it operates, or move them from one area to another as needed. So a large company prefers to make use of specialized local companies, for which start-up costs are low and there are no particular entry barriers to skills or other requirements. Mafia organizations are very familiar with such mechanisms and have, over time, created construction companies on a family basis in different parts of Italy, and especially in the North. These employ only people who are trusted, and often from the mafia organization's home territories. The 'Ndrangheta's business sector of choice is earthmoving: demolition, excavation, reclamation, disposal of waste material, and all the preparatory activities for construction. All public works – buildings, roads, bridges, hospitals – require earthmoving.

With reference to the expansion of the 'Ndrangheta in Lombardy, Judge Gennari states that

in this sector, the Calabrians are absolute masters. This means that in all the territorial districts where the 'Ndrangheta is present, that is, practically everywhere in Lombardy, there is no earthmoving contract which is not handled by or entrusted to a firm connected to the organization. The organizational structure of these mafia businesses is very simple and is based on the family unit. Each *family* creates its own little *SRL* (limited company) with a few trucks used by the same family for jobs. These little businesses are then the ones that work on the construction sites. (Gennari 2013, 54)

Mafia firms are able to offer low costs for services (saving on staff costs and taxes) and to carry out the work on time. So, assigning work to these companies seems not to increase costs for the legal companies. In addition, relying on these mafia companies ensures protection, timeliness of payments, and labor control on construction sites, as well as any required loans and control over the competition: it is in the interests of these mafia companies to delay the work of competitors who do not collude with the mafia organization, setting fire to their vehicles and equipment and obstructing – with the option of resorting to violence – the realization of their projects. The mafia organization, then (at least at the beginning), offers affordable illegal services to legal companies.

The legal firm's building contractor enters into a relationship with the mafia business in two main ways. In the first case, the boss of a mafia family approaches the entrepreneur "suggesting" the use of this or that company for work that must be performed. If the entrepreneur does not immediately understand or is not appreciative of the advice, he will promptly experience some acts of intimidation (explosives in the company, gunshots into the side of the car, vehicles or trucks set on fire, etc.).

In the case of recalcitrance, physical violence may be resorted to, but this is usually not required.

In the second case, it is the entrepreneur himself (or herself) who intentionally turns to the mafia organization in order to carry out certain activities, both to obtain the services included (protection) and to be able to perform certain tasks (Varese 2011). This could also include situations involving a sudden expansion in demand in a given territory that is not covered by an adequate supply of services, making it necessary to use business entities that are not wholly unblemished from the legal point of view. As shown by many investigations, in environments with a high density of mafia businesses, contacting them in relation to earthmoving services becomes almost natural, without any need of suggestions being made[79] (Dalla Chiesa and Panzarasa 2012; Sciarrone 2014; Dalla Chiesa 2016). This second method is also common in areas where the Triads are present, as is clear from Chu's research:

> Triads can be employed by entrepreneurs to protect their businesses against attack by other gangs, to manipulate a market by suppressing competitors, and to recover stolen property or debts. In many cases they enter a legitimate market "by invitation" rather than on their own initiative. Thus, the business community is not necessarily the victim of triad societies; companies that employ Triads to settle their business conflicts are in fact the direct beneficiaries. The victims are those who are forced out of the markets by the Triads. Consumers may suffer too because they pay a higher price for relatively low-quality goods or services. (Chu 2000, 123)

The business community is not, in many cases, a passive victim, unable to resist the threats and demands of criminal organizations, but an active subject that frequently seeks out the "services" offered by the mafias, remaining evilly and inextricably involved.

Given these important benefits, it would seem rational for a business owner, having managed to overcome any moral qualms, to go into business with the mafia organization in order to benefit from its protection as a business partner. The legal firm's alliance with the criminal organization provides short- and even medium-term benefits. However, these benefits seem to decrease in the long run and the legal business risks crisis and subsequent bankruptcy.

An interesting case in point is presented by events regarding Blue Call, an Italian company with nearly a thousand employees working in the

---

[79] Tribunale di Milano 2010, *Ordinanza di applicazione di misura coercitiva con mandato di cattura,* Ufficio del giudice per le indagini preliminari, 47816/08 R.G.N.R. mod. 21 and Tribunale di Milano 2010, *Ordinanza di applicazione di misura coercitiva con mandato di cattura,* Ufficio del giudice per le indagini preliminari, 43733/06 R.G.N.R.

sector of telemarketing, telesales, and call centers.[80] It had its head offices in northern Italy, in Cernusco sul Naviglio (Milan), but there were branches throughout Italy. In 2010, the company had a turnover of around 13 million euros, a good financial position, and good customers. Precisely because of this business vitality, it attracted the attention of the 'Ndrangheta, which began to ask for *pizzo* from the Blue Call headquarters in Rende in Calabria, the 'Ndrangheta's home territory. When the extortion demands became too oppressive, the two partners who ran the company decided that the best solution was to rely on a "protector" powerful enough to keep their tormentors at bay. Through their accountant, they were able to establish contact with the Bellocco clan of the 'Ndrangheta, and in 2011 they entered into an agreement under which the clan, through front men, became shareholders in Blue Call with 30 percent of the shares (unpaid). The protector ensured an end to the extortion at once. But he immediately began to expand: placing his own men in the company structure, putting in one of his own men as sole director, a front man in his early twenties and totally incompetent. He ousted directors and managers, not without resorting to threats; changed suppliers and forced their own on the company (even including those who looked after the cleaning). The looting of the company also went on with continuous withdrawals of money. The partners realized they had made a mistake and wanted to buy back the shares sold to the 'Ndrangheta clan, but by then it was too late. They had to endure threats and violence until the police arrested everybody, with the company ending up in state receivership. As was seen during the Maxiprocesso[81] (Great trial) against the Sicilian Cosa Nostra,

the involvement of so many entrepreneurs in judicial investigations into the mafia is the clearest demonstration, on the one hand, that the climate of mafia intimidation is so oppressive as to determine the belief in the inability of the state to ensure the conditions for peaceful coexistence; and on the other, that the protection of Cosa Nostra allows one to carry out lucrative economic activities in the most effective way possible. In this situation, it is very difficult to establish, in any concrete sense, where the action necessitated by mafia imposition finishes and where the involvement and association with mafia activities begins. (OSPA Stajano 2010, 125)

Mafia protection reduces the transaction costs of the protected enterprise, in exchange for a fee. In the medium- to long-term, however, these benefits seem destined to come to an end (not only because of the

---

[80] Tribunale di Milano 2012, *Operazione Blue Call, Misura di prevenzione nei confronti di Bellocco Umberto+5*, President Giuliana Merola, November 8.
[81] See Chapter 2, note 13.

intervention of law enforcement agencies), and there are numerous cases of bankruptcy or transfer of ownership into mafia hands. Moreover, mafia protection means increased costs for the citizen/customer, but this is not always accompanied by an increase in the quality of services and products.

Synergy with the 'Ndrangheta, on the one hand, allows the company to procure work and encourage business development thanks to mafia methods; on the other, it redistributes the work by subcontracting it to the families of the criminal organization. This symbiotic relationship often, however, ends badly for one of the two parties, the one that started out as legal: "This is the real face of the organization. Behind the screen of fictitious capital operations, the organization manages to put a foot in the company door and at that point it is the end. The virus is injected and the company becomes a zombie that is only there to serve the needs and interests of the 'Ndrangheta element" (Gennari 2013, 88). The viral metaphor aside, the pursuit of a predatory modus operandi leads over time to the company's destruction. It is different, of course, in cases when businesses pay the so-called *pizzo* in exchange for protection: they can continue to live according to the dynamics of the market in which they operate, since the relationship with the criminal organization is limited only to this specific transaction.

2.8.4   Limitation of Competition

Limitation of competition is one of the most important functions performed by the mafia: it arouses the interest of both the criminal and legal enterprises and is achieved mainly through the *creation and management of cartels*. A cartel is an alliance of organizations with sanctions applied to members who deviate from cartel policies. The creation of cartels is one of the oldest and most typical services that the mafia provides. Leopoldo Franchetti (1876) describes the millers cartel, created by a mafia group in the province of Palermo, in Sicily. The members of the cartel agreed not to compete with each other, while maintaining fixed prices. In this way profits were assured, minimizing the risks of market competition. Cartels, to remain effective, must punish cheaters. Through the threat of violence, the mafia ensured compliance with contracts, thus gaining a share of the profits.

There is an example of the offer of protection from a mafia organization through the governance of illegal markets in the events relating to the building contractor Angelo Siino, a famous figure in Palermo in the 1980s (Martocchia et al. 2014). The case illustrates well the creation and operation of a mafia cartel intent on corruption: the entrepreneur had codified a system of relationships and agreements – known as the "Siino Method" – which earned him the title of "Minister of Public Works" for the Sicilian Cosa Nostra. Siino had asked the Sicilian mafia organization to help coordinate tenders for public works in order to achieve better profit margins. Given this strong support from the mafia brand name, Siino organized a large number of entrepreneurs (up to 160), establishing agreement on the amount of each bid in order to win in rotation – a win could require a minimum reduction, even as low as 0.5 percent. Mafia protection consisted in ensuring the observance of these agreements and preventing anyone from trying to jump the queue. On each public work there was a percentage earning of 4.5 percent, with 2 percent going to the Sicilian Cosa Nostra, another 2 percent to politicians, and 0.5 percent to the public administration control bodies.

A corrupt system can work if all the actors are familiar with it, at least by reputation, and if there is mutual trust in the fact that no one will violate the agreements and behave as a *free rider*. Restrictions, therefore, must be set on the size of the undertaking. But what happens if the illegal market is potentially composed of a large number of actors – even 160 as in the Siino case – where it is not possible for everyone to know each other? Opportunities for betrayal increase, as does *free rider* behavior. In situations of this kind, with a huge number of actors, given the absence of legal protection, requests come for extralegal protection from an actor whose brand is able to ensure system governance and respect for agreements, sanctioning "dishonest" behavior. The mafia carries out this role of protection, in the sense of market *governance*.

A more recent investigation, completed in 2013, highlighted how a Camorra group, the Moccia clan (operating in Casoria, in the province of Naples), had imposed a single local company run by one businessman alone as the only provider of funeral services in the area, after removing competitors through the use of violence and even resorting to the homicide of certain recalcitrant entrepreneurs.[82] Relatives of the deceased in the area were forced to pay for the services of this firm, which charged prices that could reach twice the market value. Should any citizen attempt to resort to one of the cheaper suppliers in a neighboring municipality, these agencies would either refuse to provide the service, obviously having no wish to risk punishment from the Moccia clan, or ask

---

[82] Tribunale di Napoli, DDA 2013, *Richiesta del Pubblico ministero di misura cautelare personale nei confronti di Esposito Salvatore+8*, Public prosecutor: Marco Del Gaudio, Raffaello Falcone, Alessandro Cimmino and Ida Teresi.

double the price and pay a bribe to the mafia group. Otherwise, if the Camorra organization became aware of the situation, the entrepreneur would be risking his own life, as would anyone who wanted to set himself up as a competitor in the territory.

The formation and maintenance of cartels are favored, say Pfeffer and Salancik, by two sets of factors: "characteristics of the environment that affect the possibility of developing interfirm coordination and the motivation for organizing a cartel or belonging to one" (1978, 182). The mere presence of conditions that favor the formation of a cartel does not guarantee, however, that companies will automatically join. The need for formal coordinating organizations, add the two authors, "would be greatest when conditions of uncertainty are greatest, organizations are interdependent, and the number of organizations to be coordinated, their differences in operating characteristics, or their similarity in size all require a more formal and centralized coordinating structure" (182). In addition to these structural conditions there is the active role played by mafia organizations, which act as enablers in cartel formation.

Such practices are widespread in all mafias. Triads, for example, are active in the sector of minibus operators, protecting their lucrative routes by limiting the entry of other drivers (Chu 2011).

In conclusion, the formation of a cartel ensures a greater amount of profits for all the companies involved, keeping prices high and market shares stable for the participating firms. The cases cited confirm what was noted by Gambetta (1989–90): the mafia does not eliminate the market, without which it could not live and prosper, but tends to eliminate competition between economic operators, to the detriment of final consumers.

In fact, the colluding firms may act as a monopoly, reducing their individual output (as happened with the society of millers described by Franchetti in 1876) so that their collective output would be similar to that of a monopolist, allowing them to earn higher profits.

The case of Carlo Chiriaco – already mentioned in Section 2.8.3 with regard to the opportunity for business development offered by the mafia organization through the targeted assignation of public tenders – is an example of how relationships with political and institutional actors can reduce competition, to the advantage of entrepreneurs who accept mafia protection. On the one hand, as in the preceding example, it is a matter of exploiting (and developing new) relationships with political actors and in the context of the public administration of expanding business opportunities (for a group of entrepreneurs, for himself, and for his mafia associates) in new sectors. On the other hand, in "proposing" to entrepreneurs to participate in activities that he organized, Chiriaco specified an additional benefit other than the relative ease of procuring contracts and licenses: the business owners who placed their trust in him were promised a monopoly in business. Moreover, Chiriaco himself was recognized by the investigation as a supplier of protection to Pavia industries that were allied with him, either by organizing retaliation against enemy entrepreneurs or by (directly) managing tenders in the health care sector and manipulating bids in other sectors.[83]

Through threats and intimidation, mafias organize the elimination of competition, exercising a complementary activity to the creation of cartels. The Triads, for example, writes Chu,

tend to team up with legitimate entrepreneurs to monopolize a newly developed market. Their active participation in interior decoration; the selling of new residential flats; the intimidating of popular film actors in order to take control of the film industry during the 1990s, demonstrates that they are now able to team up with business entrepreneurs to run large projects when a lucrative market emerges. Lastly, triad members increasingly invest in legitimate businesses such as bars, nightclubs, restaurants, dance halls, and the film industry. However, it is not clear to what extent there is triad involvement in these legitimate businesses. (Chu 2005, 7)

A different form of competition limitation consists in the imposition of higher prices than those "on the market," implemented through intimidation (with the use of violence if required) by mafia groups: this represents another essential element in their service to companies. The investigation called Cerberus[84] highlights an archetypal case, again in Italy. The entrepreneur Maurizio Luraghi, active in the construction and earthmoving industry, developed his business by acting in collaboration with one of the oldest 'Ndrangheta families in Milan, the Barbaro-Papalia. The advantage for Luraghi consisted in cornering the market in the most economically substantial jobs, not at the prices set by the market (as usually happens in a normal competitive environment untroubled by 'Ndrangheta intimidation), but at prices determined and imposed by boss Salvatore Barbaro. Another investigation featuring Barbaro showed how they "obtained jobs at prices well above those of the competition and did not see their vehicles and equipment damaged, despite not having a suitable technical structure for carrying out

---

[83] Tribunale di Milano 2010, *Ordinanza di applicazione di misura coercitiva con mandato di cattura*, Ufficio del giudice per le indagini preliminari, 43733/06 R.G.N.R., 1681–2 and 1752–5.

[84] Nucleo di Polizia Tributaria di Milano 2008, *Operazione Cerberus, Comunicazione notizia di reato Barbaro Salvatore + 12*, Gruppo di investigazione sulla criminalità organizzata, June 8.

works that require specialized expertise, exactly as in the case of the present proceedings."[85]

The influence on prices is not, however, always a very evident element. In the case described, while one business owner earns, many others lose – the victims of "pure" extortion or intimidation and damage. There are, however, some cases – less discussed in the literature on the subject – in which the prices charged by the mafias are no different from those of the market. Again with reference to the Barbaro-Papalia investigation, one entrepreneur noted that

in the environment in which I work you know that if you intend to carry out earthmoving work in the Assago area, then you have to go to companies that use Calabrian company bosses. I could see for myself that our suppliers that were offered work in Assago took a step back. The prices charged by the Calabrian companies are absolutely level with those on the market, only in the area of Assago, Corsico, Buccinasco they want to have a monopoly.[86]

In the Perego case mentioned, there is further evidence of how some entrepreneurs can benefit from the mafia services of "maintaining the monopoly." In a wiretap of January 31, 2009, entrepreneur Ivano Perego talks to Salvatore Strangio about the possible involvement of a rival firm to work on a sewer in Orsenigo, in the Como province. Perego explicitly asks Strangio to act so that the rival company does not get involved: "Go and have a word with him tomorrow and tell him . . . that he shouldn't come to Orsenigo . . . that he shouldn't even set foot there, you understand? That we are already there working . . . and he mustn't come there."[87]

Another example of restriction of competition emerged from the Redux-Caposaldo operation,[88] which showed how the 'Ndrangheta in Milan had acquired a monopoly in the management of parking areas occupied by street vendors. While this was certainly no large-scale business, it did ensure a flow of money into the organization coffers on a regular basis, as well as guaranteeing control of the territory. The vendor paid a certain sum to the criminal organization in order to have a place, with the amount varying depending on the value of the location in terms of potential customers (if it was near a disco, night club, or university, it

---

[85] Tribunale di Milano 2009, *Ordinanza di applicazione di misura coercitiva con mandato di cattura*, Ufficio del giudice per le indagini preliminari, 10354/05 R.G.N.R., 335.

[86] Ibid., 335.

[87] Tribunale di Milano 2013, *Sentenza del 6 dicembre 2012*, Ufficio del giudice per le indagini preliminari, 13255/12, 1138.

[88] Tribunale di Milano 2011, *Operazione Redux-Caposaldo, Ordinanza di custodia di misura cautelare personale e decreto di sequestro preventivo di Romeo Giuseppe+34*, Ufficio del giudice per le indagini preliminari, Giuseppe Gennari.

was worth more). Under Italian law, the vendors can situate themselves wherever they want to, but not over a specific number of hours, in order to give a range of opportunity to a variety of vendors. The 'Ndrangheta, however, in its handling of an area, creates a condition of exclusivity: only the person whom the organization has chosen can occupy a specific place, thus creating an illegal market. In this way, through exclusivity and control, the mafia organization creates a "legal right" that did not exist before (Gennari 2013, 175). The vendor, a victim at first because forced to pay to operate in certain areas, becomes an accomplice, however, when he relies on mafia protection for the protection of his (illegal) right – if, for example, he finds his place occupied by someone else or if someone threatens him.

The activity of claiming territorial rights and renting out hawking spaces is present in various mafias, such as the Hong Kong Triads (Chu 2000). Unlike licensed hawkers, whose location is defined by specific bureaucratic authorization, unlicensed hawkers, who are illegal, must try to protect their own locations by themselves. Although they should not stand constantly in the same place, once a place is found that brings them good sales, they tend to keep to the same locations. This spatial monopoly is difficult to maintain, in that someone else may arrive earlier and take their place. This is where the mafia organization steps in: making use of threats, it removes the intruder, thus ensuring the monopoly rights protected through the customer's weekly fee.

By limiting access to new entrants or allocating them to areas of less commercial interest, the mafia organization reduces competition and ensures a higher level of the market to those under its protection. The new entrants could in turn pay higher fees to the mafia organization in order to make use of the commercially superior places, but this would increase production costs and reduce their ability to sell. At the same time, if the mafia enlarged the market to too great an extent, they would no longer be recognized as controllers of the competition and their reputation would be affected. The interests of the protectors, therefore, and of a limited number of the protected, tend to coincide. In addition to control of the competition, a further important service provided by the Triads consists in protection from law enforcement. The Triads warn unlicensed vendors of the arrival of hawker control teams, so that the hawkers can find safe refuge. In some cases, they threaten the members of the hawker control teams to dissuade them from implementing actions against their protected hawkers. A system of this kind has both beneficiaries and victims. The beneficiaries are the protected unlicensed hawkers. The victims are the unprotected hawkers; customers who cannot benefit from the advantages of competition and pay higher prices, which include the cost of protection; and shops, which must endure illegal competition from unlicensed hawkers (Chu 2000, 53–6).

This brief overview of competition limitation shows how mafia activities are not restricted to the provision of protection services to the actors in the market, but extend to their direct presence as actors in the markets themselves: not only, as in the cases mentioned, taking part as operating companies in the sector, but also directly involved at the head of mafia-entrepreneurial consortia. This was the case with 'Ndrangheta boss Marcello Paparo, who, in order to strengthen his role and gain a monopoly in the field of logistics for large retailers, organized the "injury to intimidate" visit to the entrepreneur Onorio Longo, the head of a cooperative porterage service, who had refused to be part of the consortium led by Paparo.[89]

While the empirical evidence shows that the relationship between legal businesses and mafia organizations frequently resolves in favor of the latter, it is equally true that there is significant bias regarding the sources in this respect, mainly of an investigative-judicial kind. That is, we learn of this relationship above all when things go wrong. We know less, however, about how things go when these relationships are good. But economic logic leads us to the conclusion that, if the relationship always finished badly, the system as a whole would disappear, or would only be episodic and residual in character. The evidence, however, points against this scenario.

2.8.5   Enforcement

The capacity of enforcement can be distinguished in specific categories depending on the activity pursued. Labor control (the extralegal regulation of relations with company employees), debt collection, and dispute resolution skills are of particular interest. The Redux-Caposaldo operation[90] highlighted the important role, among other things, of a mafia organization – the 'Ndrangheta in this case – in controlling labor. In some cases, entrepreneurs have benefited from the services of the mafia organizations by virtue of their ability to reduce operating costs through the violation of rules and regulations that often cause the costs to rise. One significant case involved the Dutch company

---

[89] Tribunale di Milano 2009, *Ordinanza di applicazione di misura coercitiva con mandato di cattura*, Ufficio del giudice per le indagini preliminari, 10354/05 R.G.N.R., 99.

[90] Tribunale di Milano 2011, *Operazione Redux-Caposaldo, Ordinanza di custodia di misura cautelare personale e decreto di sequestro preventivo di Romeo Giuseppe+34*, Ufficio del giudice per le indagini preliminari, Giuseppe Gennari.

TNT Global Express Spa, a multinational company in the logistics and package transport sector, which in Lombardy had been infiltrated by the 'Ndrangheta. In general, it is very difficult for mafias to enter, and even more difficult for them to gain control over, large companies, especially multinationals. In the case of TNT, entrance was facilitated by the fact that the company made extensive use of subcontracting for picking up packages, storage, and shipping management – activities that were entrusted to more than 100 branches throughout Italian territory. In addition, the services included a network of thousands of points for reception and delivery and external cooperative companies for home delivery. All these outsourcing activities operated under the direction of TNT, but in complete autonomy in terms of organizing work and accounting and administrative aspects. This use of external companies by the multinational giant enabled efficiency and cost reduction, faced with the need to offer competitive prices. The mafia organization found it easy to enter this market, creating a situation of efficiently functional illegality throughout the whole system, offering competitive prices and integrated services. In particular, cost limitation was made possible by the control of labor, placed in the condition of not being able to complain about the fact that they were poorly paid, with neither insurance nor social security cover. In 2008, TNT chose to reorganize the logistics network and the outsourcing system, rationalizing the system of highly fragmented businesses. When grassroots workers rebelled against the reorganization, with strikes and various complaints, the company decided to employ the "services" of a company controlled by the 'Ndrangheta to resolve internal disputes. The end result was that in the 2009–11 period the distribution service showed a net increase in efficiency and safety (Gennari 2013).

In the Perego case, too, labor control was one of the "benefits" provided by the criminal organization. Truck drivers were forced to load their vehicles with a quantity of material exceeding the allowable capacity, and were told that if by any chance they were forced to pay fines, then the company would take responsibility for payment and ensure that any points lost from their licenses were recovered. Those who did not accept this system lost the opportunity to work overtime.[91]

With reference to debt collection, some investigations into the 'Ndrangheta in Lombardy have shown that it is often the entrepreneurs themselves who turn to the criminal organization for that purpose, especially if the company is in need of liquidity. While resorting to legal action would

---

[91] Tribunale di Milano 2010, *Ordinanza di applicazione di misura coercitiva con mandato di cattura*, Ufficio del giudice per le indagini preliminari, 47816/08 R.G.N.R. mod. 21, 193.

take years, and with no certainty of a positive outcome, the involvement of a criminal organization could provide rapid results, at a cost of 50 percent of the sum to be recovered. Chu reports the case of a shoe wholesaler that tended to use triad collectors to help him settle business disputes: "If a shoe retailer deliberately refused to pay his debts or cheated him, he would employ Triads to deal with him" (2000, 78). In 1996, one retailer had ordered a large quantity of shoes from this businessman as he wanted to open a new shop. However, after six months, the shoe retailer suddenly closed down his shops and vanished without paying his debts. At this point, the businessman employed a powerful triad debt collector to chase him. The shoe retailer was found and violently punished for what he had done. Even though he was able to recover only a part of his debt, the businessman stated: "It is better than nothing. More importantly, people in the same field have learnt that I am a tough guy and they won't try to cheat me again!" (Chu 2000, 78).

However, debt collection is, very often, an illusion for the entrepreneur. On the one hand, the criminal organization does not always give the creditor what has been agreed, and, on the other, the latter are by then embroiled in a network of continuous requests and favors to which they can hardly say no. How do you say no, says Judge Gennari (2013), "when asked to give your name to a mafia-owned company, when the request comes from the same people to whom you turned in order to put pressure on your debtors, because you know that they are violent and dangerous individuals?" (129). Similar operations to debt collection combine – in a similar way to what typically happens in the areas in which they traditionally operate – with the recovery of stolen goods or equipment.[92]

Dispute resolution is another typical enforcement service in which mobsters are specialized. Referring to dispute settlements in Triads, Chu observes that

in theory, legitimate operators can use the law to settle disputes with their business partners or customers. However, the legal channel involves cumbersome procedures which are often time consuming and may prove ineffective in the end. Even if resorting to the law may pay off in some cases, operators generally prefer to use their own means to settle their business disputes. This is particularly the case in some sensitive industries, such as entertainment and financial services, whose image is essential to their business. Triads, with a

---

[92] Tribunale di Milano, DDA (*Direzione Distrettuale Antimafia*, District Anti-Mafia Directorate) 2010, *Richiesta per l'applicazione di misure cautelari*, 43733/06 R.G.N.R. 949, 1295.

reputation for violence, may be brought in by legitimate operators to resolve business disputes effectively and with minimum fuss. (Chu 2000, 77)

'Ndrangheta boss Pepè Onorato – for decades one of the most important figures in organized crime in Milan – was able to solve a variety of problems. Working out of a bar in Milan, Onorato – nicknamed "the Uncle" – had a knack for sorting out misunderstandings, establishing what was the right or wrong thing to do.[93] He was always capable of finding a solution without having to resort to violence – though this, of course, remained a latent weapon that was well known to those who took advantage of his services. It was an ability that derived from a criminal reputation built on four decades of continuous presence in the Milan area, and was a valuable asset for those entrepreneurs, and others as well, who had to solve a problem quickly. It was a reputation, however, that was only apparently used for the purpose of helping out the entrepreneur who turned to the mafia. There was the case, for example, of an entrepreneur called Bonalumi, who asked Onorato for assistance in relation to a factory premises that another 'Ndrangheta group had set on fire. Onorato carried out the required mediation from his usual bar and received the appropriate payment for the role he had played. However, according to the statements to the courts of one of the participants in the case, the whole thing was a double-cross on the part of Onorato, whose idea it had been to burn down the factory in the first place.[94] It is not surprising, however, that the entrepreneur in question here had previously taken advantage several times of the enforcement capacity of the mafia group (especially for the purposes of debt collection). Together with dispute resolution (whether real or manufactured), mobsters can offer to entrepreneurs close to them services of guarantee with regard to the claims of other criminal groups. In the case of the Blue Call, members of the Bellocco family had entered the company as shareholders in exchange for "protection against the claims of figures belonging to organized crime" with whom the entrepreneur had contracted debts.[95]

Going back finally to the case of the Perego construction company, the 'Ndrangheta's entry into the company had resulted in a number of benefits, including the resolution of disputes and problems. Another local boss, the aforementioned Salvatore Strangio, was used for the settlement of disputes or arguments that occurred on the various

---

[93] Tribunale di Milano 2008, *Ordinanza di applicazione di misura coercitiva con mandato di cattura*, Ufficio del giudice per le indagini preliminari, 35026/2006 R.G.N.R.
[94] Ibid., 282–3.
[95] Tribunale di Milano 2014, Sezione Autonoma Misure di Protezione, 124/2013 M.P., 9.

construction sites, for example, if there were objections regarding the progress of the work or similar situations. It was enough simply to drop the boss's name ("OK, I'll send Strangio over and he can sort things out") for the other party to feel intimidated and for the entrepreneur Perego to get what he wanted.[96]

Mafia as Franchising? Abadinsky (2013) argues that mafias are a type of organizational franchise. In a conception contrary to that of the mafia as a pyramidal organization, or a patron–client relationship, mafias are much more similar to the models used by large corporations, Coca-Cola, Goodyear Tires, Ford Motor Company, Benetton, etc.

A franchising is a symbiotic relationship between two legally independent businesses (Blair and Lafontaine 2005), based on an agreement or license between them. The franchisor owns a trademark or trade name and gives a person or group of people (franchisee) the right to use it to market a product or service. The franchisor receives fees from the franchisee, sometimes expanding the business by providing support for financing, advertising and marketing, and training. According to this form of relationship, the franchisor would be the boss of a family and the franchisee the members of the organization, who receive permission to make use of the "brand" in return for ensuring profits for the organization. As for legal markets, to have the right to use the trademark, the franchisee has to adopt the operating methods of the franchisor.

For example, the Mexican cartel the Zetas[97] adopted an operational system similar to that of franchising (Mazzitelli 2011). In new markets, rather than using organization members, they adopt cells of local gangsters as franchisees. The Zetas seek gangsters who will best meet their criminal characteristics, giving them the use of their trademark after a period of military training and sometimes even providing weapons. The new criminal cells are responsible for preserving the "good name" of the Zetas, punishing those who make use of the trademark without permission. The franchisee pays a portion of his revenues to the central organization, signing a pact of solidarity with the latter that ensures its military participation in case of a war against the Zetas by other cartels. This model allows the Zetas to grow rapidly, with no particular organizational and coordination costs, and with the advantage of obtaining highly

---

[96] Tribunale di Milano 2010, *Ordinanza di applicazione di misura coercitiva con mandato di cattura*, Ufficio del giudice per le indagini preliminari, 47816/08 R.G.N.R. mod. 21, 204.

[97] Unlike the Sinaloa Cartel, the Zetas do not specialize in drug trafficking. They provide protection for activities run by other criminal groups and legal operators in the territories under Zetas control (Mazzitelli 2011).

entrepreneurial behavior from the franchisees: far from being employees, they have every incentive to maximize personal earnings, which at the same time increases the earnings of the cartel. A similar branching-out strategy for the formal expansion of the organization has also been adopted by Al-Qaeda after the losses that were inflicted by the U.S. Army in response to the 9/11 terrorist attacks (Mendelsohn 2016).

Notwithstanding the obvious advantages of the organizational model described, and despite some similarities with such a system of relationships, mafias do not work as a franchise system. The typical problems encountered in legal markets would be amplified in the criminal world and in mafias in particular. First of all, the contracts in franchise systems, which define the rights and obligations between the parties, are already complex in legal markets and frequently give rise to disputes (Blair and Lafontaine 2005). The mafia world lacks a legal actor for the enforcement of contracts, and thus the situation would become even more complicated. In addition, there would be complex control problems on the part of the franchisor in relation to compliance and behavior, as well as the possible pursuit of greater autonomy by franchisees. Moreover, given an accounting system that is not especially formalized, the franchisor would be forced to trust the franchisees in terms of the earned amounts that the latter report, without tools of verification at hand. A further problem is the fact that other, unauthorized, persons could make use of the brand, designed to inspire terror and ensure impunity, without paying royalties arising from their criminal activities. To safeguard the brand[98] and to discourage this kind of opportunistic behavior, the mafia naturally resort to violence, which can lead to the killing of the impostors. In the world of legal business, when two franchising brands compete, the result is not violence (e.g., McDonald's vs. Burger King), but in the criminal world conflicts can be very violent indeed and difficult to manage. As Mazzitelli shows, with reference to the Zetas group,

the autonomy of each cell, the very nature of its core business (territorial control) and the consequent need for sustaining control and expansion through unselective recruitment lead necessarily to the atomization of the original structure and the progressive separation, and confrontation, among cells. The Zetas' model of expansion also clashes with local criminal groups that will not accept their dominance. Hence, intra-cell violence, as well as violence between cells and local criminal groups becomes the rule until one of the fighting groups

---

[98] In the case of the Zetas cartel (and others) the brand does not only have a symbolic meaning. The cartel in fact makes use of a recognizable brand sign: a shield split into three segments containing outline maps of Mexico and Tamaulipas (the gang's home state), and a letter "Z." The sign is visible on the uniforms of the members, on baseball caps, on backpacks, and on other items.

prevails. In this scenario, violence will also target innocent civilians residing in the territory under dispute. (Mazzitelli 2011, 23)

A further set of problems relates to control and coordination. In such a highly decentralized system with very loose modes of control, individual franchisees could adopt behavior that was rational and useful from their point of view but extremely harmful from the point of view of the collective organization in terms of its brand. In 2011, for example, a group affiliated to the Zetas committed a serious breach of an unwritten rule, killing Jaime Zapata, a special agent from the U.S. Immigration and Customs Enforcement. Despite the high rate of violence and homicides perpetrated by Mexican cartels, there existed the unwritten rule that absolutely prohibited violence against Americans, especially those in the police. This was certainly not due to any form of respect, but was intended to prevent the devastating consequences that would arise from such acts in terms of repression, harmful to the organization's business. In fact, after the Zapata homicide, the United States cracked down with great severity, with the arrest of hundreds of members and couriers: the damage to the cartel business was far greater than any benefits arising from the elimination of a dangerous enemy (Wainwright 2016). So, if this organizational model has many positive aspects in the short term, enabling rapid organization growth, it also presents weaknesses in the mid- and long terms.

The reasons cited discourage the use of such a model by mafias, which is, therefore, at best an analogy. Mafias have different organizational models, based on many features typical of the clan form of organization.

2.9   Between Clan and Feudal Hierarchy

James Coleman (1974; 1990; 1993) distinguishes between "primordial forms of social organization," and "purposively constructed organizations." The term *primordial forms of social organization* refers to social formations, including family, class, ethnic groups, communities, and kinship networks. They are rooted in the relations established by childbirth, above all, family. The term *purposively constructed organizations* refers to corporate actors that tend to focus around a defined purpose, and in which the elements of structure are not persons, but positions or offices. Persons are merely occupants of positions.

Mafias are a hybrid type: they are purposively criminal constructed organizations (corporate actors), with elements of primordial social organization. This original mixed model is similar to the clan form of organization. Mafias bear no relation to Max Weber's ideal type of legal-rational bureaucracy (or bureaucratic hierarchy). They are far more similar, if anything, to another form of centralized hierarchy: *feudal hierarchy*.[99] While in a bureaucratic hierarchy power is exercised impersonally through the application of formal rules, according to Boisot in a feudal hierarchy

> power translates into personal authority. Relations are face to face and to the trust required by both parties, given the unstructured nature of the information used, is added the faith needed by the weaker party that the stronger one will not abuse the power arising from the knowledge he possesses. This power is at root charismatic and yields what we shall term hierarchical-feudal transactions. Wherever leadership of the "great man" variety is required, transactions will be of this type. They can be found in the research laboratory, the sports team, the company boardroom, and even on the hustings. (Boisot 1986, 144–5)

This form is exemplified by the *fief* as social organization and encompasses personal and hierarchical relationships, just as the kind of coordination involved is hierarchical. Bureaucratic hierarchy is characterized by a high level of concentration of authority and a high level of structuring of activities, and it is managed by impersonal, formal rules and regulations. Feudal hierarchy is also based on a high level of concentration of authority, but it is characterized by a low level of structuring activities, and it is run by the leaders' personal power and influence.

Mafias are a special mix of clan form and feudal hierarchy, even though the clan is of a particular type. Clan[100] form conforms to Durkheim's meaning of an organic association (1912), which resembles a kin network but may not include blood relations (Wasen 2015). While clan societies are highly decentralized government systems, in which power is dispersed among a multitude of kin groups (Weiner 2013), mafias are hierarchical clans, with the presence, in some of them, of higher-level bodies of coordination.

There are three related phenomena, Weiner argues, that characterize the rules of a clan: (1) the legal structures and cultural values of societies organized primarily on the basis of kinship, (2) informal patronage networks (clannism), (3) an antiliberal social and legal organization that tends to grow in the absence of state authority or when the state is weak. These groups include petty criminal gangs, the mafia, and international

---

[99] Feudal hierarchy was introduced into organization studies by Max Boisot (1986; Boisot and Child 1988; 1996).

[100] *Clan* is a word of Gaelic origin (*clann*) which literally means *children* or *family* and generally identifies an aggregation of people united by degrees of consanguinity or affinity, or of common interests.

crime syndicates, which look a great deal like clans and in many respects act like them (2013, 8–9). In contrast to the societies of "contract" (Maine 1861), clans are similar to the societies of "status." These are communities in which "family groups serve as the primary basis for social organization and in which the law takes the extended family as its principal unit of concern. In these communities – societies governed by the rule of the clan – a person's social and legal role is determined by his or her place within the kinship group" (Weiner 2013, 12). Criminal gangs, racial groups, religious groups, and kin groups are some examples of clans, as are some multinational corporations.

Since mafias are illegal organizations that do not have third parties for the resolution of disputes and respect for property rights, the clan form fosters in them the creation of a highly versatile control apparatus over their members, made of rules, initiation and career rites, secrets, etc., which helps to develop a strong sense of belonging among the members.

The clan is a complex form of government in that it presupposes that the members feel connected to the organization by common values and beliefs.

Common values and beliefs, says Ouchi,

> provide the harmony of interests that erase the possibility of opportunistic behavior. If all members of the organization have been exposed to an apprenticeship or other socialization period, then they will share personal goals that are compatible with the goals of the organization. In this condition, auditing the performance is unnecessary except for educational purposes, since no member will attempt to depart from organizational goals. (Ouchi 1980, 138)

The initiation rites, rituals, rules, promotion ceremonies, etc., far from being profitless residues of the past, work in support of these organizations and are powerful and effective tools to build clan form, to enforce respect for behavioral rules, and to contain the violence that is always a possibility among participants. As emerged from the study on the transition to the market economy in China, norms based on contract compliance and mutual support, and subsequent sanctions in case of noncompliance, were at the heart of informal commercial codes. The resulting collaborative networks of entrepreneurs relying on a governance system rooted in reputation for trustworthiness among peers triggered the Chinese economic miracle (Nee and Opper 2012). Similarly, belonging to the same clan constitutes the basis on which trust between members is founded. Penalties for violating the rules that they themselves helped produce, or for noncompliance, can be severe, ranging from expulsion to "loss of face" to death, as in criminal organizations. This clan model can be inculcated and maintained through a comprehensive and complex set of practices, such as the rules, rites, and ceremonies to which we have referred. The clan form appeals, then, for the advantages that it brings in terms of trust and possibility of control, as the form most suited, compared to alternative kinds of market and hierarchy (Williamson 1975; 1985), to reduce the typical transaction costs of mafia activities. Alvesson and Lindkvist (1993, 442–3) identified three different kinds of clan. The *economic* clan focuses to a high extent on the economic relation among its members. The *social* clan, instead, responds to individuals' need to belong and communicate, rather than economic considerations. Finally, the *blood relationship* clan is based on a biological imperative, in which consanguinity structures the organization. Mafias incorporate, to some extent, all three dimensions, although in some cases, such as the 'Ndrangheta, the blood relationship dimension is dominant.

2.9.1   Organizational Control

It is well known that the success or failure of an organization depends largely on its ability to maintain control over its members. The tension between the organization's needs (for effectiveness and efficiency, for example) and those of its members (the satisfaction of their own interests) is particularly evident in the area of organizational control (Etzioni 1961). When individual and organizational needs are compatible, the need for control decreases as a consequence. Participants will tend to do what is best for the organization in order to increase their own gratification, while the organization, in pursuing its own needs, also indirectly pursues those of its participants. Organizational control would not constitute a problem if organizations could be sure of recruiting people who would conform to their standards, or if they could train them in order for them to do this. Selection, recruitment, and socialization mechanisms are of particular importance therefore for organizational control, and this explains the special care that mafias take in adhering to them. The more effective socialization is, observes Simon (1947), the less necessary is control. From an organizational point of view, the clan represents cultural values that are almost the opposite of bureaucratic control. Clan control relies on values, beliefs, corporate culture, shared norms, and informal relationships to regulate employee behavior and facilitate the achievement of organizational goals. The clan form, then, seems to be able to solve certain serious control problems that mafias, like many other organizations, have to face in order to ensure that members follow the rules and obey orders (Etzioni 1964).

To mediate transactions efficiently, each organization must reduce the ambiguity of performance evaluation[101] or the goal incongruence between parties. Market relations are efficient when there is little ambiguity over performance. In this way, the parties can tolerate high levels of opportunism or goal incongruence. Bureaucratic relationships, however, are efficient when both performance ambiguity and goal incongruence are moderately high. The clan, argues Ouchi, replaces bureaucracy "when the ambiguity of performance evaluation becomes significantly greater than that which brings about market failure" (1980, 134).

Transaction costs increase under conditions of extreme uncertainty and opportunism, and these are conditions typical of a mafia criminal enterprise. Extreme uncertainty is due to the hostile environment in which the organization operates and the low level of proceduralization possible with regard to activities. Criminal activity does not take place within a definable and observable physical perimeter, except for certain specific and limited activities. In addition, performance is characterized by a high level of ambiguity. The services provided by the mafia are, in fact, barely standardizable and routinizable and take place in conditions of high uncertainty and danger, with secrecy guaranteed. A set of standards of the performance of actions that makes it possible for superiors to evaluate, compare, and control behavior or output achieved is absent in the mafia. The absence of standards, or their lack of precision, increases the possibility of idiosyncratic interpretation. Moreover, given the structural characteristics of mafia activity, there is a problem of information asymmetry between those who carry out the actions and those who should control and evaluate them. This opens the door to opportunism, also taking into account the absence of third parties in the control and resolution of disputes, and, given the low controllability of many activities, increases the possibility of cheating for mafias, which are, inter alia, very prone to this kind of behavior, thanks to the mind-set and skills acquired.

It should be stated at this point that a clan can develop stably only as a result of a long habitual relationship between the parties. It takes a long time and costs money to set up, so it cannot be used as an instant solution in a situation of crisis. Some Japanese companies (Abegglen 1958; Dore 1973), and also American ones (Ouchi 1981), have invested

---

[101] A performance is ambiguous when it is not possible to determine with certainty the relationship between performance and reward, or when it is difficult to determine the cost of goods or services. This difficulty may depend on the intrinsic characteristics of the goods or services, or on the lack of trust between the parties to the transaction (Ouchi 1980; 1981).

in socialization processes over a long period in order to foster alignment between individual motivation and the collective interests of the organization. These socialization processes, along with other organizational mechanisms typical of mafias, make it possible to overcome, or at least restrict, a structural problem that makes it difficult for such organizations to operate: the fact that members do not share a selfless devotion to the same objectives (Barnard 1938; Mayo 1945).

This explains why the clan form (always combined, of course, with the other two forms, of market and hierarchy, given that pure forms are quite rare) is the most suitable form for, and the one adopted by, mafias. It makes it possible to minimize goal incongruence and tolerate the high levels of ambiguity in performance evaluation typical of mafia organizations. The frequent presence of groups based on ethnic and/or national-territorial ties is due to the fact that such ties reduce certain transaction costs, discouraging opportunistic behavior and desertion among members.

It should be pointed out that in mafias these objectives are not only achieved through intense socialization processes, but also through a strict system of punishment for violations, even though this form of organization minimizes the need for recourse to violence: "In some contexts, primary bonds between members of the organization, based on kinship, ethnicity, family, nationality and locality, guarantee the security and continuity of illegal transactions and minimize the need or the threat of violence" (Arlacchi 1998, 210).

According to clan rules, individuals are considered less as individuals per se, and more as members of their extended families. Individuals are therefore immersed in the social groups to which they belong and from which they cannot (easily) extract themselves. Paoli (2003) points up the brotherhood dimension, saying that mafias are based on fraternization contracts among members. Studying the gangs of Russia, Stephenson (2015) affirms that "gangs members see themselves as both businessmen and brothers" (114). Gangs are supported by a collective ethos, nurtured and supported by the leaders as well as by the ordinary members of the organization. This constitutes an element of strength for the organization, allowing gangs to succeed where modern corporations fail. However, says Stephenson, if the aspect of economic accumulation prevails over the ideals of brotherhood, its authority loses legitimacy. It is an interesting trade-off and one that we will return to later.

As Weiner affirms:

The principle of group honor ties each person's social value and moral worth to the reputation of his or her kin group. The corresponding principle of collective shame in turn means that the moral misconduct of any member of the group dishonors the group as a whole, just as the misconduct of one Marine disgraces the entire Corps ... This creates a strong incentive for the group to ensure that its members do well according to community norms. (Weiner 2013, 101)

The behavior of one member of the group contrary to the claims of honor diminishes the entire social standing of the group, and its reputation.

The use of violence is also influenced by the clan form, as in feudal society, where private vendetta for a wrong suffered was a kind of moral obligation, the most sacred of tasks of the injured party (Bloch 2014), and so in the mafia: if a group is dishonored by the action of another group, the latter must be made to pay for the offense, even with death, to restore the honor of the former. This restores equilibrium, even if only temporarily, as the frequent feuds demonstrate. To contain violence and limit damage, some mafias, as we have said, and as we will see more fully in Chapter 3, form higher-level bodies of coordination.

In some gangs, particularly in the 'Ndrangheta, blood relationships are a constitutive element in the organization both at the level of an individual organizational unit ('ndrina) and in establishing relationships and strong ties between different organizational units. In this case, rather than an economic or social clan, it is a matter of a "blood relationship clan" (Alvesson and Lindkvist 1993). As Sjöstrand says:

These can only be changed by the breaking/forming of blood relationships or death. Clans of the type mafia rely, according to Ianni, on family ties. These bonds are stronger the closer the relationship and the closer the feelings of belonging. The family is culturally influenced and incorporated in the social order preserved in history. It becomes a kind of limited altruism – only relatives and family (the collective of these) mean anything. The individual only exists as a member of the collective. (Sjöstrand 1985, 226, cited in Alvesson and Lindkvist 1993, 443)

This form of highly integrated clan not only pertains to the criminal world, but is also typical of many legal businesses, such as the Rockefeller empire in the United States, or the Agnelli family's activities in Italy. Also, in some mafias, and in the 'Ndrangheta in particular, there is a concrete matrimonial strategy aimed at increasing the power of families and clan ties. The intertwining of kin cements mafia sodality and strengthens associative links. Marriages also perform another important function: to attempt the settlement of disputes or to establish peace after a war (Ciconte 1996).

The clan form is reinforced in some mafias, for example, the Italian ones, by a relationship of internal reciprocity. Each member can count on economic assistance from the organization, in the event of situations related to criminal activity such as prison detention, legal proceedings, or being on the run (Di Cagno and Natoli 2004). To handle these events, there exists a common fund into which flow the various types of income deriving from mafia activities, and which can be drawn on when it is necessary to pay legal costs (lawyers), to support the detainee's family, and to finance a fugitive's escape. This reciprocity has the function of strengthening the associative link between members, reducing the possibility that arrested members will inform on the organization or cooperate with law enforcement agencies (see Section 2.6).

2.9.2   Clan Signs

Some mafias attempt to recreate the bonds of blood relationship through tattoos. In particular, in the Yakuza, the Russian Mafia, some triad groups, and some clans of the Camorra, members tattoo images and symbols that indicate their status. The images used vary from mafia to mafia. For example, in the Russian Mafia there are numerous religious icons, swords, skulls, or animals (cat, lion, panther, leopard, tiger, snake, eagle, etc.), together with other images. Among gangs, it is common to display membership symbols, such as clothes, hand signs, and tattoos (Decker and van Winkle 1996).

Triad members wear tattoos that represent their membership in a particular gang, and in various Camorra clans, too, the members use tattoos as signs of belonging and devotion to the clan.[102] The members of the clan led by boss Marco De Micco use tattoos on their forearms and/or back with the word "Bodo," De Micco's nickname. The latter is a young and emerging *capoclan* in Ponticelli (Naples), hugely admired by his followers. "Bodo," on the other hand, is a cartoon character: a peasant of the Middle Ages, whom schoolteachers use to make history more appealing in the eyes of their pupils. Four young people between twenty and twenty-three years who were arrested by the police in 2015 in an operation carried out in Ponticelli had instead the word "Fraulella"

---

[102] De Blasio (1905) documents how the tattoo was already widespread among the Camorra in the late nineteenth and early twentieth centuries. It was used to identify, on the one hand, the status of the members in the Camorra organization and, on the other, the clan they belonged to. To identify the status, a design similar to telegraph writing was employed: a dash and three dots to identify the Camorra, a dash and two dots to identify the *picciotto*, a dash and a dot to identify the *giovane onorato* (the lowest grade). This type of tattoo was accompanied by another that identified the clan (e.g., a pistol for the clan of the Sanità district of Naples).

(wild strawberry) tattooed on their bodies, a distinctive term associated with the D'Amico family, a historic group of gunmen allied with the Sarno clan.[103] The tattoo is a tribute to the boss Giuseppe D'Amico, currently in jail and, indeed, nicknamed "Fraulella." Each of the four men had also decided to accompany the name with other designs (bullets, the eyes of a woman, a rose, and a cross).

In another clan, members pay homage to their leader, Umberto Accurso, with a declaration of loyalty accompanied by the ZIP code of the area where the clan operates (80144). The members of the Scampia clans, meanwhile, have a scorpion painted on their skin as a means of recognition. This is the zodiac sign of the boss Raffaele Amato, the boss of bosses of the Secondigliano Camorra, and the same symbol is stamped into the cakes of hashish that the Amato-Pagano clan imports from Morocco and Spain.

Another tattoo that is very popular with clan members is the head of a Neapolitan mastiff. As Maurizio Prestieri – collaborator with justice and former right-hand man of superboss Paolo Di Lauro – explained, this is the hallmark of the members of the Licciardi clan of Masseria Cardone. Finally, the killers of the Buonerba clan tattoo a small "B" on their arms as a mark of devotion to their boss.

The message is that these men feel that the Camorra is truly a part of themselves, and that belonging to a specific criminal group is for life. Tattoos are symbols of status and of recognition, like business cards. Tattoos express belonging; they are "costly signals" (Zahavi and Zahavi 1997), or "embodied handicaps" that indicate some relevant aspects regarding the qualities of the person who bears them (Gambetta 2009). Paying these costs signals to others that the person is engaged in a long-term relationship with the group. However, situations are not uncommon where members of a clan with a specific tattoo move on to another clan, which favors a different type of tattoo.

Tattoos are an important tool of communication and of identity, a visual brand, even though stigmatized by society and dangerous in that they facilitate identification by law enforcement agencies. It is estimated that about 70 percent of Yakuza members have tattoos (Hill 2003a, 87) and that the main reasons given for them are ostentation and intimidation. In addition to being highly visible, tattoos are expensive, especially if made with traditional techniques and require a long time to be realized. The fact that they are also painful to receive is a sign of the strength of

---

[103] "Fraulella e gli altri tatuaggi della camorra", *Corriere del Mezzogiorno* (*Corriere della Sera*), March 24, 2015.

endurance of those who have them, and the fact that they are difficult to remove attests to the permanent nature of the criminal bond.[104]

While symbols and meanings vary from mafia to mafia, tattoos are a means of sociopolitical communication and act as symbols of public identity, social self-awareness, and collective memory (Baldaev and Vasiliev 2004). Of course, some might make use of these symbols without authorization to increase their power – if discovered, however, the punishment they risk can be lethal. Cases have been reported of the removal of tattoos with knives or abrasive materials, in addition to violent beatings (Baldaev and Vasiliev 2004; Varese 2017).

2.10 Organizational Structure

To understand how a mafia organization works, it is essential to analyze its power structure – how power, in other words, is distributed within the organization. The organizational structure represents a map of the formal power of an organization and depends on the choices related to the differentiation of its components and the establishment of connections between and within them (Thompson 1967). Structures are designed, says Hall (1977), to minimize and adjust the influence of individual variations on the organization. The formal organizational structure (hereafter, organizational structure) defines the division of labor, the formal allocation of authority, and the relationships between people in an organization. It identifies the grouping of individuals into organizational units and the organizational units as they exist within the organization, indicating the relationships of formal dependency, including the number of hierarchical levels and the amplitude of the control (the *span control*) of managers and supervisors. In addition, it includes the plan for the methods of communication and coordination, and the integration of efforts between the organizational units (Daft 2013). The design of the organizational structure tells us much about the power relationships within the organization: in other words, who controls whom, and not how the work is actually carried out. For this latter aspect, mafias have various ad hoc combinations, shaped in an adaptive way to the task to be performed and influenced by the need for security and secrecy.

Organizational structure, through the horizontal dimension, defines the division of labor and the aggregation of individual persons into

---

[104] It would appear that within the Yakuza many modern-minded bosses encourage their members not to have tattoos, so that in the future they will face no restrictions and will not be confined solely to the activities of the Yakuza, given that the tattoos are a barrier to entering the world of legitimate business (Hill 2003a, 214).

increasingly complex units, such as organs, functions, divisions. Through the vertical dimension, it defines the relationship of hierarchical super- and suborders that link people and the organizational subunits.

Organizations vary considerably according to their structures, with important consequences for individual and organizational results.

In the mafia, besides individual action, we can distinguish two levels of the organization:

(1) The basic *organizational unit* – called *family*, *clan*, *'ndrina*, *ikka*, *brigade*, etc. – which constitutes the basic organizational level common to all the mafias. It is composed of individuals who hold specific organizational roles, and it is always characterized by a hierarchical structure, with an authoritative center represented by a leader. The hierarchical dimension is essential both to ensure protection (Gambetta 1993) and to allow an effective and coordinated use of violence, an essential resource for the firm to establish and maintain its territorial rights (Chu 2000).

(2) The *metaorganizational* level, which includes the higher-level bodies of coordination that certain mafias develop over time to regulate specific aspects of organizational life. Where the basic organizational units are composed of individuals, metaorganizations are composed of other organizations, in the sense that the people who take part in them represent other organizational units.

While, as we will see, the organizational unit level presents numerous similarities between the various mafias, in a model with many aspects in common, the metaorganizational level (i.e., the higher-level bodies of coordination) presents several variations that require specific treatment for each mafia (see Section 3.1) and prevent the development of a common model. However, this higher-level body of coordination does implement functions that are common to the various mafias in terms of conflict reduction, the development of shared organizational strategies, and the maintenance of the unity and the unitary identity of the organization.

The two levels refer to two different logics of action and organizational rationality, in that metaorganizations operate in different conditions compared to individual organizations, since their members are organizations rather than individuals (Ahrne and Brunsson 2008). The level of the basic organizational unit regards the dimension of *government*, while the metaorganizational level, superordinate to basic organizational units, regards the dimension of *governance*.[105] This dimension relates to the

---

[105] The two terms "government" and "governance" have received sometimes very different definitions and characterizations by numerous authors in the field of social and political

various modes of social coordination to produce and implement collectively binding rules. From the operational point of view, governance consists of structures and processes. Structures consist of the various organizational components (families, districts, etc.), while processes have to do with the rules of operation and the practical means to operate and carry out coordination. Unlike government, governance is characterized by a rationality that is more of a political kind and less hierarchical in nature: nonhierarchical coordination, a second-order coordination that involves coordination among organizations whose primary function is to coordinate and to manage human activity. Persuasion and bargaining are important requirements with regard to operationality and conflict resolution.

The combination of the two levels, organizational and metaorganizational (if present), constitutes the overall mafia organization. The variety of combinations of these two levels gives rise to two different forms of government: *clan-based* and *clan-based federation*. The clan-based system is based on a plurality of organizational decision makers who can act and make strategic decisions independently of one other and without having to account to higher-level bodies of coordination (HLBC). This is the case of many – but not all – of the Camorra clans, for example. A clan-based federation, on the other hand, is not primarily a hierarchical system where those at a higher level, a supraordinate organizational unit, in other words, control those at a lower level, as happens with a boss and the members of his family. In a federal system, there is a partial cession of sovereignty by the basic organizational units in favor of higher-level bodies of coordination, but only with regard to a number of aspects of collective organizational life. These aspects may be significant, but they are not matters relating to the business methods of the individual component organization. In a federal system, the HLBC work to resolve any disputes by minimizing the negative externalities deriving from conflict and excessive violence, to develop strategies of collective interest, to

---

science (Kooiman 1999; 2003; Benz 2007; Börzel and Risse 2010). For our purposes here, we will use them to identify two different modes and two different rationalities of organizational regulation: through hierarchy and the principle of command and control (government) at organizational level, and through nonhierarchical coordination (governance) at the interorganizational level. The type of governance we are dealing with here involves the use of coercion, a requirement not contemplated in pure forms of governance. In mafias, elements of hierarchical decision can also coexist in interorganizational contexts of governance: for example, if one group acquires a particularly significant level of power over others and is thus able to make binding collective decisions without resorting to dialogue or negotiation. Or, elements of governance can coexist in the dimension of government, when hierarchical decisions are made taking into account the existing interorganizational relationships, constraints, and expectations of other organizational actors.

identify and eliminate potential enemies of the organization, and to establish and enforce rules. They cannot, as has been said, decide the life within the basic individual organizational units, even though the latter, in order to make decisions, in some way take into account the existence of the HLBC. The *clan-based* and *clan-based federation* forms vary over time, in the sense that an organization, as we will see, can shift from one system to another in the course of its organizational life, in terms of endogenous factors (degree of cohesion or conflict among clans, organizational leadership, etc.) and exogenous factors – above all, repression from law enforcement agencies.

The differences between the two levels are relevant. For example, hierarchical interdependence, or the degree to which the behavior of a subordinate organizational actor is conditioned by the actions of another superordinate organizational actor, is high at an intraorganizational level, but appears to be low at an interorganizational level.

2.10.1   The Government Dimension: The Minimal Organizational Unit

At the level of the government dimension, or basic organizational unit, the relationships between people are characterized by the presence of a boss (the principal) and subordinated actors (the agents). As already mentioned, mafias have a rather similar basic organizational model, as shown in Figure 2.1.

The names of the different roles may vary, but, apart from some differences, there is a substantial convergence among the different organizational units of mafias, notwithstanding the different cultural contexts. This happens because the different mafia organizations face similar technical, economic, and organizational problems, and will tackle them in similar ways. Joan Woodward writes that "it was possible to trace a cause and effect relationship between a system of production and its associated organizational pattern and, as a result, to predict what the organizational requirements of a firm are likely to be, given its production system" (1958, 37). These similarities at a basic organizational level are therefore attributable to the similar production systems, or rather to the same method of carrying out services that characterizes the different mafias. Variations in organizational response are referable to variations in task or task environment rather than to differences in cultural value systems.

The Principal Dimensions of Formal Structure. Formal structure has three main dimensions: (1) *centralization*, (2) *complexity*, and

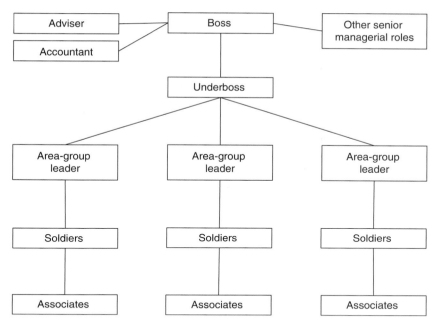

Figure 2.1 The typical organizational structure of a mafia family

(3) *formalization*; these will be analyzed with particular reference to the basic organizational units (*family*, *clan*, etc.).

(1) *Centralization*: the dimension of *centralization* regards the locus of decision-making authority within an organization (van de Ven and Ferry 1980). It refers to how much control the headquarters or center of an organization exerts over its local units. The opposite, decentralization, refers to the contrary forces and points to the degree of control those units have over their own businesses. The degree of centralization is also related to the level of participation of different groups in an organization in strategic decisions, and a quick way to evaluate it consists in the examination of the levels of discretion and real power of lower-level employees to effect change in the organization's manner of operating and to respond to unique circumstances (Southerland and Potter 1993).

According to van de Ven and Ferry (1980, 399), "When most decisions are made hierarchically, an organizational unit is considered to be centralized; a decentralized unit generally implies that the major source of decision-making has been delegated by line managers to subordinate personnel." Criminal organizations are reluctant to delegate authority vertically. This happens in extremely limited circumstances, and decisions that affect the organization's ability to protect itself and produce a profit are reserved to the top of the organization (Southerland and Potter 1993, 253). Moreover, important decisions are made close to the top for security reasons.

As stated earlier, rather than being characterized by bureaucratic hierarchy, mafias are based, at the level of the basic organizational unit, on principles typical of the feudal hierarchy (Boisot and Child 1988). This form provides a mix of personal and hierarchical relationships (similar to those of a feudal system), while the kind of coordination between the different units, individuals, and organizations is also hierarchical. While bureaucratic hierarchy is managed by impersonal, formal rules and regulations, feudal hierarchy is run by the leaders' personal power and influence.

Mafias are highly centralized within the base units (*family, clan, 'ndrine,* etc.), with the division of power similar to the "decimal organization" (Keegan 1994) typically used by the army. Three levels can be identified:

(a) The *strategic apex* of the organization is represented by the boss. His activities of control and strategic direction are supported by several advisers, senior members in the organization who help him make critical decisions as well as those relating to more operational matters. The last word on every decision remains with the boss. In the American Cosa Nostra the hierarchy is

> more rigid than most companies and even the US government. The man at the top of the pyramid – the boss of the family – is as powerful and inaccessible as any CEO or even the president. The boss is the unquestioned leader, the supreme dictator, the final arbiter, the ultimate wiseguy. His word is final, his decisions non-negotiable, his authority absolute ... You cannot understand the way of the wiseguy unless you understand the particular mystique of the Mafia boss. (Pistone 2004, 80)

The boss represents the organization in the higher-level bodies of coordination. Below the boss is the underboss, who in some mafias has a buffer position and is the direct liaison with the subordinate levels. In other mafias (e.g., the Sicilian Cosa Nostra), he has a staff position: he does not directly control the subordinate levels, but assists the boss in management and stands in for him in cases of absence or impediment.

(b) At a lower level, there is the *middle line*, consisting of managers placed between the strategic apex and the operational line. At this level, members are gathered in groups led by a group leader (who has different names: captain, *caporegime*, etc.) whose *span of control*, the number of actors coordinated by a single center (Woodward 1965), varies from several units to several dozen members, called *soldiers* (or *warriors*, or in other ways). It should be noted that, in mafias, the efficiency of span of control is higher than in other organizations, as the subordinates, the soldiers, are not "indifferent" with regard to the tasks to be performed (Williamson 1970), but are intensely involved in the work they have to do. If the boss mainly takes care of decisions of interest to the whole organization, the so-called strategic management, group leaders are responsible for operational management within the groups that they direct. These groups are characterized by local autonomy, or by a certain degree of operational freedom, which means they have the ability and capacity to carry out their own business independently. In general, these groups control a specific territory, as if they were specialized divisions for a geographic area.

(c) Finally, there is the *operating core* composed of soldiers, the regular members who make use of associates in order to carry out their activities. The latter work with the organization on a daily basis but are not "made members," although in some cases they might one day become part of the organization. The strategic apex and the middle line are the location of the element functions (direction, control, etc.), while the operational core is the location of the task functions, directed toward specific and defined purposes, coordinated to ensure a more effective pursuit of the overall objectives of the organization (Woodward 1965).

2) *Complexity:* a second dimension of the organizational structure, is constituted by *complexity*, that is, the degree of division of labor and of the structure of the subunits in an organization. A high degree of complexity (the number of subunits) involves greater need for coordination and control of subunits and the integration of their activities. Complexity is divided into (a) *horizontal*, with reference to the division of labor; (b) *vertical*, or hierarchical; and (c) *spatial*, or geographical dispersion (Tolbert and Hall 2009).

(a) *Horizontal complexity* concerns the way in which work tasks in an organization are divided into different job titles and subunits (i.e., production, marketing, etc.). The greater the number of these, the greater the complexity of the organization. (b) *Vertical or hierarchical complexity*, on the other hand, concerns the division of decision-making tasks (between line and staff operation) and supervisory responsibilities and depends on the number of hierarchical levels present in an organization. (c) *Spatial complexity* is related to the fact that the organization has, or does not have, different sites in different physical locations. This dimension may be measured by counting the number of places where the organization has offices or production facilities, or by calculating the percentage of people working far from the headquarters. The greater the geographical dispersion, the more necessary coordination and control activities will be.

Criminal organizations tend to have a low degree of complexity. As a matter of fact, according to Southerland and Potter,

tasks in criminal organizations are typically interchangeable and require little sophisticated skill or education. Specialization is usually unnecessary and counterproductive because it restricts the freedom of the enterprise to get work done on an efficient basis by using all available manpower in the process. Departmentalization makes little sense at all in illicit enterprise. The operations are simply not complex enough to either segregate production knowledge or to require a chain of command to oversee the quantity and quality of production. Departmentalization would create organizational sub-units on the basis of ceremony, not necessity. Therefore, criminal enterprises have relatively simple structures. (Southerland and Potter 1993, 254)

In mafias, horizontal complexity tends to be very low and there are no functional or divisional variations, as have been detected in some terrorist organizations, such as Al-Qaeda, before 2001 (Shapiro 2013). Vertical complexity, however, is present, although to a limited extent. The HLBC do not have hierarchical functions, but those, as the term implies, of coordination, and therefore cannot be counted as hierarchical levels and as an indicator of hierarchical complexity.

As regards spatial complexity, it should be noted that mafias tend to be very restricted in this area in terms of the core activity of organizations of this type: protection. It is carried out within a specific and limited geographical context. However, for several decades now mafias have been involved in expansion into nontraditional areas, where, however, business activity rather than protection – at least in the original meaning of the word – seems to be prevalent.

(3) *Formalization:* the dimension of formalization, in an organization, relates to the degree of explicitness of procedures and operating rules that indicate how a certain task should be accomplished, and through which steps (Tolbert and Hall 2009). The degree of formalization can be measured by the number of rules and written procedures present in an organization, or by the perception that individuals have of the importance of formalization in performing their work. Formalization makes it possible to render the behavior of participants predictable: "Formalization makes allowances for the finitude and inconstancy of human actors" (Scott and Davis 2007, 39).

Table 2.5 *Centralization, complexity, and formalization in mafias*

Structuring Dimensions	Meaning	In Organized Crime and Mafias
Centralization	Degree of concentration of authority	High (in the minimal organizational unit – *family*, *clan*, etc.)
Complexity	Vertical (hierarchy) and horizontal (division of labor) differentiation	Low (four to five levels; few different roles)
Formalization	Degree to which roles, rules, and procedures are explicitly defined	Somewhat (unwritten rules; no procedures)

Criminal organizations tend to be somewhat formalized:

Their formalization is not through manuals of standard operating procedures. The formalization occurs through careful socialization of new members of the organization. This socialization process is a vital program for these organizations, yet no documentation will be found on these programs as it would in legal enterprise. (Southerland and Potter 1993, 256)

As for mafias, they establish rules to govern the behavior of their members. These rules, mostly unwritten, are discussed in Chapter 5.

To sum up, criminal enterprises tend to be centralized and partially formalized, but not complex (see Table 2.5).

The organizational principles adopted by the mafia, at a basic organizational unit level, are very reminiscent of the classic administrative principles (Gulick and Urwick 1937; Fayol 1949): in particular, (a) the *pyramid of control* principle, which provides the hierarchical organizational form in which all participants are linked in a single pyramidal structure of control relationships; (b) the *command and control* principle, which states that no participant should receive orders from more than one superior (e.g., associate and soldier; soldier and captain; captain and boss); (c) the *span of control* principle, according to which no superior should have more subordinates than can be effectively supervised; (d) the *exception* principle, according to which routine tasks are handled by subordinates so that superiors are left free to address situations that are exceptional and new.

At the primary level, that of the basic organizational units (*family*, *clan*, *ikka*, etc.), many similarities emerge between the different mafias. All are based on the same principles of *span of control* and *pyramid of control*. With reference to the former, relating to the number of subordinates (soldiers) that a boss can control, it can be seen that the size of a group depends on the possibility of control by the leader, but also on the need for a boss to avoid the creation of groups that are too numerous. The latter could in fact acquire too much power, putting the safety of the boss himself at risk. In the organizational unit, order is based on autocracy, and certainly not on democracy, so anyone who acquires too much power is a potential threat.[106] With regard to the second principle, the *pyramid of control*, it can be seen that in mafias the levels of hierarchical variation range from a minimum of three to four in some low-structured Camorra clans and the Sicilian and American Cosa Nostra, to four to five in the Triads, the Russian Mafia, and some highly structured Camorra clans and up to five to six levels in the case of the Yakuza.

The basic units of the mafias are characterized by vertical specialization: the higher the hierarchical level of a particular role, the more this involves making decisions and the less it deals with carrying out a specific activity, a job. So there is a division between decision-making activities and operational activities: the activity of soldiers and, especially, the associates, is substantially executive (with more latitude for self-entrepreneurship in the American Cosa Nostra).

As regards the methods of division of labor and the allocation of people to organizational units, the prevailing principle is that of geographical area. The basic organizational units (*family*, *clan*, etc.) run a specific geographical area where they try to have a monopoly on illegal and criminal activities.

For example, for the three Italian mafias, control is based on geographical division, so each unit oversees a specific reference area, where it offers its "services" and realizes its activities, and has other organizational units on its borders. Other mafias, such as the American Cosa Nostra, instead adopt control through line of business.

Before proceeding, it may be useful to recall certain concepts. The analysis of organizational structures is, of course, only one aspect of the overall organizational analysis. Organizational structures highlight the power relations in the organization and the lines of control (who controls whom) but tell us little about the activities undertaken by the organization and how they are carried out. In mafias, the operational models of the organization of work are similar to the organizational principles of the Burns and Stalker organic model (1961) and Mintzberg's adhocracy (1983).

---

[106] It can also, of course, happen in the legal business world: for example, in 1978, with the dismissal of Lee Iacocca, the brilliant Ford manager who would later become head of Chrysler. The dismissal did not depend on Iacocca's performance but on the fact that Henry Ford II, grandson of the founder, did not like the level of power that the manager had achieved within the company thanks to his positive results (Morgan 1986).

They are, that is, highly flexible and task oriented and therefore define the organizational work structure according to the activity to be carried out and guaranteeing the requirement of security. For example, the clan of Camorra boss Paolo di Lauro organized the work of the production and sales of drugs according to a strict division of operational activities on several vertically arranged levels. One level was in charge of the control and supervision of the trafficking and sale of drugs; another dealt with procurement and packaging for sale; another for managing relationships with drug dealers; and another handled the level of control of the trading process in the selected locations and collected earnings from the sellers (Scanni and Oliva 2006, 44).

2.10.2 The Governance Dimension: Higher-Level Bodies of Coordination

Almost all organizational theories assume that organization members are only individuals. In their influential book, *Organizations*, March and Simon (1958) affirmed that they were interested in individual-based organizations, and over the following years organization theory developed with this as its objective. However, there are organizations whose members are not individuals but other organizations, defined by Ahrne and Brunsson (2008) as metaorganizations. Metaorganizations are associations that differ from federative states and business conglomerates. The members of metaorganizations may be states, firms, or associations and they have considerable autonomy: They have applied for membership by choice and they are free to leave any time, and members tend to be equal (Ahrne and Brunsson 2008). Examples of metaorganizations are the European Union, the World Federation of United Cities, the International Chamber of Commerce, the International Labour Organization, the North Atlantic Treaty Organization, the World Trade Organization, and many, many more.[107]

To try to reduce the Hobbesian situation of *Homo homini lupus*, in which each clan can maintain a threatening attitude with regard to all and sundry, various mafias have created, over time and in different ways,

---

[107] While there are similarities between the concepts of metaorganizations and networks, they are two distinct concepts and phenomena. In networks, unlike metaorganizations, participation is not centrally regulated and boundaries tend to be open. Metaorganizations, however, create boundaries between themselves and the outside world, explicitly deciding who is a member and who is not. Despite the great variety of metaorganizations there is a center in which some degree of authority is recognized, while this is not always so in the network. Unlike metaorganizations, networks do not make decisions and strategies are not developed explicitly, but emerge from the interaction of multiple elements.

metaorganizations – called here, for the functions they perform, *higher-level bodies of coordination* (HLBC). This is not in any way a "Leviathan" that hierarchically controls every single organizational unit, but rather metaorganizations with functions of coordination, maintenance of the regulatory system, and dispute and conflict reduction. In particular, the control and regulation of the use of violence represent the most relevant elements that favor the formation of HLBC.

While the minimal organizational units (*family*, *ikka*, *'ndrina*, etc.) are made up of people, the HLBC consist of organizations. Of course, such higher-level bodies are always composed of individuals, but they take part as representatives of organizations, as stakeholders in other organizations, and not just as individuals per se. Each level is not simply higher than the one below, but represents a more inclusive grouping that addresses aspects of coordination that go beyond the scope of any of its individual components. The HLBC operate according to different methods with respect to the subordinate units, with no possibility of recourse to the hierarchy and to the command and control mode. These bodies are examples of governance but, as mentioned, unlike the governance that characterizes political institutions and federal models, it is a governance that involves the use of coercion and of sanctions for the violation of shared rules and regulations.

If, at the government level, the cost of coordination is related to the number of individuals and subunits involved, in terms of governance, the cost of coordination relates to the number and complexity of the organizations involved. At this level, the following problem emerges: to what extent do the strategies, actions, and use of violence by an organization create spillovers (i.e., negative or positive externalities) for other organizations, so that coordination is necessary to prevent socially perverse outcomes?[108] The potential for conflict within HLBC increases in relation to the interdependence of the component organizations. As Fritz Scharpf points out: "As the number of affected parties increases … negotiated solutions incur exponentially rising and eventually prohibitive transaction costs" (1997, 70). In what way can these costs – if excessive – be reduced, given that they would increase organizational entropy and render the coordination effort vain? One solution adopted by mafias is to introduce more levels of coordination, more higher-level bodies of coordination. For example, as will be seen in Section 3.1, the Sicilian Cosa Nostra has established three levels above the approximately 150 families: district, provincial level, and regional level. Meanwhile, the

---

[108] A similar dilemma is indicated by Hooghe and Marks (2003) with reference to political institutions.

American Cosa Nostra, which has had at most twenty-four families, larger in size than its "Italian cousin," has established only one higher-level coordination body for New York, where there are five families, 20 percent of the total, and one at a national level – the Commission. The latter, however, played a very innocuous role from the operational coordination point of view with meetings every five years, unless there was an emergency.

The overall model seeks to combine the autonomy of the individual parts (the minimal organizational units) with the economics of coordination. As already mentioned, this does not mean that these bodies are perfect examples of deliberative democracy, a place of equals where everyone has the same power as everyone else. Naturally, as in a great deal of social reality, the asymmetry of power is present, and so the historically strongest groups, those that have the most members or are richer or more violent, exert an influence on the dynamics of decision-making that shapes the end result in a significantly greater way than the contribution of others. As Thompson says, "When the power is widely distributed, an *inner circle* emerges to conduct coalition business" (1967, 140), and the central power figure, Thompson argues, is the individual who can manage the coalition. In this case, there manifests a presence of government forms in contexts of governance. This was what happened with the so-called Corleonesi, an inner circle within the Provincial Commission of the Sicilian Cosa Nostra, or the central power figures of Totò Riina and Bernardo Provenzano. An excess of government can, however, kill governance: in fact, under the leadership of Totò Riina, the original function of HLBC was reduced in favor of the boss, who emptied these bodies and transformed them into personal power centers. Riina reached this goal with the physical elimination of opponents, and so thanks to forced consensus arising from the fear of the consequences of dissent. However, he also employed shrewd political power tactics typical of legal organizations (Pfeffer 1981), creating coalitions and expanding the network of people he could trust. It was a strategy that made use of interlocking directorates, where board members were appointed on the basis of their loyalty to him, rather than on a principle of territorial representation, as should have happened.

There are various reasons for, and advantages in, the creation of metaorganizations: the creation of a higher degree of order in an "organizational field" (DiMaggio and Powell 1983; Fligstein and McAdam 2012); improving economies of scale in the implementation of activities, limiting costs, and seizing opportunities beyond the reach of individual organizational units; the fact that, thanks to the creation of new collective actors, "opinions and pronouncements can also be coordinated.

A meta-organization expresses one opinion and speaks with one voice ... By joining forces, acting in a concerted way, and combining their resources, organizations can muster greater power to change their environment in the desired direction, or at least to prevent their environment from deteriorating" (Ahrne and Brunsson 2008, 69). As we will see later, in Chapter 4, this aspect has obvious implications for the use of violence, particularly in terms of the frequency and type of homicides committed.

While in organizations the *free rider* is widespread and can be a serious problem, "the problem in meta-organizations may be the opposite (Jordan 1998). Organizations may choose to join a meta-organization as a matter of precaution and because they do not like to be left outside, rather than because of a real interest in the purposes and activities of the organization" (Ahrne and Brunsson 2008, 81).

The establishment of metaorganizations, in legal organizations as well as in mafias, poses the dilemma of reconciling the autonomy of the organizational units with the power of decision of the metaorganization. Autonomy implies that the organizational unit components have the right to decide for themselves. On the other hand, if a metaorganization cannot make decisions that impact on its members, it loses its legitimacy and its existence is put at risk. It is an irresolvable tension, in that shifting the decision-making center all to one side (individual organizations) or all to another (metaorganization), can have unwelcome consequences – in particular, as we will see, for mafias.

The HLBC assume different forms and employ different methods in different mafias, in terms of number of levels, internal structure and rules, and operating practices. However, in addition to the requirement of governance, these organs share a multiplicity of functions relating to strategy, organization, and business, but especially to the containment and regulation of conflicts.[109] The activities are presented in detail in Table 2.6.

Moreover, these bodies allow movement from "little strategy," that is, limited to the single minimal organizational unit, to "grand strategy," which encompasses all the organizational units, and provides the basis of coordinated and sustained efforts directed toward achieving long-term business and organizational objectives. The HLBC give the organization as a whole, understood as the set of all (or almost all) the clan members, the right to speak on behalf of the organization (Zuckerman 2010), a very

---

[109] Pistone (and Brandt 2007) affirm that "without a Commission to protect themselves, bosses would be forever walking around with little bull's-eyes pinned to the backs of their heads. On their backs like 'Kick Me' signs would be 'Shoot Me and Take Over' signs. Who would want to assume such a vulnerable position?" (151).

Table 2.6 *Functions and activities of higher-level bodies of coordination*

Functions	Activities
Strategic	Maintaining the unity of the organization
	Making decisions regarding the interests of the whole organization
	Enhancing awareness regarding the external environment, in terms of opportunities and threats
	Identifying the organization's external enemies
	Deciding on the elimination of persons deemed to be dangerous to the life of the organization (high-profile assassinations)
	Establishing and maintaining links with local and national political system
Control and organization	Controlling territorial divisions between individual families
	Establishing standards regarding the recruitment and supervision of men of honor by each individual family
	Voting for organization laws, for example, the prohibition of certain types of crime (e.g., kidnapping)
Conflict containment	Settling and rectifying existing conflict between families
	Containing internal conflict and resolving any situations of this kind in progress
	Controlling the use of violence
	Guaranteeing succession without violence, discouraging internal feuds, and minimizing attempts to seize power
Business	Realizing activities that involve a number of families and territories
	Coordinating complex international traffic
	Organizing and sharing the main flows of public resources

important condition for a mafia organization since, because they are secret and clandestine, "there is no way – from the outside – to really know who is authorized to speak in the name of an organization [...] 'What an organization is' always depends on who is speaking *in its name, on its behalf*, or *for it*" (Stohl and Stohl 2011, 1207). Speaking on behalf of the entire organization allows, for example, the Sicilian Cosa Nostra to reachieve a unity that has been lost.

The formation of HLBC can be particularly welcome, so to speak, to those figures who seek to deal individually with the mafia subject, such as (some) politicians. Rather than strike up relationships with a plurality of organizations that could present multiple requests, for the political actor it is preferable to maintain relations with a single actor – one that represents the plurality of organizations and is able to speak in the name of all of them. Some factors favor the creation of HLBC, while others favor their dissolution. There are four main factors that can influence the creation of HLBC in mafias: *conflict, size, territory,* and *opportunity*. Many

HLBC arise as a result of wars between particularly violent clans (e.g., the 'Ndrangheta in 1991) or for control and prevention of the proliferation of *conflict* (the Sicilian Cosa Nostra in 1957 and 1975), both intraorganizational (i.e., the so-called internal climb to power) and interorganizational (between clans or cartels of clans). With regard to *size*, the smaller the average size of the mafia business, the more urgent the need to have HLBC to coordinate collective action.[110] Where *territory* is concerned, on the other hand, the more mafia businesses are contiguous, the more HLBC are required to settle any disputes. Finally, with respect to *opportunity*, the greater the number of business opportunities that are beyond the ability of an individual organization to achieve, the greater the chances are that HLBC will be created in order to obtain economies of scale and pursue business opportunities beyond the reach of the individual organization. A further dimension that could influence the presence of HLBC regards any possible *threats* that might arise from the external environment. This in fact, if anything, tends to support the creation of alliances between clans and cartels, rather than generating bodies that deal with regulation and dispute resolution.

As mafia history shows, the HLBC, once created, do not remain unchanged over time, but undergo modification and can also be dissolved. In mafias, the main reasons for this choice include repression activity by law enforcement agencies. As we will see in Section 6.4, while the creation of these bodies gives power and unity to the criminal system, at the same time it makes the leadership more vulnerable, increasing the risk of informing and the possibility that members of the organization, once arrested, will collaborate with law enforcement agencies. The latter are able to act strategically, giving priority to the capture of members who occupy top positions, thus creating problems for the overall decision-making process.

Before concluding the analysis of the size of organization structure, it should be noted that, as in legal organizations, organizational structure in mafias represents the ideal organizational design, or that which is hoped for, not that which is realized. There is, in other words, always a gap, sometimes a significant one, between the formal structure and the one that actually exists. Organization theory distinguishes between formal and informal organizational structure: "Formal organizations arise out of and are necessary to informal organizations; but when formal organizations come into operation, they create and require informal organizations" (Barnard 1938, 120). Both the formal and informal structure

---

[110] In the mafias, the Camorra appears to be an exception here.

influence the behavior of people, as was pointed out many years ago by the Human Relations school (Roethlisberger and Dickson 1939).

Rather than informal organizational structure, which seems to imply something residual and of lesser importance than the formal one, it is more suitable to talk about *real* organizational structure. Formal organizational structure relates to the explicit, formalized, and legitimate division of responsibility and authority, specifying how the work should be done and what the relations between people should be. Real organizational structure, on the other hand, includes norms, power relations, and social expectations, which possess no principle of formal legitimacy or of formalization but which can be a very powerful force in guiding the behavior of people in the organization. Real organizational structure emerges over time and can be very different from the formal version.

For example, in the Sicilian Cosa Nostra we see the presence of HLBC formed in order to represent the underlying organizational levels. Although the formal design suggests a substantial equality of importance, the real organizational dynamics show how some groups count far more than others and how certain important strategic decisions are taken, not in a shared manner respectful of the various organizational structures, but by those who, at a particular historical moment, have a leading role. Within a mafia oligarchy, therefore, a further elite is created that can significantly direct certain critical decisions for the organization. It is a matter of the replacement of the original purposes and the iron laws of oligarchy (Michels 1911). The HLBC, created as far as possible for democratic and participative decision-making about the overall destinies of the organization, can thus become the preserve of small groups, able to influence the decisional outcomes.

This is not to deny the importance of the formal dimension of the organizational structure, but to argue that, for a correct and more realistic reading of organizational dynamics, it is necessary to integrate the analysis of the formal aspects of the structure with those that organizational literature defines as informal (which here we call *real*) in order to arrive at an effective analysis of the criminal organization.

3 Organizational Orders

In order to function as effectively as possible, mafias establish organizations with particular structures. We have distinguished two organizational orders: *clan-based* and *clan-based federation*. Mafias organized according to a *clan-based* order are characterized by the absence of higher-level bodies of coordination and have distributed power and clan-based decision-making processes. In contrast, mafias organized according to a *clan-based federation* order have higher-level bodies of coordination, more centralized power, and systemic decision-making processes.

The theme of organizational orders and higher-level bodies of coordination presents analogies with, but is not reducible to, that of organizational hierarchy, a classic theme in organization studies (Coase 1937; March and Simon 1958; Thompson 1961; 1967; Williamson 1975; 1985; Miller 1992). Selznick (1948) identified stability in the lines of authority as one of the elements for the maintenance of an organizational system. Other authors have analyzed the evolution of various organizational configurations, from vertical and integrated forms to network organizations (Powell 1990; Nohria and Eccles 1992; Baker 1992; Podolny and Page 1998; Gerlach 2001; Kogut and Walker 2001; Kenis and Knoke 2002; Powell et al. 2005; Baldassarri and Diani 2007; Anand and Daft 2007; Zaheer and Soda 2009). Zuckerman (2010) points out the advantages when the hierarchy has the right to speak on behalf of the organization. However, the organizational literature has, on the one hand, privileged the analysis of legitimate organizations and, on the other, made no distinction between hierarchical organization (command tree) and clan-based federation order characterized by higher-level bodies of coordination, in which decision-making takes place through negotiation among multiple actors (i.e., clans or families). The latter is the case in some of the mafia organizations that are the object of this study. If there certainly exists a hierarchy and command tree *within a single clan family*, this does not mean that this exists *between the clan families* that are part of a mafia organization. The decision-making processes between clans are more configurable in terms of a political coalition (March 1962; Cyert and March 1963).

Mafias are complex organizations with a long history. Having looked at certain organizational aspects in the preceding pages, in this chapter we will go on to analyze the different organizational models that characterize some mafias. The following descriptions are mainly aimed at outlining the characteristics of the base structure both in terms of the minimum level organizational unit (*family*, *ikka*, *clan*, etc.) and at the level of the higher-level bodies of coordination (HLBC), where present. Attention will be paid to organizational models and how they have changed over time, while for further information the reader is referred to the many books and articles on the history and origins of mafia organizations. The analysis is essential to distinguish between the two main organizational orders, *clan-based* and *clan-based federation*. As we will see, this distinction is relevant to understanding the use of violence in mafia organizations, and there are significant differences according to the organizational order adopted, particularly in terms of the number and type of homicides.

3.1 Mafia Structures

3.1.1 The Sicilian Cosa Nostra

The Sicilian mafia, the Cosa Nostra, emerged in the mid-nineteenth century. The word "mafia" first appeared in 1865 in a report by the prefect of Palermo, Filippo Antonio Gualterio (Lupo 2011b). For many years mobsters named their criminal organization "honored society" (Gentile 1963). The term was transformed into "Cosa Nostra" (Our Thing) due to American influence.[1]

The basic unit is the *family*, a criminal group with a specific territorial base, which controls a zone of a city or an entire inhabited area from which it takes its name (e.g., the family of Porta Nuova, the family of Villabate). The term "family" denotes the fundamental importance given to the concepts of loyalty and honor: actual blood ties between the

---

[1] The term "Cosa Nostra" was introduced to the general public in the United States in October 1963 by ex-mobster and collaborator with justice Joe Valachi, who testified before Arkansas Senator John L. McClellan's Permanent Subcommittee on Investigations of the U.S. Senate Committee on Government Operations. Subsequently, the term was used in Italy for the first time in the 1980s by collaborator with justice Tommaso Buscetta. For an analysis of the similarities and differences between the Italian mafias, see Paoli 2003; Savona 2012. For a historical analysis of the Sicilian Cosa Nostra see Lupo 2011, a–b; Santino 2017.

members are not necessary. The selection of members is extremely strict,[2] unlike the selection and recruiting mechanisms of another Italian mafia, the Camorra. According to the DIA *(Direzione Investigativa Antimafia)*, there are about 100–150 families in Sicily, with a total of 2,000–3,000 members.[3]

The families are organized according to a pyramidal model,[4] a hierarchy with subdivision of power. The organizational structure of a *family* and the hierarchical chain of command work as follows: the base is formed by the *soldiers*, also known as "button men," or *picciotti*: they carry out the operational orders of the *family*. The *capodecina* (boss of ten) oversees a crew of soldiers, numbering from five to ten or twenty, with a maximum of thirty, according to the size of the family. The *representative* is the boss, he is elected *democratically* (one person–one vote) in a secret vote by the button men in specifically organized family meetings.[5] For large-sized families, the heads of ten collect the votes from the men of honor, given the high risk of bringing together a large number of people in one place. The *vice-representative (underboss)* is nominated by the representative, and he can make decisions in his absence, but this is a situation that rarely arises. The *advisers* or counselors provide advice to the boss and also serve as liaison with the soldiers (Figure 3.1).

There is a division of labor: the representative makes the decisions, the head of ten transmits the orders and has them carried out, and the soldiers performs the actions. It is essential for the Sicilian Cosa Nostra

---

[2] Members should have no left-wing tendencies and they must come from a family with a respectable, untarnished reputation. Illegitimate children, homosexuality, and divorces are not tolerated, and relatives cannot be members of the police forces or the judiciary.

[3] DIA *(Direzione Investigativa Antimafia*, Anti-Mafia Investigative Directorate), Ministero dell'Interno (Ministry of Interior) 2013; 2014; 2015, *Attività svolta e risultati conseguiti (Activities and final findings)*, http://direzioneinvestigativaantimafia.interno.gov.it/.

[4] The reconstruction of the organizational structure, regulations, and mechanisms derives from the confessions and memories of *mafiosi* such as Leonardo Vitale (1973), Tommaso Buscetta (1984), Salvatore Contorno (1984–5), and Antonino Calderone (1987–8) and from the investigative work carried out by the Antimafia pool in Palermo and by the magistrates Giovanni Falcone and Paolo Borsellino, killed by the Sicilian Cosa Nostra in 1992.

[5] Numerous collaborators with justice have emphasized this process of direct democracy for the annual election of the boss and other major organization positions. However, it is a process that over the course of time has become meaningless, and corrupted by two elements. First, the candidate for boss was selected from among the wisest men of the organization, thus restricting opportunity and effectively creating a self-reproducing oligarchy (Paoli 2003). Second, it is highly doubtful that the majority of voters chose autonomously, daring to disagree with the oligarchs, and it is unclear what would happen in the event of differences of opinion regarding the candidates for the organization's top management.

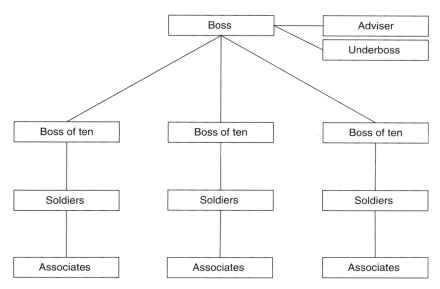

Figure 3.1 The organizational structure of a *family* of the Sicilian Cosa Nostra

to have complete control over the territory, both in economic and in criminal terms. In the territory controlled by a family, no illegal activity can take place without the agreement of its representative. This is also the case in relationships between families: no one can consider carrying out a criminal activity of a certain importance without the prior approval of the relevant family. Otherwise, sanctions, and even death, would be incurred.

Until the mid-1950s, the coordination between families within Cosa Nostra was ensured by informal meetings involving the most important and influential men of honor from the principal families. But from 1957 on, the Sicilian Cosa Nostra began to deploy higher levels of coordination.[6] The heads of the families from the same province (Caltanissetta, Catania, Enna, and Trapani) nominate a boss of the entire province, called the "provincial representative." In the province of Palermo,

---

[6] It is interesting to note that the adoption of HLBC, particularly the provincial level with the Commission, took place in the Sicilian Cosa Nostra after the adoption of the American Cosa Nostra Commission and not before (Bonanno 1983; Arlacchi 1994). This happened in 1957, when Joseph Bonanno, boss of one of the five New York families, suggested to Sicilian "colleagues" that they adopt a similar model during a meeting in Palermo. This contrasts with the idea that the organizational model of the American Cosa Nostra is derived from the Sicilian Cosa Nostra.

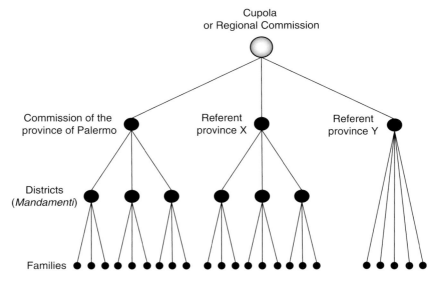

Figure 3.2 The organizational structure of the Sicilian Cosa Nostra with higher-level bodies of coordination

however (and sporadically in other provinces, such as Agrigento),[7] three or more families with adjoining territories are organized into a *mandamento* (district). It is the job of the head of the *mandamento* to coordinate the families when operations involve the territories of more than one family, and to resolve any eventual disputes. For the province of Palermo there is a "Provincial Commission," consisting of the province's various district bosses (in the past eighteen altogether, representing 54 families), which elects a provincial representative, who represents the entire province. This representative is a secretary, a coordinator, however, and not a boss with the power to command the district bosses or to give orders to the members of the families.

Starting in 1975, the Palermo model, involving a Provincial Commission, was imitated on a regional scale, forming the highest level of coordination, the so-called Regional Commission or Cupola, which comprises the representatives of the six provinces where the Sicilian Cosa Nostra operates (see Figure 3.2). This highest-level body of coordination was responsible for defining and monitoring compliance with the organization's rules, settling disputes between families of different provinces,

[7] As for Messina, there seems to be no provincial level nor representatives for the entire province, given the lower level of local density of the Sicilian Cosa Nostra.

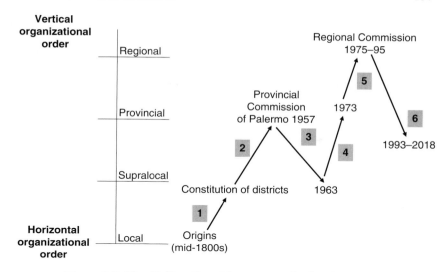

Figure 3.3 The Sicilian Cosa Nostra: organizational evolution

authorizing the eventual killing of men of honor, and, above all, eliminating high-profile figures deemed to be dangerous for the organization. One of the reasons for establishing HLBC in Sicilian Cosa Nostra was the international drug business, because it required greater coordination among the families (Morosini 2009).

The Evolution of Higher-Level Bodies of Coordination. It is important to highlight that mafia organizations differ both synchronically (between organizations at a specific historical moment) and diachronically (within the same organization over time) in relation to the level of organizational verticality that they have achieved.

As we have said, the Sicilian Cosa Nostra has moved toward a *clan-based federation*, developing higher-level bodies of coordination, first, in 1957, by creating supralocal and provincial levels, and then, in 1975, by creating the regional level (see Figure 3.3).[8] Following severe repressive measures, it broke up the regional level and, in part, the provincial level. Recent inquiries by law enforcement agencies have indicated attempts by the Sicilian Cosa Nostra to rebuild the superordinate levels of coordination.

---

[8] The regional level also oversees the activities carried out by clans that are not located in the regions under the control of the mafia organization.

Regarding the reorganization of the Sicilian Cosa Nostra, recent investigations show that

on several occasions, the Cosa Nostra has tried to renew itself through a confirmation of its governance structures, starting with those working in the area of Palermo and in particular with reference to the provincial Cosa Nostra Commission in Palermo. To confirm that, even in times of crisis, Cosa Nostra does not renounce the development of unitary organizational models and projects designed to ensure their survival in conditions of the greatest possible efficiency. With particular use of its "constitutional" patrimony and, therefore, the rules regarding its traditional structure of government that – even apart from the presence on the territory of free bosses endowed with special charisma – enables it to deal with and, unfortunately often, overcome moments of crisis such as the one which it is undoubtedly now going through.

It should once again be reiterated also here that the Cosa Nostra appear endowed with a kind of "formal constitution" and with its own "material constitution." In some historical moments, its material constitution has counted for more, in the sense that the organization's governance was carried out according to the choices of the leaders and regardless of the rules. When state investigative action led to the capture of those leaders, if the so-called material constitution of the organization underwent a crisis, the formal constitution of the Cosa Nostra regained importance and still allows the structure to survive even in the absence of important recognized leaders in a state of liberty.

The recourse to old and never abrogated rules of organizational life thus allows the mafia organization to survive in times of crisis like the present. The sources of memory, the elderly, safeguard the rules and the rules, which are used to run the organization, are constantly brought to the attention of younger subjects.[9]

The strength of the Sicilian Cosa Nostra lies, then, in its organization. Even the arrest of the most important bosses does not destroy the organization, though it may result in a change of leadership. Currently, the Sicilian Cosa Nostra is trying to reconstruct the provincial level, in particular the Palermo Provincial Commission.[10] In addition, new developments have emerged such as the creation of an additional level between the supralocal and provincial, with the establishment of a new district deriving from the union between two previous districts

---

[9] DNA (*Direzione Nazionale Antimafia*, National Anti-Mafia Directorate) 2014, *Relazione annuale sulle attività svolte dal Procuratore nazionale e dalla Direzione nazionale antimafia e antiterrorismo*, 62–3.

[10] Rapporto della Squadra Mobile di Palermo 2006, *Operazione Gotha*, April 21; DDA Palermo (*Direzione Distrettuale Antimafia*, District Anti-Mafia Directorate of Palermo) 2008, *Operazione Perseo, Decreto di fermo nr. 18038/08, R.G.N.R. Mod. 21*, December 16; Procura della Repubblica di Palermo 2008, *Sentenza di rito abbreviato 1579/07 Reg. Not. Reato 800165/07*, Reg. Tribunale di Palermo, Sezione del giudice per le indagini preliminari, Piergiorgio Morosini.

(San Giuseppe Iato and Partinico). As shown by recent investigations, the reconstitution of higher-level bodies of coordination would strengthen the organization to an alarming degree, given that it would then be able to take decisions even "for serious things."[11] This concern confirms the hypothesis that the presence of HLBC favors the process of identification and elimination of high-profile figures.

The formal structure of the higher-level bodies of coordination should not, however, overshadow the decisive role played by the area of the city of Palermo and its province, which has always hegemonized the actual functioning of these superordinate bodies. Nearly 50 percent of the approximately 100 families in Sicily operate in Palermo and its province. As noted previously, in fact, the role of formal organizational structure (*how things should be*) is strongly influenced by the existence of a real organizational structure (*how things in fact are*), a structure that in some historical periods has been particularly significant. First of all, the Provincial Commission of Palermo has always played a greater role and exercised strategic leadership in the entire associative system. In addition, starting in 1983, two important bosses of the province of Palermo (Corleone), Totò Riina and Bernardo Provenzano, introduced a verticalization of the leadership and played a decision-making role of particular importance for the dynamics of organizational life in the mafia organization. Notwithstanding the existence of several higher-level bodies of coordination, the role of these leaders meant that the organization was strongly influenced by their decisions. This occurred first with the strategy of direct confrontation with the state carried forward by Totò Riina and his command group, which led to the death of many state and institutional figures. There followed a completely different strategy, based on the idea of "submersion," promoted by Bernardo Provenzano, Riina's successor after his arrest in 1993. Provenzano preferred a quiet style of business, without homicides, except in exceptional cases, in order to avoid attracting the attention of newspapers and as a consequence of public opinion, the government and the law enforcement agencies (Dickie 2004; Morosini 2009).

In conclusion, the Sicilian Cosa Nostra is now characterized by a *clan-based federation* model at a provincial level, while there is an absence (though they could be reconstructed again in the future) of HLBC able to coordinate the entire criminal system, as instead happened for a long time in the past.

---

[11] DNA 2015, *Relazione annuale sulle attività svolte dal Procuratore nazionale e dalla Direzione nazionale antimafia e antiterrorismo*, 152.

3.1.2   The 'Ndrangheta

The 'Ndrangheta (meaning "manliness" or "courage"), or "Honored Society," founded in the Italian region of Calabria, has become the most powerful mafia in Italy.[12] It is estimated to have a membership of around 10,000, grouped into 150–70 gangs.[13] The 'Ndrangheta, unlike the Camorra and the Sicilian Cosa Nostra, is based on blood parentage, and the links between the various families are further strengthened through intermarriage. The members are prevalently recruited on the basis of blood relationship. There is a strong hierarchy within each family, and discipline is based both on respect for the rules, as with other mafia organizations, and on the rules of family and generational authority and government. There is a code that involves distinct rituals for every moment of criminal life: from the investiture of the new member, to the solemnly taken oath, to the next level in criminal ranking, up until the trials that the "tribunal" can impose on members, should they violate any of the society's rules. The organizational structure is more complex than that of the Sicilian Cosa Nostra, as visualized in Figure 3.4.

The basic organizational level consists of the *'ndrina*, made up of members of a family nucleus (this can be a few dozen) related by blood ties: a true endogamy.[14] Every *'ndrina* has its own boss, called the *capondrina*, or *capobastone*, whose surname gives its name to the *'ndrina* (as in the Camorra, but unlike the Sicilian Cosa Nostra, where it is the town or local area that gives its name to the family). Several *'ndrine* in the same area form the *locale* (the local), a consortium of families that operate in the same territorial district. In order to be founded, the *locale* must possess at least 49 members.[15] The *locale* (or *società*) takes its

---

[12] DIA (*Direzione Investigativa Antimafia*, Anti-Mafia Investigative Directorate), Ministero dell'Interno (Ministry of Interior) 2015b (*a:* first semester; *b:* second semester), *Attività svolta e risultati conseguiti (Activities and final findings)*, http://direzioneinvestigativaantimafia.interno.gov.it; DNA 2010; 2015, *Relazione annuale sulle attività svolte dal Procuratore nazionale e dalla Direzione nazionale antimafia e antiterrorismo.*

[13] DIA, Ministero dell'Interno, 2015a, *Attività svolta e risultati conseguiti (Activities and final findings)*, http://direzioneinvestigativaantimafia.interno.gov.it; Commissione parlamentare d'inchiesta sul fenomeno della mafia e sulle altre associazioni criminali anche straniere, 2010, *Audizione del Procuratore distrettuale antimafia di Reggio Calabria dottor Giuseppe Pignatone*, www.narcomafie.it/wp-content/uploads/2010/10/audizione_pignatone.pdf (last accessed on April 5, 2018).

[14] Marriage is used to settle violent feuds or to create stronger and more stable connections. Moreover, these potent and widespread family relationships make the phenomenon of informing more difficult, increasing the secrecy around the organization (see Section 6.7).

[15] Collaborator with justice Antonino Belnome says that to open a *locale* in a town, there must necessarily be a *carabinieri* or police station, given that the 'Ndrangheta is the rival body (in Barbacetto and Milosa 2011, 428). It is unclear whether this rule is actually real

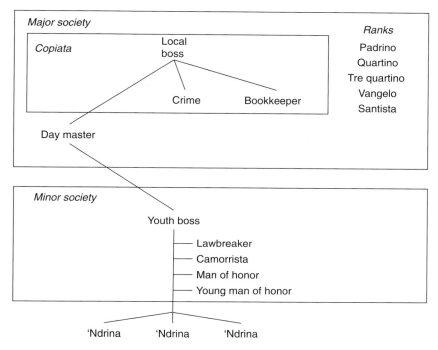

Figure 3.4 The organizational structure of a 'Ndrangheta *locale*

name from the territory in which it operates and has a boss, called the *capolocale* (local boss), who makes decisions regarding operations, calls meetings of the *locale*, decides membership and promotion, settles disputes between members, and, most importantly, directs criminal activity within the territory for which he is responsible. Each *locale* is equal in dignity to the others and is the *dominus* of its territory, with the following limitations: (a) the compliance with the interests and territory of the other *locali*; (b) the requirement to send part of its proceeds *alla Mamma di San Luca* (to the mother of St. Luke) – the "parent company," in other words, or headquarters; (c) the obligation to respect, whatever the situation, the decisions made by the top management of the Provincia (Province), the highest-level body that coordinates most of the *'ndrine* and the *locali*. The violation of these obligations involves the application

or whether there are other motivations and stipulations that lead to the opening of a *locale* in a given area. However, true or not, this rule provides a great deal of information regarding the cultural model that characterizes the lives of these *mafiosi*.

of sanctions.[16] For extra security, the *locale* is divided into two separate organizational groups: the Società maggiore (Major society) and the Società minore (Minor society). This can happen only if there are at least seven members who have reached the high level of *santista*, and who can take part in the Major society.

The roles and organizational positions held by members within the 'Ndrangheta (or "responsibilities") in the Major society include the *capolocale* (local boss), who is assisted by the *contabile* (bookkeeper), who handles the finances of the *locale*, and by the *crimine* (crime), who deals with illegal activity. Together, these three roles form the *copiata*. The *capolocale* also makes use of the *mastro di giornata* (day master) who circulates information and orders throughout the organization, reporting back with any problems or specific situations.

Minor society is headed by the *youth boss* and includes the *giovani d'onore* (young men of honor), which is not a real rank but a membership by "right of blood," a title that is assigned at birth to children of the 'Ndrangheta as a good omen that in future they may become men of honor. The *picciotto d'onore* (man of honor) is the first real step on the 'Ndrangheta "career ladder": a straightforward follower and executor of orders, who must be blindly obedient to other ranks of the clan with no hope of achieving tangible and immediate benefits. The *picciotti*, in practice, are the infantry, or rather the squad of corporals, of the Calabrian clans. The *camorrista* is already a member of some importance, after a reasonably long period of "apprenticeship," and is assigned functions that the *picciotti* cannot carry out. Finally, the *sgarrista* (or *camorrista di sgarro*, lawbreaker) is a member with significant responsibilities, the final rank in the Minor society.

Apart from the roles already mentioned, there is a system of ranks, *doti*, meaning "qualities" or "gifts," which expresses the merit accumulated by a member during his career and which increases step by step with the crimes committed. The responsibilities represent developments in the organizational structure; the *doti* are the ranks of development in the profession. The ranks are the association's status badge, and the 'Ndrangheta has a wide range of these: fourteen have been identified, three for the Minor society and many more for the Major society.[17]

---

[16] DNA 2013, *Relazione annuale sulle attività svolte dal Procuratore nazionale e dalla Direzione nazionale antimafia e antiterrorismo*, 109.

[17] Tribunale di Reggio Calabria, DDA 2010, *Operazione Crimine*, vol. I, 448; DNA 2013, *Relazione annuale sulle attività svolte dal Procuratore nazionale e dalla Direzione nazionale antimafia e antiterrorismo*. The ranks of *stella*, *bartolo*, *mammasantissima*, *infinito*, and *conte agadino* were created by the boss of the Lombardy *locale* Carmine Novella, who tried to make the 'Ndrangheta groups in Lombardy autonomous, independent of the

In the Major society there are two levels: entry ranks and senior ranks. The two entry ranks are the *santista*, a member who has achieved the Santa, a higher rank for exclusive criminal merits; the *vangelo* (gospel), also called *vangelista*, because they have sworn the oath of allegiance to the criminal organization by laying a hand on a copy of the Gospel. Then there are the senior ranks, which, from lower to higher, are *tre quartino*, *quartino*, and *padrino*. The ranks must be conferred at specific periods of the year (Christmas, Easter, August) and only with the approval of the Calabrian "parent company," even for the *locali* outside Calabria. The ability to confer ranks is a powerful "trademark" that must remain solely in the hands of the parent company.

Anyone who is not part of the 'Ndrangheta is called *contrasto* (contrast, or hindrance), while those not belonging to the 'Ndrangheta but who can be trusted and who may in future join the organization are known as *contrasti onorati* (honored contrasts). The ranks are permanent, just as in any hierarchical structure, passed through by merit or seniority, following the appropriate rite. Responsibilities, however, are temporary and are also entered into through the appropriate rite of investiture. Both responsibilities and ranks, as well as new members, occur through cooptation. One or more members are the guarantors of the figure to be given membership or promoted.

Above the *locali* there are two superordinate levels of coordination (see Figure 3.5):[18] (1) the *mandamento* (district), which groups together several *locali*. There are three main districts in the province of Reggio Calabria (Ionian, Center, and Tyrrhenian), and other districts and *camere di controllo* (control rooms) for the *locali* in other regions of Italy (Lombardy, Piedmont, Liguria, etc.) and around the world (Canada, Australia, Germany, Switzerland, etc.); (2) the *Provincia* or *Crimine* (Province, or Crime), a supreme coordinating body of criminal activity, formed only by the three Reggio Calabria districts. This highest

headquarters in Calabria. He was killed for this insubordination on July 14, 2008. Such ranks, however, are not always recognized by the Calabrian headquarters. Although there is not sufficient historical or judicial confirmation, it is believed that these ranks have been introduced progressively into the organization. In the second half of the twentieth century, the rank of *santa* was introduced and later on the others (Ciconte 1996).

[18] As we will see in the next paragraph, there were more or less formalized attempts as early as the late nineteenth century to establish higher-level coordination organs. In the 1930s a sort of HLBC called Gran Criminale (Great Criminal) was identified, with coordination functions for the clans in the province of Reggio Calabria and the management and resolution of conflicts. However, in its current structure, this body was formed in 1991 at the end of a long and violent conflict (about 700 deaths) between opposing clan groups.

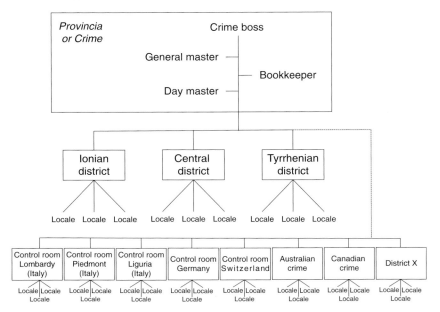

Figure 3.5 The higher-level bodies of coordination of the 'Ndrangheta

coordination body was created in 1991, even though there were attempts in the preceding decades to establish a body of this kind.[19]

The Provincia (or Crimine, crime) is the most important coordination organism of the *locali*. However, certain *locali*, both in Italy and around the world, do not appear today to be coordinated by the Provincia.[20]

This supreme coordination body controls the application of the rules, with functions of legitimation and recognition of the new *locali*, with power of life and death over the members, and with the function to prevent and/or contain conflict between the families. It also governs the overall structure of the organization, making or ratifying the major decisions that involve the interests of several clans or even the entire

---

[19] It is important to note that the highest superordinate body consists only of representatives of the three districts of the province of Reggio Calabria, while, in all other mafias, these bodies have a greater geographical representation. For example, in the Sicilian Cosa Nostra, the Cupola is formed by representatives of the Sicilian provinces where the Cosa Nostra operates, even though a dominant role has always been played by the province of Palermo.

[20] According to Sergi and Lavorgna (2016), rather than talking of an 'Ndrangheta, we should use the term '*Ndranghete* (plural), given the different characteristics of this mafia organization's behavior in different parts of the region.

organization. The Provincia does not intervene directly in the concrete criminal activity, managed independently by each *locale*, but it plays a significant role through the imposition of the basic rules of the organization – those rules that characterize the 'Ndrangheta identity and ensure its recognition through time and space, even at a distance from the Calabrian motherland. The top management also ensures the maintenance of general equilibrium, control over the nomination of local bosses and the establishment of other clans, resolution of any dispute, and passing of judgment over any wrongdoing on the part of the members. It is important to emphasize that the organizations's legitimation of a *locale* derives exclusively from the recognition of the so-called Mamma di Polsi, the highest structure in the 'Ndrangheta. So the opening of a new *locale*, in Italy as in the world, is always subject to the approval of the Provincia.

The objective that led to the establishment of higher-level bodies of coordination was to

ensure harmony, given that clash and conflict generate, like all wars, as well as grief and desire for revenge, also economic crisis, higher costs for weapons, armored vehicles, difficulties in the management of the usual criminal activities that allow the acquisition of illicit proceeds (extortion, robberies, drug trafficking), causing, in addition, repression and preventive action from law enforcement agencies and determining, also, greater control over the territory, and the desertion and defection of those belonging to the organization.[21]

---

[21] Tribunale di Reggio Calabria, DDA 2010, *Operazione Crimine*, vol. I, 63. A previous investigation in 2010, called *Meta*, already highlighted that "the urban 'Ndrangheta . . . is an organization that needs new tools and shared hierarchies, which can no longer support itself on pure consolidated horizontality which is increasingly becoming a mere façade. There is a widespread awareness that to survive it is necessary to reach a consensus that is also shared by those who suffer the worst consequences: no more wars and unnecessary deaths, no more tension between clan bosses, but strict rules to apply to all, to be applied under the control of a well-defined hierarchy in which the members of the top management join together to administer a complex and insidious machine. It is, in short, an organization that evolves, adapts to the present day, on the basis of shared principles; an organization that has an authoritative leadership for the coordination of criminal actions, which does not distinguish between parties, which finds broad legitimation in the general awareness of the criminal significance of its leaders, who are no longer only the recognized leaders of their respective territorial structures but are the expression, the result of precise agreements, of a mafia-type organization that has abandoned the antihistorical logic of division to become ever more influential, functional and recognizable. In this way, an unequivocal message is delivered to the civil society and business entities of the city: the season of war is over, the 'Ndrangheta has moved towards unification and to greater strength both internally and externally, claiming their share of all economic activity" (Tribunale di Reggio Calabria, DDA 2010, *Operazione Crimine*, vol. I, 75).

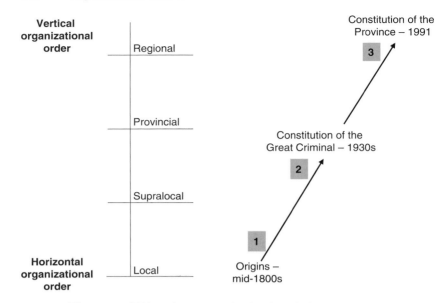

Figure 3.6 'Ndrangheta: organizational evolution

The Provincia (or Crimine) is headed by the *capocrimine* (crime boss), who is not the boss of bosses, but the speaker of an assembly, whose major role is to enforce rules and settle disputes. He is assisted by three senior officers: *mastro generale* (general master), *day master*, and *book-keeper*. Collaborator with justice Luciano Piccolo says, "Basically the *Crimine* is like a higher court where you can discuss general problems; if for example there is a feud in some *locale*, the court should intervene to pacify the situation and evaluate whether to close the *locale* or keep it open."[22]

The 'Ndrangheta is, at the moment, the only criminal organization to have such a complex structure.

The Evolution of Higher-Level Bodies of Coordination. The 'Ndrangheta has moved from a *clan-based* order to a *clan-based federation* order (see Figure 3.6). The 'Ndrangheta at its origins presented a clan-based order. As emerged from judicial investigations and sentences, the organization gradually developed attempts at coordination and verticalization. At first, in the late nineteenth and early twentieth centuries, forms of

---

[22] Ibid., 455.

territorial coordination were developed by the different *'ndrine*. Subsequently, at least from 1933 onward, two HLBC were constituted called Criminale, with coordination functions in the province of Reggio Calabria, and Gran Criminale (Great Criminal), superordinate to the Criminale and with functions of control for the monitoring of compliance with the organization rules of operation, for the management of internal justice through a court, and especially for conflict management and resolution.[23]

On October 26, 1969, during a summit meeting at Montalto (Calabria) among about 130 'Ndrangheta members from various districts, the opportunity emerged to unify the various local organizations and provide them with a management structure that could coordinate activity and resolve conflicts.[24] This body saw the light in 1991, at the end of bloody conflicts between two cartels of opposing clans[25] (Dickie 2012; Truzzolillo 2013). A supralocal (Mandamento) and regional (Provincia, Province) structure was introduced, greatly reducing – though not completely eliminating – the feuds and giving the organization a more strongly unified governance. This also included the structures of coordination (control rooms) for *locali* in areas at a distance from Calabria, in Italy (Lombardy, Piedmont, Liguria), in Europe (Switzerland, Germany), and around the world (Australia, Canada).

In conclusion, the 'Ndrangheta is now characterized by a *clan-based federation* model, with the presence of different levels of HLBC. It is now the only mafia organization capable of coordinating most of its criminal system in a tendentially unified way.

3.1.3   The Camorra

The Camorra was founded at the beginning of the nineteenth century in Campania, first in the prisons, then in the city of Naples. The criminal organization first appeared in police records in 1820, and in the same year the police discovered a written statute that contained information regarding a stable organizational structure in the underworld. In 1843,

---

[23] As emerged from investigation by certain judges in Reggio Calabria. These findings were based on the statements of a member of the organization, Antonio Musolino, brother of the more famous Giuseppe, nicknamed the "King of Aspromonte" (Dickie 2012; Truzzolillo 2013).

[24] Ciconte 1996; Tribunale di Reggio Calabria, DDA 2010, *Operazione Crimine*, vol. I, 58.

[25] As emerged in a trial against various members of the 'Ndrangheta (ASCZ, CAppCZ, *Sa, Sentenza Giovanbattista Sciarrone+95*, February 21, 1890, 137, in Truzzolillo 2013, 208). See also ASME, CAssRC, *Sentenza Abenavoli Giuseppe+32*, February 23, 1933, 442, in Truzzolillo 2013, 211.

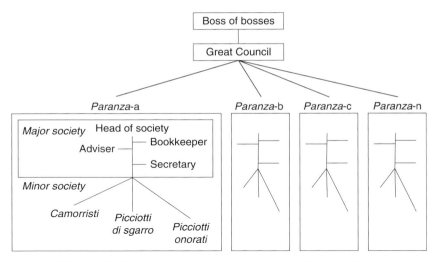

Figure 3.7 The organizational structure of the Camorra (at the beginning of nineteenth century)

another statute was discovered, indicating initiation rites and collecting funds for the families of those imprisoned (Behan 1996, 12).[26] The organization then spread out to cover the entire provincial territory, where its main pursuit was the organized extortion of the majority of economic activities in the area. The Camorra was initially organized into small, independent groups (*Memoria sulla consorteria*, 1861, in Marmo 2011; Monnier 1862; Alongi 1890; De Blasio 1897), also called *paranze*,[27] and showed a high level of organized hierarchy, in particular in Naples, where there were twelve groups, one for every district in the city, commanded by a boss (the *caposocietà*, head of society), elected by members of the group and flanked by an adviser (*primo voto*), a bookkeeper (*contaiuolo*), and a secretary (*chiamatore*). Each group was divided into two areas: the Società minore (Minor society), which included the youngest members, and the Società maggiore (Major society), with the more experienced members, which dealt with the management of the entire organization (see Figure 3.7). Career progression was rather slow. For example, to move from the role of *picciotto onorato* (the lowest rank) to that of *camorrista* (the highest in the Minor society), the member might have to wait a minimum of two years to a maximum of ten (Alongi 1890).

---

[26] For a historical account see Barbagallo 2010; Allum 2017.
[27] The term *paranza* has seafaring origins, indicating the small boats that fish in the shallows, holding the nets two by two.

The bosses of the *paranze* (*capisocietà*, head of society) formed the Great Council, headed by a *capintesta* (boss of bosses), who had absolute authority over the organization. Each week the *capisocietà* consulted with the *capintesta* regarding the progress of their respective groups (Consiglio 1959). The *capintesta* also chaired the supreme tribunal of the Camorra, known as the Gran mamma (Great mother), while the *capisocietà* themselves were presidents of the lower courts known as Piccole mamme (Little mothers), with jurisdiction limited to the territory controlled by the Camorra group. Thanks to the existence of higher-level bodies of coordination, conflicts between different groups were either prevented promptly or resolved, with violations punished by the courts.

This model vanished in the early decades of the twentieth century, and no trace remains nowadays of this original organizational structure. The Camorra today is a population of criminal organizations (clans) in competition/conflict with each other for governing power over the territory and control over the economic activities present therein. In contrast with the Sicilian Cosa Nostra and the 'Ndrangheta, the Camorra is not a unified organization, and no single higher-level body of coordination exists (such as the family or group of families) able to coordinate the entire criminal system. This *clan-based* organizational configuration is characterized by distributed power and it is similar to a *polyarchy*, a system in which there are several and competing organizational decision makers, who can undertake strategies and criminal actions independently of one another.

Rather than speak of a single mafia organization, we should speak of "Camorre" in the plural (Sales 1988), given the wide variety of organizational structures. Unlike other mafias, in fact, the Camorra presents a greater variety of basic organizational clan models. The different organizational models can be placed along a continuum ranging from models with a low level of formalization and few hierarchical levels, low differentiation of labor, low definition of the roles, and a restricted number of members to organizational models (e.g., the Casalesi cartel, the Secondigliano alliance) with greater hierarchical structure and formalization of roles and a large number of members.[28]

Unlike other mafias, where it is possible to locate one prevailing organizational model, the Camorra has four quite different coexisting

---

[28] Tribunale di Napoli 2008, *Ordinanza di applicazione della misura cautelare coercitiva personale nei confronti di Ammutinato Salvatore+132*, Sezione del giudice per le indagini preliminari, September 16; Tribunale di Napoli 2011, *Ordinanza di applicazione della misura cautelare coercitiva personale nei confronti di Buanno Fabio e altri*, Sezione del giudice per le indagini preliminari, September 27; Colletti 2016.

organizational models. (1) The *federation*, such as the Casalesi clan in the province of Caserta, made up of two historic families (Bidognetti and Schiavone) and other clans allied with one family or the other. The federation is directed by a top management that defines the organization's overall strategies, settles disputes by reducing internal violence, manages the common fund, and pays the salaries to members. Given the high level of structuration, homicides tend to be less frequent compared to other models.[29] (2) The *alliance*, tendentially unstable, temporary, like the Secondigliano alliance (including the Contini, Mallardo, and Licciardi clans), specializing in drug trafficking, or the alliance of the Alberto, Cuccaro, and Aprea clans.[30] (3) The *highly structured clan*, such as certain long-established families, characterized by greater organizational formalization (Polverino, Nuvoletta, Vollaro, Moccia, and others). (4) The *gang*, such as highly violent criminal groups dedicated to the sale of narcotics, mostly found in the city of Naples and characterized by a very low average age, in some cases with leaders in their early twenties. In some ways, more than resembling other mafias, in their way of functioning and for their frequent use of violence, they present analogies with the "violent gangs" described by Yablonsky (1962).

The more structured clans (types 1, in part 2, and 3) have an organizational structure as shown in Figure 3.8.

The *regents*, together with the boss, form the top management that defines the organization's strategies. Each *regent* oversees a number of *group leaders*, who in turn coordinate more than one *area leader*. The latter command the *affiliates*, who perform the operational criminal roles. *Regents* and *group leaders* make decisions with regard to investments, for example, for the purchase of large quantities of drugs, weapons, etc. *Group leaders* and *area leaders* decide together the extent of the salaries of the various members of the organization, depending on the roles performed, danger incurred, and seniority. The most important business is handled directly by the higher roles (e.g., the regents). The size of the groups varies from 30 to 40 units (the group of "secessionists"), up to 200 in the Misso and Lo Russo clans, 250 for the Mazzarella clan, and 300 members for the Contini and Licciardi clans (Di Fiore 2016, 316).

The different organizational models also depend on the different markets and activities of reference. Clans with low complexity and low

---

[29] In the 2010–15 period there was only one homicide within this federation (DNA 2016, *Relazione annuale sulle attività svolte dal Procuratore nazionale e dalla Direzione nazionale antimafia e antiterrorismo*).

[30] As in legal organizations (Gulati and Gargiulo 1999), alliances between clans are favored by resource interdependence.

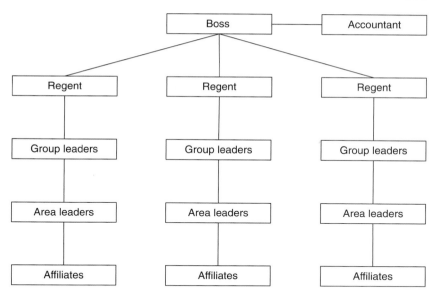

Figure 3.8 The Camorra's *clan* model

formalization are particularly active in drug trafficking and extortion. Clans with high formalization and complexity, on the other hand, tend to operate in legal markets (though in illegal ways), such as construction. The organizational structures of the Camorra clans are highly flexible and can be reconfigured depending on the various activities to be carried out. In general, two groups can be identified: the urban clan and the provincial clan. *Urban clans* are highly unstable and conflictual, making it very difficult for them to establish agreements with politicians and entrepreneurs. This leads them to prefer short-term earning activities such as extortion and drug trafficking and to restrict political-institutional or entrepreneurial infiltration. *Provincial clans*, however, exhibit greater stability and less conflict, and therefore have a greater ability to think in terms of medium-term earnings. This capability has pushed them further into the world of political-mafia interplay, into the sphere of public tenders and front men–controlled businesses, infiltration into public administration, and the search for control over political and administrative figures who hold decision-making power.[31]

---

[31] V. Galgano (Attorney general of Naples), 2005, *Relazione annuale per l'anno giudiziario* (Annual report on the administration of justice), in Di Fiore 2016, 318–9.

To indicate the criminal organization, members use the term '*o Sistema* (the System). For example, you can say, "Which system does that guy over there belong to?" to ask which clan a certain person is a member of. The answer might be, for example "He's in the Secondigliano system." So the term *system* contains both a general element (the set of all the clans in the mafia organization) and a specific item, the name of the individual clan.

From an interorganizational perspective, alliances tend to establish confederations between criminal groups and forces, but they are only partial, are contingent, and do not give rise to the configuration of a compact organization with a unified, coherent direction. Conflict prevails over agreement, especially during periods when there are no leaders blessed with special abilities to command.

The majority of the clans (around 70 percent) therefore find themselves in a situation of competition and conflict. In the Naples area, the clans no longer directly carry out many illicit activities (such as drug dealing, robbery, smuggling, receiving stolen goods, and counterfeiting). Instead, they prefer to farm these jobs out to a variety of criminal cells, which pay them a percentage of their earnings.[32] In the provinces, however, these activities are run directly by the clans.

The most significant phenomenon in the evolution of the Camorra is the multiplication of clans and families. While in 1861 there were 16 clans and families,[33] today there are around 128.[34] To organize activity and reduce conflict, some clans have established forms of coordination, either tightly coupled (cartels) or loosely coupled (alliances, nonbelligerence pacts). In the Caserta area, four clans constituted the Casalesi cartel, exerting their influence over the whole region and cooperating with satellites families.

The Evolution of Higher-Level Bodies of Coordination. At its origins in the nineteenth century, the Camorra possessed a centralized

---

[32] V. Galgano, *Relazione annuale per l'anno giudiziario*, presented at the General Assembly of the Court of Appeal, January 15, 2005.

[33] From *La memoria sulla consorteria dei camorristi esistente nelle province napoletane* (Memoir regarding the groupings of "camorristi" in the Neapolitan province), 1861, in Marmo 2011, 35.

[34] According to the latest report issued by the DIA (Investigative Anti-Mafia Directorate), Camorra clans and families are distributed over the territory as follows: 42 in the city of Naples, 47 in the province of Naples, 14 in the Caserta area, thirteen in the Salerno area, 6 in the Benevento area, and 6 in the Avellino area (DIA, *Direzione Investigativa Antimafia*/Anti-Mafia Investigative Directorate, Ministero dell'Interno/ Ministry of Interior 2017a, *Attività svolta e risultati conseguiti (Activities and final findings)*, (*a:* first semester; *b:* second semester), http://direzioneinvestigativaanti mafia.interno.gov.it).

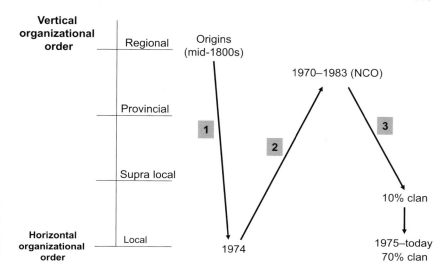

Figure 3.9 Camorra: organizational evolution

command and coordination structure for Naples and its province: thereafter it assumed a *clan-based* order without higher-level bodies of coordination (Figure 3.9).

The only attempts to organize the various Camorra clans into a clan-
based federation order were carried out at the beginning of the 1970s
with Raffaele Cutolo's Nuova Camorra Organizzata (NCO – New
Organized Camorra), which echoed the structure of the nineteenth-
century Camorra. The organizational structure designed by Cutolo was
of a pyramidal hierarchy and paramilitary kind, based on the cult of
personality of its creator.[35] Raffaele Cutolo himself was the boss of the
organization, the *caposocietà*, or *vangelo*, and he made use of an advisory
council led by certain trustworthy figures, known as *santisti*.[36] Below
these, there were the *capizona*, responsible for specific geographical areas
that included the whole of Campania. Finally, there were the members,
with the ranks of *picciotto*, *camorrista*, or *sgarrista* (lawbreaker). Cutolo
also reintroduced the oath of membership, which in previous years had
almost disappeared.

[35] Tribunale di Roma 1985, Sezione Settima, *Sentenza di primo grado contro Matarazzo
Giovanna+82*, January 19, 46/93 R.G.N.R., 18/96 RG Assise, President Rombolà
Marcello, 19.
[36] There were five *santisti*: Corrado Iacolare, Vincenzo Casillo, Davide Sorrentino,
Pasquale Barra, and Antonino Cuomo (Di Fiore 2016).

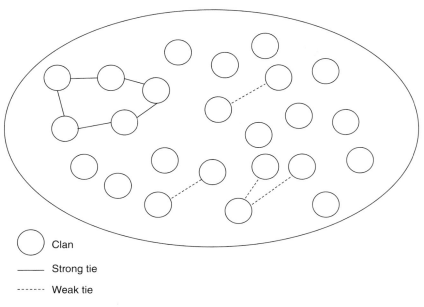

Figure 3.10 The organizational structure of the Camorra today

This attempt at centralization triggered a strong reaction from a group of clans, who in 1978 created the Nuova Famiglia (the New Family – with the Bardellino, Nuvoletta, Alfieri, and Galasso clans, and many more): a temporary federation of families with no centralizing objective who violently opposed Cutolo's NCO. In the end, this resulted in exacerbating the Camorra's "anarchic fragmentation"[37] and led to a bloody conflict that, running from 1978 to 1983, involved around 1,500 deaths. Other similar attempts were made with Carmine Alfieri's Nuova Mafia Campana during the 1980s, but these too were doomed to failure. The NCO came to an end in 1983, hopelessly weakened by political alliances, by attacks from adversaries, and above all by severe repressive measures from law enforcement agencies. The Nuova Famiglia ran out of steam around the same time, while the Nuova Mafia Campana was an aspiration rather than an achieved reality. The Camorra's organizational order today is fluid, polycentric, and conflictual (Figure 3.10), and the central unit is made up of the families.

To sum up, the Camorra had two failed attempts – in 1975–83 and in 1992 – to adopt a hierarchical structure of coordination, but in the end it has

---

[37] CPA (*Commissione Parlamentare Antimafia*, Italian parliamentary antimafia commission), *Report sul crimine organizzato in Campania*, Doc. XXIII, 46, XIII Legislatura, October 24, 2000, 22.

never been capable of doing so. The Camorra today is prevalently characterized by a clan-based model. With the exception of the Casalesi clan cartel and other alliances between clans, however unstable and temporary, the Camorra has no HLBC that are capable of coordinating the entire criminal system.

3.1.4 The American Cosa Nostra

The American Cosa Nostra[38] is a collection of Italian-American organized crime "families" that has been operating in the United States since the 1930s.[39] Originally it stemmed from the Sicilian mafia, but it has functioned as a completely independent criminal organization from the beginning. The families that make up the American Cosa Nostra all have the same organizational structure (Maas 1968; Cressey 1969; Bonanno 1983; Jacobs and Gouldin 1999; Finckenauer 2000; Abadinsky 2013; Raab 2016). At the top there is a boss, the representative of the family, who controls it and makes executive decisions (Figure 3.11).[40]

The boss represents the family in interfamily meetings and negotiations, spending much of his time on settling intrafamily and interfamiliy disputes. Normally, he conducts his criminal business from several different places, such as social clubs, bars, or restaurants. The second in command is the *underboss*; usually there is only one underboss, but sometimes there are more. The underboss is chosen by the boss himself and his role is to deliver orders to the members and provide a buffer with members. He acts as the alter ego of the boss under certain circumstances, and in many families the underboss arbitrates the less complex disputes that arise within the *family*. The underboss does not automatically succeed the boss in case of his death. In fact, the new boss normally is the person who prevails after a power struggle or is identified through compromise.[41] The boss appoints a senior adviser (*consigliere*), who is an

---

[38] The name "La Cosa Nostra" (Our Thing) was adopted mainly by New York families, while Chicago called itself "the Outfit," Buffalo adopted "the Arm," and others, especially in New England, chose "the Office" (Raab 2016).

[39] In the 1920s there were already many Italian-American gangs operating in America, but most of them had little awareness of the Sicilian Cosa Nostra's structure or rules. They were gangs mainly involved in bootlegging, a profitable illicit activity resulting from the Volstead Act prohibiting the manufacture, sale, or transportation of alcoholic beverages (Varese 2011). Compared with the Sicilian Cosa Nostra, these gangs lacked *omertà* oaths, rigid rules of conduct, and a well-defined structure (Raab 2016).

[40] "He has absolute power," affirmed the ex-mobster turned informer Salvatore Vitale (Crittle 2006, 161).

[41] Although it seems that the *capos* were empowered to elect the new boss democratically, it apparently never occurred (Raab 2016).

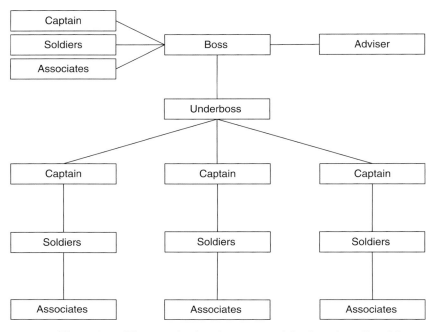

Figure 3.11 The organizational structure of the American Cosa Nostra

older member with extensive expertise and who advises the boss. And then there are a number of *capos*, or captains or *caporegime*, who supervise crews composed of *soldiers*, the *made members* of the American Cosa Nostra. The number of *capos* depends on the size of the *family*: in the Gambino family of New York, for example, there were more than twenty. The *capos* and those above them receive shares of the proceeds from crimes committed by the *soldiers* and *associates*. Made members, sometimes called *good fellows* or *wise guys*, are all male and in the past were all of Italian descent. The number of soldiers under each *capo* varies from a minimum of two to more than ten. The associates are the main regular collaborators of the soldiers, and their number can vary greatly, from only one to several units. In some families, the boss has a group of a *capo*, soldiers, and associates who report directly to him, without going through the organizational hierarchy.

The organizational structure of the American Cosa Nostra was developed by Salvatore Maranzano in 1931 in a meeting with one hundred *mafiosi*, apparently basing its model of organization on the Roman Empire and its army (De Stefano 2007, 32–3; Gosch and Hammer

2013, 133–4). Maranzano proclaimed himself *boss of all bosses*, but it was a role that soon after cost him his life.

While in the Sicilian Cosa Nostra there is a clear geographical division between the families that control specific territories in which only they may act, in the American Cosa Nostra the model is not territorial in nature. In New York especially, given the size of the city, there is a functional division of the activities (Gambetta and Reuter 1995), with some families, for example, controlling specific businesses such as the carting/waste disposal industry (Lucchese and Gambino) or the docks of Manhattan (Genovese).

Historically, there were 24 families in the American Cosa Nostra.[42] Unlike the Sicilian Cosa Nostra, the membership of the American Cosa Nostra is not limited to those with Sicilian origins; it is extended to all Italian regions. Originally, the member had to have parents who were both Italian, but this rule has experienced changes over time, probably related to difficulties in recruitment (see Section 2.1). The organization, however, makes use of thousands of associates from different countries, and there have been cases, though rare, of non-Italian members. This mafia organization was at the height of its power in the mid-1980s. Nowadays, the number of members has decreased because of both the repression by law enforcement agencies and demographic changes. It is increasingly difficult for American Cosa Nostra to recruit people of Italian origins who are skillful and willing to enter that world: if it does not change its rigid recruitment rules, the organization can become marginal in the criminal world. Indeed, to cope with this recruiting problem, the New York Gambino family has started to recruit as mobsters Sicilian immigrants who have close ties to crime families in Sicily (Raab 2016, xv). Members of the American Cosa Nostra are not employees and they do not receive a monthly salary. They are independent entrepreneurs searching for (legal and illegal) opportunities to make money.

Today, the American Cosa Nostra is a weak organization, far from its past splendor (Reuter 1995; Jacobs 1999). In the 1980s, a federal and state law enforcement campaign was launched against it. The result was that many of the 24 families have been dismantled or weakened. The most active nowadays are the five families who make up the American

---

[42] According to ex-mobster Jimmy Fratianno (*United States vs. Frank Tieri*, 1980), there were five families in New York, and one in each of the following cities: San Francisco, San Jose, Los Angeles, Denver, Dallas, Kansas City (Missouri), Chicago, Detroit, Cleveland, Buffalo, St. Louis, Pittsburgh, Steubenville (Ohio), Milwaukee, Philadelphia, Pittston (Pennsylvania), Tampa, an unknown city in Connecticut, and Providence (Albanese 2014, 150).

Cosa Nostra in New York City (Bonanno, Colombo, Genovese, Gambino, and Lucchese) and a few other families active in Newark, Philadelphia, Chicago, and the New England area (Raab 2016). Overall, there are about 3,000 *made members* of the American Cosa Nostra (Mallory 2012; FBI 2018[43]), including a total of around 700 to 800 (Raab 2016) operating in New York.[44] In addition to the made members, there are approximately 10,000 associate members working for the families in the United States. Almost entirely destroyed by the repression in the late 1980s, the American Cosa Nostra has benefited from a shift of attention in the aftermath of 9/11, when the FBI, and other law enforcement agencies as well as public opinion, have switched their focus to the threat of terrorism. However, while the American Cosa Nostra may be "down" at the present moment, it is not, as recent operations have shown, "out."[45]

The Evolution of Higher-Level Bodies of Coordination. Referring to New York families, Jacobs affirmed that "it is best to think of Cosa Nostra as a mélange of locally based crime families, each of which has exclusive jurisdiction in its territory" (1999, 9). Over time, however, three higher-level bodies of coordination emerged, with the goal to prevent bloody wars among families of the American Cosa Nostra and to arrange profitable alliances among them: (1) the National Commission, (2) the national meetings, and (3) the New York Commission.

(1) The National Commission was established in 1931 in order to prevent one single figure in command from becoming a dictator. Indeed a few years earlier, it had happened first with the leadership of Joe Masseria and then of Salvatore Maranzano and had led to conflict between the families and the long years of war for control in the late 1920s.[46] The National Commission was proposed by Lucky Luciano,

---

[43] This figure is reported in the FBI website section on Transnational Organized Crime, at www.fbi.gov/investigate/organized-crime (last accessed on April 5, 2018). According to several scholars, however, this value is an overestimation of the real number of members.

[44] In the 1950s there were approximately 5,000 members in New York City (Hortis 2014, 195). At the turn of the century, Capeci (2004) estimated a total of 1,375.

[45] In early August 2016, an FBI operation led to the arrest of 46 members of the American Cosa Nostra, including four of New York's five mafia families (Genovese, Gambino, Lucchese, and Bonanno), in a conspiracy that spanned from Springfield, Massachusetts, to South Florida ("Feds indict 46 in mob sweep, including reputed Philly boss," *The New York Times*, August 4, 2016): just one sign that the organization is still active today.

[46] Besides creating the commission, Lucky Luciano set the maximum membership numbers to prevent families from suddenly reinforcing ranks and igniting wars. New members could therefore be added only upon the death of an existing member and had to be approved by all New York families to prevent both unreliable affiliations and attempts to gain manpower advantages (Raab 2016).

who refined and americanized Maranzano's Castellammare del Golfo exile unit in New York, resembling Sicilian gangs. The Commission was initially made up of seven people, the heads of the five New York families plus the heads of the families in Chicago and Buffalo. In 1956, at the request of the other families, the membership of the Commission was extended to two other families, from Detroit and Philadelphia, while the others were represented by those present.[47]

The main objective of this body was to encourage mediation between different families, settle disputes, and prevent violent conflict. It could not interfere in the affairs of individual families unless this was explicitly requested by the boss or members of a family: "The Commission would have influence but not direct executive power ... More than anything else, the Commission was a forum" (Bonanno 1983, 159). An important role regarded control over the number of new members, which could either be hindered or encouraged, and establishing organization rules and ensuring compliance with them. Given the large number of families in New York, the city was always overrepresented, so the history of the Commission, says Bonanno (1983), is above all the history of the New York families, a rather similar situation, in fact, to the Sicilian Cosa Nostra's HLBC, where the role of Palermo and its province has always been decisive.

The Commission normally met every year to discuss national strategy and any business that could involve a number of families and territories, to contain conflict and clarify any situations of tension between families, and to ratify the Commission membership for the following five years. The Commission ratified the appointment of a new boss at the head of a family as well as that of a new made member and could authorize the elimination of high-ranking organization figures, such as a boss, when there were valid reasons.[48] Unlike the New York Commission, there is no evidence with regard to the effective functioning of this governing body today.

(2) As well as the meetings of the Commission, there were the "national meetings" involving all, or nearly all, of the American Cosa

---

[47] The families making up the Commission have changed over the years. For example, the Buffalo family lost its seat at the Commission table after the death of the boss Stefano Magaddino in 1974. Due to the infiltration of the undercover FBI agent Joseph Pistone, the Bonanno family lost its seat at the Commission until the 1990s, when Joe Massino was elected as the new boss (Capeci 2004).

[48] As in the case of the homicide of Carmine Galante, authorized by the Commission in order to resolve a power struggle within the Bonanno family (*United States vs. Salerno*, in Jacobs et al. 1994).

Nostra families in a kind of general assembly, held every five years starting in 1936 (although there is evidence of national mob conferences already being held in 1928 and 1929, Repetto 2004). Afterward, they were held less frequently. The meetings carried out an important function of coordination and gave the bosses a chance to see each other, the only opportunity they really had to meet in person. This was, of course, extremely risky, given the large number of people involved. In fact, the Apalachin meeting (New York), in 1957, was discovered by police and most of the participants were identified (Reavill 2013).

(3) Over time, the National Commission turned into the Commission of New York's five American Cosa Nostra families, formed by the five bosses of the New York families with, from time to time, the addition of a new member (e.g., New Jersey, the Chicago Outfit). Meetings of all the mobs operating in New York were held from the beginning of the twentieth century. The New York Commission regulated and facilitated the relationship between and among families, resolved disputes, and assigned areas of activity for each *family*. The Commission decided that all new members proposed by one of the five families had to be made known before induction and approved by all five families. Even this HLBC, however, is characterized by a certain weakness when compared to those of other mafias, such as the Yakuza, the Sicilian Cosa Nostra until a few years ago, or the 'Ndrangheta. It functions intermittently, like a court called on to solve occasional disputes (Jacobs and Gouldin 1999). The New York Commission was more a consultative rather than ruling body (Repetto 2004), its main objective to settle disputes and to prevent internal revolts within families. The former FBI agent Philip Scala, head of the FBI's Gambino Squad, affirmed that family bosses now tend to confer on a one-to-one basis (in Raab 2016, xv).

Of these three coordinating bodies, therefore, the only one that with any probability is still in existence is the New York Commission.[49] A recent investigation has found that members of the Gambino, Bonanno, Lucchese, and Genovese crime families from New York, along with a crew allegedly led by Joseph Merlino in Philadelphia, were collectively labeled the "East Coast La Cosa Nostra Enterprise." Members of the American Cosa Nostra in New York, Philadelphia, Springfield (Massachusetts), and Boca Raton (Florida) allegedly committed a variety

---

[49] *United States vs. Salerno*, in Jacobs et al. 1994. A meeting was definitely held in 2000 with representatives of the five families, which was attended by three bosses, one *consigliere*, and a member of the Genovese ruling panel (J. Marzulli, "Boss rat Joseph Massino admits to court that Mafia Commission hasn't met in 25 years," *New York Daily News*, April 16, 2011).

of crimes including extortion, fraud, arson, and selling of illegal cigarettes. Interestingly, they also pooled their resources and income streams. Despite trials that are still ongoing, this investigation could prove the persistence and evolution of some sort of HLBC.[50] According to the ex-boss of the Bonanno family, Joe Massino, the last known Commission meeting held with all the bosses was in November 1985. The National Commission has not held a summit in more than twenty-five years,[51] and the national meetings have also disappeared, having become too risky. Instead, there are mini and ad hoc meetings. The American Cosa Nostra's HLBC are not, then, today, able to coordinate the entire criminal system in the United States, and little is known with regard to their operation. As Jacobs points out, "The mechanism of (New York) Commission and Cosa Nostra decision-making are similarly obscure" (1994, 90). It is also unclear how the Commission functions (let alone how the National Commission worked), whether according to the rule of majority decision or unanimity. If it is true that the Commission must approve the possible murder of a boss, what happens if the boss is one of the members of the Commission? How is it possible for the information not to get out? Does the Commission have the power to quell disputes or must it first be endowed with this by the parties involved? These are just a few questions that help us understand how much there is still to know about the real functioning of this governing body: sometimes, however, it seems that it ratifies decisions already taken and actions already carried out.[52] In any case, we may conclude that, unlike other mafias, the American Cosa Nostra has so far remained free of significant and relevant higher-level bodies of coordination.

3.1.5   The Triads

The origin of the Triads[53] is unclear, being a mixture of fact and myth. They were founded for patriotic, religious, or criminal reasons in the

---

[50] The investigations identified three of the most prominent members within the organization: two Genovese capos (i.e., Pasquale Parrello of New York and Eugene Onofrio of Connecticut, and Joseph Merlino of Philadelphia). While Parrello was among the 44 of the 46 members of the organization who pleaded guilty, the trial for Onofrio has been postponed indefinitely due to undisclosed health concerns, and recently the judge in Merlino's case declared mistrial for hung jury after nearly four days of deliberation (see for instance J. Roebuck, "On trial again, Joey Merlino claims he's left the mob behind", *The Philadelphia Inquirer*, January 26, 2018, and R. Fenton and B. Golding, "Reputed mob boss' trial ends in hung jury", *New York Post*, February 20, 2018).

[51] See Marzulli, Note 49.

[52] Like the homicides of the boss Vincent Mangano by underboss Albert Anastasia; of Carmine Galante; and of the boss of the Bonanno family Paul Castellano by John Gotti.

[53] There is no evidence of a unitary, worldwide "Chinese Mafia," but there are different mafia groups, which include the Hong Kong Triads, the Taiwan gangs, the China-based

seventeenth century in feudal China (Morgan 1960; Ip 1999a; Chu 2000; Lee 2004; Chin 2014). Initially, triad societies were mainly mutual associations meant to protect job opportunities for their members. Afterward, they engaged in different types of criminal activities, such as organized robbery, piracy, salt and opium smuggling, and protection rackets (Sinn 1989). According to Chu (2000), Triads specialize in trading the commodity of protection. The distinctive role of triad societies, Chu argued, is neither extortion nor the monopolization of illegal goods and services, but "providing protection services" to illegal entrepreneurs in order to smooth their activities in a risky business environment.

According to the Hong Kong Police (Ip 1999a) there were more than 300 triad societies in the region. Most of them were established between 1914 and 1939, and they were divided into eight major groups operating in Hong Kong (Chu 2011). Each society group consisted of a headquarters branch and a number of subbranches operating in their respective areas. The organizational structure was verticalized and centralized and the headquarters maintained strict control over its subordinates.

The structure of the headquarters (in which the roles are also indicated by numbers), as shown in Figure 3.12, gave the role of chairman to the *mountain master* (*shan chu*), the supreme leader, responsible for all final decisions on the issues that concerned the organization. The leader was assisted by the *deputy chairman*, a kind of underboss. Staff functions were carried out by two officers of the same rank, the *incense master* and the *vanguard*, responsible for ceremonies of initiation, promotion, and recruiting. Below the *deputy chairman* there were three officers, respectively, in charge of the relationship between headquarters and its branches (*liaison officer*), military command during wars and the punishment of traitors (*fighters manager*), and general administration functions and adviser, thinker and planner (*mastermind*). The senior officers were in charge of five departments: (1) the general affairs section, (2) the recruiting section, (3) the organization section, (4) the liaison section, (5) and the education and welfare section (Morgan 1960). For the implementation of activities, the senior officers could make use of the collaboration of a number of senior ordinary members as assistants.

---

mafialike gangs, and United States–based tongs and street gangs (Chin 2014). In this book, we will mainly refer to the Hong Kong Triads. The word "triad" is an English designation for the sacred symbol of the societies, a triangle enclosing a secret sign derived from the Chinese character HUNG. The resulting symbol represents the triangular union of heaven, earth, and man.

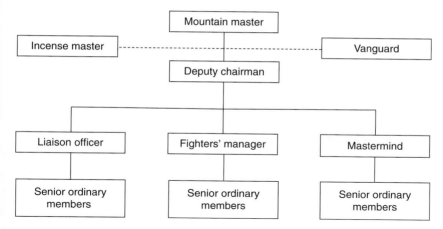

Figure 3.12 Structure of a traditional triad headquarters

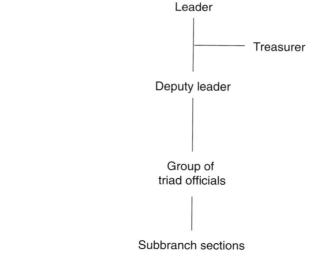

Leader

Treasurer

Deputy leader

Group of
triad officials

Subbranch sections
(general affairs, recruitment, organization, liaison, education, welfare)

Figure 3.13 The structure of a traditional triad branch society

Below headquarters, there were the branch societies (similar to the families for other mafias, see Figure 3.13), in some cases even several dozen, divided into *leader, deputy leader,* and *treasurer,* with the last only responsible for the economic management of the branch society.

Finally, there was a group of triad officials responsible for the activities of the sections, which were similar to those at headquarters, but concerned with problems limited to the level of the branch society (Morgan 1960, 96).

The structure of the branch societies lacked the figure of the *vanguard* and the *incense master*, responsible for recruitment, as these aspects were managed and authorized at a central level. Territoriality, codes of conduct, initiation rites, oaths, rituals, and respect for the hierarchy completed the organization's operating rules (Lo and Kwok 2012).

Over time, the role and power of headquarters, whose name has become *Central committee*, has gradually declined. Since the 1950s, and especially since 1974, there has been a decentralization of corporate power by the Central committee to the advantage of the branch societies, which have become increasingly autonomous. The role of the Central committee has become limited to the functions of initiation of new members and arbitration when threatened with intersociety and intergroup warfare. For this reason, the highest positions of the Central committee were occupied by senior figures with solid reputations, well respected by the other members. In addition, decisions regarding recruitment began to shift progressively from the center to the periphery (*branch society*), thus limiting central power to ceremonial functions, carried out by the *incense master* and *vanguard*, while the decisions were taken by the branch societies.

Subsequently, the organizational structure underwent further changes with the aim of simplification. The eight groups became four (i.e., the Chiu Chow/Hoklo, 14K, Wo, and Luen), each of which includes several triad societies, about fifty in all, of which a dozen are actually active today (Chu 2011).[54] The number of members varies widely: some triad societies can be very small, with only 100 members, while at the high end of the range, each of the four major groups would have 30,000 members.

The modern Triads' organization, as shown in Figure 3.14, is the result, then, of a process of power decentralization, streamlining of organizational structure, fragmentation, and laicization (Chu 2000).

Today, the triad structure may be *well organized (structured)* or *fragmented* (Chu 2011). A structured Triad may have a *Central committee* (the former headquarters), with functions of coordination of a number of

---

[54] According to Chu (2011, 226) the most active triad societies are Sun Yee On, 14K Hau Group, 14K Tak Group, 14K Ngai Group, Wo Shing Wo, Wo Hop To, Wo On Lok (Shui Fong), and Luen Ying Sh'e. In terms of membership, 14K is believed to be the largest triad society in Hong Kong.

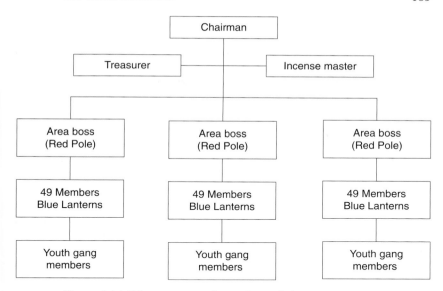

Figure 3.14 The structure of a modern triad society

gangs operating under its name, elected annually or biannually and composed of a *chairman*, a *treasurer*, and an *incense master*, who in general is the most elderly member. This coordination body has a very different role from the past, devoid of hierarchical command and mainly dedicated to initiation and promotion ceremonies, to respect for the rules and to settlement of disputes. It does not deal with the organization of actual activities or assign tasks to people, and its members receive their incomes from the organization. A fragmented triad society, such as the 14K, has no Central committee, and the gangs can cooperate on an ad hoc basis (Chu 2011).

Even though the various triad societies belong to one of the four existing groups, there is no higher-level body of coordination or effective command as there was in the past. Each triad society is an independent organization consisting of several autonomous gangs. The organizational structure has become more flexible and decentralized and the traditional ranking system has been reduced to three levels: area boss (*red pole*), *49 members* and *blue lanterns*, and youth gang members (Chu 2005).[55]

---

[55] "Hanging the blue lantern" is the lowest rank for a person who is verbally accepted as a member of a Triad without going through a formal initiation ceremony. It is a rank similar to that of an associate in other mafias and precedes the real entrance into the Triads that occurs with the rank known as "49."

In both variants, well organized and fragmented, today the most important part of the triad operation is located in the level below the Central committee, consisting of a cartel of street gangs, each with about fifteen to twenty members. Each gang, headed by a *area boss*, controls and operates in a specific territorial area. Under the supervision of the area boss, the *49 members* and the *blue lanterns* manage the activities and the recruitment of youth gang members.

The Triads exert a growing attraction over juvenile gangs. In this regard, Lo (2012) defines the process of the submission of youth gang members to triad subcultures and values as "triadization." This process allows the organization to continue its survival across different generations over time. Once they are members, the area boss becomes their protector (*big brother*), and young members must faithfully obey his orders, fighting for the triad society to which they belong (Kwok and Lo 2013). The income generated by criminal activity stops at the level of the area boss, and does not pass up the hierarchy. Not all triad societies have a Central committee. Some are freelance and are therefore incapable of carrying out any kind of coordination or settling disputes between gangs.

In addition to this process of decentralization of power and organizational rationalization and simplification, there was also a "laicization" process involving simplifying the rites and ceremonies, which had lost their "symbolic" importance and were thus abbreviated. The "brotherhood" elements, too, gradually gave way to the prevalently economic aspect of organization activity. Such simplification processes were also encouraged by the tightening legislation that prompted the Triads to reduce the risk of exposure of their activities, particularly after the approval of the Organized and Serious Crime Ordinance of 1994 and other related legislation (Lo and Kwok 2012).

On the one hand, the Triads have become extremely flexible and able to respond better to rapid change in the social and economic environment in which they operate (Broadhurst and Lee 2009), on the other, they do not hesitate to resort to violence to solve (or even expand) conflict. The structure of the Triads today, argues Chin (1995), is loosely organized, driven by self-interest and with a decreasing emphasis on brotherhood. There is a lack of central control and coordination over the operation of their branches. As Lo points out (2010), "Gang cohesiveness and members' loyalty and righteousness have begun to diminish" (852).

The number of triad members in Hong Kong has declined over time: in the past they were estimated at almost 160,000 (Chin 1995, 47), then 100,000 (Ip 1999b; Hong Kong Police in Lee 2004, 2; Mallory

2012, 161), while recent estimates range from 50,000 (Liu 2001) to 120,000.[56] Probably such a high number of members with respect to the population as a whole (around 7 million) also includes older-generation Triads and those who are no longer active members. In addition, only a part of them is dedicated to criminal activities in a continuous manner. In relation to population, however, Hong Kong certainly has the highest per capita number of mafia members on the face of the earth.

The Triads are also present in numerous countries, including China, the United States, Canada, Australia, and the United Kingdom. In the new millennium, Lo and Kwok argue, Triads in Hong Kong

> have gone through a process of mainlandization, which is defined here as the process of making Hong Kong triad societies more reliant on mainland China for financial gain through social networking with Chinese officials, enterprises and criminal syndicates and taking advantage of legitimate and illegitimate business opportunities resulting from China's economic growth and rising demand for goods and services. (Lo and Kwok 2012, 83)

The Evolution of Higher-Level Bodies of Coordination. From an organizational point of view, modern Hong Kong Triads are decentralized (McKenna 1996; Xia 2008) but not disorganized (Kwok 2017). They are neither a centrally structured nor an unorganized entity. There is no godfather nor central body able to direct the entire criminal organization (Chu 2011). Rather, Triads today constitute a set of clans organized in the pyramid style of typical mafia families, with a boss who exercises a hierarchical role of leadership within the clan.

Triads today are characterized by a *clan-based* organizational model, and the lack of HLBC to coordinate the entire criminal system is associated with a greater frequency of conflict, between both gangs belonging to different triad societies and gangs belonging to the same Triad. The Central committee's role involves ritual more than organizational leadership and it is unable to give rise to unitary strategies. The organizational form, therefore, is that of a hierarchical clan with relationships with other clans in the form of a cartel.[57]

3.1.6   The Yakuza

The Yakuza, the Japanese mafia, is a semilegitimate organized crime group and is the only mafia that is not illegal. The Yakuza has operated

---

[56] G. Schloss, "Triads spread their wings", *South China Morning Post*, December 24, 2000.
[57] For an analysis of the most recent organizational changes of three major triad societies (Wo Shing Wo, 14K, and Sun Yee On), see Kwok (2017).

openly for centuries. The headquarters of the clans are marked with the symbol of the clan; their office addresses are listed in phone books, on their business cards, and in the National Police Agency (NPA) annual report on crime. Senior members carry business cards engraved with the organization logo and wear ornate platinum badges on their suits.[58] All of this despite the fact that their primary sources of revenue are extortion, racketeering, financial fraud, blackmail, stock market manipulation, and drug trafficking. Many gangs publish their own magazine or newsletter with articles containing legal advice or information regarding community life:

Weekly and daily Yakuza fan magazines, the 'de facto trade publications' of organized crime in Japan, are available at newsstands, convenience stores, and public libraries. Yakuza techniques and etiquette are also popular themes for self-help and management books aimed at businessmen. Films, documentaries, and video games portraying the Yakuza as code-adhering gentlemen capable of ninja-like assassinations have also become a staple Japanese cultural export. (Reilly 2014, 805)

In the aftermath of particularly visible conflicts, the leaders of the gangs organize press conferences to apologize for any inconvenience that they may have caused (Kaplan and Dubro 2003). The Yakuza has always tried to promote its image as protector of the people. For example, Yakuza groups delivered aid to the victims of the Great Hanshin Earthquake in 1995 and again following the Great Tohoku Earthquake and Tsunami in 2011. With this state of semilegality, the Yakuza has never killed high-profile figures (judges, politicians, journalists, etc.), unlike other mafias, and especially the Sicilian Cosa Nostra.

The number of members was very high, especially in the past, with a peak of 184,091 members and associates in 1963 (NPA 2017).[59] According to data from the Ministry of Justice (MOJ) and the National Police Agency (NPA), the number of members steadily decreased until 1987, and then again was reduced by the implementation of the

---

[58] A clear indicator of the legitimacy of this criminal organization is the fact that in 1946 an order was issued that gave the Yakuza Tekiya bosses formal control over the open-air markets in Tokyo (Wildes, 1948). The situation has gradually changed since 1991, with the approval of a law, the Bōtaihō. While not as effective as the laws passed in the United States (such as the RICO – Racketeer Influenced and Corrupt Organizations Act of 1970), or in Italy (416 bis of the Penal Code, approved in 1982), the legislation has started to reduce the space of legitimacy and action of the Yakuza by providing law enforcement agencies with more effective courses of action.

[59] National Police Agency (NPA) 2017, *Heisei 29-nen kamihanki ni okeru soshiki hanzai no jōsei* (The situation of organized crime in the first half of 2017). Retrieved from www.npa.go.jp/sosikihanzai/kikakubunseki/sotaikikaku01/h28.sotaijyousei.pdf (last accessed on April 5, 2018).

Anti-Boryokudan Act in 1992,[60] which has hindered some Yakuza's activities. The decline continued with the start of the new millennium, and in 2010 the estimated population was between 78,600 and 80,000 members and associates, with a majority of part-time gang members rather than full-timers.[61] As of the end of 2016, Yakuza members and associates were estimated to be approximately 39,100 (NPA 2017).

Among them, the estimated 17,470 Yakuza members are organized in 22 groups.[62] Most members (76.7 percent) are affiliated with the four main Yakuza groups: the Yamaguchi-gumi includes 29.8 percent of Yakuza members, the Sumiyoshi-kai 17.7 percent, the Kobe Yamaguchi-gumi 14.9 percent, and the Inagawa-kai 14.3 percent. The Yamaguchi-gumi used to account for nearly half the members of the Yakuza until 2015, when some of them formed a new group, the Kobe Yamaguchi-gumi. Since the split, several shootings and other accidents occurred due to the ongoing turf war between the two groups (NPA 2017).

There are two types of organizational structures in the Yakuza syndicates (Huang and Vaughn 1992; Gragert 2010): (1) the *pyramidal power structure*, which is followed by the two largest syndicates in Japan: the Yamaguchi-gumi and the Inagawa-kai; (2) the *federation*, or *conglomerate structure*, which is followed by the Sumiyoshi-kai syndicate.

(1) The *pyramidal power structure* is characterized by a flow of power that is vertical in nature, with, at the very top, the *kumi-chō*, the supreme chief of the syndicate (Figure 3.15).

---

[60] Boryokudan is commonly referred to as Yakuza and is defined in the Anti-Boryokudan Act as "any organization likely to facilitate its members to collectively or habitually commit illegal acts of violence" (Art. 2.2).

[61] It should be remembered that, although the Yakuza is a legal organization, the number of members may be higher if those active members who are not known are taken into account.

[62] According to the latest report by the NPA (2017), current Yakuza groups are Rokudaime Yamaguchi-gumi (based in Hyogo, with approximately 5,200 members, corresponding to 29.8 percent of total Yakuza members), Sumiyoshi-kai (Tokyo, 3,100, 17.7 percent), Kobe Yamaguchi-gumi (Hyogo, 2,600, 14.9 percent), Inagawa-kai (Tokyo, 2,500, 14.3 percent), Matsuba-kai (Tokyo, 650, 3.7 percent), Kyokuto-kai (Tokyo, 590, 3.4 percent), Dojin-kai (Fukuoka, 540, 3.1 percent), Godaime Kudo-kai (Fukuoka, 420), Gyokuryu-kai (Okinawa, 360), Namigawa-kai (Fukuoka, 240), Godaime Kyosei-kai (Hiroshima, 180), Sandaime Fukuhaku-kai (Fukuoka, 150), Soai-kai (Chiba, 140), Nidaime Azuma-gumi (Osaka, 140), Taishu-kai (Fukuoka, 130), Rokudaime Aizu Kotetsu-kai (Kyoto, 110), Sandaime Kyodo-kai (Hiroshima, 100), Godaime Asano-gumi (Okayama, 90), Nanadaime Goda-ikka (Yamaguchi, 90), Yondaime Kozakura-ikka (Kagoshima, 70), Nidaime Shinwa-kai (Kagawa, 40), and Kyudaime Sakaume-gumi (Osaka, 30).

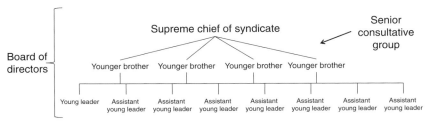

Figure 3.15 The pyramidal structure of the Yamaguchi-gumi and Inagawa-kai syndicates

Under the *kumi-chō* rule is a group of usually four *shatei* (younger brothers). Next follows a group of eight directors called *wakashira-hosa* (assistant young leaders), one of whom will be appointed a *wakashira* (young leader). The *shatei*, *wakashira*, and *wakashira-hosa* function as a board of directors who meet monthly, and decide on syndicate policy and divide up the syndicate's income accordingly (Gragert 2010, 165).

This board makes use of the advice provided by a senior consultative group called the *sanro-ka*.

(2) The *federation structure*, unlike the pyramidal structure, is characterized by greater gang autonomy and a horizontal distribution of power among the different gang bosses, who select a *kumi-chō* from among the group members.

All these syndicates are composed of *ikka*, the minimal organizational units of the Yakuza, organized as in Figure 3.16. The gangs have to ensure a monthly payment to syndicate headquarters. The formal hierarchy of the *ikka* is similar to the other mafia organizational structures[63] and consists of a highly structured leadership that is pyramidal and stratified.

Internal cohesion is favored by quasi-blood relationships: "Gangs are based on fictive family ties of father-son (*oyabun–kobun*) and brother–brother (*kyōdai*) relationship" (Hill 2014, 236). The role of boss is covered by *kumi-chō*, who is responsible for all the important decisions for the life of the *ikka* and who makes use of a series of advisers (*kōmon*) and senior executives (*saikō-kambu*), one of whom also performs the functions of underboss (*waka-gashira*). The executives (*kanbu*) form

---

[63] There are variants described by others (e.g., Kaplan and Dubro 2003, 116), but they do not change the hierarchical pyramid structure.

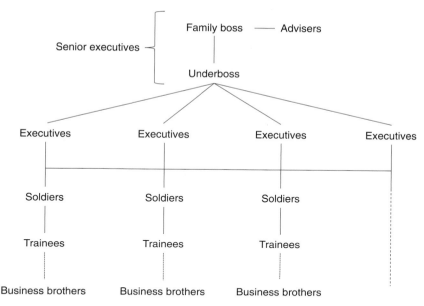

Figure 3.16 The typical organizational structure of the *ikka*
(*Source:* Hill 2003a, 66)

and command groups of soldiers (*kumi-in*) that perform all the operational activities, both legal and illegal, of the *ikka*. Finally, the trainees
(*jun-kōsei-in*) and business brothers carry out the activities that do not
require much skill and carry little prestige.

Unlike other mafias such as the Sicilian Cosa Nostra, but similar to the
'Ndrangheta, the Yakuza is characterized by career progression based on
seniority rather than on merit.

The Evolution of Higher-Level Bodies of Coordination. The Yakuza
today is characterized by a kind of *clan-based federation* model, with the
presence of higher-level bodies of coordination, albeit different from
those of the past. The objectives of the superordinate coordination
bodies of the three main Yakuza syndicates are to manage conflicts,
resolve disputes, and organize the rotation of leadership (so as to prevent
internal power climbing), territorial expansion, punishments, and gang
dissolution. The role of president of these bodies is not the boss of
bosses, nor even the superordinate command levels of the *ikka*'s internal
business. The HLBC are limited to coordinating individual Yakuza

societies, and there is no higher level that can coordinate the entire criminal system, as there is in the case of the 'Ndrangheta, and as occurred in the case of the Sicilian Cosa Nostra.

3.1.7   The Russian Mafia

The Russian Mafia has its origins in a series of political and economic tumults that characterized the Soviet Union in the early 1980s, as a consequence of an imperfect transition to the market (Varese 2001). The transition from the planned economy of the USSR to a market economy allowed citizens to start business ventures and run activities that were prohibited before. However, the increase in wealth and economic transactions, coupled with a sort of institutional vacuum and the absence of protection for property rights, favored fraudulent entrepreneurs and new types of crime, such as fraud and financial crimes (Varese 2001). While the new state was not able to provide protection, a class of men who were expert in violence (soldiers, police officers, career officers, ex-KGB agents, etc.) and were largely unemployed as a result of the regime transition constituted the highly skilled human capital needed to meet the demand for extralegal protection.[64]

By Russian Mafia we mean here "the sum total of the criminal leaders who went through the *vory* ritual" (Varese 2001, 188) – those, in other words, who share the ideology of reference of *Vor-v-zakone* (thief in law, man who follows the code of honor), a kind of criminal elite that emerged in the Soviet Gulag from the 1920s on (Varese 2001; Slade 2013, 11; for a historic overview see Galeotti 2018). Unlike other organized crime groups, not all members undertake the initiation rite: in the Russian Mafia this is a prerogative only of leaders. Only those who have proved their criminal conviction and skills, as well as their organizational skills and ability to establish connections, can reach the positions of leadership in the governing bodies of these criminal groups, and are therefore entitled to the initiation rite and the title of *Vor-v-zakone* (Dolgova 2003, 361). This title is therefore reserved for those networking criminal leaders involved in mafia activities (Slade 2013, 17). According to

---

[64] Underlying the criminal-political nexus, Shelley warns against a misinterpretation of the concept of Russian Mafia due to the "mafia" label. She claims that Russian organized crime groups involve both the widest range of participants and the most diverse forms of criminal activity of almost any criminal group. She underlines how they differ from the Italian mafias, mainly because it is not a unique or homogeneous entity, but also because of the different role that family ties and initiation rituals play within them (Shelley 2004; 2016).

Galeotti (2018) a modern Russian boss may avoid the term *vor*, preferring the term *avtoritet*. Although the number of criminals and criminal groups is very high in Russia, only a subgroup of these should be regarded as mafia organizations, namely, those that are capable of providing protection (Sukharenko 2016). According to the Russian news agency PrimeCrime.ru, there were 485 *Vor-v-zakone* in 2015, and 118 of these were behind bars (in Varese 2017, 21).

The Russian Mafia groups share some general rules of reference (see Section 5.2), have an ideology in common, and coordinate among themselves to carry out activities of mutual interest. These groups are organized internally in a hierarchical structure (Varese 2001; Volkov 2002; Mallory 2012), typical of other mafias. However, unlike other gangs such as the Yakuza and the Sicilian Cosa Nostra, they are substantially autonomous, without control or coordination from a higher-level body. The organizational architecture is *clan-based*, with some mechanisms of coordination between the bosses and meetings to manage potential conflicts and resolve disputes. However, such forms of coordination do not constitute higher-level bodies of coordination comparable to those present in other mafias. There are some major governing structures, at least eight according to Galeotti (2018). These bodies are different among them, some are more hierarchical, others are like loose networks (the prevalent form), others again are anchored around individuals or based on a specific territorial focus. All of them provide benefits, services and criminal opportunities for their members, whether individuals or gangs (2018, 126–7).

The basic organizational unit is called the *brigade* and is structured hierarchically (Figure 3.17).

At the top there is the boss (*avtoritet*, authority, or *pakhan*), who controls four criminal cells in the working unit through four intermediary captains (*brigadier*); each of them is in charge of a small group of men. A senior adviser (*sovietnik*), a member who has extensive expertise, advises the boss, while the *obshchak*, the bookmaker, collects funds from the brigadiers and bribes the government. The adviser and the bookmaker are the boss's most trusted people.

A *brigade* is composed of soldiers (*boyevik*, warrior), to whom the *brigadiers* assign jobs. Soldiers are also in charge of finding new members and paying tributes to the captains. Finally, there are four other types of members: *kryshas*, literally "roofs or covers," cunning and violent individuals employed to protect the business from other criminal organizations; *torpedos*, contract killers; *byki*, bodyguards; *shestyorka*, associates to the mafia organization, often playing the role of errand boy, the lowest rank in the mafia.

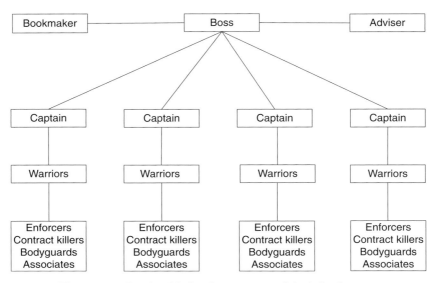

Figure 3.17 Russian Mafia: the structure of the brigade

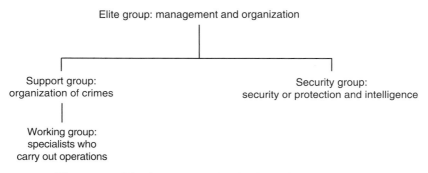

Figure 3.18 The four separate levels of Russian crime groups

From the point of view of activities, members of the organization are divided into four groups (Mallory 2012, 94) (Figure 3.18).

The *elite group*, made up of leaders who plan out operations and crimes for lower ranks to commit, could be equated with the top management of a company. It is led by a boss (*pakhan*), who is involved in management, organization, and ideology. This group controls both the support group and the security group. The *security group* looks after the security or protection and intelligence. It is comparable to lower management or the senior executives. It is led by one of the boss's spies, whose job is to make sure the organization keeps running smoothly. He also keeps the peace between the organizations and other criminal groups and makes sure to pay off the right people. This group works with the *elite group* and is equal in power with the *support group*, which is also led by a spy of the boss. In this case, his job is to watch over the working unit, collecting the money while supervising their criminal activities. They plan a specific crime for a specialized group or choose the resources necessary to carry out the operation. The working unit consists of the individuals who carry out crimes (kidnapping, human trafficking, thefts, prostitution, extortion, and others). Every organization has an accounting system separate from the private accounts of its members.

The Evolution of Higher-Level Bodies of Coordination. The Russian Mafia is characterized by a *clan-based* model, today lacking in higher-level bodies of coordination.

3.1.8   Comparison of the Mafias' Organizational Orders

Although they are very similar in terms of activity carried out, the number of organizational units involved and the overall number of members, mafia organizations still differ in numerous important ways, such as organizational structure and the methods of coordination and power management. This is summarized in Table 3.1.[65]

On the basis of the empirical evidence available at the moment and taking into account that organization models change, albeit slowly, over time, we can say that the 'Ndrangheta, the Sicilian Cosa Nostra (until 2000), some Camorra clans, and the Yakuza are characterized by a *clan-based federation* model. In contrast, the Triads, the Russian Mafia, and most Camorra clans are characterized by a *clan-based* model.

Some mafias have done away with or weakened their higher-level bodies of coordination (e.g., the Triads, the Camorra, the Sicilian Cosa Nostra); others, such as the 'Ndrangheta, have gradually strengthened them. Moreover, mafias with a clan-based federation model are characterized by more systemic decision-making processes: these mafias are thus more able to develop tendentially unitary strategies, involving

---

[65] The data refer to the current situation of the mafias analyzed. Numbers may change over time, just as the presence of higher-level bodies of coordination may not remain constant.

Table 3.1 *Summary of the main characteristics of analyzed mafia organizations at the beginning of the twenty-first century*

	Sicilian Cosa Nostra	Camorra	'Ndrangheta	American Cosa Nostra	Triads	Yakuza	Russian Mafia
Members	Around 3,000	Around 6,000	Around 10,000	Around 3,000	From 50,000 to 120,000	Around 39,100 (17,470 members)	Around 485 *Vor-v-zakone*
Organizational units	Around 100–150	Around 130	Around 150–170	Around 8–10	Around 50; 12–15 active (with hundreds of gangs)	Around 22 (4 largest have 76.7 percent members)	Around 167
Organizational order	(semi) Clan-based federation now	Clan-based for many gangs, clan-based federation in others	Clan-based federation	Clan-based	(semi) Clan-based	Clan-based federation	Mainly clan-based
HLBC	Present (at district level)	Absent	Present	Present but weak (in New York)	Absent now	Present	Absent
Decision-making processes	Partly systemic	Clan-based	Systemic	Clan-based	Clan-based	Partly systemic	Clan-based
Strategy	Coordinated	Emergent	Coordinated	Emergent	Emergent	Coordinated	Emergent

across-the-board interest for all the clan components. In mafias charac-terized by a clan-based model, on the other hand, decision-making processes are mainly based on individual clans and consequently there is no unified strategy, but rather an emergent one, in the sense that it arises from the interaction of the different strategies pursued by individual clans.

4 Organizational Orders and the Use of Violence

4.1 Conflict and Violence

Even if conflict is present in every organization, the few studies of conflict within and between organizations have principally, if not exclusively, regarded legitimate organizations (Ackroyd 2009). There are many reasons for conflict in organizations: for example, tension between organizational subunits arising from different perceptions on the priority to be given to organizational problems and the different solutions proposed, or from attempts to control scarce resources. Another source of organizational conflict is the situation in which two subunits have common responsibilities for the same set of tasks, or where people further down the organizational hierarchy try to climb to higher positions in search of status, prestige, and monetary rewards.

Whatever the reasons that give rise to conflict, or the form it takes, its source is always located in some perceived or real divergence of interests (Morgan 1986, 155). Conflict in organizations grows, therefore, when individuals or groups perceive the differences in their preferences involving decision outcomes and make use of the power they have to try to promote their own preferences over those of others.

Sociological studies of conflict have analyzed a wide range of individual and relational factors that account for violent and criminal activities (Collins 2010). Studying a Chicago youth gang named Vice Lords, Keiser (1969) analyzed the use of violence and retaliation, and the reasons for it. Vice Lords were a structured gang with a division of labor and different hierarchical levels, and Keiser identified two types of conflict: intraorganizational conflict, within the gang, and interorganizational conflict, between the gangs and other gangs. Intraorganizational conflict consisted mainly in several feuds among various subgroups within the federation, some between different branches, others within the same branch, due to competition for leadership. When senior leaders were arrested, the resulting vacancies at the top encouraged attempts by younger members to launch internal power climbs.

Of particular interest are the interorganizational conflicts, involving the Vice Lords and other gangs. For example, if a Vice Lord was beaten up by members of another gang, retaliatory raids became highly probable. The likelihood of such violent events was linked to several factors, first, whether tension had already existed between the Vice Lords and the gang involved (arguments, individual fights). A second set of reasons had to do with the internal dynamics of the gang, especially in terms of the competition for leadership: if someone aspired to climb to a better position in the hierarchy, retaliation was an opportunity to show the group his skills and value. Strong competition increased the chances of retaliation, therefore, while lack of competition decreased these chances. Finally, a third factor concerned the status of the person involved: if the position held was not important, retaliation was not inevitable. Conversely, if the person held high positions in the organizational order of the Vice Lords, or was a member of prestige and influence, then retaliation was certain. The higher in rank the person involved, the greater the involvement of the organization. The fact that the threat of violence by another gang increased solidarity within the threatened gang was seen in different gangs (Decker and van Winkle 1996).

Retaliation and vengeance have moral legitimacy in most tribal societies, while they are outlawed in modern societies with formal legal systems (Boehm 1984). In some situations, there are rational motivations for revenge. Mary Durham (1928) relates the story of a tribal leader who failed to take revenge and, as a consequence, lost his right to speak in a meeting of the tribe. Members of many tribal societies, Boehm affirms, consider it "to be a legitimate moral prerogative of an individual or group to take homicidal revenge for the death of a close relative" (1984, 65).

The type of market in which the illegal organization operates also plays an important role in the genesis and dynamics of conflict. For example, of illegal markets, the drug market appears to be one of the most violent. However, certain recent research studies have produced results of a different kind. Analyzing 31 police investigations in the Netherlands, Soudijn and Reuter (2013) show a variety of nonviolent dispute resolution methods in drug retailing. They found data on 33 incidents involving failures in transactions related to cocaine smuggling and the subsequent outcome. In many cases, the methods of dispute resolution (for example, following a failure to deliver a load of drugs or its loss) are similar to those used by legitimate businesses. Criminals initiate an investigation to check whether the balance of evidence favors an interpretation of bad luck or incompetence as opposed to an effort to defraud. The result of these investigations in most disputes is that they are resolved with neither threats nor violence. However, when negotiations break down, because there is evidence that someone stole drugs or was guilty of deliberate betrayal, then threats and violence are often used.

Recent studies of violence have brought to the fore the importance of moving from a focus on the individual determinants of crime, to the analysis of its relational and social network basis. Gould (2003) argued that interpersonal violence is a property of relations, and most often emerges from disputes over dominance, demonstrating how conflict is more likely to occur in symmetrical relationships, in which there is ambiguity concerning the relative status of the contenders, than in hierarchical ones. Papachristos (2009) applied this relational approach to the study of organized crime, explaining the spread of violence in gangs through the patterns of interaction and conflict among gang members. While this scholarship has successfully documented the role of interpersonal relationships and social networks in explaining violence in organized crime, in this book the focus is switched to the *formal* organizational structure of criminal organizations – their organizational order.

Given that it is impossible for mafias, as it is for other criminal organizations, to resort to the legal system, violence is the method frequently employed to enforce contractual agreements and resolve disputes. The use of violence in the mafia is heavily dependent on the type of organization adopted, whether clan-based or clan-based federation. Clan-based federation organizational order is characterized by collusion between criminal organizations, while clan-based organizational order is characterized by competition. It follows that a high degree of violence is an indicator, not only of conflict, but of a high degree of competition in a criminal system, while a low degree of violence indicates the prevalence of collusion between the clan members of the criminal system. There are obvious advantages in practicing collusion. In a situation of oligopoly, in which there are few companies present, agreement is preferable, with a sharing of the market, especially if the takeover is complicated and very expensive to implement. In criminal systems that practice collusion, "clients" are prevented from turning to other suppliers, and competitors are prevented from entering their territory to provide services. In addition, the cost of conflict is minimized, with enormous savings in terms of people and resources, and time and money can be dedicated mainly to maximizing business. All this produces organizational stability and longevity; it is not, however, always possible.

The conflicts in Mexico between cartels of drug traffickers and in El Salvador between gangs are very eloquent with regard to this (Wainwright 2016). There is a high level of competition among the drug dealers in Mexico to control access to the limited border crossing with the United

States. Agreement between them is extremely difficult, as some passages are very profitable (70 percent of the drugs that enter the United States go through Juàrez), and it is therefore hard to divide the market equally. In contrast, in El Salvador, the two most important gangs, Mara Salvatrucha and Barrio 18, managed to sign a truce – temporarily – in 2012, after years of feuds and murders (with about 50,000 people killed in the 1990s), reducing the number of deaths by an average of 15 a day to 5.[1]

Competition and collusion may be favored by endogenous factors, arising from within the criminal system, or exogenous, arising from outside, law enforcement action, for example. In the cases of Mexico (competition) and El Salvador (collusion), external factors were prevalent, with the role of the police – whether intentionally or unintentionally – decisive. Paradoxically, in Mexico, the more law enforcement agencies obtained results by limiting the number of accesses to the United States, the more the violent competition between criminal organizations increased in order to take control of the remaining channels.[2] In addition, the extremely ragged and complex structure of law enforcement agencies, from the federal level to the local level, prevented the effective coordination and unity of action. In the case of the Salvadorian gangs, on the other hand, the government played a role (flirting with the limits of legality) in facilitating the cease-fire, "softening" the prison conditions of gang leaders and moving them from top-security prisons to facilities where they could communicate with their members, so that they could work out a possible way to form a truce with the rival gang. Endogenous factors, too – those generated within the criminal system itself – influence and determine situations of collusion rather than of competition; each solution is influenced by both types of factor, but the main factor is still identifiable.

In the case of the Italian mafias, we will see how, for some, an endogenous strategy, built through the establishment of higher-level bodies of coordination, is particularly important in controlling conflict.

---

[1] The truce was signed thanks to the support of politicians and police. In 2016, however, the government arrested many of the truce mediators, including top officials in the previous government, with requests for the impeachment and suspension of immunity of MPs and ministers who were accomplices to the negotiation. The accusation was that the truce was used by the gangs to regroup and increase their illegal trafficking (A. Arce, "El Salvador throws out gang truce and officials who put it in place", *The New York Times*, May 21, 2016). The cost for Salvadorans of extortion and criminal activities of gangs is about 3 percent of GDP for a total, including the amount households spend on extra security and the lost income of people deterred from working, of nearly 16 percent of GDP (Source: Central Bank of Salvador and UN Development Programme; "The gangs that cost 16% of GDP", *The Economist*, May 21, 2016, 29–31).

[2] Reuter (2009) shows how action aimed at fighting drug trafficking can generate violence by creating instability among the participants.

One major difference in the use of violence is very clear: homicides involving high-profile figures. In some mafias this is strictly prohibited and very rarely occurs (the American Cosa Nostra, the Yakuza), while in others, especially certain Italian mafias, it has been a characteristic feature of the use of criminal violence.

The Mexican cartels, for example, have made, and continue to make, use of violence against high-profile figures, even though they try to avoid using violence against U.S. military or police, in order to prevent significant retaliation. As mentioned in Section 2.8, in 2011 a serious violation of this unwritten rule was committed, with the killing of Jaime Zapata, a special agent of the U.S. Immigration and Customs Enforcement. The devastating consequences for the life of the cartel clearly outweighed any benefits deriving from the elimination of the threat posed by Zapata's activity.

In gangs, using violence plays a significant role from the initiation, which marks the entrance into these organizations, onward. The use of violence conveys a message to both gang members and nonmembers: violence is a constituent part of gang life and the members are unafraid to use and to undergo it (Padilla 1992). Violence, moreover, increases solidarity between members of the organization, reinforcing the boundaries between those who belong and those who do not. Some gang studies have highlighted the relationship between the level of organization of a gang and the use of violence, particularly homicide. Examining gang homicides during their peak in the mid-1990s in St. Louis, a city with high homicide rates and large gang problems, Decker and Curry found that

well-organized gangs (e.g., groups that function in corporate-like fashion) will engage in relatively few acts of homicide against their own members, preserving group solidarity and cohesion. For such groups, cohesion, solidarity, and leadership mitigate against internecine violence. Correspondingly, gangs with low levels of internal organization are expected to experience higher levels of intra-gang homicide. It is likely that the inability of these groups to control the behavior of their members may reflect a lower level of organization and control. (Decker and Curry 2002, 344)

In the Italian mafias, different organizational structures affect both conflict, in terms of magnitude and frequency, and homicides. Clan-based mafias, characterized by competition between clans, present significantly greater presence of conflict with respect to clan-based federation mafias, characterized by collusion between clans. The different organizational structures affect their capacity to contain internal conflicts, strategize, and react to external threats, and clan-based federation structures are better able to contain violence and conflict. Available historical accounts support this idea. Table 4.1 reports the major conflicts that have occurred in the three Italian mafia organizations since the 1960s, distinguishing between interclan conflicts and intraclan conflicts.

The former include (a) *mafia wars*, which involve all the criminal groups in a bitter struggle between two opposing sides; and (b) *feuds*, which involve two clans in conflict with each other for the control of a specific territory, but do not extend to include other clans and other territories. Intraclan conflicts, on the other hand, are violent *internal conflicts* that may, in certain cases, lead to (c) *division*. The Sicilian Cosa Nostra has had three mafia wars (in 1962, 1981, and 1991) and very few other instances of conflict. The Camorra, in contrast, has had only one mafia war, but an extremely violent one (in 1979, with about 1,500 deaths). It has, however, had numerous instances of feuds between clans, internal conflicts, and divisions. The 'Ndrangheta has had two mafia wars (1974 and 1985), and a number of clan feuds, though fewer than the Camorra, and practically no divisions.

4.2   Collusion or Competition? Italian Mafia Murders and Conflict Resolution

Analyzing the use of violence, particularly homicides, in the three Italian mafias, there emerge obvious differences in the homicide rate – significantly higher in some – and in the kind of homicide: whether they mainly concern organization members or figures who can threaten their existence (judges, journalists, etc.). While many observers relate these different outcomes to different strategic choices, it is argued here that they are due to variations in organizational order – that these differences, in other words, are due to different ways of organizing cooperation among the various criminal groups, and to the different organizational orders adopted.

As we have already seen, one form of structure is a *clan-based federation* characterized by collusion between the clans, with the presence of higher-level bodies of coordination able to define unitary, overall organization strategies and to limit conflicts and the use of violence. A second form of structure is the *clan-based* model, characterized by competition between clans, especially if they operate in the same territories, without higher-level bodies of coordination and therefore unable to define unitary strategies or to limit the use of violence. Unlike the clan-based model, the clan-based federation is characterized by the presence of a leadership able to speak on behalf of the organization.

Table 4.1 *Types of conflict in three Italian mafia organizations (a selection of the most relevant)*

Type of Conflict		Sicilian Cosa Nostra	Camorra	'Ndrangheta
Interclan	Mafia wars	1962–9: Barbera Torretta vs. Greco et al. 1981–3: Bontade, Inzerillo, Badalamenti, Buscetta, vs. the Corleonesi (Leggio, Provenzano, Riina, Bagarella) 1991–2: the Corleonesi war	1979–83: NCO (Cutolo) and the Nuova Famiglia (18 clans: Bardellino, Nuvoletta, Zaza, et al.)	1974–6: Cataldo, Piromalli, De Stefano, Mazzaferro, Mammoliti clans 1985–91: De Stefano, Libri, Tegano, Barreca, Paglianiti, Zito clans vs. Imerti, Condello, Serraino, Fontana, Saraceno, and Rosmini clans
	Feuds	1962–3: Barbera vs. Greco 1987–91: the Partanna feud in Trapani (Ingoglia vs. Accardo)	1984–8: Bardellino, Alfieri vs. Nuvoletta, Gionta 1998–9: the Secondigliano Alliance (Contini, Licciardi, and Mallardo) vs. the clan alliance (Misso, Mazzarella, Giuliano, and Sarno); Rinaldi vs. Mazzarella; Misso, Pirozzi vs. Tolomelli, Vastarella, Mariano, Di Biasi, Giuliano, and Misso clans 2012: Abete, Abbinante, Notturno clans vs. Mennetta, Magnetti, Petriccini clans	e.g., Palamara vs. Mollica; the S. Luca feud: Nirta and Strangio clans, vs. Pelle and Vottari clans
Intraclan	Divisions		2004–5: the Scampia feud: the Di Lauro clan vs. the "Separatists" or the "Spanish" (former Di Lauro clan); 2006: the Sarno clan; the Misso clan; the Mariano clan in Naples; the Bidognetti clan, with the separation of the Setola group	

204

These are, then, two different organizational structures that give rise to different responses and strategic actions.[3] Without necessarily sharing a deterministic idea of social and organizational structures, it is clear that the range of possible strategies is limited by the structure of an organization. Without proper structure, a strategy could not be realized. Therefore, strategies that involve the elimination of high-profile people, due to the complexity required to perform the action, and to contain the repression that results as a consequence, are in some way conceivable and achievable mainly by organizational systems characterized by a *clan-based federation* model, with collusion prevalent between clans. Of course, organizational structures are artifacts; they are not born and do not modify themselves naturally – they derive from specific and conscious choices of strategy.

4.2.1 Ordinary Murders

The different organizational orders have consequences for mafia behavior, namely, with respect to their capacity to govern conflict and contain violence. From this, the following proposition can be derived:

> *Proposition 1* – There exists a correlation in Italian mafias between organizational order (*clan-based federation* vs. *clan-based*) and the frequency of conflict and violence: the clan-based federation order, due to the presence of higher-level bodies of coordination, should lead to fewer conflicts and homicides.[4]

---

[3] The concept of structure is closely linked to that of strategy, in the sense of the determination of the fundamental goals and long-term goals of an enterprise, the definition of the criteria for action, and how to allocate the resources necessary to achieve the objectives (Chandler 1962). On the strategy–structure relationship there are three major characterizations: (1) *structure follows strategy*: structure is determined by strategic decisions; thus organizational form follows strategy of development (Chandler 1962) as its implementation tool, and organizational design is modeled according to the strategies; (2) *strategy follows structure*: the specific organizational structure influences strategic decisions, tending to condition and preselect them (Normann 1977; Hall and Saias 1980); (3) *strategy and structure coevolve*: due to accentuated environmental turbulence and the growth of competitive intensity; the strategy–structure relationship is configured more as a process of interaction and circularity between the different phases (Ansoff 1984) than as a rational design in one direction (from strategy to structure) or the other (from structure to strategy).

[4] Data regarding homicides carried out by the three Italian mafia organizations began to be recorded by police forces and ISTAT (the Italian Institute of Statistics) in 1983. Only since 1982, in fact, has the legislature provided a definition of the concept of "mafia," with the approval of a new article in the Criminal Code (416 bis), which identifies a new type of crime: criminal association with the mafia. For this reason, data relating to homicides prior to 1982 are not always reliable, because mafia homicides were not clearly differentiated from other kinds of homicide.

A problem common to both clan-based and clan-based federation organizations is conflict control and the use of violence – which is an instrument, a resource (Gambetta 1993), and not the objective, of these organizations. Violence is often used by mobsters to establish their reputation in their groups and in the area. In Triads, for example, "violence is used to build up and maintain a Triad's reputation as a credible protector. Since Triads have established their reputation for violence, some people are able to use this 'trademark' to make profits" (Chu 2000, 39). As an instrument, this cannot be eliminated, but must be managed and contained in order to prevent (a) destructive conflict throughout the whole organization and (b) greater repressive action from law enforcement agencies following the escalation of violence. As we will see, the way conflict control and violence are managed (both within and outside the organization) differs between the two organizational orders, in both quantitative (the number of crimes) and qualitative terms (the types of homicides), and this depends on the presence, or lack thereof, of higher-level bodies of coordination. Following a similar line of argument, Leeson and Rogers (2012) argue that criminal organizations establish collusive interfirm institutions designed to internalize the externalities of violent criminal activity and, in so doing, increase the criminal profits of participating mafia families.

The control pyramid that characterizes all basic units of the mafias (*family*, *clan*, *'ndrina*, *ikka*, etc.) makes it possible not only to manage and govern the organization, but also to manage and resolve intraorganizational conflict, which, if not dealt with in time, could undermine the organization's effectiveness. For example, as indeed also happens in legal firms, those in charge of suborganizational units (*captain*, *head of ten*, etc.) might be tempted to pursue subgoals of their own unit, in terms of resources and prestige, even at the expense of the collective interest of the organization. The task of those who run the organization is to minimize these events, reducing the possibility of violent conflict. However, the intraorganizational hierarchy does not guarantee effectiveness in resolving interorganizational conflict between clans. That is why specific organizational units developed by some mafias are required: the higher-level bodies of coordination.

Mafia groups that are based on a *clan-based federation order*, thanks to the presence of higher-level bodies of coordination, should, in general, have greater capacity to speak with a single voice, to make collectively binding decisions, and to strategize, compared to mafia groups that present a *clan-based order*. This should increase their capacity to govern conflicts and contain violence, and to defend themselves better from external enemies. Paradoxically, the monopolistic tendency of organized crime may bring about positive externalities compared to disorganized crime, because the monopoly over criminality guarantees greater control over violence (Buchanan 1980). Paraphrasing Adam Smith, "It is not from the public-spiritedness of the leader of the Cosa Nostra that we should expect to get a reduction in the crime rate, but from their regard for their own self-interest" (Buchanan 1980, 132). All organizations, both legal and illegal, try to maximize their profits in the environments in which they operate. Mafias accomplish this goal by providing illegal goods and services as well as operating in legal markets through illegal activities.

These considerations apply both to conflict within the mafia organization and to the use of violence toward the general population. The constitution of higher-level bodies of coordination not only makes it possible to increase power *within* the organization (Ocasio 2005), settling disputes and containing internal conflict (feuds between clans and attempts to seize the position of leadership within a *family*); it also makes it possible to increase the power *of* the organization (Mizruchi and Yoo 2005), exercised with regard to the external environment and in relation to other organizations. A clan-based federation mafia organization will have a strong influence on its territory and will not need to use violence to control the local population.

The formation of higher-level bodies of coordination makes it possible to control violence. Boulding (1964) affirmed that one of the main roles of hierarchy is to establish a mechanism for dealing with disputes that cannot be resolved at lower levels, and whose resolution is required for the organization to act. In mafia organizations, the control of internal conflict, violence, and homicides should depend, therefore, on the presence, or lack thereof, of higher-level organizational structures. The greater the intimidating force and authority of a mafia, the less need there is to resort to violence. As magistrate Giovanni Falcone stated:

The more the organization is centralized and clandestine, the greater the threat it poses, because it has the means to effectively control the market and maintain order in its territory, with only an extremely brief period between a decision being taken and the ensuing action. It's a different kettle of fish when you're dealing with a fragmented organization with a number of centers of power. (Falcone and Padovani 1992, 100)

My first proposition is that the type of organizational order, clan-based federation, as in the case of the Sicilian Cosa Nostra and the 'Ndrangheta, or clan-based, as in the case of the Camorra, impacts upon the nature and frequency of homicides. Strong evidence in this direction comes from Figure 4.1, reporting the total number of homicides by mafia

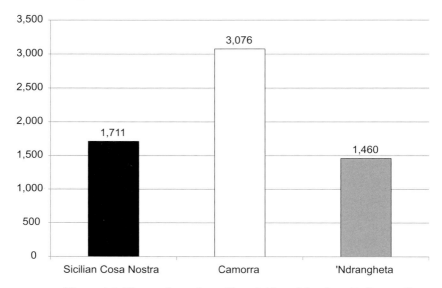

Figure 4.1 The total number of homicides of the three Italian mafias, 1983–2016
(Elaboration of data sourced from: DIA; Ministry of Interior; ISTAT, Italian Institute of Statistics)

organizations. In the period 1983–2016, the Camorra killed a total of 3,076 people,[5] while the death toll for the Sicilian Cosa Nostra was 1,711, and for the 'Ndrangheta 1,460. Of all the mafia-related assassinations (6,247) that have occurred in Italy since the 1980s, almost 50 percent were carried out in Camorra territory, while the remaining half were split between the Sicilian Cosa Nostra (27%) and the 'Ndrangheta (23%).[6]

---

[5] It is important to point that the highest number of murders by Camorra clans were committed by clans with a low-level organizational structure (such as gangs and alliances), while the more highly structured clans have made a more economical use of violence. For example, the Casalesi federation committed a single murder between 2010 and 2015 (DNA, *Direzione Nazionale Antimafia*/National Anti-Mafia Directorate, 2016, *Relazione annuale sulle attività svolte dal Procuratore nazionale e dalla Direzione nazionale antimafia e antiterrorismo*, 80). However, when the more formalized structures come into conflict, the power unleashed is greater, and consequently the number of deaths is high, such as during the climb to the top of the Camorra by Cutolo or during conflicts within the Casalesi federation itself.

[6] The recording of crimes reported by law enforcement agencies in Italy to judicial authority began in 1955, but the classification of the crimes (which drew on the Penal Code for titles and headings) did not make it possible to single out the type of murder.

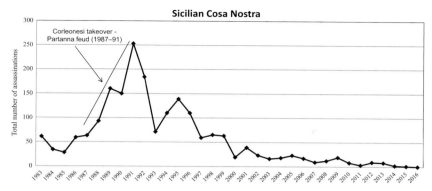

Figure 4.2 Sicilian Cosa Nostra homicides, 1983–2016
(Elaboration of data sourced from: DIA; Ministry of Interior; ISTAT)

The analysis of the data for each mafia organization over time provides additional insights in line with my hypothesis. Figure 4.2 shows the trend for the total number of assassinations by the Sicilian Cosa Nostra. On average, the number of deaths per year is 50. There is a peak in killings in the early 1990s, explained by two main events: first, the internal war within the Sicilian Cosa Nostra, due to the attempt of one group, the Corleonesi, to take over control of the organization, eliminating their adversaries, as in the violent feud in Partanna (Trapani), which lasted from 1987 to 1991; second, the Supreme Court's confirmation in 1992 of the sentence of the Maxiprocesso (Great trial), which condemned many Sicilian Cosa Nostra bosses to life imprisonment, creating a series of power vacuums. This peak was followed by a steady decline, which was also due to severe repressive measures by the law enforcement agencies, culminating in the arrest of Totò Riina, boss of the Corleonesi.

Many statements by the Sicilian Cosa Nostra leaders highlight the importance of avoiding internal conflicts, in that they are opposed to the "common good," the collective interests of the organization. It emerges, for example, in some statements by important bosses of the Sicilian Cosa Nostra such as Bernardo Provenzano (in 2001) and Matteo Messina Denaro (in 2004), who intervened to quell some internal conflicts between clans, which if not managed in time, could also have led to

From 1983 to the present day (1983–2003 survey model 165 Istat/Ministry of Interior, since 2004 Information System of the Ministry SDI) there appears instead the information "murders for reasons of mafia, Camorra and 'Ndrangheta." It is therefore possible to make use of the geographical location (available at a provincial level) to attribute the reported homicides to the various organizations.

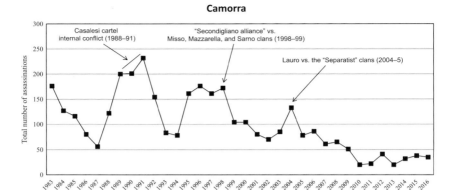

Figure 4.3 Camorra homicides, 1983–2016
(Elaboration of data sourced from: DIA; Ministry of Interior; ISTAT)

violent wars. The so-called common good, "good for all of us ... and our cause" (Pignatone and Prestipino 2013, 220), is more important, in the words of the bosses, than the violent resolution of the conflicts, precisely because of the negative consequences this could bring with it.

In contrast, in the case of the Camorra, the absence of higher-level bodies of coordination, the fragmentary nature of the organization's clans, and the fluidity of alliances made it impossible for the conflicts to be negotiated and managed in a nonviolent manner within the organization. The principal enemy of a Camorra clan always remains the rival territorial clan, as shown by the high rate of homicides, 92 per year. The trend shows several peaks concomitant with various conflicts (Figure 4.3).

In recent years, in different parts of the city of Naples and especially in the municipalities of the province, a new phenomenon involving the use of violence has become popular, called the *stese* (knockdowns). Groups of at least four people, two per motorcycle, armed with pistols and machine guns, burst into opposing clan territory, guns blazing against buildings, shops, and other random targets, even in broad daylight, causing panic among residents, and, very often, innocent victims – a kind of *camorrista* terrorism. The perpetrators hired by the clan to carry out such actions are often minors, referred to as the "paranza babies" – in other words, a gun squad composed of youngsters barely older than children.[7]

---

[7] Dugato et al. (2017) apply the Risk Terrain Modeling approach to analyze and forecast the Camorra homicides in Naples. The approach is based on the identification and evaluation of the underlying risk factors able to affect the likelihood of a homicide. Their findings demonstrate that past homicides, drug dealing, confiscated assets, and

Finally, until the 'Ndrangheta introduced higher-level bodies of coordination, a command structure capable of controlling disputes, there was a great deal of internal conflict, with numerous feuds and deaths. In 1985, the second war began between 'Ndrangheta clans, a war triggered by attempts to control contracts and tenders and by one clan's desire for territorial expansion.[8] This conflict extended further, involving other clans and yielding around 700 deaths among members. Although the construction of HLBC had begun decades before (as we have seen in Figure 3.6, in the 1930s at least; Dickie 2012; Truzzolillo 2013), it was only in 1990–1 that such structures achieved effective institutionalization in their current form. Previous structures and coordination mechanisms had proved unsatisfactory and not capable of avoiding bloody feuds.

The power and autonomy of each individual *'ndrina* remained unaltered, but this superordinate structure made decisions regarding the most important matters involving the entire organization – in particular, with regard to control of violence. The Province, stated collaborator with justice Giacomo Lauro,

established the principle that if disputes arise, of any kind and for whatever reason, between the different *locali*, there would be no recourse to arms before the disputes had come before the Commission for evaluation. This explains why, as of September 1991, all the wars in the province of Reggio Calabria ended. The 'Ndrangheta had managed to find a unifying moment, a centralization of the power of command that was able to function and to enforce the rules and the decisions taken. (in Ciconte 1996, 151)

The special nature of this organism lay in the balance between centralization and autonomy: on the one hand, the controlling structure forced all the *'ndrine* to respect its decisions; on the other, they were allowed total autonomy with regard to the rest of their activities. This temporary solution then became a permanent one, beginning a process of progressive verticalization and centralization in the 'Ndrangheta, with the constitution of the provincial Cupola, and in particular with regard to centralization relating to the most crucial and delicate decisions.[9] The

---

rivalries among groups made it possible to predict up to 85 percent of 2012 mafia homicides. They also identify city areas at highest risk. See also Brancaccio 2009.

[8] The cause of the conflict was economic in nature, relating to the interest of the various clans in the public contracts concerning Villa San Giovanni (Calabria), in view of the proposed construction of the bridge that would connect Calabria with Sicily.

[9] DIA, *Direzione Investigativa Antimafia*/Anti-Mafia Investigative Directorate, Ministero dell'Interno/ Ministry of Interior 2010b, *Attività svolta e risultati conseguiti (Activities and final findings)*, (a: first semester; b: second semester), http://direzioneinvestigativaantimafia.interno.gov.it.

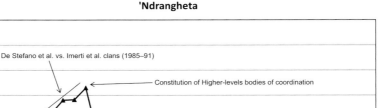

Figure 4.4 'Ndrangheta homicides, 1983–2016
(Elaboration of data sourced from: DIA; Ministry of Interior; ISTAT)

provincial level also became superordinate with respect to the structures operating outside Calabria. Thus, the process of centralization and the creation of superordinate bodies of coordination and conflict resolution had their origin in a violent clan war within the 'Ndrangheta.

A model of coordinated organization, with stable HLBC and specific rules applicable to the entire organization, is not, of course, as previously mentioned, even remotely similar to the model of a multinational company, with a CEO who gives orders and organizational units that carry them out. The closest model is always that of the "political arena," with frequent negotiations between peer groups to reach shared decisions.

Thanks to this new organizational structure, the number of 'Ndrangheta feuds and homicides (Figure 4.4) dropped sharply.

Moreover, the leading body decided to do away with kidnappings, which generated a low level of income compared with the severe measures of repression they triggered from the state. The existence of a guiding structure taking responsibility for issuing and ratifying decisions has been confirmed by recent law enforcement agencies' inquiries.[10] It should be specified that the unitary character of the 'Ndrangheta cannot in any way be considered belied

by the fact that feuds may periodically arise between the various gangs operating in a certain geographical area: on the one hand, because in any complex organization, and even more so in those that are criminal in nature (one only

[10] DNA 2011, *Relazione annuale sulle attività svolte dal Procuratore nazionale e dalla Direzione nazionale antimafia e antiterrorismo*, 109.

has to think of the events of the Sicilian Cosa Nostra, marked by severe "turbulence" and by the numerous homicides even during the years of the *pax mafia* organized by Bernardo Provenzano), there are pathological stages in which internal conflict and serious crimes can occur; and on the other because it is still a matter of incidents which, when they occurred ... did not call into question the overall equilibrium in the general terms that have been described so far.[11]

While rates of homicides are the most compelling indicator of the capacity of clan-based federation orders to contain violence, there are other considerations that strengthen the argument advanced in Proposition 1. Namely, the average age of the Sicilian Cosa Nostra's family heads is in general higher with respect to that of the Camorra (Gambetta 1993). This is an indicator of greater organizational stability in the Sicilian mafia and suggests, according to Gambetta, that the Sicilian Cosa Nostra bosses are older because their positions of power are acquired through a more organized selection process – one that discourages younger members from challenging the internal hierarchy. The main route for professional promotion in the Sicilian Cosa Nostra therefore passes through internal channels, not through direct competition in the market, with the selection of top leaders taking place largely according to a hierarchical logic and not through the violence of the marketplace. The presence of superordinate bodies not only reduces conflict *between* clans, or families, but also *within* the individual clans themselves, discouraging in-family disputes and attempts by the dissatisfied or impatient to seize power. As one Sicilian Cosa Nostra informant, Vincenzo Marsala, states:

When disputes of various kinds between members come to the attention of the representative, if the latter cannot settle the matter himself, he turns to the district boss, who intervenes to find an agreement between the members and reach a decision regarding the particular problem. When the matter is a serious one that involves the entire family territory, the representative seeks the help of the district boss and the latter intervenes through the Provincial Commission of Palermo. (OSPA Stajano 2010, 102)

In the case of the 'Ndrangheta, the family is a criminal organization based on blood ties and this relationship automatically dictates the chain of power, with a rigid succession through the direct male line. This is an important element of stability in the organization, given that matters relating to succession render mafia organizations vulnerable to conflict, fostering feuds, division, and internal wars. In the case of the 'Ndrangheta, the issue is resolved through the principle of the family law of dynastic male succession.

---

[11] Tribunale di Reggio Calabria, DDA 2010, *Operazione Crimine*, vol. I, 80.

Higher levels of coordination come about for various reasons. Regarding the 'Ndrangheta, such levels were introduced to control conflict *between* clans and violent feuds, especially in the 1985–91 period. Where the Sicilian Cosa Nostra is concerned, however, according to the informant Tommaso Buscetta, the Commission was originally created in order to settle conflict *within* clans, and only thereafter to discipline the activities and possible disputes *between* families. The Commission was an arena, states the informant Antonino Calderone (Arlacchi 1993, 126 and thereafter), where it was possible to resolve such important matters as homicides or whom to support at political elections, and to decide punishment for those who made mistakes and violated the rules. For example, if a Sicilian Cosa Nostra family head disappeared for some reason, this would create a dangerous power vacuum that might generate conflict. The superordinate bodies would therefore intervene to make a decision regarding succession, bestowing stability upon the system. In the case of the Camorra, however, the disappearance of a clan boss would create a sense of opportunity both within the clan itself (with various members claiming power) and in neighboring clans. This behavior is not regulated by any superordinate force and can therefore break out into particularly violent conflicts, as shown in Figure 4.2. For all these reasons, clan-based federation mafia organizations, due to the creation of higher-level bodies of coordination, were overall more capable of containing conflict and homicides than the Camorra, as the history of the three organizations demonstrates.[12]

4.2.2   High-Profile Assassinations

As a response to repressive actions by law enforcement agencies, mafias resort sometimes to the killing of people in an institution or in the public sphere (magistrates, members of the police force, politicians, trade unionists, priests, newspaper reporters) whose activity in some way threatens the legitimacy and interests of the mafia organization. Different from the "ordinary" killings discussed in Proposition 1, these *high-profile assassinations* are more likely to be conducted by organizations with a clan-based federation order. In fact, the decision to eliminate such

---

[12] Studying homicides committed by Italian mafias, Moro et al. (2016) show that there is a clear link between the structure of the political markets and the severity of violence. In particular, the authors argue that the fragmentation of the political market is negatively associated with the strategy of criminal groups to exploit violence. By contrast, single-party dominance and bipartisanship seem to lead to an increase in homicides, since these organizations have few opportunities to access the political arena.

relevant targets[13] requires considerable strategic and operational capacity to be carried out, and organizational resilience to manage the consequences of the inevitable retaliation from the law enforcement agencies. The presence of higher-level bodies of coordination provides mafia organizations with the ability to strategize, identify external enemies, and coordinate action in response to external threats. This brings me to my second proposition:

> *Proposition 2* - The presence of higher-level bodies of coordination in the clan-based federation order increases the capacity to respond to the threat of law enforcement agencies, resulting in a greater number of high-profile assassinations involving figures from institutions, politics, and the public sphere.[14]

Higher levels of coordination have been created to settle disputes and violent conflicts. However, in addition to conflict containment, the presence of HLBC in mafia organizations makes it possible to create organizational strategies and to identify and eliminate external enemies of the organization. This ability becomes significant when, for example, the state increases repressive measures in relation to mafia organizations. We therefore expect that, in the case of intense investigative activity by law enforcement agencies or public attack by members of the civil society (e.g., politicians, priests, newspaper reporters), clan-based federation mafia organizations will commit more high-profile homicides.

In theory, an alternative argument might be advanced: namely, that a well-coordinated vertical structure could represent a better partner for politicians and therefore foster collusion, thus *reducing* high-profile assassinations. However, this alternative hypothesis relies on the assumption that both actors involved (i.e., mafia organizations and the state) are unified actors, which act in a coherent and coordinated manner. While the Sicilian Cosa Nostra (after 1957 and 1975) and the 'Ndrangheta (after 1991) were, in general, unified organizations, this has never been the case for the state (Lupo 2011a; Dickie 2012). At any point in time,

---

[13] Excluded from this category are those who, though politicians or pertaining to the sphere of institutions, have been collaborators with, or associated with, a mafia organization. There are other types of homicide and criminal action that, due to their brutality, may also trigger state retaliation on a level similar to that caused by high-profile assassinations, such as bombs, mass murders, killings of children or women.

[14] *Data regarding high-profile assassinations.* Integrating different sources, from historical and official reports to websites, I have compiled an original dataset of high-profile assassinations, which goes back to the second half of the nineteenth century. For each murder, I controlled across multiple sources to verify its nature, ensuring that the victim was a recognized mafia enemy.

political and institutional actors (the state, magistrates, politicians, political parties, law enforcement agencies, etc.) acted in different ways, with some that, through fear or interest, preferred to collude with mafia organizations, and others that chose to fight the mafia (e.g., figures such as the politician and trade unionist Pio La Torre, General Carlo Alberto Dalla Chiesa, magistrates Giovanni Falcone and Paolo Borsellino). As a consequence, sometimes mafias made agreements with the former and killed the latter. To sum up, the fact that the state has always presented itself as a fragmented actor makes this alternative framework unlikely to apply to the Italian case.

The Sicilian Cosa Nostra and the Camorra have been targeted by law enforcement agencies and other institutions for a long time, while the 'Ndrangheta has only been an object of attention in fairly recent years. Taking the value of the assets seized and confiscated from a mafia as an indicator, we can see that, in the 1992–2011 period, assets worth about 7.4 billion euros were confiscated from the Sicilian Cosa Nostra, assets worth 4.8 billion euros were taken from the Camorra, while assets worth only 1.2 billion euros were seized from the 'Ndrangheta.[15] The magistrate Giovanni Falcone (Falcone and Padovani 1992), mentioned earlier, believed that the 'Ndrangheta, and to a certain extent the Camorra, given their clan-based organizational model, were less dangerous than the Sicilian Cosa Nostra. The 'Ndrangheta was really recognized as a dangerous mafia organization starting from around the year 2000 – the most dangerous, indeed.[16] Only in 2010 was the 'Ndrangheta included in the Italian antimafia laws. Following this growing attention from law enforcement agencies, the 'Ndrangheta recently initiated a reaction with a series of attacks on, and intimidatory acts toward, illustrious people.[17]

My hypothesis is that the Sicilian Cosa Nostra was able, in particular from 1975 on, with the constitution of the regional level, the *Cupola* – precisely because of its organizational model with higher-levels bodies of coordination – not only to reduce and contain conflict (as we have already seen) but also to identify its true adversaries in the state outside its organization, or, rather, in that part of the state or civil society that refuses to cooperate with it (magistrates, politicians, public administrators, etc.). Figure 4.5 reports the number of high-profile assassinations

[15] DIA, *Direzione Investigativa Antimafia*/Anti-Mafia Investigative Directorate, Ministero dell'Interno/ Ministry of Interior, 2012, *Attività svolta e risultati conseguiti (Activities and final findings)*, http://direzioneinvestigativaantimafia.interno.gov.it

[16] DNA 2010; 2011, *Relazione annuale sulle attività svolte dal Procuratore nazionale e dalla Direzione nazionale antimafia e antiterrorismo.*

[17] DNA 2010, *Relazione annuale sulle attività svolte dal Procuratore nazionale e dalla Direzione nazionale antimafia e antiterrorismo*, 89.

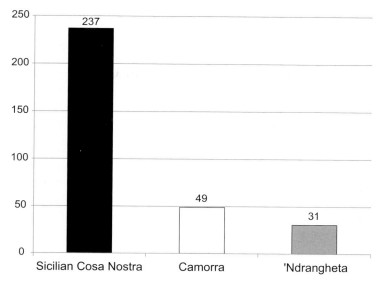

Figure 4.5 High-profile assassinations committed by three Italian mafia organizations, 1861–2016
(Elaboration of data sourced from: DIA; Ministry of Interior; ISTAT)

carried out by the three organizations (1861–2016). In Table 4.2, the same information is presented, distinguishing among institutional, political, and public sphere killings. The Sicilian Cosa Nostra is the organization that has killed most high-profile people by far (237), the first dating back to the second half of the nineteenth century. The Camorra, in contrast to the Sicilian Cosa Nostra, has carried out a significantly smaller number of high-profile assassinations (49). In addition, more than half of them (33 out of 49) occurred in the eight years from 1975 to 1983, in which the Camorra was organized in a clan-based federation order. The fragmentary nature of the Camorra organization hinders the elaboration of unified strategies and makes it difficult to identify the entire criminal organization's common enemies on the outside.[18] Moreover, the Sicilian Cosa Nostra stands out as having killed a

---

[18] Only the Casalesi cartel, composed of ten clans, is able to think in these terms. The informant Salvatore Venosa has stated that the Casalesi bosses Giuseppe Setola and Nicola Schiavone were planning the murder of high-profile people, such as magistrates and members of law enforcement agencies. The construction of a cartel with a leading

Table 4.2 *High-profile assassinations committed by three Italian mafia organizations, 1861–2016*

		Sicilian Cosa Nostra	Camorra	'Ndrangheta
	Magistrates and professionals in the legal world	15	0	3
Institutions	Law enforcement agencies	122	32	14
	Officials pertaining to institutions	4	1	1
Political parties, social movements	Politicians (activists and elected)	47	11	11
Trade unionists	Trade unionists	35	3	0
Public sphere	Journalists	8	1	1
	Priests	6	1	1
	Total	**237**	**49**	**31**

Elaboration of data sourced from: DIA; Ministry of Interior; ISTAT

high number of magistrates, certainly the targets with greatest media impact, and the most costly in terms of state retaliation.

Finally, the 'Ndrangheta, which until 2007–8 was not the focus of attention of the repressive action of the state,[19] has limited itself to just 31 murders.

Further support for Proposition 2 comes from the analysis of the Sicilian Cosa Nostra's high-profile assassinations over time. In the years before the creation of the Cupola (1965–75), the Sicilian Cosa Nostra killed "only" 10 prominent individuals, while in the following years (1976–86) the death toll of high-profile victims reached 56, a 560 percent increase. Moreover, while only 1 magistrate was killed in the decade preceding 1975, 6 were killed in the following ten years. The same considerations hold if we look at larger time windows: focusing on the 1957–75 window, which corresponds to the period in which the Sicilian Cosa Nostra had a

---

group in command constitutes an attempt to control internal conflict and violence and makes it possible to identify external enemies who could cause problems for the organization. Up until today, this is a possibility limited to the Casalesi clan ("Gomorra. Il progetto stragista. Colpire magistrati e carabinieri," *la Repubblica*, July 31, 2012).

[19] DNA 2010, *Relazione annuale sulle attività svolte dal Procuratore nazionale e dalla Direzione nazionale antimafia e antiterrorismo*, 89.

provincial structure of coordination, the overall number of high-profile killings is 25, with only 1 magistrate among the victims. In the eighteen years after 1975, however, there were 82 high-profile assassinations, including 13 magistrates.

The importance of having higher-level bodies of coordination to carry out such notable killings has been repeatedly acknowledged. No murder of a significant person could be carried out without being authorized from the highest level. The informant Leonardo Messina has said:

If a normal person has to be killed, or if normal interests are involved, it's enough for the town bosses to communicate this to the local *mandamento*. But if a journalist or magistrate has to be murdered, orders have to come from the *Region*. ... Policemen, too, cannot be killed without orders from the *Region*. To kill a "man of honor," you need an order from the *Provincia*. To kill a "head of ten," you need orders from the *Region*.[20]

No high-profile homicide can be carried out, then, without the deliberation and the order of the Commission, and anyone who violates this provision commits a serious violation of the basic rules of the Sicilian Cosa Nostra, with grave consequences within the organization.

The informant Antonino Calderone stated:

If ... an important man has to be hit – a politician or policeman or judge – the decision has to come from above, from the highest level, namely from the Regional Commission ... This is logical. A murder of this kind can cause harm to everyone. True, the killing is done in a given territory, but its consequences will be paid later by everyone. (Arlacchi 1993, 36)

The collaborator with justice of the Sicilian Cosa Nostra Tommaso Buscetta says:

When the Commission decides to commit a homicide, it is the Commission itself that forms the team that will have to carry out the decision; it is entitled to choose the participants in any one of the families without informing the boss. The organization of the crime, then, is exclusive to the Commission and should be unknown by everyone, except, of course, those called to do it. In practice, however, it may happen that a member of the Commission informs his most trusted collaborators of the decision, but this will not minimally affect either the design or fulfillment of the homicide. (OSPA Stajano 2010, 114)

Former Sicilian Cosa Nostra mobster, now collaborator with justice Antonino Giuffré explained how the mafia organization carried out a real kind of opinion poll before moving on to the execution phase of the high-

---

[20] CPA (*Commissione Parlamentare Antimafia*, Italian parliamentary antimafia commission), *Audizione del collaboratore della giustizia Leonardo Messina*, XI Legislatura, December 4, 1992d, 517.

profile murders. It was a sort of "pulse check," not of the criminal world but of those in contact with it (politicians, masons, businessmen) to evaluate their reactions to crimes of this sort: a "preliminary study" in order to understand the degree of "legitimacy" of the murder, to acquire elements that could provide a more rational assessment of the action (Di Matteo and Palazzolo 2015).

In general, the constitution of higher-level bodies of coordination gives the Sicilian Cosa Nostra and the 'Ndrangheta's leadership the right to speak, and act, on behalf of the organization (Zuckerman 2010). This not only enhances their capacity to carry out high-profile assassinations, but also ensures their ability to perform several important organizational functions (see Section 2.10 and Table 2.6): *strategic*, making decisions regarding the interests of the whole organization; *control and organizational*, such as the control of territorial division between the families; *conflict containment*, containing conflict in progress and preventing any that might arise; and *business*, identifying business opportunities that exceed the capacity of an individual family and fostering economies of scale.

4.3   War and Peace in Other Mafias

Mafias, as we have seen, have to manage and make use of violence in a skillful way. In such organizations, the opportunities for conflict abound. Nick Gentile (1963) has shown how, in the American Cosa Nostra, for example, a simple altercation could give rise to a long chain of revenge and conspiracy.

This mafia does not tolerate a "boss of the bosses" and the formation of higher-level bodies of coordination impacts upon the rate of conflict and the use of violence. For example, the Commission in the American Cosa Nostra was not a ruling council, but a tool for containing violence and mediating disputes that would otherwise strongly "disturb" the family affairs. The absence of major conflicts between the various American Cosa Nostra families is an indicator of the organizational rationalization achieved with the formation of the Commission and the consequent reduction in gang wars.

Prior to the formation of HLBC (see Section 3.1.4), conflict among the different families operating in the United States, particularly in New York, was very high. For example, the American Mafia rebellion (1928–31) originated in conflict over money and power (Maas 1968; Critchley 2006; 2009; Dash 2009; Hortis 2014; Raab 2016). It was not a "war," given the, in a certain sense, "low" number of deaths (fewer than 20 in the period 1930–1, compared with an average of 76 per year from

1920 to 1930), but rather a gang fight over issues of power and money. The families were opposed to the dominance of Salvatore D'Aquila, Giuseppe Morello, Joe Masseria, and Salvatore Maranzano, who tried to become the boss of bosses, each one eliminating his predecessor and taking his place. Maranzano, in particular, designed an organizational structure that gave New York City's five families noncompeting jurisdictions, either in territories or in spheres of operation (Gosch and Hammer 2013). The only problem was that he placed himself at the head of the whole system, thus relegating the bosses of the five families to the simple role of captains, since they would be responsible only to Maranzano. The four bosses were killed in just three years, in 1928 (Salvatore D'Aquila), 1930 (Giuseppe Morello), and 1931 (Joe Masseria in April and Salvatore Maranzano in September). To prevent further dangerous and destabilizing conflict, in the fall of 1931 the general assembly of the American Cosa Nostra abolished the title of "boss of bosses." They decided that there would never be a "monarchy," and that nobody would ever again assume the role of boss of bosses: giving this kind of title "to just one, could swell the head of the elected person and induce him to commit unjustifiable atrocities" (Gentile 1963, 119). No boss would ever be able to be a kind of dictator of all the families of the American Cosa Nostra. In place of such a role, a Commission was set up in 1931 composed of the heads of the various families, with a forum to discuss the major issues and to resolve disputes and conflicts. A few years later, the attempt by Albert Anastasia, boss of one of New York's families, to assume greater power and to take on the role of boss of bosses, interfering with the affairs and decisions of individual families, ended with the killing of the aspiring dictator on October 25, 1957 (Hortis 2014).

Unlike the Sicilian Cosa Nostra, the American mafia generally did not target journalists or government officials, or other high-profile people. The first recorded mafia killings of important figures in America happened in Lousiana, on October 16, 1890, when David C. Hennessy, the police chief of New Orleans, was killed by two members of two Sicilian clans in conflict with each other for the control of the laborforce and import of fruit (Repetto 2004; Lupo 2008). Subsequently, in 1909, Joe Petrosino, head of the Italian team against mafia crime of the New York Police Department, was killed in Palermo. In 1933, an FBI agent and two Kansas City detectives were killed while they were trying to arrest a bank robber named Frank Nash, recently escaped from a federal prison in Leavenworth (Kansas). This event, called the "Kansas City Massacre," attracted national public opinion to organized crime and its activities. In response to this growing attention from law enforcement agencies, which could hamper business, the national American Cosa Nostra Commission decided that reporters and policemen would be off-limits (Repetto 2004). Former American Cosa Nostra mobster Tony Accetturo tells how during his initiation ceremony into the New Jersey faction of the Lucchese family of New York, he had been given a list of a number of organizational and behavioral rules, including the policy that police and other law enforcement agents could never be "whacked" – killed, in other words (Raab 2016). In fact, the American mafia's history contains very few incidents involving high-profile murders. There were some rare exceptions, such as that of Carlos Tresca, an Italian-American newspaper editor, who was assassinated in 1943 (though it was never proven that he was killed by *mafiosi*), and Victor Riesel, a journalist, who was blinded by an acid attack in 1956 on gangsters' orders. Another exception is the American labor movement: according to Jacobs (2006, 107–8), there are at least 34 homicides of low-level union officials and union dissidents that can be attributed to labor racketeers. On July 30, 1975, the former president of the International Brotherhood of Teamsters Jimmy Hoffa was killed by the American Cosa Nostra. This was probably the most important high-profile murder ever committed by the organization, even if Hoffa was not a union dissident, or an opponent of the mafia: he had, instead, a career-long history of alliances with organized crime groups.

When compared to other mafias, the Yakuza has always maintained a low rate of homicides, and indeed of particularly violent episodes in general. Given its status as a semilegitimate organization and the muted opposition offered by the state,[21] there has been little need for it to carry out the elimination of high-profile people. According to Hill (2003a) this also depends on the mafia organization's greater degree of maturity, which has led over time to higher organizational stability and consequently fewer internal conflicts: certainly never anything as sanguinary as happened with other mafias, especially the Sicilian Cosa Nostra.[22] Thus, greater organizational stability has led to a reduction in internal violence, less attention from law enforcement agencies, and less need to eliminate judges or civil servants physically. The introduction of the anti-Yakuza law, the Bōtaihō, has further encouraged the Yakuza to search for diplomatic ways to resolve internal conflicts and to reduce certain violent activities, in order to preclude prosecution by law enforcement agencies.

[21] The arrests of Yakuza members are certainly consistent, with up to about 30,000 a year out of a total of 80,000 members in the various Yakuza groups. However, the duration of these arrests is not very long.

[22] The Hachiōji war in Tokyo, which took place in February 1990, was one of the major conflicts in the Yakuza. There were "only" two people killed and a number of revenge shots fired (Hill 2003a, 140).

The Yakuza has demonstrated a high awareness of intraorganizational costs and of the high negative externalities resulting from the use of violence, and homicides in particular, both due to the loss of social visibility and to the increased repression by law enforcement agencies. As Rankin has noted:

In the late 1980s the Yakuza were responsible for 30% of Japan's murders. Today they are responsible for 15%. During the first decade of this century, Yakuza gang members and Yakuza-connected persons were arrested in connection with an average of roughly 170 murders and attempted murders each year. Almost all Yakuza murder victims are civilians: according to the NPA, in the same period only 32 Yakuza were murdered by other Yakuza. These extremely low figures mean that the Yakuza are among the least murderous crime gangs in the world today.[23] (Rankin 2012a)

Since 1972, to manage and resolve conflicts better, the Yakuza in Tokyo have established the Kanto Hatsuka-kai, an association comprising all of the groups in the capital, with the purpose of providing a mechanism for the speedy resolution of conflict and the prevention of misunderstandings. The members of all groups are prohibited to using firearms against each other (Hill 2004, 110).

As Rankin points out,

the Yakuza generally specialize in non-violent forms of coercion. Yakuza land sharks put pressure on tenants by sending them unpleasant objects in the mail or playing music at uncomfortably loud volume outside their buildings. Yakuza enforcers and blackmailers scrawl obscenities on debtors' doors or embarrass them at their workplace. Businesses that refuse to pay protection money may have their premises vandalized: emptying the contents of a septic waste truck through a window is a trademark tactic. (Rankin 2012a)

However, the continuous search for new sources of earnings, partly due to pressure from the police, increases the possible situations of conflict, at the same time reducing space for peaceful resolution. Moreover, the situation of instability increases internal tensions. In 2015 there was a major split within the largest of the Yakuza syndicate, the Yamaguchi-gumi, which gave rise to another syndicate, Yamaguchi-Kobe Gumu. This split originated with 13 groups of members who questioned some decisions made by the supreme and senior boss Shinobu Tsukasa: in particular, a nepotistic attitude in relation to career

---

[23] MOJ 1989: Ministry of Justice, MOJ, Heisei gannen hanzai hakusho – White Paper on Crime 1989; MOJ 2011: MOJ, Heisei 23-nen hanzai hakusho – White Paper on Crime 2011; in Rankin 2002a.

progression, leading him to favor people in whom he had trust rather than in terms of merit, and the intention of moving the clan headquarters to his hometown. These choices were exacerbated by tensions within the Yamaguchi-gumi, due to pressure placed on clan members regarding the payment of membership fees and contributions toward the cost of the headquarters (water and basic necessities) or for gifts for the boss at parties and celebrations. All this further reduced the coffers of the federation clan.

It was a schism that alarmed the police, given that it could lead to conflict and even violence (unusual, as we have seen for the Yakuza), such as that which occurred in 1984, when, following another split inside the group, more than 25 people lost their lives and 70 others were injured as a result of a war between clans.

As for the Triads, studies and research on the use of violence are fairly rare and research into the homicides committed by these organizations has been very limited. Lacking real and effective higher-level bodies of coordination, incidents of internal conflict and clashes between triad gangs have increased (Lo 2010). For example, the largest triad society in Hong Kong, 14K, is relatively disorganized compared to other triad groups. Each subgroup is set up as a separate and independent triad society. With this lack of effective higher-level bodies of coordination, "gang fights among different sub-groups are not uncommon" (Chu 2011, 232). Peter Yam Tat-wing, director of operations of the Hong Kong Police, affirms that triad societies are

a collection of loose-knit groups or gangs who operate independently. They are mainly local area gangs, each active in certain areas and activities. Their disputes sometimes result in fighting and it is not uncommon that gangs within the same triad society often fight with each other over a disputed interest or territory. (Chu 2011, 28)

In one of the few pieces of research on the subject, Lee (2004) conducted a detailed analysis of 95 triad-related homicide cases (124 victims) over ten years, from 1989 to 1998: they were about one in eight (11.9 percent) of all homicide events, involving 13.2 percent of all homicide victims recorded in the ten-year period. Triad homicide victimization averaged 0.206 per 100,000 persons in Hong Kong.[24] The main reasons for these homicides were (399):

---

[24] The homicide rate in the United States was 10.2 per 100,000 persons in 1980, 5.6 homicides per 100,000 in 2002, and 4.7 homicides per 100,000 persons in 2011, the lowest level since 1963 (Smith and Cooper 2013).

- Turf war and status and honor contests among lower-rank triad gang leaders, members, and nontriads (47 cases, 49.5 percent).
- Competition among illegal syndicate entrepreneurs, syndicates, businessmen, and senior triad leaders (20 cases, 21.1 percent).
- Discipline of illegal trade customers (often also triad members, and resulting in status or honor contests), extortion of victims, theft of illegal services or goods (16 cases, 16.8 percent).
- Internal discipline within organized crime among illegal syndicates (7 cases, 7.37 percent), such as cases of dishonesty during transactions.
- Internal discipline within a triad gang as ordered by leaders (5 cases, 5.26 percent).

Lee (2004, 3) shows that more than half of the analyzed murders were not motivated by economic or profit motives (e.g., rational or instrumental), but derived from what Lee referred to as subcultural triad status and reputation/honor contests. The murders were more associated with notions of expressive motives (emotional or nonrational). Violence, then, was primarily status or reputation driven.

In any case, irrespective of the reasons, the Triads are characterized by a very low level of use of homicide (estimated today around one or two homicides a year), in particular if compared with the Italian mafia and especially given the high number of members (between 50,000 and 120,000) and when compared to the population (about 7 million inhabitants). The overall homicide rate in Hong Kong seems to be fairly low, 1.5 per 100,000 inhabitants. Finally, while there were a few assault and wounding cases involving high-profile people, such as politicians and journalists, nothing lethal has taken place in recent years.

5   Mafia Rules

How can criminal organizations that lack legal mechanisms of dispute resolution and are unable to establish binding contracts work efficiently? They establish and enforce organizational rules. Rules are an essential aspect in the life of any organization. Paradoxically, organizational rules are especially important for criminal organizations, such as mafias, for two main reasons. First, mobs cannot rely on law and government to enforce norms and settle disputes (Reuter 1983; Gambetta 1993). Reliance on norms and their enforcement is positively associated with trust (Nee, Opper, and Holm 2018), which in turn plays a major role for a second reason: mobs need to cooperate among themselves in order to achieve their economic interests. They do not live in anarchy; they are subjected to the law of the outlaws. Over time they have developed a set of rules in order to perform different functions: to establish organizational order (e.g., organizational roles and the chain of command), to cooperate, to regulate various issues in organizational life and individual behavior (e.g., mobsters should always show respect to those who can command them), to coordinate intra- and interorganizational relationships, to manage silence and secrecy (e.g., mobsters should introduce themselves to other mobsters in a specific way; they should never ask for the last name; they should not use the telephone), to contain internal conflicts, retaliation, and violence (e.g., it is forbidden to touch the women of other mobsters; mobsters should never resort to violence with other mobsters). These rules are, with rare exceptions, passed on orally. While legitimate organizations can rely on the rule of law to enforce contracts and solve disputes, mafias cannot resort to external authorities. Therefore, they establish organizational rules as a form of private governance in order to address these problems.

Organizational rules are a foundational theme of organization theory (e.g., Weber 1922; Gouldner 1954; March and Simon 1958; Crozier 1964), but have been rarely studied in recent years, with a few exceptions (e.g., March and Olsen 1989; Zhou 1993; March et al. 2000). The latter, however, focused mainly on legitimate organizations, and principally on formal and written rules. Much of the organizational literature based on legitimate business firms and public bureaucracies also applies to mafia organizations. Although they are "outlaw" organizations, they have created an apparatus of rules to deal with the various aspects of organizational life. Studying mafias, therefore, makes it possible to investigate an important topic of organizational theory: the role of rules in guaranteeing stability, adaptation, and longevity. This is particularly important in that while organizational studies have dedicated a great deal of attention to the theme of routines in organizations (see, for example: Cyert and March 1963; Nelson and Winter 1982; Feldman 2000; Feldman and Pentland 2003; Pentland and Feldman 2005; 2008; etc.), less attention has been paid, at least in recent times, to rules.

This chapter unveils the organizational rationality of mafia rules. In general, I argue that mafia rules represent a rational way to regulate behavior, to impose self-constraint, and to create preventive obligations. In sum, they create social order (for a similar argument, see Skarbek 2014 on California prison gangs, and Leeson 2009 and 2011 on pirates). In particular, I show how a set of general rules, often expressed in the form "Do X, do not do Y," serve three vital functions for the self-governance of these criminal organizations.

Even if the context of criminal organizations is radically different from the context of legitimate organizations, mafias use organizational rules for the same reason legitimate organizations do: (1) to ensure organization, coordination, and cooperation among their members and their organizational units. In addition to this function, however, mafias also need rules (2) to settle conflicts and to contain violence that, otherwise, could be destructive for the organization; and (3) to maintain secrecy and conceal information regarding their illegal activities from the outside. Legitimate organizations, on the other hand, do not need rules to settle disputes, given that they can rely on government and courts, and require secrecy only in relation to a limited number of activities (usually concerning patents, innovation, etc.).

In this chapter, I expand the theory of rules in organizations, by showing that organizational rules do not only perform organizational functions, but may also serve to maintain secrecy and contain violence. I speculate on the scope conditions of these functions: while organizational functions are common across all types of organizations, secrecy is mainly a concern of legal and illegal secret societies, and containment of conflict is mainly a concern of criminal organizations (because they cannot rely on third parties to solve disputes).

5.1   A Theory of Mafia Rules

Mafia organizations have to solve many critical organizational problems. Some of these are typical only of criminal organizations, while others are common to all organizations. For example, mafias exist in a relatively hostile environment in which a serious error may result in the crippling of the organization (Potter 1994). As extralegal organizations, they have information, communication, and trust problems; they have high transaction costs, have difficulties in finding reliable people, cannot keep meticulous books and records, and suffer from adverse selection in recruiting people (Spence 1974). They must stay small and closely monitor their members to avoid police infiltration; they lack a legal dispute resolution mechanism (Gambetta 1993), and they have to defend themselves from internal takeover, etc. Some of these problems also characterize legitimate organizations (e.g., managing transaction costs), but the modalities of management and solution are different (e.g., mafias cannot decide to externalize some activities exclusively on the basis of economic considerations, because they also have to maintain secrecy, as we have seen in Section 2.8). To cope with these complex problems, and to facilitate internal governance, mafias establish organizational rules.

5.1.1   Rules in Organizations

Rules consist of explicit or implicit norms, regulations, and expectations governing individual behavior and interaction among individuals. The term "rule" is often used in a broad sense to denote different things, such as personal ethic, recurrent observable behavior, habits, normative expectations, procedures, organizational rules, contracts, and laws. In this chapter I mainly consider *organizational rules*.

Organizational rules share some common aspects with social norms: they both identify the permitted, obligatory, and forbidden behavior of people with particular attributes in a given context (Crawford and Ostrom 1995). Despite some similarities, organizational rules are substantially different from social norms (Coleman 1990; Ellickson 1991; Posner 2000; Hechter and Opp 2001; Elster 2007). Social norms are "non-legal mechanisms of cooperation" (Posner 2000, 4), and a "prescribed guide for conduct or action which is generally complied with by the members of a society" (Ullmann-Margalit 1977, 12). They are unplanned, and spontaneously emerge from social interactions; they are public and shared, and are not necessarily supported by formal sanctions (Bicchieri 2006). Organizational rules, instead, are stipulated by the organization with the purpose of constraining the behavior of its members. Whereas social norms rely, at best, on informal and decentralized punishment systems (no specific individual is formally designated to punish norm violators), organizational rules are often characterized by centralized punishment systems. Moreover, social norms may affect a large social system, whereas organizational rules are valid only for the organization that has established them. Even if there are overlaps between the two (e.g., norms on extramarital affairs exist not only within some organizations but also in the larger society), organizational rules may differ from social norms in the functions performed, the reasons for which they were established, the context in which they operate, and the sanctioning mechanisms.

Rules in organizations are defined as actions, regulations, prohibitions, and policies and concern how members of the organization are supposed to execute their jobs (March et al. 2000). Formal organizations are governed by rules (Zhou 1993), and in case of problems, organizations rely on existing rules. Nevertheless, an organization can never specify all the rules necessary to cope with all possible decisions. Rather, it specifies a small set of rules to cover routine decisions, while exceptions are referred to individuals at the top of the hierarchy. Under certain conditions of uncertainty or complexity, as Galbraith (1973) has pointed out, the amount of exceptions may become so numerous that the hierarchy becomes "overloaded" and the quality of decision-making suffers. Organizational rules are independent of the single actors that carry them out and can survive a considerable turnover of individuals. March and Olsen (1989) distinguish "choice-based" behavior, where the logic of consequence prevails as motivation for action, from "rule-based" behavior, where the individual decides to act according to what he believes to be the appropriate normative behavior (March and Simon 1958; Burns and Flam 1987; March and Olsen 1989).

Rules are a distinctive feature of modern business and bureaucracy (Weber 1922). They constitute a superior instrument of organization, in that they are able to ensure stability, reliability, equity, predictability, and discipline in complex organizations. Rules carry out an important role in organizations and perform a wide range of functions (March et al. 2000; Schulz and Beck 2002): from organizational and coordinational functions between people and organizational units, linking activity to organizational objectives (van de Ven et al. 1976; March et al. 2000; Okhuysen and Bechky 2009), to functions involving sense-making and the transmission of organizational memory (March et al. 2000). Stabilizing expectations, rules reduce uncertainty – a fundamental problem for all organizations (Thompson 1967) – and ambiguity in conducting activity (Meyer and Rowan 1977), as well as imposing limits on rational individual opportunism (Williamson 1975; 1996). Rules, however, may also have negative consequences for an organization. For example, an excessive number of rules and procedures can result in inefficiency, conformism, lack of innovation, and goal displacement (Blau 1955; Merton 1968), as well as low motivation and performance (Gouldner 1954). Other consequences may include vicious circles, and an inability to change (Crozier 1964) and to react to unexpected events (Weick and Sutcliffe 2007).

Rules are functionally equivalent to personally issued orders (Gouldner 1954), thus avoiding the repetition of orders from a superior to subordinates and facilitating control at a distance. However, rather than mechanically determining the behavior of participants, according to Friedberg (1993), rules structure spaces of negotiation and deployment between actors, and are not able to make uncertainties completely disappear – in fact, new uncertainties tend to be created.

Rules are relevant in organizational decision-making (Cyert and March 1963; March et al. 2000), in learning processes, and especially in routine-based learning (Cyert and March 1963; Levitt and March 1988; Schulz 2001). The environment outside the organization impacts on rules, which are established and determined by symbolic compliance with externally legitimated institutions, for example, political movements, laws, the state (Meyer et al. 1988; Sutton et al. 1994; Sutton and Dobbin 1996; Dobbin and Dowd 2000). Organizations adapt to their environment by creating rules that retain valuable solutions, by revising rules that encounter problems, and by suspending rules that have ceased serving a useful purpose for the organization (Schulz and Beck 2002). Moreover, rules are not immutable and can adapt to history through empirical learning (Levitt and March 1988). They can change, or they can cease to exist if, for example, the results they produce are unsuccessful. They can, however, continue to exist even though they produce unsuccessful results, if they protect the interests of specific people within the organization.

Rules may be written, and explicit, or unwritten, and implicit. Written rules are impersonal, explicit, and predictable and are a distinctive feature of formal organizations. They define the procedures to be followed and the sanctions for noncompliance with such procedures; they are visible in documents such as contracts, organizational charts, operational procedures, and regulations. One advantage of written rules is that they are "bearers of history" (March et al. 2000), fixing the experience of the individual in the organization. Unwritten rules, although they are not formalized, can carry out important functions within an organization and, sometimes, have a force and cogency that are superior to written rules, to which they may often bestow meaning, in that they reinterpret or fill a gap with regard to formalization. Written rules can therefore bring about an increase in those unwritten rules, which are sometimes necessary in order to give the former a practical sense.

It is normally assumed that written rules are formal and unwritten rules informal. This is not the case with mafias, where it is prohibited to leave written evidence regarding the organization: all the rules are therefore unwritten, except on rare occasions, which we will look at later – a single document pertaining to the Sicilian Cosa Nostra in more than 150 years of its history. Consequently, the degree of formalization of a mafia rule does not depend on whether it is written or not but, if anything, on its effective application and the mechanisms of sanctioning relating to it.

A second important distinction for the study of organizational rules is the one between two main different conceptualizations of the idea of rule: *rule as a way of doing things* and *rule as a way to regulate behavior*. The first conception emphasizes the procedural dimension, and it is close to the concept of routines (Cyert and March 1963; Nelson and Winter 1982; Cohen and Bacdayan 1994; Feldman 2000; Feldman and Pentland 2003; Becker 2004; Pentland and Feldman 2005; 2008; Hodgson 2008; Weichbrodt and Grote 2010). In this perspective, rules are artifacts and routines are behavior (Pentland and Feldman 2005); rules are abstract and general and need to be translated into concrete actions, establishing organizational routines. The second conception is normative and defines what people should do and what they should not do. As we will see, this latter conception is more appropriate for understanding the role of rules in mafia organizations.

5.1.2   Rules in Mafia Organizations

As for other secret societies, mafias also possess normative codes, in some cases complex and variegated, employed to regulate behavior both within the organization and outside. It is of particular interest to try to understand why different organizations, with radically different ethnic groupings, adopt a similar set of rules.

One important legal expert, Santi Romano, who had a certain – controversial – influence on the debate in Italy regarding the mafia as a juridical system states that

every form that is effectively social and is thus bound to be organized is transformed by that very fact into law. That it, as sometimes happens, may come to be in opposition with another institution, may constitute a reason why its juridical character is denied or that it is even considered by the other institution as anti-juridical – in other words, by that organization against which it works and to which it acts as a disorganizing and anti-social force. However, it is itself conversely a legal system when it excludes itself from this relationship and from this point of view and considers itself as it actually is, in terms of the regimenting and disciplining of its own elements. As has been said, a revolutionary organization or criminal association is not considered legal by the state they want to tear down or whose laws they violate, just as a schismatic sect is declared anti-juridical by the Church. However, this does not exclude the fact that, in these cases, they could be considered as institutions, organizations, orders, which, taken in isolation and considered intrinsically, are legal. Conversely, it is not legal that and that only which does not have a form of social organization. (Romano 1918, 41–2)

Romano goes on to say that

it is known that under the threat of state laws, there often live in the shadows associations whose organization one could call analogous, on a small scale, to that of the state: they have legislative and executive authorities, courts that settle disputes and punish, agents that inexorably carry out the punishment, statutes that are as elaborate and precise as state laws themselves. They therefore implement their own form of order, just as the state and lawful state institutions do. To deny that order the character of legality can only be the result of an ethical appreciation, given that such entities are often criminal or immoral; which would be admissible, if the necessary and absolute dependence of positive law on morality were proved, which, in our opinion, in this sense, which seems a very naïve one, is instead non-existent. (Romano 1918, 111)

Without ever employing the term "mafia," but referring rather to criminal organizations, the lawyer argues that there is always law where there exists a society given order through an organization. It follows that criminal organizations, being equipped with an organizational structure, have their own legal order. This is, of course, juridical analysis that has nothing to do with the legitimization of a criminal association, even though such assumptions have been deployed by certain lawyers working for the Sicilian Cosa Nostra.

Operating in hostile environments and unable to resort to legal protection, mafias have to create their own rules and monitor their effective implementation. These rules govern organizational life from the stage of recruitment and are in part common to the various mafias (Gambetta 1993; Hill 2003a; Catino 2015; Varese 2017), suggesting the consideration that such criminal groups are subject to similar pressures, and that these structural conditions transcend specific cultural differences.[1]

---

[1] Rules and codes of conduct are present in many other organizations, such as gangs (Anderson 1999; Densley 2013; Stephenson 2015).

The Camorra had its own code throughout the nineteenth century[2] (Monnier 1862; De Blasio 1897; Mastriani 1889–90; Marmo 2011), suspending it in the aftermath of the Cuocolo trial in 1911.[3] It was then restored in 1974, borrowed from that of the 'Ndrangheta by Raffaele Cutolo, who considered it essential to the founding of the Nuova Camorra Organizzata (Ciconte 2008; Di Fiore 2016). Many codes and texts of oaths of various organizations have come down to us thanks to the transgression, by certain mafia members, of the rule that nothing relating to the organization must ever be written down – a rule that was necessary to protect secrecy from the outside world and above all from judiciary investigations.

The formation of rules for the control of individual conduct is a feature of both the upperworld and the underworld, as in the case of outsiders (Becker 1963), or prisoners (Cressey 1967; Skarbek 2011; 2012; 2014), and gangs (Decker and van Winkle 1996). The rules in the mafia establish what is right and what is wrong and violation is sanctioned, in extreme cases, by death. Since, as already said, they cannot rely on the law and government to solve a series of problems, and need to cooperate with each other in order to achieve their economic interests, mobs create rules as a form of extralegal self-organizational governance. As Gambetta (2009) argues, if cooperation between honest people is difficult, it is even more difficult in the underworld, where criminals have manifold reasons not to trust each other. In fact, one of the general problems that mafias have to solve regards trust, the latter defined as the probability that others will engage in beneficial or at least nondetrimental action (Gambetta 1988). "Our entire system of cooperation and connections depended on trust," stated Joseph Bonanno, one of the bosses of the five New York families (1983, 155). Organizational rules can be an important instrument to solve – at least in part – the trust problem.

These rules, far from being a subcultural by-product of a specific geographical context (i.e., Southern Italy), as maintained by several mafia scholars (Lestingi 1880; Hobsbawm 1959; Ianni and Reuss-Ianni 1972; Hess 1973; Schneider and Schneider 1976; Blok 1988), are in fact rational (Abadinsky 2013) and intentionally designed to govern specific problems typical of secret criminal organizations. Operating in hostile environments and with no possibility of resorting to legal forms of protection, mafias must create their own rules, explicit and implicit, and supervise their effective implementation.

---

[2] The first code that we know about is the Frieno – brake, or check – of the Camorra, dated September 12, 1842.

[3] See Chapter 2, note 49.

Mafias, refusing to recognize the state's superiority and supremacy, create their own system of regulations, an alternative legal order independent to that of the state (Romano 1918). This system of rules is a binding one for a *mafioso* from the moment of his affiliation and he is honor-bound to respect it for the rest of his life. Some criminal organizations have rules similar to state constitutions, and they adopt these "criminal constitutions" because they facilitate cooperation and enhance profits (Leeson and Skarbek 2010). Other criminal organizations, such as gangs, also have recourse to regulations in order to enforce discipline on certain aspects of organizational life (Sanchez-Jankowski 1991; Densley 2013). Referring to an American mafia family, Ianni and Reuss-Ianni identified three basic rules of conduct:

(1) Primary loyalty is vested in family rather in individual lineages or nuclear families, (2) each member of the family "must act like a man" and do nothing which brings disgrace on the family, and (3) family business is privileged matter and must not be reported or discussed outside the group. (1972, 139)

The generality across different cultural contexts of these basic rules, as well as other organizational characteristics, can be explained, following Hill (2003a, 73), by the fact that these criminal groups are subject to the same sorts of pressures and that these structural conditions transcend cultural differences.

In this chapter, I take these general considerations to the next level, and show, through a systematic analysis of mafia rules, that these perform a set of functions that is partly different from that of most legal organizations. In addition to the basic goal of achieving coordination and cooperation among members, mafia organizations need to settle disputes, control violence, and maintain secrecy. In fact, as anticipated, my analytical classification led to the identification of three major functions ensured by mafia rules:

(1) to establish organizational order
(2) to contain conflict and violence
(3) to maintain secrecy.

While the latter two goals may also be present, to some degree, in some legal organizations, they are vital for illegal, secret organizations.

5.2   Mafia Rules: Types and Functions

5.2.1   *Written Codes*

Some criminal organizations, such as 22 of the 37 street gangs studied by Sanchez-Jankowski (1991) or La Nuestra Familia in Californian prison gangs (Leeson and Skarbek 2010), set down their rules in writing. Unlike other forms of organized crime, mafias have always tended to communicate only by word of mouth. On occasion, however, this prohibition has been violated and some written codes have come to light. Most of the rules that govern mafia members had no specific point of origin.

Sicilian Cosa Nostra. The most detailed description of the rules of the Sicilian Cosa Nostra was provided by collaborator with justice Antonino Calderone in 1987[4] with a list of the various rules that are communicated to the new member during the initiation procedure:

(1) Not to touch the women of other men of honor.
(2) Not to steal from other men of honor or, in general, from anyone.
(3) Not to exploit prostitution.
(4) Not to kill other men of honor unless strictly necessary.
(5) To avoid passing information to the police.
(6) Not to quarrel with other men of honor.
(7) To maintain proper behavior.
(8) To keep silent about Cosa Nostra around outsiders.
(9) To avoid under all circumstances introducing oneself to another man of honor. (The presence of a third man of honor is necessary: he has to know them both, and introduce them as men of honor, saying, "This is our friend," or "This is the same thing.")

In 2007, during the arrest of the boss Salvatore Lo Piccolo, a list entitled "Rights and Duties" was discovered in his hideout. This contained ten rules relating to membership of the Sicilian Cosa Nostra and to a large extent echoed those reported by Calderone two decades before.[5] It was the first time in the history of the Sicilian Cosa Nostra that a document of this kind had been found:[6]

---

[4] Testimony of Antonino Calderone given to Michel Debacq (Investigating Judge of Marseilles), and to the Commissione Rogatoria Internazionale (International Investigating Committee), with Giovanni Falcone (Investigating Judge of Palermo) et al., March 19, 1987–June 25, 1988, vol. III, 734–8.

[5] M. Nizza, "Sicilian Mafia Fades but Legend Continues", *The New York Times*, November 9, 2007.

[6] A few years before the discovery of the document on the rules of the Sicilian Cosa Nostra in the lair of the boss Lo Piccolo, the former mobster Salvatore Facella, as a collaborator with justice, said in 2003 that a statute written by the Cosa Nostra had existed for some time. It had been drawn up before the Second World War by a lawyer called Panzeca, from Caccamo in the province of Palermo, Sicily. The statute would eventually end up in the hands of Totò Riina (Palazzolo and Prestipino 2007).

(1) No one can present himself directly to another of our friends. There must be a third person to do it.
(2) Never look at the wives of friends.
(3) Never be seen with cops.
(4) Don't go to pubs and clubs.
(5) Always being available for Cosa Nostra is a duty – even if your wife's about to give birth.
(6) Appointments must absolutely be respected.[7]
(7) Wives must be treated with respect.
(8) When asked for any information, the answer must be the truth.
(9) Money cannot be appropriated if it belongs to others or to other families.
(10) People who can't be part of Cosa Nostra: anyone who has a close relative in the police, anyone with a two-timing relative in the family, anyone who behaves badly and doesn't hold to moral values.

It should be made clear that, even though these rules are presented as being cast in iron, empirical evidence suggests that their actual application is characterized by many exceptions and their apparent hard-and-fast nature is a far from realistic representation.

Apart from the "Rights and Duties" document found in Lo Piccolo's hideaway, a second document was also discovered that specified certain organizational rules:

(1a) The head of the family is elected by all members of the family. The same for the adviser.
(2a) The deputy head is chosen by the head of the family. The same for the *capodecina*.
(3a) The head of the family has the final word.
(4a) The deputy head acts when the head is absent.
(5a) The adviser strives to keep everybody united in the family, and gives advice for the good of the family.
(6a) The soldiers are directed by the *capodecina* and serve the needs of the family.

---

[7] Pistone (and Brandt 2007) affirm: "That's one of the principal grounds for a death sentence – disobedience. And especially failing to come when called. It's actually a part of the mafia oath when an associate is made; you always come when called. Period" (57). Mobster Gino Gillespie of the Bonanno family was targeted for punishment because he was disrespectful: he sometimes failed to show up at meetings and sometimes arrived thirty minutes late (Cicale and Scarpo 2014).

Other rules refer to the training and tasks of the higher-level bodies of coordination:

(7a) The Commission is formed by all the *capimandamento*.

(8a) The Commission elects the head of the Commission and his deputy, and a secretary who fixes the time of the meetings.

(9a) The Commission has been created to ensure that there is equilibrium within the families and within Cosa Nostra, and to discuss and decide the most delicate matters.

We have already dealt with these rules in Section 3.1, with reference to the Sicilian Cosa Nostra, but here it is important to emphasize the simplicity and linearity of the line of command that characterizes the rules for its organizational structure – the same linearity that we find in other mafias.

American Cosa Nostra. Cressey (1967) presents two succinct summaries of the mafia families code, one made in 1892 and the other written in 1900.[8] More recently, based on previous evidence (Valachi in Maas 1968; Coffey and Schmetterer 1991; Jacobs 2002; Capeci 2003), and in particular on the transcriptions from the 1992 trial of John Gotti, Abadinsky (2013, 93) reports the following main rules of the American Cosa Nostra:

(1) Always show respect to those who can command it.

(2) Report any failure to show respect to one's patron immediately.

(3) Violence must be used, even if only of a limited type, to ensure respect.

(4) Never ask for surname.

(5) Never resort to violence in a dispute with a member or associate of another family.

(6) Never resort to, or even threaten, violence in a dispute with a member of your family.

---

[8] From Cressey (1967, 47): (a) 1. Reciprocal aid in case of any need whatever. 2. Absolute obedience to the chief. 3. An offense received by one of the members to be considered an offense against all and avenged at any cost. 4. No appeal to the state's authorities for justice. 5. No revelation of the names of members or any secrets of the association (1892). (b) 1. To help one another and avenge every injury of a fellow member. 2. To work with all means for the defense and freeing of any fellow member who has fallen into the hands of the judiciary. 3. To divide the proceeds of thievery, robbery and extortion with certain consideration for the needy as determined by the *capo*. 4. To keep the oath and maintain secrecy on pain of death (Cutrera 1900).

(7) Do not use the telephone except to arrange for a meeting place, preferably in code, from which you will then travel to a safe place to discuss business.

(8) Avoid mentioning specifics when discussing business – for example, names, dates, and place – beyond those absolutely necessary for understanding.

(9) Keep your mouth shut – anything you hear, anything you see, stays with you, in your head; do not talk about it.

(10) Do not ask unnecessary questions. The amount of information given to you is all you need to carry out your instructions.

(11) Never engage in homosexual activities.

(12) If your patron arranges for two parties to work together, he assumes responsibility for arbitrating any disputes between the parties.

(13) The boss can unilaterally direct violence, including murder, against any member of his family, but he cannot engage in murder-for-hire, that is, make a profit from murder.

(14) The boss cannot use violence against a member or close associate of another family without prior consultation with that family's boss.

(15) The principal form of security in the American Cosa Nostra is an elaborate system of referral and vouching. Vouching for someone who turns out to be an informant or undercover officer entails the death penalty.

Yakuza. According to Hill (2003a, 72–3), the Yakuza has "five cardinal rules which have remained unchanged for centuries":

(1) Do not disobey, or cause a nuisance to your superiors.
(2) Do not betray your gang or your fellow gang members.
(3) Do not fight with fellow members or disrupt the harmony of the gang.
(4) Do not embezzle gang funds.
(5) Do not touch the woman of a fellow gang member.

The generality across different cultural contexts of many basic rules, as well as other organizational characteristics, can be explained, following Hill (2003a), by the fact that these criminal groups are subject to the same sorts of pressures and that these structural conditions transcend cultural differences (73). Given the "legitimacy" of the organization, there are no special rules regarding the maintenance of secrecy.

Russian Mafia. The Russian Mafia has its own code of conduct (Serio and Razinkin 1995; Finckenauer and Waring 1998; Varese 2001) that relates to many aspects of the criminal life. This code, the *Vor-v-zakone,* consists of a number of rules designed to control the behavior of clan members (Varese 2001, 151–2; Serio 2008; Mallory 2012, 91; Siegel 2012, 33). The main rules are the following:

(1) Members cannot have a family (no wife or children) but can have a lover.
(2) Members forsake all relatives.
(3) Members cannot have a legitimate job.
(4) Members must assist other thieves – by both moral and material support, utilizing the commune of thieves.
(5) Keep secret information about the whereabouts of accomplices (i.e., dens, districts, hideouts, safe apartments, etc.). Members can never reveal information about thieves' activities, identities, or locations.
(6) Members must make good on promises to other thieves.
(7) Members do not gamble if they cannot afford to pay.
(8) Members must teach young thieves the trade.
(9) Members cannot help the authorities or testify in court.
(10) Members should not take weapons from the hands of authorities; not serve in the military.
(11) Members cannot cooperate with law enforcement agencies. Have nothing to do with the authorities, particularly with the ITU (Correctional Labor Authority), nor participate in public activities, nor join any community organizations.
(12) Members carry out punishment against any rule-offending thief.
(13) Members do not resist carrying out the decision of punishing the offending thief who is found guilty, with punishment determined by the convocation.
(14) Members must participate in an inquiry to settle disputes between thieves in the event of a conflict between themselves and other thieves, or between thieves.
(15) If necessary, participate in such inquiries.
(16) Members should not lose the ability to reason by using drugs and alcohol.
(17) In unavoidable situations (if a thief is under investigation) take the blame for someone else's crime; this buys the other person time of freedom.
(18) Have good command of the thieves' jargon (Fehnay).
(19) Have, if possible, informants from the rank and file of thieves.
(20) A member must refrain from using violence.
(21) A member must not have a family of his own, but he can have as many women as he wishes.

(22) Never and under any circumstances is a member allowed to have a job or property.

(23) A member does not adhere to the Soviet laws.

(24) A member is not allowed to be involved in political activities.

(25) A member must not participate in public activities or organizations, or serve in the army.

(26) A member must not be a witness in a court.

(27) A member is not allowed to leave the brotherhood.

Triads. Finally, the triad societies also have their own code of conduct. Graham (1997) cites a code belonging to one of the largest Triads (around 10,000 members), the United Bamboo.[9] The code consists of ten articles:

(1) Harmony with the people is the first priority. We have to establish good social and personal connections so as not to create enemies.

(2) We have to seek special favors and help from uncommitted gang members by emphasizing our relationships with outside people. Let them publicize us.

(3) Gambling is our main financial source. We have to be careful how we handle it.

(4) Do not take it upon yourself to start things and make decisions you are not authorized to make. You are to discuss and plan all matters with the group and the elder brother first.

(5) Everyone has an assigned responsibility. Do not create confusion!

(6) We must not divulge our plans and affairs to outsiders, for example to our wives, girlfriends, etc. This is for our own safety.

(7) We have to be united with all our brothers and obey our elder brother's orders.

(8) All money earned outside the group must be turned over to the group. You must not keep any of it for yourself. Let the elder brother decide.

(9) When targeting wealthy prospects do not act hastily. Furthermore, do not harass or threaten them. Act to prevent suspicion and fear on their part.

(10) If anything unexpected happens, do not abandon your brothers. If arrested, shoulder all responsibility and blame. Do not involve your brothers.

---

[9] The code was found by Los Angeles police (the Los Angeles County Sheriff's Department) when they arrested a member who was trying to enter the United States.

5.2.2   Types and Functions of Rules

A comprehensive classification of both written rules and those rules that have emerged from other sources (i.e., declarations of informants and collaborators with justice in interrogation reports, investigations, and biographies/autobiographies), has led to the identification of different types of rules (Table 5.1).[10] As regards the three main functions performed by the rules (1, *to establish organizational order*; 2, *to contain conflict and violence*; 3, *to maintain secrecy*), while the first goal is common to all organizations, the second and third goals are more typical of illegal and secret organizations.

Rules as a Way to Establish Organizational Order. A relevant part of mafia rules pertains to the organizational dimension. These "organizing" rules define organizational assets, coordination methods, and "vertical" and "horizontal" functions. In *vertical* terms, rules define organizational roles (boss, underboss, *consigliere*, etc.), their activities, the hierarchical structure and chain of command, the higher-level bodies of coordination (districts, provincial level and regional level for the Sicilian Cosa Nostra; the Commission for the American Cosa Nostra), careers, etc. In *horizontal* terms, they define the territories relating to each family and the mechanisms of coordination between the various organizational units that make up a mafia organization. Organizing rules confer legitimacy on the decisions taken by the leadership: "a clear sense of organization was the only way to manage so many men" (Bonanno and Abromovitz 2011, 131).

Some rules define decisional processes, for example, the election of a boss or procedures relating to meetings of the Commission. In the Sicilian Cosa Nostra, the boss of a family is elected democratically, one vote per person. In families with a large membership, the votes are collected, in order to avoid having to assemble a large number of people in one place (Arlacchi 1993). Bonanno describes the procedural rules and strict protocol employed for the meetings of the American Cosa Nostra's highest level of coordination, the Commission (Bonanno and Abromovitz 2011). There are rules about the voting quorum, who can attend (family bosses and highest-ranking members), who can speak (only family bosses), the frequency of the meetings, the dress code, the table for the meeting (circular, signifying that each member has

---

[10] See also "John Gotti's Rules of Leadership," in Anastasia 2015, 327–8, and Gratteri and Nicaso (2013a) for the 'Ndrangheta.

Table 5.1 *Classification of the main explicit rules of some mafias according to their different functions*

	Rules
Establish organizational order	**Sicilian Cosa Nostra:** Always being available for Sicilian Cosa Nostra is a duty – even if your wife's about to give birth. Appointments must absolutely be respected. When asked for any information, the answer must be the truth. The head of the family is elected by all members of the family. The same for the adviser. The deputy head is chosen by the head of the family. The same for the *capodecina*. The head of the family has the final word. The deputy head acts when the head is absent. The adviser strives to keep everybody united in the family, and gives advice for the good of the family. The soldiers are directed by the *capodecina* and serve the needs of the *family*. The Commission is formed by all *capimandamento*. The Commission elects the head of the Commission and his deputy, and a secretary who fixes the time of the meetings. **American Cosa Nostra:** Always show respect to those who can command it. Report any failure to show respect to one's patron immediately. **Yakuza:** Do not disobey, or cause a nuisance to your superiors. **Russian Mafia:** Members cannot have a family (no wife or children) but can have a lover. Members forsake all relatives. Members cannot have a legitimate job. Members must assist other thieves – by both moral and material support, utilizing the commune of thieves. Members must teach young thieves the trade. Members carry out punishment against any rule-offending thief. Members do not resist carrying out the decision of punishing the offending thief who is found guilty, with punishment determined by the convocation. In unavoidable situations (if a thief is under investigation) take the blame for someone else's crime; this buys the other person time of freedom. Have good command of the thieves' jargon (Fehnay). Have, if possible, informants from the rank and file of thieves. **Triads:** We have to seek special favors and help from uncommitted gang members by emphasizing our relationships with outside people. Let them publicize us.

Table 5.1 (*cont.*)

	Rules
	Gambling is our main financial source. We have to be careful how we handle it.
	Do not take it upon yourself to start things and make decisions you are not authorized to make. You are to discuss and plan all matters with the group and the elder brother first.
	Everyone has an assigned responsibility. Do not create confusion!
	We have to be united with all our brothers and obey our elder brother's orders.
	All money earned outside the group must be turned over to the group. You must not keep any of it for yourself. Let the elder brother decide.
	When targeting wealthy prospects do not act hastily. Furthermore, do not harass or threaten them. Act to prevent suspicion and fear on their part.
	If anything unexpected happens, do not abandon your brothers. If arrested, shoulder all responsibility and blame. Do not involve your brothers.
Containment of conflict and violence	**Sicilian Cosa Nostra:**
	Not to quarrel with other men of honor.
	Not to touch the women of other men of honor.
	Not to steal from other men of honor or, in general, from anyone.
	Not to kill other men of honor unless strictly necessary.
	The Commission has been created to ensure that there is equilibrium within the families and within Sicilian Cosa Nostra, and to discuss and decide over the most delicate matters.
	American Cosa Nostra:
	Never resort to violence in a dispute with a member or associate of another family.
	Never resort to, or even threaten, violence in a dispute with a member of your family.
	If your patron arranges for two parties to work together, he assumes responsibility for arbitrating any disputes between the parties.
	The boss can unilaterally direct violence, including murder, against any member of his family, but he cannot engage in murder-for-hire, that is, make a profit from murder.
	The boss cannot use violence against a member or close associate of another family without prior consultation with that family's boss.
	Yakuza:
	Do not betray your gang or your fellow gang members.
	Do not fight with fellow members or disrupt the harmony of the gang.
	Do not embezzle gang funds.
	Do not touch the woman of a fellow gang member.
	Russian Mafia:
	A member must refrain from using violence.
	Members should not lose the ability to reason by using drugs and alcohol.

Table 5.1 (*cont.*)

	Rules
	Members must participate in an inquiry to settle disputes between thieves in the event of a conflict between themselves and other thieves, or between thieves. If necessary, participate in such inquiries.

Triads:
Harmony with the people is the first priority. We have to establish good social and personal connections so as not to create enemies.

Maintain secrecy

Sicilian Cosa Nostra:
To maintain proper behavior.
To keep silent about Sicilian Cosa Nostra around outsiders.
No one can present himself directly to another of our friends. There must be a third person to do it.
Never be seen with cops.
Don't go to pubs and clubs.
People who can't be part of Sicilian Cosa Nostra: anyone who has a close relative in the police, anyone with a two-timing relative in the family, anyone who behaves badly and doesn't hold to moral values.

American Cosa Nostra:
Keep your mouth shut – anything you hear, anything you see, stays with you, in your head; do not talk about it.
Never ask for surname.
Do not use the telephone except to arrange for a meeting place, preferably in code, from which you will then travel to a safe place to discuss business.
Avoid mentioning specifics when discussing business – for example, names, dates, and places – beyond those absolutely necessary for understanding.
Do not ask unnecessary questions. The amount of information given to you is all you need to carry out your instructions.
Vouching for someone who turns out to be an informant or undercover officer entails the death penalty.

Russian Mafia:
Keep secret information about the whereabouts of accomplices. Members can never reveal information about thieves' activities, identities, or locations.
Members cannot help the authorities or testify in court.
Members cannot cooperate with law enforcement. Have nothing to do with the authorities, nor participate in public activities, nor join any community organizations.

Triads:
We must not divulge our plans and affairs to outsiders, for example to our wives, girlfriends, etc. This is for our own safety.

equal status), how to start and how to conclude the meeting, the time to begin, and other rules.

The importance of the (mafia) family outweighs that of the single individual. Should a *mafioso* find himself in a difficult situation, even one of extreme urgency, he must still put the organization's interests first. Even if someone's wife is about to give birth or "your child is dying and has only twenty minutes to live, and your boss sends for you, you must leave that kid and come. If you refuse, you will be killed. When the boss sends for you it precedes everything else" (Maas 1997, 88). This rule, that the mafia organization comes before everything else, is common to all the mafias.

Other rules were designed to avoid an excessive concentration of blood relatives in one family. The informant Antonino Calderone stated that, in 1975, in order to avoid a concentration of familial relationships that might introduce unduly opportunistic elements into organizational life, the Sicilian Cosa Nostra decided that there "couldn't be more than two brothers in the same family, and two brothers or blood relatives couldn't be at the top of one family or of a provincial organization" (Arlacchi 1993, 128). Other mafia organizations, such as the Triads (Chu 2000) and the Yakuza (Iwai 1986), also adopted the same rule. This provides the mafia family with an organizational strength that goes far beyond the necessarily limited links offered by real family relationships: "These are the rules that can make an institution's reputation and thus its longevity independent of the fate of its individual member" (Gambetta 2009, 208). This rule about the composition of the highest leadership is not only an organizing rule, however. It is also aimed at limiting possible conflicts within the same family between blood-related members and other members with no blood relationship. Blood ties, in fact, can facilitate the formation of factions, especially when critical decisions have to be made.

A further organizing rule that is fundamental for a secret organization such as the Sicilian Cosa Nostra is the rule of truth. This is not due to reasons of sincerity but for the functional requirements of a secret organization. According to collaborator with justice Antonino Calderone, "The crucial thing is precise information. The information that circulates in the mafia must be accurate and exact. Otherwise, you can't understand anything and the result is great confusion" (Arlacchi 1993, 24). That the news that circulates among men of honor is true

is an essential fact for the mafia organization and lies are punished with severe penalties. Therefore, if a man of honor learns from another member that a third man is a man of honor, that is the truth. It is not physically necessary to meet the man of honor; it is enough just to know that he is one ... When a man of honor speaks of another person as belonging to the Cosa Nostra, you can be sure that this is not idle gossip, nor corridor chatter, but very serious information regarding which any superficiality is prohibited. (OSPA Stajano 2010, 86–7)

As Falcone and Padovani state:

The man of honour is obliged to tell the truth because truth constitutes for him a law of survival when he is free and all the more so when he is in prison. If a mafioso does not respect the obligation to tell the truth in the presence of another man of honour, it is a sure sign that either one or the other of them is soon to die. (Falcone and Padovani 1992, 41–2)

This categorical imperative of speaking the truth can cause some paradoxes to arise. For example, the son of a man of honor killed by the Sicilian Cosa Nostra cannot join the organization since, due to this obligation to speak the truth, should the son ask for information about his father's death, it would not be possible to lie to him.

The rule "Always show respect to those who can command it" is aimed at ensuring the legitimacy of the chain of command and the execution of orders: "A mafia boss's words have the inviolability of a papal bull," the American Cosa Nostra ex-mobster Dominick Cicale affirms (Cicale and Scarpo 2014, 8). As Cressey (1969) states, although the code of organized criminals is purportedly for the protection of the people, it is administered and enforced for the protection of each boss.

Finally, rules and protocols exist that establish correct behavior toward other hierarchical levels and that make a distinction between "respect" and "equality." The first involves a demonstration of honor, esteem, and courteous regard to someone and something. Equality, by contrast, means possessing the same rights, privileges, and responsibilities. Mafias are based upon the principle of equality among members, but "confusion between respect and equality could affect one's behavior, and lead to unfortunate consequences" (Bonanno and Abromovitz 2011, 279). People of a different hierarchical level and organizational status are equal within the same organization, but a member of an inferior status and level must always show respect to a member of a superior level, even in informal situations. Otherwise, the consequences could be extremely dangerous. Bill Bonanno states:

If my father (a family boss) or Albert or Frank, were sitting at their tables, the family's *sottocapo*, or a leader from another family, or perhaps a group leader might join them. But a soldier would never sit down at the leader's table unless specifically invited. Without such an invitation, a soldier would simply sit at his own table with other soldiers. (Bonanno and Abromovitz 2011, 266)

The rules also establish the communication process that follows the chain of command. For example, in the American Cosa Nostra, as explained by the former underboss of the Gambino family, later collaborator with justice Sammy Gravano: "You don't run to the boss. You go to your captain. That was the protocol. Your captain will go to the administration of the family..." (Maas 1997, 87). Pistone (Pistone and Brandt 2007) says that when he operated undercover in the Bonanno family, as an *associate* he had to report to a soldier and not a captain.

More than a matter of "respect," however, this strict regulation of the communication chain solves a fundamental organizational problem. Since families are made up of a large number of members, in particular those of the American Cosa Nostra, communication can only take place in a selective manner, with the hierarchy constituting an effective criterion of implementation.

Rules as a Way of Containing Conflict and Violence. Rules channel aggression, providing legitimate methods for its expression as well as making punishment legitimate (Gouldner 1954). As seen in Section 4.2, for mafia organizations, violence is an instrument, not an end in itself (Gambetta 1993). Violence and the threat of using it are necessary for mafias to maintain, protect, and expand their business. For instance, given their illegal status, they cannot appeal to the law to enforce agreements. Violence can also increase cooperation, as it functions as a viable sign of "credible commitment" (Campana and Varese 2013). As an instrument, then, violence cannot be eliminated, but must rather be managed and contained. It must be adequately employed toward the right target and to the right extent. Excess due to errors increases the possibility of negative consequences to the detriment of the results. Precisely for these reasons, mafias define basic rules to discipline violence and reduce opportunities of conflict, and to regulate various activities and behaviors that can generate negative externalities for the entire organization.

Given the impossibility of turning to the law, mafias have designed a series of rules to manage the tensions that can arise in running an illegal activity. First, the hierarchy can be appealed to. For example, if there is a dispute between two members of the same family who belong to two different crews, the two members must consult their respective lieutenants. If no agreement is possible, the case is referred to their boss. If the matter involves members belonging to different families, the lieutenants refer the case to the respective bosses, who will then try to work out an agreement. If this turns out not to be possible, a higher level is consulted. For the American Cosa Nostra, this means referring directly to the Commission, while for the Sicilian Cosa Nostra, recourse is made to the *mandamento*, or, if that still leads to no solution, to the Provincial

Commission. For the Sicilian Cosa Nostra, if the matter regards different *mandamenti* (districts) in the same province, and the two heads of the *mandamenti* involved are unable to come to an agreement, then recourse is made to the Provincial Commission. If the matter involves different provinces and the respective provincial heads cannot find an agreement, then recourse is made to the Regional Commission. The presence of higher-level bodies of coordination is, therefore, an important instrument for the containment of violence, through "sit-downs" that can facilitate the discussion and resolution of disputes. Resorting to violence is thus discouraged as an instrument of conflict resolution (Catino 2014). In fact, since these higher-level bodies of coordination were set up (in the 1930s for the American Cosa Nostra; in 1957 and 1975 for the Sicilian Cosa Nostra), possibilities for conflict resolution have increased and the number of homicides has decreased (for the Sicilian Cosa Nostra, see Catino 2014). This is not of course always possible and the resulting conflicts can be extremely violent.

Containment of retaliation and violence, both within the organization and toward the outside world, is fundamental for the mafias, for reasons of organizational stability (internal feuds are destabilizing) and, above all, because it might attract the attention of the law enforcement agencies. It is therefore prohibited for any member to resort to violence, in order to prevent an uncontrollable escalation that could threaten the organization. "Do not betray your gang or your fellow gang members" establishes a Yakuza law. Only the boss can decide whether and how to employ violence. The first collaborator with justice from the American Cosa Nostra, Joe Valachi (Maas 1968), states that it was forbidden for a *mafioso* to raise his hand against another *mafioso*, in order to avoid starting a war between families. This rule prohibits "vigilante" justice:

It is hard rule in this thing of ours from the days of Mr. Maranzano that one member cannot use his hands on another member. In New York the no-hands rule is most important. It ain't all peaches and cream like in Buffalo, say, or them other cities where there is only one family and everybody is together. In New York there are five families – really you must say there are six because when you mention New York, you got to mention Newark, New Jersey – and in New York we step all over each other. What I mean is there is a lot of animosity among the soldiers in these families, and one guy is always trying to take away another guy's numbers runner or move into a bookmaking operation or grab a shylocking customer. So you can see why it is that they are strict about the no-hands rule. (Valachi in Maas 1968, 207)

And violations were punished: "A murder that had not been authorized invited immediate retribution" (Maas 1997, 46). Valachi himself violated this rule, beating up a member of the Gambino family who had stolen money. A sit-down was arranged chaired by the underboss Albert

Table 5.2 *Rules on use of violence in the American Cosa Nostra*

Perpetrator	Victim	Rule
Boss	Member, associate, nonmember	The boss of a family has sovereign authority over all family members and associates. He can unilaterally direct violence, including murder, against any member or associate of his family, or against a nonmember, except that he cannot engage in "murder-for-hire." He cannot use violence against a member or associate of another family without prior consultation with that family's boss.
Member	Member	A member cannot use violence against another member of his own family without permission from his boss. This prohibition is even stronger when it involves a member from another family.
Member	Associate	It appears that a member cannot use violence against an associate of another family. A member can murder an associate of his own family with the permission of his boss. He can use nonfatal violence, however, to enforce family discipline. It appears that he also cannot use violence against an associate of another family (although the prohibition would not be as strong as in the case of an actual member).
Associate	Associate	Associates cannot use violence against other families' associates. It is not known whether they are permitted to use violence against other associates in their own family, although this would seem unlikely.
Member	Nonmember	No restriction.
Associate	Nonmember	No restriction.
Associate	Member	Prohibited (except on orders from the boss).

Anastasia to address the issue with a captain of the Genovese family. Anastasia rebuked Valachi for his behavior:

What the fuck's the matter with you? After all, you been in this life of ours for twenty years. There is no excuse for you . . . A rule is a rule. You know you can't take the law in your own hands. You know you could start a war with the kind of thing you pulled. (Valachi in Maas 1968, 214)

Abadinsky (1983, 160–1) summarizes the rules on the use of violence in the American Cosa Nostra, distinguishing between perpetrator and victim, as in Table 5.2.

The use of violence is the legitimate monopoly of the family boss within the family, but the boss must still consult with others in cases where violence is used against the member of another family.

Other rules designed to contain violence regard the relationship between genders, such as "Never look at the wives of friends" and "Wives must be treated with respect." This is not a matter of *male culture*, typical of Southern Italy, which expresses a form of respect toward women: it rather addresses the fact that any eventual betrayal might easily lead to violent conflict between members – conflict that could prove to be dangerous for the organization and dysfunctional for business. It is more a problem of organizational stability than moral choice. This passage well exemplifies the distinction between organizational rules and social norms. Even though these specific organizational rules resemble some social or moral norms that exist in the larger society, they perform a different function (i.e., to contain violence, rather than to relate appropriately to women), they were established for a different reason (namely, after actual conflicts generated by extramarital affairs within the mafia family) and operate in a specific organizational context (the mafia organization).

Overall, the goal of these rules is, therefore, to increase the rational and legitimate aspect of violence and to avoid any form of conflict between members, since this might possibly degenerate into an uncontrollable escalation.

Rules as a Way to Maintain Secrecy. Knowing how to say nothing is a required ability of secret societies' members (Simmel 1906). As secret associations, mafias have to deal with a fundamental dilemma: how to carry out their own (illegal) objectives in conditions of secrecy. To do so, they establish norms to ensure the state of secrecy of the organization and its activities as it pursues its economic goals, while guaranteeing its longevity. Mobs cannot keep any written record about their activities and this, of course, is a serious problem with regard to having a reliable report on their economic situation. For example, an investigation into the DeCavalcante family of the New Jersey American Cosa Nostra revealed that Sam DeCavalcante managed thousands of dollars without any written accounting document (in Zeigler 1970).

Mafia organizations are frequently associated with one particular term, *omertà*, which refers to a specific kind of behavior dedicated to informational reticence. The etymological significance of the term refers to the idea of a "strong man," while the current meaning denotes a specific type of behavior – *omertoso* – implying secrecy, reticence, and an attitude of silence. Above all, it signals a refusal to collaborate with the state, in particular with regard to investigations into criminal acts. This concept of *omertà* and the silence that is such a feature of this type of organizations are more than mere cultural codes of behavior: rather they are necessary requirements for the life of an illegal secret organization, just as for other secret organizations (Hutin 1955; Davis 1977). For a mafia organization, handling secrecy means above all handling information, a containment of the diffusion of what is known, in that remaining silent is a necessary requisite to the selling of protection (Gambetta 1993).

Sicilian Cosa Nostra collaborator with justice Tommaso Buscetta says that

every "man of honor" must respect the "order of silence." He must not reveal to strangers his membership of the mafia, or, above all, the secrets of Cosa Nostra; this is, perhaps, the most strict Cosa Nostra rule, the one that has allowed the organization to remain impervious to judicial investigation and the violation of which is almost always punished with death. Within the Sicilian Cosa Nostra, loquacity is not appreciated: the circulation of news is reduced to a minimum and the man of honor should refrain from asking too many questions, because this is a sign of unseemly curiosity and arouses suspicion in the other party.[11]

Omertà, on the one hand, binds the members of the organization to secrecy and, on the other, makes it impossible for men of honor to have any type of relationship with state authorities in order to ensure that their rights are respected. The mafia code of *omertà* establishes the first duty of a man to be that of taking justice into his own hands against any kind of wrong perpetrated against him. Only infamy, public execration, and public vendetta can await anyone who should resort to justice in any way, whether with information or action (Colajanni 1900). In relation to this aspect, collaborator with justice Salvatore Contorno states that "it is a fundamental rule for every man of honor never to report a theft or crime to the police."[12]

This prevention of collaboration with, or recourse to, either the police or the judiciary is not only a rejection of legitimate state structures, though it is certainly also this, or a necessity motivated by issues of organization security and secrecy. It is a prohibition designed primarily to protect the reputation of the organization (Gambetta 1993): if the state and its bodies are resorted to in order to deal with issues of interest to mafia members or "clients," then the power of the mafia as a solver of disputes is weakened.

Only in the 1970s was it possible for Sicilian Cosa Nostra members to report the theft of their car, in order to avoid being associated with any crime involving the stolen vehicle. Should any other property belonging

---

[11] OSPA 1985, *Ordinanza Sentenza della Corte di Assise di Palermo contro Abbate Giovanni +706*, Palermo, November 8, 1985, vol. VIII, 817–8.

[12] Testimony of Salvatore Contorno given to Giovanni Falcone (Investigating Judge of Palermo), *et al.*, October 1984–June 1985, 121.

to the member be stolen, however, even if it has nothing at all to do with his mafia activities, he cannot report the matter to the authorities.

The rule regarding marital fidelity, meanwhile, which requires the *mafioso* to respect his wife and forbids him to take a lover, has little or nothing to do with an ethical concept of the matrimonial state: more crucially, it is a matter of containing possible conflict and the maintenance of secrecy: "Having an affair is thought to be a signal of a disorderly and weak character, and an occasion for a *mafioso* to risk dangerous pillow talk with lovers as loose with their tongues as they are with their mores" (Gambetta 2009, 52). This rule, however, is one of the least likely to be observed: the important point is to be discreet.

In the following section, we will see how rules regarding secrecy govern certain fundamental organizational processes.

Introductions and Recognition. Being members of mafia secret societies, mobsters have to establish reliable rules to introduce and recognize themselves, even if it is forbidden for a member of the mafia to reveal to the outside world that he belongs to a mafia organization. Situations may arise in which two individuals suspect each other of being men of honor, but, in the absence of certainty, nothing can be said regarding this. To resolve the matter, a third person, who knows both the individuals and is also part of the Cosa Nostra, is required to introduce them to one another. The first rule of the ten commandments of the Sicilian Cosa Nostra affirms: "No one can present himself directly to another of our friends. There must be a third person to do it." In such a case, the third individual will say, "This one is the same," or "This one is Cosa Nostra," or "This one is like you and me"[13] (in Arlacchi 1993, 20; OSPA Stajano 2010). The same procedure applies in the American Cosa Nostra (Anastasia 1991; Maas 1997). Joseph Pistone, the FBI agent who operated undercover in the Bonanno family for six years, reported the rules governing the introduction of other *mafiosi*:

Now, when a wiseguy introduces you to another wiseguy, he will say, "Donnie is a friend of mine." That means Donnie is okay, and you can talk in front of him if you want, but he's not a made guy, so you may not want to talk about certain business or family matters in front of him. That's the way I introduce you, see. When a wiseguy is introducing another made guy, he will say, "He's a friend of

---

[13] Testimony of Antonino Calderone given to Michel Debacq (Investigating Judge of Marseille), and to the Commissione Rogatoria Internazionale (International Investigating Committee), with Giovanni Falcone (Investigating Judge of Palermo) et al., March 19, 1987–June 25, 1988, vol. III, 734–8.

ours." That means you can talk business in front of him, because he's a member of la Cosa Nostra. (Pistone and Woodley 1987, 134)

In the 'Ndrangheta, mobsters usually say: *Questo è un cristiano* (This is a christian) to say that he is one of them, a member of the organization.

This rule ensures that people who have never met before can recognize each other without making a mistake. This means that the organization has grown quantitatively and that the bonds of friendship and knowledge are no longer sufficient to distinguish a mafia member from a nonmember correctly. In addition, this rule (a) provides a way to protect the mafia copyright (Gambetta 1993), making it less likely that impostors can make use of the mafia organization "brand" without actually being members; (b) makes it difficult for law enforcement agencies to infiltrate agents; and (c) places responsibility on the person making the introduction, since, in the event of an error, he will be the one to pay the price. As ex-mobster, Sammy Gravano, underboss of the Gambino family, explains:

If I introduced somebody as a friend of mine, that's all he was. But if I'm with a made member and we meet another made member, I would be introduced as a friend of ours. You needed that third party to do this, so there wasn't any way to break into that circle. (Maas 1997, 87)

Other mafias, such as triad societies

have developed numerous methods, such as passwords, phrases, poems, hand signs, gestures, slang and jargon to show their identities ... Since the new triad member is generally allocated a "protector," the most common practice adopted by triad members is to identify their links to such protectors. A triad member challenged by another will generally be asked: Where are you from? In reply he will state that he is of a certain triad society and follows with the name of his protector. (Chu 2000, 35–6)

This practice is particularly relevant because many young people like to claim that they are triad members in order to seek criminal prestige and reputation in their peer groups.

5.2.3 *Sanctions, Reinforcement, and the Ambivalence of Rules*

As instruments of organizational control, rules are associated with sanctions and penalties for violations (Gouldner 1954). The strength of a rule lies in its sanctioning capacity, concerning both the severity of the sanction and the probability that it will be imposed. A rule, says Friedberg (1993), deprived of the sanctioning power that sustains it, becomes in the long run an empty form.

Just as honest individuals may violate legitimate rules (and laws), mafias may violate their own criminal rules. Toleration of violations is unacceptable; otherwise there would be increasing risk of organizational instability, internal violence, and discovery by the police. Since mafias cannot resort to external parties to obtain discipline over their members, only two other principal instruments are available: sanctions and the termination of relationships with problematic members. The latter solution is an extremely dangerous one, since it could lead the expelled member to become an informant. As for sanctions, the mafias have created systems of sanction assigned to specific bodies (rule supervisors) that either correspond to specific levels of hierarchical articulation in the organization or are ad hoc bodies established to assess individual cases and issue sanctions, after which they are broken up. Penalties can be quite severe, including downgrading of role, physical punishment, or death. Assistant U.S. Attorney Greg Andres asked Frank Lino, former *caporegime* in the Bonanno family, who later became an informant: "What are the penalties for a soldier if the soldier doesn't follow the order?" "You know, you can get killed," answered Lino (Crittle 2006, 90). This is what in fact happened to Dominick "Sonny Black" Napolitano (*caporegime*) for unwittingly allowing FBI agent Joseph Pistone, aka Donnie Brasco, to infiltrate the Bonanno *family*.

The same punishment is involved for those who refuse to go to a meeting ordered by the boss. Greg Andres asked Frank Lino: "If you are called to a meeting and you choose not to go?" "You'll be gone ... You're dead," answered Lino (Crittle 2006, 74). This seems to be one of the reasons for the death of Joey Gallo (aka "Crazy Joe"), who had refused to go to a meeting with the American Cosa Nostra boss Joe Colombo to discuss some business and certain aspects of his behavior. Two years later, in 1972, he was killed. The same thing happened to Louie DiBono, a member of the Gambino family, who was killed on the orders of boss John Gotti in December 1989, since he had failed to show up at a meeting.[14]

In the Yakuza, violation of the rules may give rise to various sanctions, depending on the severity of the violation. In the case of light offenses, they include shaving off hair, confinement, fines, and temporary expulsion from home. In cases of serious violations, the punishment might be beatings, finger amputation, expulsion from the *ikka*, or death (Hill 2003a, 74). While, in the past, physical punishment was predominant, over time this seems to have given way to economic sanctions.

---

[14] J.C. McKinley Jr., "Gotti Underboss Fights for Audiotapes He Says Prove He Didn't Plot Murder", *The New York Times*, May 7, 2016.

In the 'Ndrangheta, the components of the Province (the highest level of coordination in the Reggio Calabria province) are chosen for the formation of the "court," the body that decides on the charges laid against the members, divided into (1) *Trascuranze*, minor offenses, and (2) *Sbagli*, more serious sanctions that can be punished by death and are divided into:

> *Tragedia* – "Tragedy," a term that refers to the activities of a 'Ndrangheta member who, for personal purposes, indulges in conduct that causes his own wrongdoings to fall on other members or triggers internal feuds or wars with other clans.
>
> *Macchia d'onore* – Tarnished honor, the behavior of a member or someone allied to the organization that brings about the loss of the member's personal honorability, so as to be deemed unworthy to remain part of the organization.
>
> *Infamità* – Infamy, when the member betrays and denies the fundamental principles upon which the criminal organization is based, does not respect the covenant of brotherhood by helping but rather denounces his comrades, and breaks the bond of *omertà* by revealing the functioning and dynamics of the organization.[15]

Similarly, in the 1980s, some Camorra clans established a series of sanctions for violations imposed by a court composed of three to five people. The severity of the penalty depends, of course, on the seriousness of the violation. For so-called *trascuranze*, or actions of a less serious nature, from one to twenty-four days of exclusion from the organization's activities results. For more severe *trascuranze*, from five to ninety days of exclusion from the organization or three cuts on the spine is the punishment. For more serious violations, defined as *tragedie*, the exclusion from the organization can be for life. Finally, the so-called *infamità* brings with it, in addition to lifelong exclusion from the organization, the risk of death as well as punishment for the family of the member who violated the rules (De Gregorio 1983).

Rules are relevant for illegal secret organizations, such as mafias. Obviously, even if they are followed, this does not eliminate all organizational problems and internal conflict. But they are certainly an important instrument that *mafiosi* can employ to attempt to maintain social order, reduce uncertainty, and foster coordination between people and the organizational unit, imposing limits on rational individual opportunism

---

[15] Tribunale di Reggio Calabria, DDA (*Direzione Distrettuale Antimafia*, District Anti-Mafia Directorate) 2010, *Operazione Crimine*, vol. I, 450.

(Williamson 1975; 1996). But when a rule is not a written one, the possibilities of ambiguity increase. A great deal of research has demonstrated that tacit knowledge and difficult-to-articulate knowledge (Polanyi 1962; Winter 1987; Cattani et al. 2013) are difficult to transfer with respect to explicit knowledge. If rules are not codified in written form, there is an increasing likelihood of ambiguity in the interpretation of correct behavior. The following case is a very significant example of this. A member of the American Cosa Nostra's Bonanno family discovered that his wife was being unfaithful to him with another member of the organization, thus violating a fundamental organization rule. As soon as he found out about this, the member asked to meet the boss to apprise him of the situation and describe the serious embarrassment it had caused. During the interview, he asked the boss whether they could be killed as a matter of vendetta. The boss, however, did not agree with this solution. Namely:

> If the member sincerely had such strong feelings about both the infidelity and the embarrassment, (the boss) said, he should have made his own decision, dispatched them both, and then presented himself to the family administration with the facts and let the family decide his fate. ... either his feelings about the matter weren't strong enough, or he didn't trust the administration enough, to put his faith in whatever decision they would make after the fact. By asking permission, the member was trying to make the family responsible for his decision to act – "wiping his potentially bloody knife on the sleeves of others." (Bonanno and Abromovitz 2011, 275)

A problem emerges, therefore: how can a *mafioso* know for sure whether he is correctly respecting or in fact violating a rule? The answer, stated Bonanno, is that what is right and what is wrong are determined on a case-by-case basis:

> *Mafiosi* learn the distinction by listening, learning and applying the traditional teaching of their elders. Punishment for violations depends upon the facts of each case. As a result, it's incumbent on each member to be sure he is correct in his decision – lest it be his last. (Bonanno and Abromovitz 2011, 278)

As in the case of organizational structures, with rules, too, there is a natural tension with leadership. A leader can exert pressure on the strictness of the rules, trying to modify them in order to increase his own field of action, to strengthen his own power. Collaborator with justice Leonardo Messina tells how one of the most important twentieth-century bosses of the Sicilian Cosa Nostra, Totò Riina (the instigator of the murders of magistrates Falcone and Borsellino, as well as many others), of the Corleone family, tried to subvert and use the rules to his own advantage during his mafia leadership. For example, in the 1980s, he introduced a rule whereby every mobster arrested would lose the "man of honor" status, in order to prevent the prisoner from remaining in touch with the organization leadership and to prevent the circulation of information. This rule, a modification of the previous one, was not just a matter of security, but derived from the fact that Riina wanted to exclude old leaders and their role in the decision-making process. Once it was his own men who were arrested, the rule fell immediately into disuse.[16] In the 1980s, the system of rules of the Sicilian Cosa Nostra had become, in Riina's hands, a highly flexible instrument, losing its character of organizational detachment and impartiality.

Sometimes, rules are not applied very rigidly. For example, the rule regarding the prohibition of membership for ex-cops was broken in the case of Ron Previti in the 1990s. As an ex-cop, Previti was not eligible for membership in the American Cosa Nostra: despite this, he was permitted to join the John Stanfa family in Philadelphia. This "elastic" application of the rules, in which business requirements prevail over the origins and skills of the new member, can be put down to a matter of opportunity – business opportunity, of course – or to contingent requirements or to a perceived situation of relative calm and security that can lead to a certain relaxation toward their rigid application, as in this particular case of recruitment.

A rule may also be suspended. Sicilian Cosa Nostra collaborator with justice Vincenzo Sinacori affirms that "even though rules exist, it doesn't necessarily mean that they'll be applied ... rules exist when they're applied ... I mean, at the moment that they're applied, they exist."[17] The collaborator with justice Antonino Calderone says:

Cosa Nostra has its rules, but then there are special cases with their own shadings and complications. There are those who follow the rules, and there are exceptions and abuses. There are those who are tolerated, those who are made examples of, those who come to be punished. (Arlacchi 1993, 110)

However, compliance with the rules is often dependent on the arbitrariness of those who hold positions of power within the organization and who administer the rules according to the convenience of the moment. The strength of a rule in the mafia is always in relation to the power of those who decide to apply it or not to apply it, and their sanctioning power.

---

[16] Procura della Repubblica di Palermo, DDA (1992), *Verbali di Interrogatorio del collaboratore di giustizia Leonardo Messina*.
[17] Corte di Assise di Trapani, Sezione Procedura penale, *Sentenza contro Agate Vito+22*; June 22, 1998 (Dino 2006, XXI).

5.2.4   Some Concluding Remarks

Despite the relevance of rules in organizations, in recent years there have been relatively few empirical studies that analyze how they work. I have given an account of how organizations that lack a legal mechanism of dispute resolution, and cannot create binding contracts, can work efficiently by establishing and reinforcing explicit and implicit organizational rules. I showed how rules work in mafia organizations and the functions that they perform. I have demonstrated that rules play an important role in secret organizations such as mafias and that, since they are essential to ensure secrecy and the concealment of illegal activity as well as to regulate the use of violence, they are important instruments of *governance* in these criminal organizations. Rules in mafias are mainly a way to regulate mob behavior rather than a way of doing things, and, far from being mere folklore, or the remains of an ancient cultural heritage, they exhibit a certain degree of organizational rationality. They are a way to constrain mobs' behavior, in order to avoid those possible options that are most detrimental to the life of the organization.

The similarity of the rules throughout the different mafias analyzed means that these criminal organizations, despite their historical and cultural differences, share common organizational problems.

To what extent do these findings apply to legitimate organizations? There are relevant similarities and differences between mafia organizations and legitimate organizations. As organizations, mafias share many characteristics with legitimate organizations. For example, like firms, mafias are motivated by the pursuit of economic profit, and they "are shaped by the same environmental and technological forces as are the enterprises of legitimate businesses" (Potter 1994, 153). Moreover, even legitimate firms can commit criminal acts, as the Enron case shows.

Nevertheless, mafias substantially differ from legitimate organizations along several dimensions: they are secret organizations, illegal in every act that they commit, even when they operate in legal markets. Moreover, they lack legal mechanisms of dispute resolution and are unable to establish binding contracts. Because mafias operate in illegal markets, or are outlaw actors in legal markets, they are subject to a series of constraints that limit their organizational structure, size, mode of operation, etc. Operating both in the underworld and in the upperworld, they have to manage a fundamental organizational dilemma: they have to pursue economic activities under secret conditions. On the one hand, lacking much of the paperwork that is common to legitimate organizations, criminal organizations can rapidly evolve and reorganize when the opportunity or need arises. They are quick to capitalize on newly opened markets, and quick to rebuild themselves under another guise when caught by authorities. On the other hand, mafias are not really efficient organizations. As discussed previously, they cannot operate as legitimate organizations because they face a variety of additional problems, from the hostility of the environment, to information, communication, and trust problems; challenges in member recruitment; and lack of legal institutions for dispute resolution.

In the light of these commonalities and differences, the working hypothesis for an extension of these findings to legitimate organizations is the following. Of the three functions performed by mafia rules – establish organizational order, contain conflict and violence, and maintain secrecy – organizational functions are common to all organizations, both legal and illegal. Rules in legitimate and criminal organizations perform the same organizational functions (e.g., to favor cooperation among members; to establish hierarchy and command and control systems). Instead, rules relating to the containment of violence are especially typical of criminal organizations, but also of terrorist, police, and military bodies. In legitimate business organizations, we would not expect to find many rules about the containment of violence, since regulation in this respect is guaranteed by law enforcement agencies. Finally, rules regarding the maintenance of secrecy, which are specific to mafias in their nature as secret societies, are also partly necessary in many legitimate organizations. High-tech organizations, for example, may need to maintain a high level of secrecy about their inventions, patents, and manufacturing processes. Legitimate organizations that derive benefits from secrecy will adopt rules that are similar to those of criminal organizations: for example, high-tech companies have a tacit rule of not hiring people from other companies without a period of unemployment; innovative industries have strict rules for their patent departments. In addition, there are trade and corporate secrecy, military secrecy, intelligence, secrets of state, etc. (see Bok 1989).

Moreover, in mafias, these three functions are closely interrelated. For example, to manage violence, an organization must equip itself with an organizational structure featuring forms of higher-level bodies of coordination (Catino 2014). The final balance is, however, not a stable one. Violence cannot be wholly eliminated, and secrecy can be violated (for example, through collaborators with justice). Mafia rules are stratagems of preventive obligation that mobs intentionally deploy to prevent themselves from making unwise decisions, and engaging in dangerous behavior.

6   Mafia Organizational Dilemmas

Mafias have to undertake the complex task of pursuing their economic interests in conditions of secrecy, while containing internal violence and working in hostile environments. It is a task that sets them certain organizational dilemmas.[1]

Organization theory has frequently interpreted and explained organizational activity by referring to pairs of opposites, seen as alternative courses of organizational action: rational model vs. natural model (Gouldner 1959); closed system vs. open system; mechanical system vs. organic system (Burns and Stalker 1961); market vs. hierarchy/organization (Williamson 1975), etc. Thompson (1967) warned of how organizational reality is too complex a thing to be represented in the dichotomous structure of such examples. He suggested abandoning the construction of simplified contrasting models, and instead analyzing how organizations manage, and reconcile, the antithetical elements that arise within them. Less attention has been paid to the fact that, very often, rather than choices that are dichotomous or positioned along a continuum, it is often a matter of polar opposites that have to be managed, with the solution at neither one pole nor the other. These pairs of opposites constitute organizational dilemmas.

Organizational dilemmas are like "oppositional pairs," the presence of which generates tension in an organizational system (Touraine 1973). These are contradictory needs and goals that all complex organizations must in some way balance and deal with. Every requirement carries both advantages and disadvantages. They exist in a state of tension – moving one objective upward automatically moves the other downward. There is no single optimal answer that solves a specific dilemma once and for all: there is no universal panacea for dilemmas (Handy 1999). Each solution,

---

[1] A dilemma (from the Late Latin *dilēmma*, which derives from the Greek *dilēmma*, consisting of *dis* – twice – and *lēmma* – premise) is a problem that is difficult to solve, involving a situation where it is necessary to choose between two alternatives.

rather, stems from an attempt to find a synthesis between opposing elements and is chosen on the basis of the evaluation of existing contingent conditions in a given context at a certain historical moment. Organizational order is the result of this equilibrium between various dilemmas. It may vary over time, shifting the balance toward one pole rather than the other.

Porter (1996) attributes trade-offs[2] to problems of strategy and strategic positioning in an organization. They occur when activities are incompatible and arise when it is difficult for an organization to do two different things just as well as two separate organizations would. An organization that has, at the same time, to undertake two different and sometimes conflicting tasks, A and B, will produce a worse performance than two different organizations dedicated to A and B exclusively. A possible solution for an organization that needs to address both tasks is to entrust the latter to two different suborganizational units.

Some dilemmas are present, with various forms and contents, in other organizations, while others are typical of, and integral to, mafia organizations.[3] Analyzing mafia organizational action with fundamental dilemmas constantly present makes it possible to escape a rigid determinism, both environmental and involving external factors – organizational constraints – and a rigid organizational subjectivism, according to which mafias are omnipotent and can do whatever they want.

To understand the logic of organizational action, it is necessary to understand the calculations that organizations carry out in order to identify which choices to pursue and which to avoid: calculations that are characterized by bounded rationality. In the case of the mafia, these calculations, and the choices that ensue, are understandable through the analysis of mafia organizational dilemmas. Let's have a closer look at the main dilemmas.

---

[2] A trade-off is a situation that implies a choice between two or more possibilities, where the loss of value in one represents an increase in value in another. It defines a situation in which there arises a compromise choice between two objectives that are equally desirable but in conflict with each other.

[3] In certain cases, there can be more than two contradictory objectives. Obstfeld et al. (2004) introduced the term "policy trilemma" in international macroeconomics, to say that is it impossible to have at the same time (1) free capital mobility, (2) monetary autonomy, and (3) exchange rate management. Similarly, analyzing the economic implications of globalization on democratic systems, Rodrik (2011) used the term "trilemma" to highlight the difficulty of having hyperglobalization, democracy, and national self-determination all at once. At most, says Rodrik, we can have two out of three.

6.1   Small vs. Large

The size of an organization, in terms of the number of participants, is an important variable in explaining its operation (Michels 1911; Pugh et al. 1968; Child 1972; Child and Mansfield 1972). Is there an optimal size for a criminal organization like the mafia? It is preferable to stay small or, instead, to increase in size in order to make the most of its activities?

From the point of view of internal cohesion, it would be preferable to stay small. Van Doorn (1966) states that only small organizations (like small parties and *kibbutzim*) may exhibit the characteristics of a "sect," while larger organizations are necessarily of the "coalition" kind, characterized by a type of organization with a diffuse power structure that functions through negotiation between a plurality of internal groups. The sect, however, works as a highly centralized organization with a high degree of consensus required from participants, where deviation from its central values is regarded as heresy and apostasy. In sects, continues van Doorn, the tolerance of independence within the group is minimal, with a high level of control over various aspects of individual behavior. Michels (1911) has shown that the magnitude of a political party was the main independent variable in explaining the formation of oligarchies. The increase in size increases organizational complexity, which favors the centralization of decision-making but makes democratic decisions difficult. In fact, as the number of participants increases, direct democracy becomes impossible, for reasons of space, time, distance, etc., and so it is necessary to resort to delegates.

A limit to size, however, could be a drag on growth. Enterprises in all sectors, from automobiles, to consumer products, to the media, attempt to grow in order to acquire the necessary resources to compete on a global scale, to invest in new technologies, and to ensure access to markets (Potter 2000). There is the belief that the interruption of growth leads to stagnation and the progressive crisis of a business: customers might not see their needs completely met and competitors would take advantage to gain market shares at the expense of the organization that intends to remain stable. The larger size of a company increases its power in its respective markets, helps to increase revenues, and is a way to reduce dependence on the environment. There are obvious advantages of size, as summarized here:

Organizations that are large have more power and leverage over their environments. They are more able to resist immediate pressures for change and, moreover, have more time in which to recognize external threats and adapt to meet them. Growth enhances the organization's survival value, then, by providing a cushion, or slack, against organizational failure. (Pfeffer and Salancik 1978, 139)

Other strategies include (a) co-option, with the incorporation of representatives of external groups into the decision-making or advisory structure of an organization or (b) the formation of alliances and joint ventures.

In addition, the larger the organization, the greater the career opportunities, as larger organizations tend to have a greater number of positions and development paths, both professional and managerial. Only large companies can make large investments in order to compete globally and only large companies can realize large-scale works and infrastructure. Large dimensions also favor the maintenance of resources for the economic support required in times of crisis. They may, on the other hand, encourage processes of structural inertia in relation to change, and processes of bureaucratization and rigidity that render the organization sluggish with respect to environmental challenges and shortsighted in the face of external threats (new competitors, new products, changes in consumer taste, etc.).

In contrast, small companies are more responsive and flexible and therefore more suitable for highly dynamic markets. They require less hierarchy, and are therefore flatter, so decision-making processes are more rapid. They suffer less from bureaucratization, and the personal involvement of employees stimulates motivation and commitment, as it is easier for participants to identify with the company's mission. This fosters entrepreneurial and innovative behavior in participants. Several alternatives exist to the small vs. large dilemma, with some hybrid forms that offer the benefits of both (e.g., Apple organizes its R&D in limited-size autonomous groups with a low level of hierarchy).

Taking the basic organizational unit (family, *ikka*, clan, etc.) as the unit of reference analysis, what form does the dilemma of size in mafia organizations take? A large size allows the criminal organization to pursue economies of scale and to maintain a high reputation resulting from the strength of the number of members. However, this also considerably increases the costs of coordination, especially given the impossibility of resorting to the typical modes of communication that legal companies employ, as well as the costs of control, increasing the risk of exposure to law enforcement agencies.

According to Schelling (1967), there are many different incentives to organization in a large-scale criminal firm. The high costs of overheads and other elements of technology make small-scale operation impractical. A large firm may internalize a number of costs and negative externalities, such as the excess of violence that attracts law enforcement agencies. A single organization has fewer incentives than a large one to reduce violence connected to its own crimes, while a large organization will profit by imposing discipline and reducing excess of violence. There are also other external economies, Schelling affirms, that can become internalized to the advantage of the centralized firm. Finally,

large criminal business firms provide governmental structure to the underworld, helping to maintain the peace, setting rules, arbitrating disputes, and enforcing discipline, they are in a position to set up their own businesses and exclude competition. Constituting a kind of "corporate state," they can give themselves the franchise for various "state-sponsored monopolies." They can do this either by denying the benefits of the underworld government to their competitors or by using the equivalent of their "police power" to prevent competition. (Schelling 1967, 118)

However, a large size entails obvious risks and inefficiencies. As Weinstein says:

The most efficient organizational form for committing crime may be that of a small, tight-knit mafia family, for a number of reasons. A crime family has the capability to run its local operations while protecting the safety of its members. Its small size facilitates its secret operations: members' defection can be credibly punished by death. Thus, to survive and avoid police information, crime families must stay small and maintain a capacity to control their members. (Weinstein 2007, 128)

Therefore, a small size would be the most appropriate solution for a mafia organization, with structures that are simple (Southerland and Potter 1993), "localized, fragmented, ephemeral and undiversified" (Reuter 1983, 131). This helps it to maintain the secrecy required by the environment in which it operates, as well as the ability to maintain a high level of internal control. And the importance of internal control in mafias is made evident by the complex recruiting practices.

A large size complicates the decision-making processes, such as the election of the top management. In large families of the Sicilian Cosa Nostra, unlike in the small ones, the election of the boss does not take place through a direct vote (one member one vote), but through delegates. This is also due to reasons of secrecy, as the assembly of a *family*, with hundreds of members present at the same place, constitutes a danger to security.

In addition, a sudden and very substantial growth in the number of members in an organization can threaten its stability, as we have seen in the case of the Camorra during the Raffaele Cutolo era, between 1975 and 1983. His attempt to centralize the Camorra, together with the rapid growth in the number of members, led to a reduction in internal cohesion, with differences in socialization between the old members and new members creating an identity crisis. This favored the formation of a fiercely oppositional cartel, in addition to the repression by law enforcement agencies.

As we have seen, there are two important elements that require a large-scale organization: investment in technology and competition at a global level. Mafias, however, adopt "simple" technologies (except in the field of narcotics production and trafficking) and tend to operate in defined territories, although they may also expand into other nontraditional areas (Varese 2011; Sciarrone 2014; Dalla Chiesa 2016) or operate in far-flung geographical contexts. They would seem, therefore, to be less inclined to meet the demands of an increase in size.

Analyzing a great deal of research regarding criminal organizations, Bouchard and Morselli (2014) demonstrate that small organizations are the typical configuration of organized crime in the majority of industrialized countries. It seems that "small is beautiful" in organized crime, and that a smaller scale appears to be safer, easier, and more efficient than a larger one (Bouchard and Morselli 2014, 289).

There exist, in fact, two natural barriers to growth (Paoli et al. 2009). The first is that criminal enterprises have to operate without the benefit of the state – without the enforcement of contracts and property rights, and with a lack of secured loan mechanisms. The second derives from the fact that they operate *against* the state, with the constant risk of arrest, seizure of property, etc. These barriers, and in particular the second, would suggest that remaining small is preferable, given that a larger scale favors vulnerability and infiltration by law enforcement agencies (Moore 1977). In addition, larger groups usually mean a lower level of trust.

Studying gambling and loan-sharking in New York City, Reuter (1983) argues that a criminal enterprise derives positive advantages from remaining small. One reason is the security of an organization in a hostile environment.[4] According to Reuter, the most precious asset of a criminal enterprise is information about its activities. Information is critical because it can lead to the arrest of members. To avoid this and protect themselves from information leakage, criminal organizations do three things, as we have seen in Chapter 2. First, they restrict the number of people with comprehensive knowledge about the organization's business and they restrict information given to lower-level employees. Second, they restrict the number of total employees in the organization. Third, they restrict the geographical size of the organization to make

---

[4] A *hostile* environment is one in which a serious error may result in the crippling of the organization (Potter 1994). For example, a utility company that uses nuclear power to generate electricity is subject not only to possible damage to production, but also to a nuclear accident.

person-to-person communication easier and more efficient, avoiding written instructions and telephones as much as possible.

There are, therefore, both incentives to increase in size, and incentives to remain small. Of course, it is necessary to clarify how size, and how the boundaries of a criminal organization, are defined. For example, if we consider only the made members of a mafia organization, or only those who have followed a specific career path, especially with reference to the rite of initiation; or if we also include the associates, the first line of organization collaborators; or if we consider the entire network of those who work together in various capacities with the criminal organization, including the white-collar workers, politicians, public officials, corrupt members of law enforcement agencies, and the whole so-called gray area. To understand the functioning of these organizations, it is necessary to understand what lies *outside* these organizations: otherwise it is impossible to explain how they work. However, it is also necessary to distinguish the organization from its environment, in order to understand more clearly the interactions that take place. It is therefore necessary to distinguish between the mafia organization, composed of made members and associates, on the one hand, and the world of the collaborators, on the other. When it comes to the size of the criminal organization, therefore, reference is made to the number of actual members and associates.

Given the characteristics of uncertainty and hostility that characterize the mafia environment, some considerations are possible regarding the relationships among organizational structure, size, and environment. Decentralization, for example, would require high formalization, with a large number of rules and procedures that organization members would have to follow in order to reduce the need for control over the actions they carry out and the decisions that they make. But this formalization might endanger security, leaving evidence with regard to the organization and its illegal activities. On the other hand, centralization in hostile environments can also be problematic, as it would require top-down communications that would always carry the risk of being intercepted. Hence, both centralization and decentralization create security problems, particularly in a large-scale organization.

Based on the preceding analysis, the best organizational structure for a criminal organization seems to be one that is small- or medium-sized, with decentralization based on mutual understandings and agreements on relatively few operating procedures (Potter 1994). This explains why mafias carry out extremely targeted and selective recruitment, involving long periods of observation of the criminal and economic ability of the initiand, someone who already frequents the community that he is about to enter formally. It also explains why they tend to develop the clan form of organization – a hierarchical clan in this case – in order to increase the sharing of objectives and thus reduce problems of control, given the risk to security that these activities entail.

6.2   Security vs. Efficiency

How are groups that operate in clandestine conditions organized? How do they manage to combine efficiency of activity and pursuit of goals while concealing their actions from the outside world? Do they adopt similar organizational models? According to Duverger (1966), groups that operate under such conditions are forced to adopt a cell-form organizational structure, employing basic units composed of the smallest possible number of elements (usually three to five) and rigidly separated from each other. At each level, only the head of each unit is in contact with the level above. Ties are thus minimized, so that if a member of the organization is arrested and tortured, only very few people can be named. The same applies should the police manage to infiltrate spies into the group.

Mafias have to balance maintenance of secrecy, both internal and external, with the need for communication (without which intraorganizational cooperation could not be realized) and for the outward visibility required to control their territory and support their reputation. Criminal groups indeed face a constant security/efficiency trade-off: criminal members reduce the levels of communication as a strategy to shield their illicit activities, but they still must take some risks to ensure the management of their businesses (Morselli et al. 2007). In this regard, Gambetta (2009) identifies three main problems that characterize criminal communication. The first is the *communication problem* – the need to interact with criminal colleagues without others (police, rivals) intercepting and understanding the message. The second is the *identification problem* – the need to identify other members of the organization and to be identified as such, without being recognized by others. The third problem is the *advertising problem* – the fact that criminal organizations cannot promote their goods and services in traditional ways, despite needing to attract the interest of others and obtain resources. The use of names and trademarks is particularly relevant for organized crime, says Gambetta, as they help to establish a reputation with customers and other organizations.

The 'Ndrangheta, for example, favors *comparaggi* – a sort of very close cronyism – and weddings for those who enter the organization, partly in order to reduce the danger of informing. Close blood ties make collaboration with justice more problematic, even if they are still present in this organization. For the American Cosa Nostra, Bill Bonanno says that in such cases, when several crews are sent to do the same job, the member who actually commits the murder is rarely known – thus concealing the actual perpetrators for purposes of security. Sometimes even the person who orders the hit never knows who fires the fatal shot. A group leader might simply call several members of his crew together and tell them, "This has to be done." The crew members assign the job or contract, then decide on their own whether it will be done independently or jointly . . . Preserving maximum deniability is especially important, because information is temptation: somewhere down the road, a person who knows too much just might crack, implicating others or himself. (Bonanno and Abromovitz 2011, 245)

Information sharing is strongly regulated on the basis of the hierarchical level occupied in the organization. In the American Cosa Nostra, for example, there are rules and protocols called *respect* that establish how a member should behave toward other hierarchical levels: "When you were around a captain or a boss, you didn't speak or join in the conversation unless asked to" (Pistone and Woodley 1987, 134). This is not only a rule of respect toward the hierarchy, but a way to control the flow of information to other subjects, the associates, whom the organization is not yet completely sure about, thus preventing the circulation of relevant information.

In carrying out their activities in illegal and legal markets, mafias must deal with a fundamental dilemma based on two opposing needs: the need for efficiency, common to all organizations, and the need for security, typical of criminal and secret enterprises. The need for security favors compartmentation. This is an organizational strategy to manage secrecy and is based on the breaking down of information by allocating knowledge, and the activities related to it, to various units, individuals, and/or organizations, making it difficult for one subject, whether internal or external, to form an idea of the picture as a whole. As in the structure outlined by Duverger (1966), members at an operational level are organized into cells (family, clan) and each one of them knows only the other members belonging to the same cell. In this way, information and the knowledge of specific events are reduced to a minimum.

The logic of compartmentation is well known to, and widespread among, many clandestine organizations, including terrorist groups. The Red Brigades, an Italian terrorist group, formalized various organizational and behavioral rules in documents in order to ensure effective compartmentation.[5] On the basis of these rules, no militant knew the

---

[5] One document stated that compartmentation was the basis for organization security: "Compartmentation is a general law for revolutionary war in the metropolis, and is one of the fundamental principles of security in our organization. Our experience has made it abundantly clear that those who neglect this law and fail to apply it with absolute rigor are inevitably destined to defeat and destruction" (*Risoluzione della Direzione Strategica delle Brigate Rosse*, 2, 1975, in Petrillo 2013, 245–6).

exact organizational chart of the group, but only the bare minimum – the name of the person immediately above or below in the hierarchy. Compartmentation was both vertical, within the structure that each single militant belonged to, and horizontal and geographical, between the various territorial structures. It not only was a matter of not knowing the names of various members of the organization, but also real information that was compartmentalized. Each activist had to know the indispensible information, with knowledge limited to what was necessary for the performance of his work.

While this organizational practice, common to all guerrilla organizations, limited efficiency and daily functioning, considerably lengthening the time devoted to action and execution, it also ensured less vulnerability over time to the repressive activity of law enforcement agencies, limiting the consequences of any possible arrests. In addition, as they grew accustomed to such a system, the militants, always in safe conditions, could limit time needed for operations and improve efficiency in the operating processes (Petrillo 2013).

To contain the excesses and risks of an organizational logic of this type – such as isolation, the loss of significance, and motivation, which could be extremely damaging to an ideological organization such as the Red Brigades – a certain amount of "discretion" was allowed to the militants in terms of the application of security precepts. Also, organizational compartmentation did not mean the compartmentation of political debate and information in general. There was, therefore, extensive production and circulation, both within the organization and in the outside world, of written documents that defined the group's strategic lines and ideas.

However, in order to be performed efficiently, a complex activity requires a certain amount of coordination between the different cells, and this results in the communication and exchange of information. These requirements may be hindered by excessive compartmentation. Mafia organizations have to deal with this trade-off, ensuring the secrecy of activities through compartmentation, but also coordination, both intraorganizational (within a family/cell), and interorganizational (between families and other parties outside the organization). The latter, in mafias, is ensured by the higher-level bodies of coordination, which, albeit with different forms and methods, almost all the mafias have developed over time.

Morselli (Morselli et al. 2007; Morselli 2009) analyze the efficiency/ security trade-off in criminal and terrorist organizations. The aspect of trade-off that must receive the most attention depends, say the authors, on the objectives of the criminal group. While terrorist networks are ideologically driven, criminal enterprises pursue monetary ends. The result is that time-to-task[6] is shorter in criminal enterprises compared to terrorist networks and thus group efficiency is prioritized over group security. Criminal groups are forced to act even when security is less than optimal. Terrorist networks, in contrast, have longer horizons and security is prioritized over the execution of any single attack.

In line with these findings, a systematic comparison between the behavior of leaders of 'Ndrangheta networks involved in drug trafficking and their behavior in more traditional illicit activities (e.g., extortion, fraud, corruption) highlights how drug trafficking networks prioritize efficiency, whereas the 'Ndrangheta networks engaging in traditional crimes prioritize security (Superchi 2018). The latter type of activities indeed allow the 'Ndrangheta to continue existing, expanding, and engaging in several types of illicit activities, among which drug trafficking is one of most profitable (Paoli 2004).

The degree of compartmentation in a mafia organization is also related to the degree of repression by state agencies (the judiciary and the police), attention from political forces and the media, and informing by former members.[7] With regard to the Sicilian Cosa Nostra, says collaborator with justice Salvatore Cancemi, not all men of honor know what happens within Cosa Nostra. And according to collaborator with justice Antonino Calderone, after a murder had been committed, not all family members were made aware of who had done the shooting, and usually only the *capodecina* knew the identity of the killer (Arlacchi 1993).

In the Sicilian Cosa Nostra,[8] compartmentation consisted in the obligation to turn to your superior for any requirement. The superior then decided whether to put the applicant in contact with other figures higher up in the hierarchy. In this way, there is a pattern that tends to maximize secrecy, limiting the degree of anyone's knowledge of the organizational structures to the minimum necessary degree. Collaborator with justice Tommaso Buscetta says that some families (Resuttana, Corleone) did not disclose the names of their followers, thus limiting the possibility of pursuing the members from a legal point of view.

According to collaborator with justice Leonardo Messina, the circulation of information within the Sicilian Cosa Nostra is very limited. This

---

[6] With the term "time-to-task," the authors "refer to the interplay between time and action. Time-to-task is shorter in criminal enterprise networks than in terrorist networks. Time-to-task is longer for covert networks pursuing ideological causes because they are less often in action than are criminal enterprise networks" (Morselli et al. 2007, 145).

[7] The Red Brigades adopted compartmentation to maintain secrecy, everyone knowing only a few aspects of a broader fact. Whoever ended up in jail automatically gave up every official responsibility, as the Tupamaros did (Fasanella and Franceschini 2004).

[8] Corte di Assise di Palermo 1986, *Sentenza contro Abbate Giovanni+459*, December 16, 1384–6.

process of limiting the circulation of information was further developed along the lines of verticalization and the apical concentration of power in the strategy of Totò Riina, one of the most significant figures in the recent history of the organization (Paoli 2003). Forms of "confidential affiliation" were also introduced for new members, in order to limit the possibilities of discovery and informing. The increased intraorganizational secrecy was in fact due to the negative consequences for the organization arising from informing. While in the past it was permitted for the members of one family to know the identity of "colleagues" in other families, this is now no longer possible. Information concerning the composition and number of members of individual families is known only to the members at a higher level. The higher the level occupied by a member of the organization, the higher his level of familiarity regarding important organizational details and the greater his knowledge concerning the members of the other families. Furthermore, the practice was introduced to employ common criminals for simpler crimes and for the ones with the highest level of risk, in order to reduce the possibility of informing in case of arrest (De Lucia 2015).

Control over the flow of information was used by top management to manipulate internal politics, such as the spread of false information regarding an opponent. Such misinformation was often a prelude to subsequent delegitimization and physical elimination.

The 'Ndrangheta, too, has resorted to a process of compartmentation in their management of kidnapping. Collaborator with justice Antonio Zagari (1992) says that to manage kidnappings, the 'Ndrangheta organized participation in "separate cells." The people who worked on the kidnapping did not know each other and during the delivery stages took the precaution of remaining hooded. The hostage's prison itself was kept secret from almost all of the kidnappers. This confession is consistent with the findings of an empirical study focusing on the information structure that optimizes criminal organizations' security/efficiency trade-off and, in particular, how the information structure reacts to two external authorities' detection models (Baccara and Bar-Isaac 2008). The agent-based detection model relies on the independence between the likelihood of an agent's detection and his level of cooperation within the organization, whereas in the cooperation-based detection model an agent's probability of detection is dependent on his level of cooperation within the organization. In the former model, the optimal information structure is that of "binary cells" (i.e., pairs of agents with mutual information on themselves and no information links with other members). In the latter model, the optimal information structure resembles a hierarchy with an agent acting as an information hub that does not cooperate with other members, thus remaining undetected. If each individual agent's contribution to the organization is sufficiently high, the optimal organization can also be a binary cell structure.

In the past, the 'Ndrangheta had had a lower level of secrecy in terms of recruiting: so much so that the former Sicilian Cosa Nostra member informant Tommaso Buscetta could say that it "represents an entity *sui generis*, from our point of view, because of the lack of seriousness in recruitment and its very low level of secrecy – almost non-existent, really" (Arlacchi 1994, 53). The 'Ndrangheta has certainly been the organization that has most increased levels of secrecy and reduced circulation of information, as a result of the rising level of interest from law enforcement agencies since the end of the 1990s. This process of progressively augmenting secrecy led, on the one hand, to the creation of higher-level bodies of coordination (*mandamenti*) to contain internal feuds, which produced a higher level of pressure on the part of law enforcement, and, on the other, to a process of compartmentation to decrease the impact of informing. Collaborator with justice Gaetano Costa states that to increase privacy and security, an organizational system of hermetic compartments was created, so as to eliminate the possibility of knowing the components of each single *locale* and to prevent members from referring to data regarding the organization and its employees in the outside world (Ciconte 1996). In line with this process of compartmentation, starting in the second half of the 1970s, a secret organization, a kind of lodge, was established within the 'Ndrangheta itself: the Santa – the Holy. It is composed of the highest positions in the organization, authorized not only to forge links with the outside world, with the sphere of politics, but also to be an actual part of it, violating one of the association's fundamental rules. Collaborator with justice Giovanni Gullà says about this:

The *Santa* is like a kind of area that allows contacts, relationships and ties with other organizations of power. With the *Santa* the 'Ndrangheta made itself open to compromise with powers deviated by institutions. Up until the rank of *sgarrista*, there is a complete ban on being part of any kind of public structure, to have relatives in the police and even to have any type of membership card relating to Public Administrations; the *santisti* instead can, and perhaps should, form relationships with politicians, civil servants, professionals and masons. Indeed, one of the main tasks of the *santisti* is to infiltrate or take over public institutions, making use of electoral support. It is clear that with the *Santa* the rules of the traditional mafia have been completely overturned, even while this continues to subsist as a prerequisite for the existence and profitable operation of the *Santa*.[9]

---

[9] Tribunale di Reggio Calabria 1999, Corte di Assise, *Sentenza contro Condello Pasquale +282*, January 19, 46/93, 18/96 RG Assise.

It is, therefore, a matter of a secret organizational unit within a secret organization, with the knowledge of its members restricted to the actual participating members themselves. Gullà goes on:

The level of *Santa* is marked by a fundamental peculiarity: it is known exclusively to those who achieve it. It creates a kind of group of mutual assistance, in the sense that every situation regarding the *santisti* must be resolved within the *Santa* itself. It is important to emphasize that the *Santa* represents a "hidden" sphere within the 'Ndrangheta, since the relative level is known only to other *santisti* and they occupy no visible role of significance within the 'Ndrangheta hierarchy. To give an example, if a *'ndranghetista* presents himself to other *'ndranghetisti* of another *locale*, he must make known his level, *picciotto*, *camorrista*, *sgarrista*, etc., but not that of *santista*, should he also occupy that position, because he can only make that known exclusively to other *santisti*.[10]

The dynamics of compartmentation are similar in other criminal organizations. In the Sacra Corona Unita (Sacred United Crown), an Italian mafia operating in Puglia, the process of secrecy and compartmentation due to intense repression led to hidden membership and the creation of power substructures whose identity is known only to the top management (Massari 1998).

The top leaders of the Yakuza, meanwhile, developed a system called *jōnōkin,* which effectively insulated them from repression by law enforcement agencies. This system consists of payments from subordinate gangs, in such a way that the bosses receive income without being directly involved in any criminal activities (Hill 2003a, 48).

Similar dynamics are present in the organization of the Colombian drug cartels. These cartels make use of the network form of organization known as *wheel,* also called *hub* or *star networks* (Kenney 2007). This involves a core group that manages and oversees the entire process and a series of peripheral nodes that perform operational tasks, sometimes for more than one core group. Through this compartmentation of activities into separate cells, those who manage the networks hope to reduce any potential damage arising from investigative activity and the possible collaboration/betrayal of employees. The organizational structure is fairly streamlined, with only three or four management levels. From top to bottom, a typical network includes core group leaders, cell managers, assistant managers, and cell workers (Kenney 2007, 34).

The degree of concealment of a mafia organization also depends on the degree of "social consensus" and of repression by law enforcement agencies. In response to intense repression and numerous arrests, the five New York American Cosa Nostra families profoundly altered their

---

[10] Ibid.

methods of communication to the outside world, avoiding certain crime "star" behavior, like that of John Gotti (head of the Gambino family), and trying to become as invisible as possible. In the Genovese family (American Cosa Nostra, New York), for example, to reduce visibility to the outside, they introduced the rotation of those who direct daily activities, or made use of people who were less well known for conducting such activities. Finally, some families are imitating terrorist organizations, where a cell (in this case a group within a family) has no knowledge of the activities conducted by another cell. A similar cell type model is deployed by the Sinaloa cartel, the most important Mexican organization specializing in the production and trafficking of drugs.

Those who fight these organizations suffer from the same problem. The difference is that law enforcement agencies also suffer from the typical problems of bureaucratic organizations, such as information jealousy in sharing information and long chains of command that require decision-making time and approval of specific investigations (e.g., wiretapping) that are often not adequate to reach the desired goal and hopelessly unsuitable in terms of taking advantage of opportunities that may arise and that only rapid action would achieve. Mafias, on the other hand, do not suffer from the typical problems of bureaucracy and can also make decisions, even important ones, very quickly. Therefore, the "red tape traps" and the problems caused by excessive regulation or rigid conformity to formal rules affect law enforcement agencies' activities, conferring a host of advantages on mafia organizations and explaining, in part, their resilience.

6.3   Concealment vs. Consensus and Visibility

The mafia organizations must balance a need for privacy with a need for visibility. The logic of secrecy is required to operate clandestinely and to reduce exposure to the oppositional activity of law enforcement. Illegal as they are, mafias must try to keep their activities and their membership secret, but at the same time, in terms of reputation, must in some way make themselves visible.

If secrecy were absolutely strict, the organization would be protected from law enforcement agencies, but would have little power over the territory in which it operates. In order to maintain this, it must make use of actions involving threats and intimidation, and so make itself visible. A balance must be found, therefore, between these opposing requirements. If the absurd situation of total secrecy were, in fact, a reality, with the mafia organization operating in absolute secrecy both internally and externally, it (a) would have a significantly adverse effect on its level of credibility and reputation and (b) might increase the risk of organizational dissolution.

(a) Negative consequences would be felt on external credibility, as there would be neither knowledge nor the circulation of appropriate information regarding actions undertaken, such as intimidation implemented to support extortion. Serious problems would, in fact, exist in terms of the construction and maintenance of the mafia's reputation, and the organization would have to replicate the offense with each subject, increasing organizational costs while reducing the symbolic value of the criminal action. Instead, as we know, mafia associations make use of iconic messages (methods, for example, involving damage, a physical attack or murder) that define the reasons for the gesture, while the media provide (free) advertising for the message and the identity of the culprit remains secret (Gambetta 2009).

(b) Second, conditions of total secrecy would expose the organization to the risk of organizational dissolution, given that its members would be confused by the growing levels of uncertainty generated by lack of information. This could undermine the sensation of belonging instilled in organization members since the initiation rite, increasing the risk of a loss of confidence, reducing external consensus, and increasing opportunities for informing.

A particular aspect of the concealment vs. consensus trade-off relates to the problem of communication. Mafias, like other criminal groups, must necessarily exchange communication in order to operate, but they must do so under certain conditions of secrecy. Members must "identify and experiment with forms of communication and modes of interaction that are able to combine the demands for secrecy with the need for communicative exchange" (Dino 2006, ix). They live in a situation of absence, in terms of institutions that can provide help, and the cost of error in communication can be very high indeed:

Because of the nature of their business, criminals have a lot to lose by misreading signs or by emitting signals that are misread ... In the world of regular business, failures of communication can lead to a loss of business, but in the underworld they can result in years behind bars, or worse. (Gambetta 2009, xxi)

It follows that the criminals must be able to communicate with extreme care and astuteness: this is as important a skill as knowing how to use violence.

Communication is a structural element for criminal organizations and in general for all forms of organized crime, as it allows cooperation between people. Mobsters resort to different modes of communication:

face to face (meetings, meetings between two people); from a distance, through technology (phone); and through written messages. Each method has its strengths, weaknesses, and trade-offs in ensuring both the effectiveness of the message and conditions of security.

The famous *pizzini* of Provenzano (see Section 2.2; Palazzolo and Prestipino 2007) made it possible for the mafia boss to evade capture for a long period, reducing the possibility of interception. But they can mainly be used for one-way, top-down communication; do not allow for easy feedback; and, in cases of doubt or ambiguity, may be less effective than other means – they can, also, of course leave traces and be discovered.

The problem of effective communication in conditions of secrecy assumes different connotations depending on the organizational model. If the organizational model is of a *clan-based federation* type, with higher-level bodies of coordination, then efficiency is high, as is pervasiveness, since a decision taken by top management can reach all the members of the different families through the various connecting nodes, keeping the message substantially unchanged. This is the case whether the communication mode is a top management meeting or whether it takes place through a *pizzino*.[11] Where the organizational model is *clan-based*, in the absence of higher-level bodies of coordination, communication mainly takes place within individual organizational units (clan) and, in the case of communications of collective interest that involve a number of clans, then it is necessary to resort to the face-to-face meeting – a very dangerous solution, given that it would require, in the absence of higher-level bodies of coordination, the presence of numerous *capiclan*. However, the vertical model is also more vulnerable compared to the horizontal model, in that, should law enforcement agencies manage to intercept communications, they may obtain valuable information about the whole organization's governing bodies and top positions.

---

[11] The *pizzino* is only one of the means used to communicate at a distance, and is used in particular to protect the fugitive from justice. *Mafiosi* continue to rely on traditional methods such as face-to-face meetings and general meet-ups to exchange information and orders to be executed. However, since the spread of the phenomenon of collaborators with justice and the use of interceptions, "it is no longer the time of the plenary committee meetings, which marked the history of the (Sicilian) Cosa Nostra until the 1980s. Other modes of discussion, acquisition of consent and organizational allocation of crimes therefore prevailed, even when such a decision would inevitably involve dozens of people. This explains the fragmentation and group meetings of no more than five or six people that characterized all the preparatory stages of the massacres of Capaci (in the Palermo province, where judge Giovanni Falcone, his wife and bodyguards died) and of Via D'Amelio (in Palermo, where the judge Paolo Borsellino and his bodyguards were killed)" (Di Matteo and Palazzolo 2015, 145).

Tension between concealment and visibility helps explain some apparently paradoxical events. In 1962, the funeral of an important American Cosa Nostra boss, Lucky Luciano, one of the main architects of the American Cosa Nostra organization in the twentieth century, was held in Naples. It was a funeral fit for a boss, an opulent event with the coffin carried in a hearse drawn by eight horses. About fifty years later, history repeated itself, once again in Italy. On August 20, 2015, in Rome, the funeral of Vittorio Casamonica took place – a boss of the eponymous clan with Sinti origins, with more than 1,000 members and close links to other Italian mafias and criminal organizations operating in Rome and Lazio.[12] The Casamonica clan has been repeatedly investigated and several of its members arrested for various offenses, including usury and drug trafficking. For the death of one of its leaders, only the best would do: a mass and a funeral were organized with more than 500 participants (some estimates say about 1,000) with Jaguars, Ferraris, Rolls-Royces, and other luxury automobiles; six SUVs packed with flowers; and a procession of motorcycles, their riders helmetless in honor of the boss. There was an old-style hearse, drawn by six black horses (two less than for Lucky Luciano), and specially made posters hung in front of the entrance to the church, portraying the dead man smiling and dressed as the pope: on one, there was written *the King of Rome* and on another, rather more threateningly, *You conquered Rome, now conquer heaven*. Meanwhile, a helicopter – violating a number of air traffic safety regulations – disgorged rose petals and a band – conducted by a former *carabiniere* – played the soundtrack from the film *The Godfather*.

An event of this type poses some questions of particular interest. Being a secret criminal organization, the clan should really have been trying to avoid any sort of visibility, especially given that at the time it was at the center of a criminal investigation of national importance called *Mafia Capitale*. The whole event appears to be a kind of self-accusation, behavior designed to confirm the charges of being a criminal organization.

Obviously, this is not actually the case. On the one hand, a criminal organization knows it is possible to do such a thing thanks to the substantial tolerance given to them by law enforcement agencies. Several traffic policemen were in fact present to manage the flow of transport and ensure public order, and the son of the deceased and two other relatives, all under house arrest, had special permission to attend the

---

[12] It was not the first time, either. In 1967, and then in 1977, the funerals of Vittorio Casamonica's parents, Virginia Spada and Guerino Casamonica, were held in a similar way.

event. Furthermore, an event like this is a great publicity opportunity for the organization, signaling to the clan members, its clients, its competitors, and everyone else involved, both individually and collectively, the strength and wealth of the clan, even at a moment when it has lost one of its bosses. Challenging law enforcement is a way to reaffirm who exactly is in command in that particular territory, to demonstrate the enormous consensus available to the clan and, therefore, to consolidate its reputation.

It is interesting to note that the title of *King* attributed to the boss stemmed from an article by a journalist who some years earlier[13] gave this appellation to the four heads of organized crime in Rome, including the Casamonica family, of whom the deceased was one of the chiefs. This confirms what Gambetta points out (1993) regarding the fact that the media, as well as the movies,[14] can enhance the reputation of these organizations and their leaders. In fact, after the publication of the article, some telephone interceptions revealed that the members of one of the four criminal organizations involved had taken to referring to their boss, Massimo Carminati, as *King*. In practice, it was a matter of the public and media recognition of the power of the boss, a form of free advertising.

The ex-mobster of the Sicilian Cosa Nostra Gaspare Spatuzza says that

> language is very important in the Cosa Nostra, as is the use of encrypted codes that allow the mafia to communicate with each other … In communication between *mafiosi*, the strategies of divulgation are never casual. Great attention is paid to what you communicate and how you do it. Especially when communicating in public. (Dino 2016, 23–34)

The mobs are very interested in what appears in the press, not only with reference to their own activities, but regarding how they are talked about, stepping in where necessary to prevent inquiries being made[15] or

---

[13] L. Abbate, "I quattro re di Roma", *L'Espresso*, December 12, 2012.

[14] Regarding how Japanese cinema has helped define the image of the Yakuza, see Varese 2006.

[15] In the 2006–14 period there were a total of 2,060 threats, attacks, and warnings aimed at thousands of journalists. More than thirty journalists were forced to get police escorts following threats received from mafias. The repertoire of warnings consists of bullets delivered to their home, unexploded bombs, letters and threatening phone calls, and media lynching on social networks. There was also real physical violence involving attacks and damage, and even legal abuse, with hundreds of spurious lawsuits brought forward by rich law firms, with the sole purpose of intimidating journalists and distracting them from their original purpose (CPA, *Commissione Parlamentare Antimafia*, Italian parliamentary antimafia commission, *Relazione sullo stato dell'informazione e sulla condizione dei giornalisti minacciati dalle mafie*, XVII Legislatura, August 5, 2015, 3).

to "correct" certain statements, as in the following case. In November 1998, one of the most important Camorra bosses, Michele Zagaria, on the run and on the Ministry of Interior's "most wanted" list, called the journalist Carlo Pascarella of the *Corriere di Caserta*, a local newspaper in Southern Italy. He wanted to complain about certain falsehoods and inaccuracies – as he termed them – that the journalist had included in an article. In particular, Pascarella had written that two bosses of the Camorra, Antonio Iovine and Zagaria himself, were in competition to take over the position as leader of the clan after the arrest of the boss Francesco Schiavone, known as "Sandokan." During the phone call, Zagaria asked the reporter not to write any more inaccuracies of this kind, and to show that there was no tension between the clans, actually passed the phone over to his supposed enemy, Antonio Iovine.[16] The event is of particular interest also because, some years before, the journalist Giancarlo Siani had been killed in a very similar situation, reporting on internal wars in the Neapolitan clans. The fact that two Camorra bosses, fugitives being hunted by the police, should decide to meet to make a phone call together to a journalist from a provincial newspaper to ask him to publish more "correct" information about them, demonstrates how keen mobsters are to be talked about in the press, even in a newspaper that is not particularly prominent in terms of national coverage and sales.

But it is not just a matter of *mafiosi* reading what is written about them – their behavior can also be influenced by it.[17] Abadinsky (1981) states that "the news media, newspapers, periodicals, books, movies, and television influence persons in organized crime – a case of life imitating fiction. We need to consider the extent to which criminals reflect or even act out roles that are inspired by the popular media" (119). Undercover Special Agent Joseph D. Pistone recounts that during the trial in which

---

[16] Here are some excerpts from the phone call: "This is Michele Zagaria. No, it's not a joke. It's me personally. This is the way I do things because I am a serious person and you are not... Wait a minute and I will pass you over to Antonio Iovine as well... OK? So you can get it out of your head to keep on writing bullshit, bullshit ... I think a serious professional, right, does not write all this bullshit. Is that clear? Now I'm passing you over to Antonio Iovine." "*Pronto*, this is Antonio Iovine. Listen, we are not kidding here because we are getting tired of doing all this crap."

[17] The media, the cinema in particular, play an important role in defining mafia modes of behavior and choices (Gambetta 2009). A boss of the Camorra, Francesco Schiavone, and one of the 'Ndrangheta, Rocco Morabito, both decorated the interiors of their homes by imitating details from the house of the main character – Tony Montana, played by Al Pacino – in the film *Scarface*, including his bathtub. Ianni (1974) notes that a narcotics operator in Newark decided on the paramilitary organizational model to adopt after seeing the movie *The Battle of Algiers*, "and it worked" (95).

he was a witness against the Bonanno family of the American Cosa Nostra, a defendant who knew that a Hollywood movie was in the making (*Donnie Brasco* 1997) asked: "Hey Donnie, who is going to play me in the movie?" (Pistone 2004, 146).[18]

6.4   Centralized vs. Decentralized Structure

The problem of centralization and decentralization is a classic theme in organizational studies (Simon et al. 1950; Etzioni 1964). The fundamental question is: What decisions should be left to the lower organizational units, and what to the upper levels? In mafias, as we saw in Chapter 2, government decisions pertain to the level of basic organizational units, while those of governance are made by superordinate levels. It is not a matter, therefore, of a hierarchical relationship, but of a functional diversity, even though in some mafias these bodies have been used by specific groups to try to control the entire set of organizations, as in the Sicilian Cosa Nostra with the Corleonesi group led by Totò Riina. The superordinate bodies do not command the subordinate ones, do not enter into their economic activities, but carry out other functions: coordination, strategy, conflict resolution, and maintenance of the regulatory system.

The logic of centralization increases the power of the organization, but exerts pressure in order to reduce internal differences (the diversity of the mafia enterprises represented) in favor of a greater homogeneity, centralizing decision-making processes, and strategy. The logic of decentralization, on the other hand, tends to favor the shift of power and decision-making process to the level of the single organizational unit (families, clans, etc.).

Studying a completely different context, Sinno (2010) shows that in armed groups only centralized organizations can make use of sophisticated strategies such as "divide and conquer" and "co-option" and can engage in successful peace agreements. At the same time, centralized organizations are vulnerable in the absence of a safe haven, because they rely on close coordination between their specialized branches and depend strongly on a few key leaders.

---

[18] The TV series *The Sopranos* is set in New Jersey, where the DeCavalcante family operates. A group of members was taped by the FBI talking about their newfound status – a rise in fortunes that seemed to be reflected on TV: "Hey, what's this fucking thing, *Sopranos*. Is that supposed to be us?" asked soldier Joseph "Tin Ear" Sclafani. "What characters. Great acting" responded *capo* Anthony Rotundo (J. Capeci, "What's Left of the Mob", *New York Magazine*, January 17, 2005, nymag.com/nymetro/news/crimelaw/features/10870/, last accessed on April 5, 2018).

What is the optimal structure for a criminal organization in terms of control and making decisions? An economical option consists of the figure of the dictator ("the boss of all bosses") who makes the decisions for everyone. Decisional centralization lowers the cost of the decision. However, dictators in large organizations might not have access to a great deal of important information on which to base their decision-making. The pyramid headed by a single person who has all the power has become a symbol of complex organizations, but it is a misleading picture – more an aspiration than actual reality: "The all-powerful chief can maintain such control only to the extent that he is not dependent on others within his organization; and this is a situation of *modest complexity*, not one of a high degree of complexity" (Thompson 1967, 132). The idea of an all-powerful individual who controls everything is rendered impossible by a number of factors: "When complexity of the technology or technologies exceeds the comprehension of the individual ... When resources required exceed the capacity of the individual to acquire ... When the organization faces contingencies on more fronts than the individual is able to keep under surveillance" (Thompson 1967, 133).

In any case, the high costs of communication make some form of decisional decentralization desirable. Dictators, in fact, cannot make effective decisions as they lack the necessary information about the issues, the people involved, and other important aspects of organizational life, particularly at an operational level. The alternative is total consensus through the broadest possible participation. But to achieve this objective is extremely expensive.

An articulated division of labor could separate the members of a secret society (Simmel 1906; Goffman 1969), with the organization's top management roles making decisions about activities and the subordinate levels carrying these out. This decentralization of activities or "compartmental insulation" (Goffman 1969, 78) limits exposure, making it difficult to identify members, especially the leaders. It is the strategy pursued, at the level of individual families or clan, by many mafias: the top management orders and the subordinate levels carry the orders out. For the Sicilian Cosa Nostra and the 'Ndrangheta, the establishment of higher-level bodies of coordination introduces additional decisional elements. Certain actions, such as the murders of high-profile figures (magistrates, journalists, politicians, etc.), are decided at the highest levels of the organization, such as the *Regione* or *Cupola* for the Sicilian Cosa Nostra. These processes of centralization allow better internal coordination, faster decision-making, the reduction of conflict, and containment of violence (as discussed in Section 2.10). Furthermore, centralized organizations are more capable of quickly adapting their strategies in response to changes in the environment or the strategies of enemies, such as the law enforcement agencies. Finally, centralized organizations also have the advantage that the possibility exists to speak on behalf of the entire organization (Zuckerman 2010). This aspect is quite critical in clandestine organizations, where the legitimacy of the spokesperson is always deeply problematic and contested (Stohl and Stohl 2011), unlike in legitimate organizations, public and private, where there is a clear consensus on who can speak on behalf of the organization (e.g., public relations managers, CEOs). In clandestine organizations, the problem assumes different connotations depending on the organizational models. While this is not possible for mafias with a *clan-based* organizational order, it is possible for those with a *clan-based federation* order.

According to organizational theory, secrecy requires decisional decentralization, while pursuing efficiency requires centralization (Baker and Faulkner 1993, 844). Compared to centralized forms, the decentralized organization provides greater protection against investigation by regulatory agencies. Mafias, however, with the exception of the Camorra after the Cutolo phase, have more centralized organizational models, both within individual organizational units (*cosca*, family, clan) and at an interorganizational level, with the establishment of higher-level bodies of coordination (*mandamenti*, Commissione provinciale, Cupola, Provincia). There emerges, therefore, a trade-off. On the one hand, centralization and the creation of higher-level bodies of coordination increase power toward the outside, internal control, a greater control over negative externalities, and the efficiency of the criminal organization as a whole. On the other hand, organizational leaders are rendered more exposed to the possibility of informing. For example, collaborators with justice made it possible to reconstruct the organizational chart of the Sicilian Cosa Nostra, contributing to the arrest of all the members of the Cupola, effectively decapitating the top management of the mafia organization. Noncentralized mafias are more resilient than centralized ones in hostile environments. Many clans of the Camorra, in fact, lacking higher-level bodies of coordination, on the one hand, are more vulnerable to internal conflicts and unable to formulate overall strategies; while, on the other, their leaders, and the organization as a whole, are less vulnerable to repressive action, with each clan like a separate organization, less dependent on coordination.

Mafias cannot tolerate a "boss of bosses," as we have seen with the American mafia rebellion (1928–31). When Raffaele Cutolo tried to impose a totally clan-based federation model on the Camorra, assigning the role of "boss of bosses" to himself, the end result was to trigger the opposition of a number of families who formed a coalition in order to fight the centralizing project.[19]

Historically, the experience of extreme hierarchical centralization seems destined to fail. Thompson (1967) has pointed out that the pyramid headed by an all-powerful individual is possible only in simple situations. The hypothesis one might derive from the existent historical evidence is that mafia organizations are not suited to a hierarchical leadership. In fact, the existence of a "boss of bosses" is incompatible with an organizational order based on families, since it tends to compromise the interests of many and provide advantages to few, and increases conflict by triggering attempts to seize the leadership position by other families and by mafia leaders. The creation of higher-level bodies of coordination through consensus and without the atypical "boss of bosses" role seems to have greater possibility of success and duration compared to the creation of "impositions," with a boss who commands the entire organization as leader.

Given that mafias will not tolerate a boss of bosses, and at the same time that the vertical organizational order has obvious advantages in terms of organizational peace and control over disputes, the fundamental question emerges: with all its advantages, why don't all mafias converge on a *clan-based federation* organizational order?

Clan-based federation orders have their own downsides, the most important of which is their great vulnerability to repressive action and the collaboration of informers. Having a hierarchical organigram makes it easier for law enforcement agencies to establish strategic priorities and to target its leaders. In addition, informer collaboration can cause great damage by revealing crucial information about organizational structure. In contrast, *clan-based* orders are less vulnerable to informer collaboration, and the arrest of members of one clan does not weaken the organization as a whole.

In the light of these considerations, we can argue that mafia organizations have to deal with an organizational dilemma, a trade-off, between the benefits of one model and the other. The historical reconstruction of the mafia organizational orders presented in Chapter 3 shows that mafias exist in an unstable dynamic equilibrium, moving between a *clan-based federation* model and a *clan-based* model, which gives greater autonomy to individual families.

---

[19] This attempt should not be confused with a clan-based federation organizational structure as we see in Sicily or Calabria, where no single family is controlling the others.

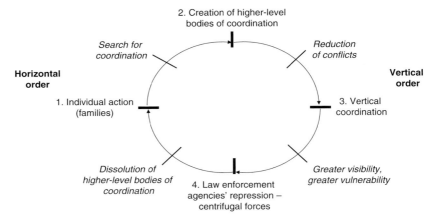

Figure 6.1 The cycle of mafia organizational action

Analytically, this dynamic equilibrium is captured by the cycle of mafia organizational action presented in Figure 6.1. This dynamic cycle goes (1) from individual organizational action (the family, clan, '*ndrina*), to the search for forms of greater coordination. This leads (2) to the creation of higher-level bodies of coordination (based on municipality, province, region), which makes it possible to reduce conflict and seize greater opportunities for complex business.

If, on the one hand, *clan-based federation* coordination increases the power of the organization (3), making strategy development possible, on the other, it engenders greater visibility and vulnerability, since law enforcement agencies can prioritize repressive action, with primary emphasis on the search for the higher-ranked members. In addition, (4) excessive centralization increases discontent and can lead to centrifugal forces, generating often-violent clan conflicts (mafia wars). The superordinate levels are thus delegitimized and/or undermined by repressive action (arrests), they are broken up, and the organization returns to a stage where individual organizational action prevails.

If the organizational structure is *clan-based federation*, repression fosters the breakup of superordinate bodies, in order to make the organization less visible and less vulnerable. In fact, in *clan-based federation* mafias, the contribution of a member in a position of leadership is *complementary talent*, since it can have a disproportionate impact on the performance of the entire organization. This is different from *clan-based* mafias, where the individual contribution is *additive talent* – it is proportional, in other words, to the collective outcome.[20] Thus, the arrest of top management figures in a clan-based federation system has considerably more destructive consequences for the organization than arrests carried out in a clan-based system.

In two cases in the Sicilian Cosa Nostra's recent history, higher-level bodies of coordination have been dismantled. First, following the repressive measures brought into play during the first mafia war (1962–3), the Sicilian Cosa Nostra decided to dissolve the Palermo Provincial Commission in the summer of 1963 (OSPA Stajano 2010). Second, in 1995–6, following severe repressive measures with significant arrests and differing strategic visions within the *Cupola,* the Sicilian Cosa Nostra abolished the regional level and the provincial level in certain provinces. At the moment, the organization is based on families and the *mandamenti,* while there is no evidence of provincial (excepting perhaps Trapani) or regional levels.[21] In addition, in a *clan-based federation* order, where the leadership is weakened by the actions of the law enforcement agencies, the organization becomes more exposed to attempts to seize power, thus increasing internal conflict.[22].

According to collaborator with justice Tommaso Buscetta, in the Sicilian Cosa Nostra, because of the increased repression following the first mafia war (1962–3), the Provincial Commission of Palermo was dissolved.[23]

The process of vertical coordination and decisional centralization confers greater stability on an organization, allowing it to pursue long-term

---

[20] In a completely different context, studying the salary differences between full and associate professors, and between associate professors and assistant professors in a sample of universities, Abrahamson (1973) found great differences in salary in research universities rather than in teaching universities. The explanation is that in research universities, activities are complementary talent: a teacher can make a contribution with a very high impact on the organization, unlike in teaching universities, where contributions are additive talent, with less disparity among the various colleagues.

[21] DIA (*Direzione Investigativa Antimafia,* Anti-Mafia Investigative Directorate), Ministero dell'Interno (Ministry of Interior) 2011, *Attività svolta e risultati conseguiti (Activities and final findings),* http://direzioneinvestigativaantimafia.interno.gov.it

[22] A similar argument has been advanced by the Chicago police to justify a 38 percent increase in the number of murders in 2012, even as killings have held steady or dropped in New York, Los Angeles, and some other cities. The majority of the killings have been tied to Chicago's increasingly complicated gang warfare (M. Davey, "Rate of killings rises 38 percent in Chicago in 2012", *The New York Times,* June 25, 2012). These wars were caused by their organizational changes: from monolithic gangs to hundreds of smaller, less organized, and decentralized factions and crews. According to Sgt. Matthew Little of the Chicago Police Department's gang enforcement unit, "in the past the gangs were very organized from the top down." As more gang leaders are arrested, convicted, and sent to prison, the gangs they left behind have become "very splintered" (D. Babwin, "Fractured gangs behind Chicago homicide surge", *NBC News,* December 6, 2012).

[23] Procura della Repubblica di Palermo, *Procedimento Penale contro Greco Michele ed altri,* 3162/89, vol. VIII.

interests, since the capacity of the organization to persist over time ensures the participating actors who incur costs today will be compensated tomorrow. In contrast, in situations where processes of decentralization and autonomy prevail, short-term logic ("everything at once") tends to be prevalent, since there is no sense for the actors to postpone the satisfaction of their own interests.

It is worth pointing out that a clan-based federation mafia organization – as with the Sicilian Cosa Nostra after 1975, with the formation of the Regional Commission, and the 'Ndrangheta after 1991 with the formation of the Provincia – does not imply a totally top-down decisional process. Rather, a clan-based federation mafia organization is still composed of autonomous parts (the families, the minimal organizational units). Membership, in fact, is always passed through the families: a member belongs to a family, not to the Sicilian Cosa Nostra or the 'Ndrangheta in general. The Sicilian Cosa Nostra and the 'Ndrangheta have created higher-level bodies of coordination with functions that work more in terms of controlling relationships and resolving disputes than of hierarchical chain of command. In these governance bodies, goals are not given but bargained and members operate in a situation of biased information, bounded rationality, and opportunism (Simon 1947; Williamson 1975). They are configurable rather as a political arena, with actors who are stakeholders with diverging objectives, who establish relationships with one another, in terms of either alliance or conflict (March 1962; Cyert and March 1963).

In conclusion, it should be emphasized that the type of organizational architecture influences the types and magnitude of the errors committed. If, on the one hand, centralized architecture reduces the possibility that the organization does not make decisions when required, on the other hand, the possibility increases that a misjudgment on the part of the inner leadership could bring about potentially disastrous strategic decisions for the entire mafia organization (as happened, for example, with the strategy of confrontation in relation to democratic and judicial institutions carried out by the Sicilian Cosa Nostra from the 1980s on). Conversely, decentralized architecture reduces the ability to make strategic decisions involving collective interest, but also decreases the possibility that errors of judgment will lead to decisions that have a negative effect on the entire organization.

6.5   The Use of Violence vs. Containment

An organization is never merely a system of cooperation: a balance of power is always present (Touraine 1973). In mafias, the balance of power is expressed through violence, a fundamental resource that is nevertheless a tool, not an end in itself. It is a tool that is necessary in order to perform the role of guarantor and to offer protection (Gambetta 1993). It is not only a matter of the actual use of violence, but also the threat of its use. In fact, violence is most purposive and most successful when it is threatened and not used. As Schelling noted: "To be coercive violence has to be anticipated. And it has to be avoidable by accommodation. The power to hurt is bargaining power" (Schelling 1966, 2). It is a resource, then, that makes it possible for these organizations to pursue their goals. The success of mafia groups is not measured in terms of number of people killed, but of economic profit gained. Killing people is not a main goal of mafias. Mafias distinguish "between violence that is legitimate and violence that is not; murder that is not legitimate is an act of war" (Anderson 1979, 46). The problem of organizing in mafias is how to transform a conflict system, in which people have objectives that are not jointly consistent, into a cooperative system in which individuals act rationally to achieve common objectives.

If they exaggerate, if they use too much violence or hit the wrong target, they suffer the consequences in terms of increased repression from the law enforcement agencies and loss of social consensus. The difficult task for these organizations is to control violence, both internally and externally. As Schelling says:

The willingness to hurt, the credibility of a threat and the ability to exploit the power to hurt will indeed depend on how much the adversary can hurt in return; but there is little or nothing about an adversary's pain or grief that directly reduces one's own. (Schelling 1966, 3)

The level of violence depends on factors that are endogenous and exogenous to the organization. Endogenous factors, for example, are related to tension regarding the leadership and the attempt to seize control of roles at the top of the organization. Not for nothing, as highlighted in Chapter 3, were higher-level bodies of coordination created to reduce these attempts to seize power. Exogenous factors are dependent on the external environment and the degree of legitimacy and consensus (high for the Yakuza) and of "balance" with the system of actors. The more these organizations play a role that is not merely predatory, the more the public perception is of victimless crime and the more tolerance increases on the part of the authorities.

Mafia organizations operate in a complex, hazardous, and uncertain environment: "perturbed by anomalies, uncertain borders, incongruent circumstances, breached norms, and biased information" (Gambetta 1993, 256). They must constantly adapt to sudden change, manage unexpected events, and respond to developing problems, in particular in relation to repressive measures from law enforcement agencies. Repressive action by the law enforcement agencies can sometimes produce unintended consequences for the criminal organization. In particular, the repressive measures of law enforcement agencies induce organizational change and innovations in the system. To put it simply, repression may trigger certain strategic responses by mafia organizations, the nature of which depends on the prevailing organizational order, vertical or horizontal.

Chu (2000) noted that after the establishment of the Independent Commission against Corruption (ICAC), in 1974, Triads were fragmented. Hill (2003b) highlighted that the change in strategy of the police had a real impact on the size and number of Yakuza gangs. For example, the introduction of an antimafia law, the Bōtaihō, imposed new restrictions on the activities of Yakuza members, making these sources of income more expensive and, therefore, forcing gangs to find new sources of income, such as the amphetamine market (Hill 2003b).

The consequences of this type of action for mafia organizations are not restricted to weakening the organization itself: significant change is also brought about in the actual organizational structure.

These repressive measures do however have different effects according to the prevailing type of mafia organizational order. In particular: in *clan-based federation organizational orders* (1), the organization can implement two actions, one internally and one externally. Internally, it may decide to dissolve the higher-level bodies of coordination in order to reduce vulnerability. Outwardly, it can implement two opposing strategies, (1.1) increasing high-profile murders or (1.2) choosing a low-profile strategy, a submerged (or sunken) strategy.

In the presence of *clan-based organizational orders* (2), however, increased repression predominantly tends to generate responses within the criminal system, in particular with an increase in violence, both intraorganizational and between clans.

Let's look at the different strategies in more detail.

An example of 1.1 (increasing high-profile murders) is a frontal attack on the law enforcement agencies and the political system in order to seek a new equilibrium and pacts of nonaggression. This was the path invariably followed, for example, by the Sicilian Cosa Nostra, especially in the years 1991–3 with the massacres that brought about the deaths of magistrates Giovanni Falcone and Paolo Borsellino; the murder of a politician, Salvo Lima, in retaliation for pacts that were not respected; and a number of bomb attacks without specific targets, as part of a strategy of tension. It was a path that proved to be the result of a miscalculation by the organization: repression against the Sicilian Cosa Nostra increased, and the number of arrests and sentences to life imprisonment was among the highest in its history. With hindsight, it can be said to have been a wrong move that, if anything, favored other Italian mafias: with the law enforcement agencies focusing their attention mainly on the Sicilian Cosa Nostra, far less attention was devoted to other organizations, the 'Ndrangheta in particular.

An example of a low-profile strategy (type 1.2) from a mafia organization characterized by higher-level bodies of coordination is that of the Sicilian Cosa Nostra from the 1990s on, in the aftermath of the massacres and the killing of magistrates Falcone and Borsellino. Given the extremely harsh reaction of the state and law enforcement agencies, the strategy developed by the organization was to avoid any conflict with these bodies, abstaining from high-profile homicides and reducing the number of ordinary murders, with the aim of lowering the level of attention from oppositional agencies. This strategy was promoted in particular by an important Sicilian Cosa Nostra boss, Bernardo Provenzano. With regard to this, collaborator with justice Antonino Giuffrè said in 2002:

Let's say that Provenzano along with other people . . . began to put the process of submersion into action, making the Sicilian Cosa Nostra invisible so it could get on quietly with reorganization. (in Pignatone and Prestipino 2013, 227)

The reduction of violence is an excellent strategy for the pursuit of doing good business. And that is exactly what happened for the Yakuza, after the approval of the Bōtaihō in 1991, with the reduction of certain types of crime and of violent activity particularly disagreeable, and visible, to the population, and then also of the media coverage that harmed the organization's image; for the 'Ndrangheta, with the establishment in 1991 of a committee for the reduction of feuds that were attracting the attention of magistrates and law enforcement agencies; and it was the same for other organizations.

(2) If the organization is characterized by a *clan-based organizational order*, repression increases the fragmentary organizational structure, encourages the breaking up of cartels (following the arrest of the bosses), and produces an increase in the number of clans, as in the case of the Camorra. Arrests in a clan increase the possibility of division and foster the competitiveness of other neighboring clans, which attempt to take over the territory of the clan weakened by the repressive measures. The fragmentary nature of the Camorra's organization represents a point of weakness with respect to the Sicilian Cosa Nostra; it is also, however, a strength. A point of weakness, in the sense that clans are constantly at

war with each other, and this explains the high rate of violence and internal conflict within the Camorra criminal system. A strength, since it is especially difficult to act against an entire organization that is split up into a number of different clans. The high level of conflict between clans constrains the law enforcement agencies to concentrate their efforts on the clans fighting against each other, in order to try to reduce violence. As a consequence, the law enforcement agencies determine priority not on the basis of the general dangerousness of the clans in relation to the economy and public administration, but on the basis of the level of violence deployed.

Moreover, repressive action, with the arrest of a clan boss and members, creates a) the possibility for some clan members to attempt to seize the clan leadership; b) areas of opportunity for other competing clans to take over their territory and run their affairs; c) the phenomenon of membership diaspora. The arrest of the bosses means that delegation is handed on to younger, less expert members, with less capacity for reflection and ability to mediate, and with a greater tendency toward the use of violence. For example, the arrest of about 110 *camorristi* of the Giuliano clan operating in the Naples suburb of Forcella favored the rival Buonerba clan, an offshoot of the Mazzarella family, which had already operated on the territory in the past before being expelled by the clan Giuliano. The successes of the law enforcement agencies thus handed over control of illegal activities in the area (extortion and drug trafficking) to the new Buonerba clan.[24]

The defeat of the Camorra boss Raffaele Cutolo constitutes an illuminating example of how the legal and law enforcement system itself becomes an element of innovation of the system. The sentence of the Naples court[25] indicated how Cutolo's aim to centralize the Camorra failed because the growth of the organization was too fast, with costs increasing as rapidly as desertions. Moreover, the pyramidal structure rendered the Camorra organization more visible to the outside and more vulnerable, both to the law enforcement agencies and to other rival clans. The Cutolian clans, defeated by severe repressive measures in 1983, as well as pressure from rivals, had given way to the clans of the Nuova Famiglia: the state, having *intentionally* defeated the Cutolian Camorra, had *unintentionally* assisted in the changing of the guard (from Cutolo to

---

[24] DNA (*Direzione Nazionale Antimafia*, National Anti-Mafia Directorate) 2016, *Relazione annuale sulle attività svolte dal Procuratore nazionale e dalla Direzione nazionale antimafia e antiterrorismo*, 75.

[25] RPMNA, Tribunale di Napoli 1986, *Sentenza del Pubblico ministero, Corte di Assise di Napoli, contro Abagnale+101*, vol. I, April 23.

Alfieri et al.) and had caused the further disintegration of the Neapolitan organizations (Falcone and Padovani 1992, 100). Repressive action by law enforcement agencies may therefore generate "unanticipated consequences" (Merton 1936), favoring change and innovation in the system.

As we said earlier, this leads to a deepening of the relationship between mafia organizations and the state apparatus with law enforcement agencies. This is a very complex topic, due to the presence and interaction of two levels of motive: (1) the risk of reification, given the nonuniformity of corporate actors and (2) the situation with multiple equilibria.

(1) The actors involved, the state with the law enforcement agencies, and mafia organizations, are not unified actors. In this case there is a high risk of reification – for the state to be considered as a unitary actor with a clear intention and a unified, coherent strategy, and similarly, to consider the mafia organization as unified and centrally governed, so as to express a unified strategy. Reality shows, as has been pointed out several times, that mafia organizations are not centrally governed and there is no "boss of the bosses." If anything, some mafias have developed higher-level bodies of coordination (which tend to be constantly unstable and not always long-lasting) with the possibility of developing strategies only tendentially unitary and that can speak on behalf of the organization. In other mafias, meanwhile (e.g., the Camorra), the strategies are emergent on the basis of the interactions of the various component families, and there is no person or body able to speak on behalf of the organization. The state, moreover, is also not a unitary actor, but is composed of a plurality of organizational units – units that are not always well coordinated among themselves and above all possess different strategies, interests, and modes of behavior.

Therefore, if certain sectors develop oppositional strategies, other sectors may, on the other hand, develop rather a logic of peaceful coexistence and nonaggression.

(2) The situation of relationship that is created between these two groups of actors, fragmented internally, is of the multiple equilibria type,[26] with strategic interdependence that is difficult to predict.

It should be noted that relations between the mafia and law enforcement and other state agencies are not always antagonistic and conflictual – sometimes, indeed, quite the opposite. With reference to the Yakuza,

---

[26] Multiple or fragile equilibria derive from incorporation within a dynamic system, characterized by given initial conditions and past experience of various types of shocks that disrupt the system. Such equilibria can also be unstable.

Ames points out that there may be mutual interest in nonaggression and finding a mode of coexistence:

Police and gangsters each find it advantageous to maintain rapport and to enhance it with a façade of cordiality. This nucleus of goodwill and understanding seems to remain when the police must severely crack down on a gang after a major incident. A complete rupture in the relationship would be counterproductive for both sides. (Ames 1981, 107)

It is perfectly rational, then, for both actors to adopt nonaggressive policies, if conditions allow. And it is not necessarily a matter of corruption, although this may be present, in part because "police and politicians have used gangsters throughout Japan's modern history to help maintain social order, especially to counterbalance the burgeoning strength of leftists" (Ames 1981, 107).

Of course it is an unstable and temporary equilibrium, one that is subject to changes induced by various factors. For example, an increase in violence by criminal organizations may require immediate repressive action by the security forces. Or an actor may emerge, on one side or another, who does not agree with the line of nonaggression and initiates a different, more aggressive, policy, thus shattering any implicit pacts. Or there might be a transformation in public perception and the media, bringing greater awareness of the role played by criminal organizations.

It should be noted, however, that over time the relationship between law enforcement agencies and the state, on the one hand, and mafia organizations, on the other, has progressively evolved from tolerance to a more intense hostility. This happens, at different periods, in all mafias.

This has been the case, for example, in Japan since the mid-1960s, and then with greater intensity since 1991 with the approval of Bōtaihō law. Even earlier, the United States brought in the RICO law (1970) and there was a significant change in policies by the FBI to combat organized crime. In Italy, since the early 1980s, one of the strictest laws in the fight against the mafia has been approved (416 bis of the Criminal Code in 1982) and the Direzione Investigativa Antimafia (DIA, Anti-Mafia Investigative Directorate) established, together with other regulations to combat organized crime. In Japan, the tightening of regulations was prompted by a series of conflicts within groups of the Yakuza and the resulting increase in violence that took place in 1990, with murders, continuous shootings, and violent clashes in the city of Tokyo. The inability of the Yakuza to control internal violence provoked a hostile reaction from the press and damaged its public image, forming the background for the enactment of more punitive laws with regard to the criminal organization.

In conclusion, for better enforcement strategy it is important to know the physiology of criminal organizations, and especially the characteristics of the markets in which they operate. Studying the dynamics of violence in Mexico, Calderón et al. (2015) show that the increase in repression promoted by the Mexican government between 2006 and 2012 to weaken the drug trafficking organizations actually produced an increase in violence and not a decline. The capture or killing of the drug cartel leaders led in the following months to an increase both in violence and in homicides within the criminal organizations and in the population as a whole. The capture or killing of 25 *capos* and 160 lieutenants over six years led to an escalation in homicides of more than 300 percent.

As the authors state:

(The) captures of *capos* have strong "hydra" effects in the locality where these take place, presumably increasing both intra- and inter-cartel fighting as well as violence within the population not directly involved in drug trafficking ... we find substantial spillover effects in the medium-term (six to twelve months after the intervention) after the capture of a leader in homicides within the general population. As discussed previously, these increases in general violence might be explained by leadership removals damaging the chain of command that keeps local criminal cells more or less under control. (Calderón et al. 2015, 27)

This poses serious problems and questions for law enforcement agencies with regard to the powerful negative esternalities produced by successful repression.

While the considerable increase in controls on the border between Mexico and the United States has not reduced the number of illegal entries, it has increased the use by Mexican migrants of "coyotes" – as people smugglers are nicknamed – to cross the border. If 40–50 percent of migrants in the 1970s resorted to this "service," today it is virtually compulsory and it is used by about 95 percent of them. And the price of the service is considerably more expensive. In other words, the increase in U.S. enforcement has meant good luck for the traffickers, transforming an initially unproductive activity into a high-earning market without, among other things, reducing the number of illegal entries.[27]

It is, in other words, a situation of products characterized by inelastic demand, where a rise in price does not reduce consumption (e.g., drugs). The consequence is that an increase, even a significant one, in repressive activity does not, on the one hand, have equally significant results and

---

[27] B. Roberts, G. Hanson, D. Cornwell, and S. Borger (2010), "An Analysis of Migrant Smuggling Costs along the Southwest Border," Department of Homeland Security, Office of Immigration Statistics, working paper, November, at: www.dhs.gov/xlibrary/assets/statistics/publications/ois-smuggling-wp.pdf, last accessed on April 5, 2018.

does not reduce the number of consumers; and, on the other, by increasing the prices of the product sold, it increases the profits of the criminal organization.

6.6   Recruitment: Kinship vs. Skills

In Section 2.1, we analyzed the various strategies deployed by mafias to try to reduce informational asymmetry in recruiting processes. In this section, we will analyze a particular dilemma associated with these practices and the various modes of management.

The main organizational dilemma with regard to recruiting is characterized by the following: to what extent should recruitment solutions based on blood or ethnic ties (that can provide greater reliability on secrecy and less willingness to cooperate with law enforcement agencies, but with the risk that familial interests will be placed above organizational concerns) be favored, and to what extent should choices based on merit (which can ensure a better pursuit of organizational goals, but at the same time can increase security risks and opportunities for informing) be adopted?

To begin with, at the first level, in mafias, as well as in many gangs and other criminal groups (for example, Albanian organized crime, Arsovska 2015), recruiting is based on the ethnic – or, as with the Italian mafias, regional – dimension. To be a made member of the Sicilian Cosa Nostra, a person must be Sicilian; to be part of the Yakuza, Japanese, etc. At a second level, there are two different criteria:

1) *kinship*, a selection based primarily on blood ties, typical for example of the 'Ndrangheta;
2) *skills*, a selection based on merit, on skills and capabilities, even though blood relationships may be present.

The first criterion ensures greater trust and reduces transaction costs. As Smith argued, "Ethnic ties provide the strongest possibility of ensuring trust among persons who cannot rely on the law to protect their rights and obligations within cooperative but outlawed economic activity" (1980, 375). This is a situation of trust based on generalization (von Lampe and Johansen 2004), in which trust is linked to the characteristics of a social group rather than to the characteristics of a particular individual. It is assumed that common ethnic and/or geographical features ensure confidence and reduce the possibilities of mistrust. Family businesses, for example, are rich in scarce resources such as loyalty, motivation, commitment, and flexibility. Also, as some research shows, families control many businesses in the world, even in advanced economies (La Porta et al. 1999). Campana and Varese (2013) argue that the likelihood of cooperation is higher among members who are related: "Even mafias that do not rely on kinship recruit locally (Varese 2011, 18–19). In this way, they have more information on the members and can punish their families in the case of defection; recruiting locally is thus a weaker form of hostage-taking" (Campana and Varese 2013, 283).

At the same time, there exist problems such as family feuds. As we have already said with regard to recruiting processes (Section 2.1), a way to reduce informational asymmetry and avoid dangerous mistakes in recruiting is to recruit people in the area where the organization operates. In this way, more information and knowledge about the candidate and his biography can be obtained (Pizzini-Gambetta and Hamill 2011).

Much research shows that people tend to place more trust in other people from the same ethnic group (Cohen 1969; Brewer 1981; Macharia 1988; Landa 1994; Fearon and Laitin 1996; Habyarimana et al. 2009). There are several possible explanations for this; Habyarimana et al. (2009) analyze three: (1) the *other-regarding preferences rationale*, in which trust stems from the belief that the trustee cares about the truster; (2) the *incentives rationale*, in which trust derives from the belief that the trustee is motivated to act in the interests of the truster; (3) the *competence rationale*, in which trust stems from the belief that the trustee is capable of acting in the interests of the truster. A person who places more trust in a coethnic than a noncoethnic does so inasmuch as (a) he believes that the coethnic cares more about him than the noncoethnic does or (b) he simply thinks that the coethnic has stronger incentives to carry out an action in his interest (42–3). In any case, explanations about motivations aside, coethnicity encourages greater trust than noncoethnicity.

However, this poses a resource dependence problem, in that hereditary selection criteria, where the recruitment base is more restricted, do not ensure quality of membership and skills relevant to the organization. Italian mafia organizations have low human capital, and this undermines their capacity for conducting complex business in the legal world. Mobs have extremely low levels of education, with a large majority of them stopping before high school. For instance, of the 13,882 people who have received a final conviction for mafia-related crimes between 1982 and 2017, 82 percent have five to eight years of schooling (Savona et al. 2018).

Research in other fields has shown that skill in a certain type of work does not depend on lineage – indeed, the opposite is often the case. The economist Luigi Zingales[28] has for example analyzed research carried out

---

[28] L. Zingales, "State alla larga dai gestori figli di papà," *Il Sole 24Ore*, September 18, 2016, 22.

on investment fund managers in the United States that has highlighted the fact that managers with "humble origins" have annual returns up to 2.16 percent higher than a manager who has inherited the activity from his father.

However, the second selection method in mafias, based on merit and skills, makes for greater choice and quality of selection for the mafia organization, also allowing it to search for more appropriate skill profiles. As in legal organizations, outside recruiting may bring new blood to an organization, even when the new members do not have major skills or superior knowledge.

We saw in Chapter 2.1 how a criminal organization such as the Nigerian cartels bases its recruitment on race but has, over time, for reasons of necessity, "opened" itself to other kinds of collaboration: given that airport controls were more frequent and assiduous in their attention to Nigerians, they began to use white women as heroin transporters from Europe to the United States, since they tended to attract less attention from airport authorities (Naim 2005).

In the Sicilian Cosa Nostra, there are more restrictive and "merito-cratic" criteria for promotion and career advancement. Italian descent, however, is crucial. As former mobster Vito Palermo (a pseudonym) claims:

If one is not an Italian, or at least part Italian, there is less trust. Italian organized crime elements are very clannish; they put a great emphasis on the feeling that is something inborn; it's the macho thing again. The Italian is a stand-up guy, a quality they apparently do not believe exists in other ethnic groups ... My meaning of mafia is that there are in fact a group of people who are tightly knit by virtue of ethnic and family ties who participate in all forms of criminal activity on a highly organized basis. (in Abadinsky 1981, 92–3)

Regarding selection, the co-opting process of the Sicilian and American Cosa Nostra involves the observation of the public and private behavior of the potential candidate over a period of years: not only his criminal potential, but also his private life, his sense of discretion. A careful observation of his bloodline family is carried out if the candidate does not already belong to a mafia family. The candidate is then employed in criminal activities of increasing levels of complexity in order to evaluate his courage, reliability, ability to cope with unforeseen events, even, eventually, his willingness to commit murder. All this, as mentioned previously, is not only for purposes of evaluation, but also for putting together a typical criminal CV – the "skeletons in the closet" that will help reduce the person's likelihood of informing in the future.

These complex selection and recruitment procedures explain the low number, compared to other mafias, of the actual members of the two

Cosa Nostra organizations. To prevent an excessive number of blood ties, fathers and brothers are forbidden to participate in the collegial bodies, in order to avoid the presence of too many people who might put blood ties above the interests of the organization they belong to.[29]

Starting in 1900, the American Cosa Nostra developed several methods of recruitment (Critchley 2009). In particular, such changes occurred in the transition from the first to second generation of mobsters and led to three different pools: (1) being a made member of the Sicilian Cosa Nostra, (2) being born in Sicily in areas controlled by mafia families able to establish the reputation and provide guarantees for the initiand, (3) being part of an American street gang active in a territory controlled by an American Cosa Nostra family (Critchley 2009, 89).

In the 1920s, in New York, Giuseppe "Joe the Boss" Masseria was one of the first to introduce meritocratic criteria in recruiting family members. While rivals limited recruitment to specific geographical areas (the Brooklyn *castellamarese* clan limited membership only to men from Castellammare sul Golfo, in the northwest of Sicily), Masseria did not set limits on their origins but sought the best bootleggers and racketeers he could find (Hortis 2014). To be a made member, however, both parents were required to be Italians, or, better still, from Sicily or a region in the south of Italy. This rule was later modified and it became possible to be a made member with only one parent of Italian origin, the father, so that the surname was Italian, and there have even been cases of membership of Americans without any familial ties to Italy at all.

Kinship ties are however very widespread in the American Cosa Nostra. When undercover agent Joseph Pistone infiltrated the Bonanno *family*

these individuals that become members of the Mafia, they are not people that start out later in life to be Mafia members. They are individuals that have grown up in the neighborhood, have been associated with crime as youngsters and associated with Mafia members as youngsters. As a general rule, there is some type of family bond, real family, not Mafia family, a father, an uncle, a cousin.[30]

However, it is much easier for a *made member*'s son to become a *made member* than for other candidates. Of course, for the children of the boss of the American Cosa Nostra, entry is virtually guaranteed: there are at least fifteen cases of the sons of bosses who have in turn become members of the organization (Capeci 2004, 18).

---

[29] Procura della Repubblica di Palermo (1989), *Procedimento Penale contro Greco Michele ed altri*, 3162/89 vol. VIII, 1300.
[30] www.americanmafia.com/Pistone_Testimony.html, last accessed on April 5, 2018.

The Sicilian Cosa Nostra established a rule to prevent an excessive concentration of blood relatives in one family. Other mafia organizations, such as the Triads Chu 2000) and the Yakuza (Iwai 1986), with a few exceptions, adopted the same rule. This provides the mafia family with an organizational strength that goes far beyond the necessarily limited links offered by real family relationships: "These are the rules that can make an institution's reputation and thus its longevity independent of the fate of its individual members" (Gambetta 2009, 208). This rule regarding the composition of the highest level of leadership is not only an organizing rule, however. It is also aimed at limiting possible conflicts within the same family between blood-related members and other members with no blood relationships. Blood ties, in fact, can facilitate the formation of factions, especially when critical decisions have to be made.

At the beginning of the twenty-first century, the Sicilian Cosa Nostra partially modified membership requirements with "greater rigor in recruiting systems, since the Cosa Nostra has taken into account the negative effects determined by the methods of membership not linked to pertaining to a family bloodline of proven mafia tradition, and with the necessity for a rigorous verification of the requirements of solidity and reliability of the members" (Di Cagno and Natoli 2004, 71).

In the American Cosa Nostra, the problem of recruitment and promotion through merit or kinship has created a great deal of tension. The boss of one of the five New York families, Joseph (Joe) Bonanno, appointed his son Bill as family adviser (*consigliere*). Many family members complained that Bill lacked experience to be an effective leader, and the situation worsened when Bill advised his father against involving the family in the illegal narcotics trade.

Of all the mafias, the 'Ndrangheta is the organization that makes bloodline recruiting the foundation of the organization. The sons of a man of honor are, in fact, budding *'ndraghetisti*. For them, access to the organization is a right. If, then, they turn out not to be up to the task, their career will be brought to a halt and they will be set aside.

Over the years, the Camorra has alternated moments of favoring greater meritocratic selection with times, especially during the Cutolo era (1975–83), of favoring greater associative openness, with less demand for specific criminal requirements. In general, in the Camorra there is no "amoral familism" (Banfield 1958) with regard to recruiting. Naturally, access to the organization is easier for sons who are following in their father's footsteps, as it is for husbands of daughters of a boss, friends, cousins, and other relatives, close or otherwise. However, command is not hereditary – and, should this in fact happen, it is far less frequent there than in some liberal professions, such as notaries, doctors, and lawyers.

Briefly, then, succession can occur, but it is the exception, not the rule. And when it does take place, it is not necessarily a good thing for the organization. Passing the scepter of clan command from father to son, while, on the one hand, ensuring continuity in managing the organization, can, on the other, be very dangerous and damaging to organization life. Camorra clan boss Paolo Di Lauro (aka *Ciruzzo 'o milionario*, "the millionaire"), decided to pass on command to his sons after 2002, thus privileging bloodline over merit. This triggered one of the bloodiest wars ever seen in the Neapolitan districts of Scampia and Secondigliano.

In conclusion, mafias prefer to recruit highly homogeneous people, in terms of ethnic, national, or regional criteria, which increases the bonding dimension of ties between members. However, it may also undermine the search for the most appropriate skills, especially for those mafias for which such criteria might have become overly restrictive and binding, as with the American Cosa Nostra, given the progressive reduction of the catchment area from which it is able to draw. The bonding dimension, characterized by interaction between homogeneous groups of people, reinforces standards of reciprocity, while solidarity and trust may reduce openness toward the outside world, making business more complicated and decreasing business opportunities for the organization. Mafias, however, though characterized by a strong dimension of internal bonding, are capable of bridging social capital, building external networks with people, groups, and organizations that are very different from them, even in geographical areas at a distance from their places of origin. For example, studying certain triad gangs, Lo (2010) highlights how bridging social capital helped the triad leader to locate both legitimate and illicit business opportunities: "bonding social capital does not necessarily facilitate contemporary triad activities. Rather, it is the linking social capital and bridging social capital that are the prerequisites to the triad-organized crime" (867). This is a topic that requires further investigation, in particular regarding how such capabilities are put into practice.

6.7 Trust vs. Distrust

Trust has been widely recognized to play a central role in the functioning of social systems (Simmel 1906; Arrow 1974; Luhmann 1979; Putnam 1993; Fukuyama 1995; Möllering 2006), and of organizations (Zand 1972; Kramer and Tyler 1996; Rousseau et al. 1998; Bachmann et al. 2001; Reed 2001; McEvily et al. 2003; Nee and Opper 2012; Jiang and Probst 2015; Nee, Opper and Holm 2018). The attention of organizational scholars, however, has been mostly focused on legal organizations. What happens in extralegal organizations? How can organizations that are unable to establish binding contracts and lack a third party acting as a rule enforcer develop organizational trust? Trust is an essential element for extralegal organizations such as mafias. In fact, they need to rely on both internal and external support to conduct their activities properly, but they cannot rely on legal mechanisms of dispute resolution to guarantee the enforcement of their rules and "contracts." A thorough understanding of intraorganizational trust dilemmas in mafias is, however, missing.

According to Hardin (2002), trust is a kind of expectation, grounded in reason, about whether another party or parties will cooperate in the future. Gambetta defines trust as: "a particular level of the subjective probability with which an agent assesses that another agent or group of agents will perform a particular action, both before he can monitor such action (or independently of his capacity ever to be able to monitor or enforce it) and in a context in which it affects his own action" (1988, 217). These two definitions point out that trust can be understood only when embedded in a relationship. They also imply that different elements can underpin trust. Dyer and Chu (2003) argued that trust minimizes transaction costs in organizations. For example, trust can function to reduce transaction costs operating as a default social decision heuristic (Uzzi 1997; Kramer 2003). Certainly, trust can smooth social and economic relationships and in many cases account for how markets really work.

A recent study by Nee, Opper, and Holm on China's transition economy, in a contest of weak property rights and enforcement of contracts, experimentally demonstrated how mechanisms embedded in personal relationships can influence generalized trust, defined as the inclination to believe that strangers will act cooperatively. Results from a trust game coupled with survey data conducted on a random sample of 540 entrepreneurs of private manufacturing industries in China showed that the crucial factors positively associated with generalized trust are reliance on relational exchange and cooperation in dyadic relationships, as well as reliance on the effectiveness of community business norms. It derives from the situation that in communities where confidence in local norm enforcement is weak, actors are less likely to trust strangers (Nee, Opper, and Holm 2018). Criminal organizations operate in a similarly stateless environment, implying that they cannot rely on third parties to adjudicate their controversies and their actions must be conducted in secrecy. Hence the scarce level of trust permeating illegal environments. However, paradoxically, trust is even more important for criminal organizations than for legal ones. In order to pursue their interests, mafias must overcome challenges in recruitment and planning, as well as in their everyday organizational operations. In all these aspects, compliance of group members and larger "constituencies" is needed. Although violence is a key organizational resource to guarantee compliance, it cannot be constantly used, and, thus, in both types of groups trust becomes essential to perform key activities and maintain secrecy (Gambetta 2009).

"Our entire system of cooperation and connections depended on trust," stated Joseph Bonanno, one of the bosses of the five New York families (1983, 155). But: "Trusting anyone is a fatal mistake for a wiseguy," stated FBI agent Joseph Pistone, aka Donnie Brasco (Pistone 2004, 111), and, because of this, "wiseguys have no friends" (Pistone 2004, 181). Even though they spend most of their time together, gambling, eating, participating in parties and marriages, greeting each other with a kiss on their cheeks as a sign of friendship, and so forth, mobsters, says Pistone, are not friends and have no friends: being someone's friend implies trusting him and sharing secret thoughts and fears – something a *mafioso* cannot afford to do, because it would make him vulnerable. So, even though they may behave like friends, they are not friends:

Friends are good for one thing in the mob: they can be counted on to kill you when your number comes up. One of the first things Lefty (*Ruggiero, a soldier of the Bonanno family, A/N*) taught me is that the guy who kills you will most likely be the guy who's closest to you. (Pistone 2004, 182)

In his memoirs, Nick Gentile (1963) tells of some murders committed by the American Cosa Nostra. Once the decision to eliminate a particular person had been taken, the people nearest the designated victim were automatically involved in the crime, with tactics deployed to quash any suspicions the target might entertain. For example, they might try to involve him in a bit of business, allowing him to choose the place and time for a meeting to reassure him, even in the presence of his trusted friends. Or they might even take the victim sociably by the arm, as in the case of the murder of Terry Burnes, fellow organization member and "brother" to Nick Gentile, who did just that to guide his friend directly toward his killers.

The former underboss of the Philadelphia family of the American Cosa Nostra Philip Leonetti aka "Crazy Phil," tells (Leonetti et al. 2012) how a member of the organization, Vincent Falcone, a criminal associate and contractor, was killed in 1979. One afternoon, along with other mobsters, including the family boss, Nicky Scarfo, they were sipping whiskey and celebrating the upcoming Christmas in advance. As the laughter and amiable conversation went on, Leonetti asked Falcone to get some ice, and as the latter turned, Leonetti shot him in the head at close range. Leonetti and the others were Falcone's "colleagues" – was there any reason not to trust them? The "crime" that Falcone had committed was to voice aloud his personal opinion regarding Scarfo: shortly before, in an informal conversation, he had said that Scarfo was crazy and should be barred from the cement contracting business. Just a few words casually uttered in a moment of relaxation, but they cost him his life. Some of those present had relayed Falcone's opinion to their boss, Scarfo himself, and he had instructed his nephew, Phil Leonetti, to carry out the sentence for betrayal, only verbal though it was. Ironically, it would be this same nephew, having become underboss, who would truly betray his uncle, collaborating with the FBI after his capture and condemning the boss to life imprisonment. Previous cases suggest that suspicion and distrust are not always bad things, but necessary conditions for survival. An excess of suspicion can lead to organizational paranoia: something considered in a positive light by some authors (Goodwin 1988; Grove 1996), since it encourages individuals to remain on the alert, observing and listening carefully for potential signals of danger. However, an excess of paranoia can also destroy the organization. Mobsters need to learn how to practice what Kramer (2003) calls "prudent trust," meaning "trust balanced with prudent wariness and reserve" (350) – a required state for operating in these criminal organizations.

The issue of trust is therefore a major issue for mafias, and one closely linked to the problem of control. As Handy points out, however, excessive control can damage trust: "If control is increased, trust is decreased" (1999, 332). Mafias must, therefore, control the behavior of their members by (1) detecting whether undesirable behavior has been implemented and (2) punishing it. This, however, could undermine trust, as "trust implies giving someone the right to make mistakes" (Handy 1999, 332). It could also prove particularly expensive and dangerous. On the one hand, in fact, control involves constant monitoring of the members of the organization. On the other, it requires an increase in communications, undermining conditions of security. In addition, if the organization is demonstrating suspicious behavior, exhibiting constant concern that someone on the inside might betray it, then a climate of suspicion with false negatives is created (if the suspected infiltrators are actually innocent). If, however, trust prevails, then doors are opened to false positives (infiltrators are regarded as loyal members).

The 'Ndrangheta has developed a way to lessen the chances of infiltration and unauthorized use of the mafia "brand." Each new member, after baptism (the initiation rite), is provided with the *copiata* – a list of the main management roles in the organization (of the *locale*). This knowledge becomes a kind of password that the member can use when going to a different *locale*. This makes it impossible for someone not in the organization to pass himself off as a *'ndraghetista*.

The issue of trust regards not only internal dynamics, but also external ones, toward the "customers": "A permanent tension between trust and violence seems to be present in every illicit transaction ... Violence is employed as a sanction when contracts are violated, and as an instrument to solve disputes and to regulate the market activities" (Arlacchi 1998, 210).

As is well known, there are online sites that have, for a long time now, been selling illegal products such as drugs. To ensure anonymity, special browsers are used and payment is made in bitcoins. Buying and selling illegal products and substances are always dangerous, and often unpleasant as well. Online shopping therefore eliminates many of the negative aspects of the transaction. But there is a problem of trust. Since the purchase takes place between anonymous subjects, and the buyer in particular has no way of tracing the seller, and given the impossibility of having recourse to an authority in case of dispute, fraud is a constant threat. However, some sites are introducing feedback systems similar to those on eBay, where buyers can evaluate sellers with a rating and/or leave comments (Wainwright 2016). Furthermore, some sellers compensate buyers for unsuccessful deals or for products that do not fulfill their purpose (stolen credit cards, for example), even offering an insurance with sales. Some studies also show that drugs purchased online (synthetic cannabis, in this case) have a level of quality equal to that purchased in traditional ways.[31] The general idea seems to be that there exists a sense of honor among thieves. However, more than honor, this is absolutely rational behavior in terms of building a necessary reputation, given the continuity of transactions. If the market were based on one-shot transactions, behavior of this kind would be costly for the seller. But since the market is based on repeated transactions over time, customer retention is necessary in order to earn. It follows that cooperation can also emerge between self-interested actors (Axelrod 2006).

6.7.1 Trust, Mistrust, Betrayal

The first internal relationship that is essential to a secret society, writes Simmel (1906), is the mutual trust of its members. This is particularly necessary as the purpose of maintaining secrecy is, above all, protection. Of all the protective rules, Simmel continues, the most radical one is to be invisible. But trust can be betrayed, with disruptive effects for a secret society. If secrecy is its constituent element, its possible violation is the biggest threat. The weakness of secret societies consists in the fact that

---

[31] G. Ginsburg et al. (2012), "Purity of synthetic cannabinoids sold online for recreational use," *Journal of Analytical Toxicology*, 36(1), in Wainwright 2016, 179.

secrets are not permanently kept: therefore, a secret known to two is no longer a secret (Simmel 1906). With reference to Chinese secret societies at the end of the nineteenth century, Davis (1977) states that an obsession with betrayal is quite understandable. Not only did members of a secret society live in constant danger of being denounced, they were also psychologically paralyzed by the rejection of official society. Disciplinary sanctions not only had a negative function, as punishment for those who had not carried out their duties, but also constituted a sort of code of honor.

Secrecy and trust are endangered by two types of actor: the infiltrator and the informer. An example of the infiltrator is the case of FBI agent Joseph Pistone who, under the name of Donnie Brasco, worked undercover in the New York Mafia for six years, disclosing secrets and illegal dealings (Pistone and Woodley 1987). With regard to Italian mafias, no operations of great significance are known: the phenomenon of collaboration, however, has become very important over the years. Collaborating with justice constitutes a particular form of *exit* (Hirschman 1970), similar to desertion (Sciarrone 2009) – a form of betrayal of the organization and cooperation with the (external) enemy.

The so-called *pentiti*[32] – former mobsters who become collaborators with justice – have always existed in mafia history. With regard to the Italian mafias, the first collaborator with justice in history was probably Gennaro Abbatemaggio, a witness in the Cuocolo trial in 1911, the most important trial in history against the Camorra. As for the Sicilian Cosa Nostra, there is no example until 1973, with the *pentito* Leonardo Vitale, who, despite the relevant information he provided (OSPA Stajano 2010), was not believed and was then killed by the organization. It was, however, Tommaso Buscetta, in 1984, who started a new period of collaboration by members of the organization, before the definition of a law dealing with the phenomenon. Subsequently, Salvatore Contorno, Gaspare Mutolo, Leonardo Messina, Pino Marchese, and others provided fundamental information about the organization as well as details regarding a number of crimes.

According to Hortis (2014), the code of *omertà* was more of a myth than a reality for the American Cosa Nostra. Before the confessions of Joe Valachi, incorrectly considered as the first mobster to break *omertà*, there were twelve collaborators with justice who violated the code

---

[32] The protection system for collaborators with justice (improperly defined as *pentiti* – penitents) was introduced by law no. 82 of March 15, 1991, then amended in the summer of 1992 and with a new law, no. 45, February 13, 2001. Regarding the phenomenon of collaborators with justice, see Dino (2006).

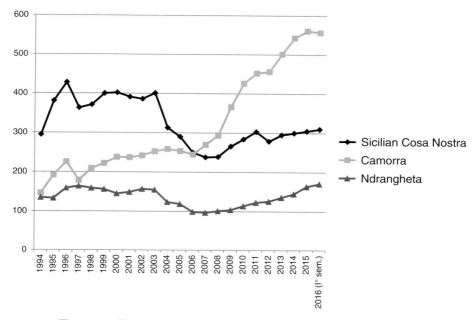

Figure 6.2 The evolution of the collaborators with justice phenomenon
in Italian mafias, 1994–2016
(*Source:* Ministry of Interior – author's elaboration)

between 1890 (Charles "Millionaire" Matranga) and 1963, the beginning of Valachi's cooperation with the Justice Department.

If we look at the number of collaborators in the period from 1994 to
the first semester of 2016 (Figure 6.2),[33] a twofold pattern emerges. On
the one hand, while the values for Sicilian Cosa Nostra and, above all,
Camorra varied a lot across years, the ones for the 'Ndrangheta remained
more stable.[34] On the other hand, while the Sicilian Cosa Nostra and,
in the last decade, the Camorra produced several collaborators, the
'Ndrangheta produced fewer.[35] According to the latest report, of the

---

[33] Reports comprising information on collaborators are issued each semester since the end
of 1994 and available on the Italian Senate webpage, www.senato.it/Leg17/2880 last
accessed on April 5, 2018.

[34] This is evident when comparing the mean and standard deviation for each mafia: Cosa
Nostra 326 (st.d. 59), Camorra 319 (st.d. 132), and 'Ndrangheta 136 (st.d. 23).

[35] It should be noted that each year the report provides the total number of collaborators,
thus including both new collaborators and those who were present in previous years and
are still in the protection program. Although this way of reporting data hinders the
identification of the actual number of new collaborators by mafia for each year, this
limitation applies to all mafias. It is therefore possible to evaluate the overall trend over
time, and to compare across mafias.

1,277 collaborators under protection in June 2016, 557 (43.6 percent) were from the Camorra, 310 (24.3 percent) from the Sicilian Cosa Nostra, 239 (18.7 percent) from other criminal organizations (i.e., Apulian Mafia and other organized crime groups), and only 171 (13.4 percent) from the 'Ndrangheta.[36]

According to law enforcement estimates, the 'Ndrangheta has almost twice as many members as the Camorra and perhaps three times as many as the Sicilian Cosa Nostra. Nonetheless, 'Ndrangheta's number of collaborators with justice is much lower than that of the other two Italian mafias. There are many factors that can encourage or hinder collaboration with law enforcement agencies. These include (1) the degree of repression by law enforcement – greater repression can encourage a greater level of collaboration and (2) the presence or absence of blood ties between members – the greater the number of blood ties, the less willingness there is to collaborate.

The Calabrian mafia, for example, suffered less in numerical terms from the phenomenon of *pentitismo* because, until about 2000, no significant attention was paid to the organization by law enforcement agencies.[37] This did occur, however, with the Sicilian Cosa Nostra from the 1980s and then even more so after the 1992 massacres. If, moreover, we also analyze the amount of goods confiscated or seized from the various mafias as a contrast indicator for the three organizations, then we can see that in the period 1992–2016 the value was approximately € 16.2 billion for the Sicilian Cosa Nostra, about € 6.8 billion for the Camorra, and about € 4.7 billion for the 'Ndrangheta.[38]

Additionally, for a 'Ndrangheta member, collaborating with justice and law enforcement agencies means, given the nature of their recruiting methods, betraying blood ties. In an interview recorded on January 5,

---

[36] Ministero dell'Interno (Ministry of Interior) 2017, *Relazione sui programmi di protezione*, Camera dei Deputati, http://documenti.camera.it/_dati/leg17/lavori/documentiparlamentari/IndiceETesti/091/008_RS/INTERO_COM.pdf, last accessed on April 5, 2018.

[37] DIA (*Direzione Investigativa Antimafia*, Anti-Mafia Investigative Directorate) 2004, *Attività svolta e risultati conseguiti* (*Activities and final findings*), http://direzioneinvestigativaantimafia.interno.gov.it; CPA (*Commissione Parlamentare Antimafia*, Italian parliamentary antimafia commission), *Relazione annuale sulla 'Ndrangheta*, Doc. XXIII, 5, XV Legislatura, February 19, 2008; DNA (*Direzione Nazionale Antimafia*, National Anti-Mafia Directorate) 2008; 2010, *Relazione annuale sulle attività svolte dal Procuratore nazionale e dalla Direzione nazionale antimafia e antiterrorismo*, vol. III.

[38] DIA (*Direzione Investigativa Antimafia*, Anti-Mafia Investigative Directorate) 2016, statistical surveys (http://direzioneinvestigativaantimafia.interno.gov.it/page/rilevazioni_statistiche.html).

2006, in prison,[39] Francesca Crisalli, the daughter of a boss killed in the 1960s, says to her son, Domenico Novella:

Nowadays, the structure of the 'Ndrangheta is completely different. Those who enter are immediately involved in *comparaggi*, a system of weddings and close relationships, a vast network that can come to include several hundred people and is a shield against the danger of informing. The tight blood ties on which the 'Ndrangheta is based, in fact, make cooperation with justice more problematic. There aren't many who decide to speak out; it would mean betraying your own blood. And blood must never be denied, even if they tear out your eyes.

Furthermore, the informer and his family run greater risks, since, thanks to such close blood ties, they can easily be traced by the other members. With regard to the results of informing, this has different consequences depending on the organizational model, vertical or horizontal. It is possible to assume that the consequences are less relevant in organizations with a horizontal structure (such as the Camorra). Here, the structure, centered around the clans and with a smaller role played by higher-level bodies of coordination (unlike the Sicilian Cosa Nostra and the 'Ndrangheta), limits the damage to the organization and to the top positions from any eventual collaboration by members.

To counteract the phenomenon of *pentitismo* – informing and collaboration – that undermines the essence of the secrecy of these organizations, some Italian mafias are changing strategy, moving from the physical elimination of the family members of collaborators with justice (ten of Buscetta's relatives were killed, and even more in the case of Contorno) to forms of assistance and psychological support for those who have been arrested. By recreating a climate of solidarity and sense of belonging within the prison, it makes it harder for the potential informer to begin collaborating, as well as increasing the psychological pressure of this kind of action.

A phenomenon that characterizes some organizations, such as political parties, is that which involves the progressive transition over time from systems of solidarity to systems of interest (Panebianco 1982). In the first case, interests and goals tend to coincide between participants and the organization has the appearance of a community. In the second case, however, interests tend to diverge and bring about an increase in internal inequalities. Mafias, like many organizations, start out as brotherhoods, as communities characterized by systems of solidarity. Over time, this feature is joined by a system of interests. If the latter ensures efficiency

---

[39] Interview recorded on January 5, 2006, between Francesca Crisalli and her son, Domenico Novella, in Cuneo (Piedmont, Italy) prison. Corte di Assise di Locri, *Sentenza per l'omicidio di Francesco Fortugno*, February 2, 2009.

and the achievement of economic results, the former is the organizational "glue" required to hold the whole thing together. In other words, in the absence of a common conception of solidarity and a clear prevalence of interests, particularly in a situation of being an extralegal organization, as mafias are, the push towards dispersion can take over and lead to organizational dissolution.

If the dimension of economic accumulation prevails over the ideals of brotherhood, the organizational authority loses legitimacy. When, in a mafia, the rational character of economic action becomes dominant, the practices and rituals that foster integration lose their value and the magical aspect disappears.

References

Abadinsky, H. (1981), *The Mafia in America*, New York: Praeger.
  (1983), *The Criminal Elite: Professional and Organized Crime*, Westport, CT: Greenwood.
  (2013), *Organized Crime*, 9th edn, Belmont, CA: Wadsworth.
Abegglen, J. C. (1958), *The Japanese Factory: Aspects of Social Organization*, Glencoe, IL: Free Press.
Abrahamson, M. (1973), Talent complementarity and organizational stratification, *Administrative Science Quarterly*, 18, 186–93.
Ackroyd, S. (2009), Organizational conflict. In S. R. Clegg et al., eds., *The Sage Handbook of Organizational Behaviour*. Vol. II: *Macro Approaches*, London: SAGE, 192–208.
Ahrne, G. and Brunsson, N. (2008), *Meta-Organizations*, Cheltenham: Edward Elgar.
  (2011), Organization outside organizations: The significance of partial organization, *Organization*, 18(1), 83–104.
Akerlof, G. A. (1970), The market for "lemons": Quality uncertainty and the market mechanism, *The Quarterly Journal of Economics*, 84(3), 488–500.
Albanese, J. S. (2014), The Italian-American mafia. In L. Paoli, ed., *The Oxford Handbook of Organized Crime*. Oxford: Oxford University Press, 142–58.
Albini, J. L. (1971), *The American Mafia: Genesis of a Legend*, New York: Appleton-Century-Crofts.
Albini, J. L. and MacIllwain, J. S. (2012), *Deconstructing Organized Crime: An Historical and Theoretical Structure*, Jefferson, NC: McFarland.
Aldrich, H. E. (1979), *Organization and Environments*, Upper Saddle River, NJ: Prentice Hall.
Aldrich, H. E. and Ruef, M. (2006), *Organizations Evolving*, London: SAGE.
Allum, F. (2017), *Camorristi, Politicians and Businessmen: The Transformation of Organized Crime in Post-War Naples*, London: Routledge.
Alongi, G. (1890), *La camorra, studio di sociologia criminale*, Turin: Edizioni Bocca.
Alvesson, M. (2002), *Understanding Organizational Culture*, London: SAGE.
Alvesson, M. and Lindkvist, L. (1993), Transaction costs, clans and corporate culture, *Journal of Management Studies*, 30(3), 427–52.
Ames, W. (1981), *Police and Community in Japan*, Berkeley: University of California Press.

Anand, N. (2005), Rituals. In N. Nicholson, P. G. Audia and M. M. Pillutla, eds., *Organizational Behavior*. Oxford: Blackwell, 352–3.

Anand, N. and Daft, R. L. (2007), What is the right organization design? *Organizational Dynamics*, 36(4): 329–44.

Anand, V. and Rosen, C. (2008), The ethics of organizational secrets, *Journal of Management Inquiry*, 17, 97–100.

Anastasia, G. (1991), *Blood and Honor: Inside the Scarfo Mob, The Mafia's Most Violent Family*, Philadelphia: Camino Books.

(2015), *Gotti's Rules: The Story of John Alite, Junior Gotti, and the Demise of the American Mafia*, New York: Dey Street Books.

Anderson, A. (1979), *The Business of Organized Crime: A Cosa Nostra Family*, Stanford, CA: Hoover Institution Press.

Anderson, E. (1999), *Code of the Street: Decency, Violence, and the Moral Life of the Inner City*, New York: W. W. Norton.

Ansoff, H. I. (1984), *Implementing Strategic Management*, New York: Prentice-Hall.

Ardituro, A. (2015), *Lo Stato non ha vinto. La Camorra oltre i Casalesi*, Bari: Laterza.

Argyris, C. and Schön, D. (1996), *Organizational Learning. II: Theory, Method, and Practice*, Reading, MA: Addison-Wesley.

Arlacchi, P. (1986), *Mafia Business: The Mafia Ethic and the Spirit of Capitalism*, London: Verso.

(1993), *Men of Dishonor: Inside the Sicilian Mafia: An Account of Antonino Calderone*, New York: William Morrow.

(1994), *Addio Cosa Nostra. La vita di Tommaso Buscetta*, Milan: Rizzoli.

(1998), Some observations on illegal markets. In V. Ruggiero, N. South and I. Taylor, eds., *The New European Criminology: Crime and Social Order in Europe*. London: Routledge, 203–15.

Arquilla, J. and Ronfeldt, D., eds. (2001), *Networks and Netwars*, Santa Monica, CA: RAND.

Arrow, K. (1974), *The Limits of Organization*, New York: W. W. Norton.

Arsovska, J. (2015), *Decoding Albanian Organized Crime*, Oakland: University of California Press.

Axelrod, R. (2006), *The Evolution of Cooperation*, rev edn, New York: Perseus Books.

Baccara, M. and Bar-Isaac, H. (2008), How to organize crime, *Review of Economic Studies*, 75(4), 1039–67.

Bachmann, R., Knights, D., and Sydow, J., eds. (2001), Special issue: Trust and control in organizational relations, *Organization Studies*, 22(2), v–viii.

Baker, W. E. (1992), The network organization in theory and practice. In N. Nohria and R. G. Eccles, eds., *Network and Organizations: Structure, Form and Action*, Boston: Harvard Business School Press, 397–429.

Baker, W. E. and Faulkner, R. R. (1993), The social organization of conspiracy: Illegal networks in the heavy electrical equipment industry, *American Sociological Review*, 58(6), 837–60.

Baldaev, D. and Vasiliev, S. (2004), *Russian Criminal Tattoo Encyclopaedia*, Vol. I, London: Fuel Design & Publishing.

(2006), *Russian Criminal Tattoo Encyclopaedia*, Vol. II, London: Fuel Design & Publishing.

(2008), *Russian Criminal Tattoo Encyclopaedia*, Vol. III, London: Fuel Design & Publishing.

Baldassarri, D. and Diani, M. (2007), The integrative power of civic networks, *American Journal of Sociology*, 113(3), 735–80.

Bandura, A. (2016), *Moral Disengagement: How People Do Harm and Live with Themselves*, New York: Worth.

Banfield, E. C. (1958), *The Moral Basis of a Backward Society*, Glencoe, IL: Free Press.

Barbacetto, G. and Milosa, D. (2011), *Le mani sulla città*, Milan: Chiarelettere.

Barbagallo, F. (2010), *Storia della Camorra*, Bari: Laterza.

Barnard, C. I. (1938), *The Functions of the Executive*, Cambridge, MA: Harvard University Press.

Baum, J. A. C., ed. (2005), *Companion to Organizations*, Oxford: Blackwell.

Baum, J. A. C. and Amburgey, T. L. (2002), Organizational ecology. In J. A. C. Baum, ed., *Companion to Organizations*. Oxford: Blackwell, 304–26.

Becker, H. S. (1963), *Outsiders: Studies in the Sociology of Deviance*, New York: Free Press.

Becker, M. C. (2004), Organizational routines: A review of the literature, *Industrial and Corporate Change*, 13(4), 643–77.

Behan, T. (1996), *The Camorra*, London: Routledge.

Bell, M. P., ed. (2011), *Diversity in Organizations*, 2nd edn, Boston: Cengage Learning.

Benz, A. (2007), Governance in connected arenas: Political science analysis of coordination and control in complex rule systems. In D. Jansen, ed., *New Forms of Governance in Research Organizations Disciplinary Approaches, Interfaces and Integration*, Dordrecht: Springer, 3–22.

Berends, H., Boersma, K., and Weggeman, M. (2003), The structuration of organizational learning, *Human Relations*, 56(9), 1035–56.

Bicchieri, C. (2006), *The Grammar of Society: The Nature and Dynamics of Social Norms*, Cambridge: Cambridge University Press.

Blair, R. D. and Lafontaine, F. (2005), *The Economics of Franchising*, Cambridge: Cambridge University Press.

Blau, P. M. (1955), *The Dynamics of Bureaucracy*, Chicago: University of Chicago Press.

Blau, P. M. and Scott, W. R. (1962), *Formal Organizations*, San Francisco: Chandler.

Bloch, M. (2014), *The Feudal Society*, Abingdon: Routledge.

Block, A., ed. (1991), *The Business of Crime: A Documentary Study of Organized Crime in the American Economy*, Boulder, CO: Westview Press.

Blok, A. (1988), *The Mafia of a Sicilian Village, 1860–1960*, New York: Polity.

Boehm, C. (1984), *Blood Revenge*, Philadelphia: University of Pennsylvania Press.

Boh, W. F., Ren, Y., Kiesler, S., and Bussjaeger, R. (2007), Expertise and collaboration in the geographically dispersed organization, *Organization Science*, 18(4), 595–612.

Boisot, M. (1986), Markets and hierarchies in a cultural perspective, *Organization Studies*, 7(2), 135–58.

Boisot, M. and Child, J. (1988), The iron law of fiefs: Bureaucratic failure and the problem of governance in the Chinese economic reforms, *Administrative Science Quarterly*, 33, 507–27.

(1996), From fiefs to clans and network capitalism: Explaining China's emerging economic order, *Administrative Science Quarterly*, 41(4), 600–28.

Bok, S. (1989), *Secrets: On the Ethics of Concealment and Revelation*, New York: Vantage Press.

Bonanno, B. and Abromovitz, G. B. (2011), *The Last Testament of Bill Bonanno*, New York: HarperCollins.

Bonanno, J. (1983), *A Man of Honor: The Autobiography of Joseph Bonanno*, New York: Simon & Schuster.

Bonini, S., Court, D., and Marchi, A. (2009), Rebuilding corporate reputations, *McKinsey Quarterly*, 3, 75–83.

Börzel, T. A. and Risse, T. (2010), Governance without a state: Can it work? *Regulation & Governance*, 4, 113–34.

Bosmia, A. N., Griessenauer, C. J., and Shane Tubbs, R. (2014), Yubitsume: Ritualistic self-amputation of proximal digits among the Yakuza, *Journal of Injury and Violence Research*, 6(2), 54–6.

Bouchard, M. and Morselli, C. (2014), Opportunistic structures of organized crime. In L. Paoli, ed., *The Oxford Handbook of Organized Crime*. Oxford: Oxford University Press, 288–302.

Bouchard, M. and Ouellet, F. (2011), Is small beautiful? The link between risks and size in illegal drug markets, *Global Crime*, 12(1), 70–86.

Boulding, K. E. (1964), A pure theory of conflict applied to organizations. In G. Fisk, ed., *The Frontiers of Management Psychology*. New York: Harper & Row, 41–9.

Bourdieu, P. (1982), Les rites comme actes d'institution, *Actes de la Recherche en Sciences Sociales*, 43, 58–63.

Bourne, P. G. (1967), Some observations of the psycho-social phenomena seen in basic training, *Psychiatry*, 30, 187–96.

Brancaccio, L. (2009), Guerre di camorra: I clan napoletani tra faide e scissioni. In G. Gribaudi, ed., *Traffici criminali. Camorra, mafie e reti internazionali dell'illegalità*. Turin: Bollati Boringhieri, 65–89.

Brewer, M. B. (1981), Ethnocentrism and its role in interpersonal trust. In M. Brewer and B. E. Collins, eds., *Scientific Inquiry and Social Sciences*. San Francisco: Jossey-Bass, 345–60.

Broadhurst, R. and Lee, K. W. (2009), The transformation of Triad "dark societies" in Hong Kong: The impact of law enforcement, socio-economic and political change, *Security Challenges*, 5(4), 1–38.

Buchanan, J. M. (1980), A defence of organized crime? In R. Andreano and J. J. Siegfried, eds., *The Economics of Crime*. New York: John Wiley & Sons, 119–32.

Buffett, W. E. (1995), *Buffett: The Making of an American Capitalist*, New York: Broadway Books.

Burns, T. R. and Flam, H. (1987), *The Shaping of Social Organization. Social Rule System Theory with Applications*, London: SAGE.

Burns, T. and Stalker, G. M. (1961), *The Management of Innovation*, London: Tavistock.

Burton, R. C. (1972), The organizational saga in higher education, *Administrative Science Quarterly*, 17, 178–84.

Calderón G., Robles, G., Díaz-Cayeros, A., and Magaloni, B. (2015), The beheading of criminal organizations and the dynamics of violence in Mexico, *Journal of Conflict Resolution*, December 1–31.

Campana, P. (2011), Eavesdropping on the mob: The functional diversification of mafia activities across territories, *European Journal of Criminology*, 8, 213–28.

Campana, P. and Varese, F. (2013), Cooperation in criminal organizations: Kinship and violence as credible commitments, *Rationality and Society*, 25(3), 263–89.

Capeci, J. (2003), *Gangland*, New York: Alpha Books.

(2004), *The Mafia*, New York: Alpha Books.

Carley, K. (2006), Destabilization of covert networks, *Computational and Mathematical Organization Theory*, 12, 51–66.

Catino, M. (2014), How do mafias organize? Conflict and violence in three mafia organizations, *European Journal of Sociology*, 55(2), 177–220.

(2015), Mafia rules: The role of criminal codes in mafia organizations, *Scandinavian Journal of Management*, 31, 536–48.

Catino, M. and Patriotta, G. (2013), Learning from errors: Cognition, emotions and safety culture in the Italian Air Force, *Organization Studies*, 34(4), 437–67.

Cattani, G., Dunbar, R. L. M., and Shapira, Z. (2013), Value creation and knowledge loss: The case of Cremonese stringed instruments, *Organization Science*, 24(3), 813–30.

Chandler, A. D. (1962), *Strategy and Structure: Chapters in the History of the American Industrial Enterprise*, Cambridge, MA: MIT Press.

Child, J. (1972), Organization structure and strategies of control: A replication of the Aston Study, *Administrative Science Quarterly*, 17, 163–77.

Child, J. and Mansfield, R. (1972), Technology, size and organization structure, *Sociology*, 6, 369–93.

Chin, K. (1995), Triad societies in Hong Kong, *Transnational Organized Crime*, 1(1), 47–64.

(2014), Chinese organized crime. In L. Paoli, ed., *The Oxford Handbook of Organized Crime*. Oxford: Oxford University Press, 219–33.

Chu, Y. K. (2000), *The Triads as Business*, London-New York: Routledge.

(2005), Hong Kong Triads after 1997, *Trends in Organized Crime*, 8, 5–12.

(2011), Hong Kong Triads. In C. J. Smith, S. X. Zhang and R. Barberet, eds., *Routledge Handbook of International Criminology*. New York: Routledge, 226–36.

Chun, R. (2005), Corporate reputation: Meaning and management, *International Journal of Management Reviews*, 7(2), 91–109.

Chwe, M. S. Y. (2003), *Rational Ritual: Culture, Coordination, and Common Knowledge*. Princeton, NJ: Princeton University Press.

Cicale, D. and Scarpo, E. (2014), *Cosa Nostra News: The Cicale Files*, vol. I, Dublin: GCN.

Ciconte, E. (1996), *Processo alla 'Ndrangheta*, Bari: Laterza.

(2008), *Storia criminale. La resistibile ascesa di Mafia, 'Ndrangheta e Camorra dall'Ottocento ai giorni nostri*, Soveria Mannelli: Rubbettino.

(2015), *Riti criminali. I codici di affiliazione della 'Ndrangheta*, Soveria Mannelli: Rubbettino.

Ciconte, E. and Macrì, V. (2009), *Australian 'Ndrangheta*, Soveria Mannelli: Rubbettino.

Ciconte, E., Macrì, V., and Forgione, F. (2010), *Osso, Mastrosso, Carcagnosso*, Soveria Mannelli: Rubbettino.

Clark, R. P. (1983), Patterns in the lives of ETA members, *Terrorism: An International Journal*, 6, 423–54.

Clegg, S. R., Hardy, C., Lawrence, T. B and Nord, W. R., eds. (2006), *The Sage Handbook of Organization Studies*, London: SAGE.

Coase, R. H. (1937), The nature of the firm, *Economica*, 3, 386–405.

Coffey, J. and Schmetterer, J. (1991), *The Coffey Files: One Cop's War against the Mob*, New York: St. Martin's Press.

Cohen, A. (1969), *Customs and Politics in Urban Africa: A Study of Hausa Migrants in Yoruba Towns*, Berkeley: University of California Press.

Cohen, M. D. and Bacdayan, P. (1994), Organizational routines are stored as procedural memory: Evidence from a laboratory study, *Organization Science*, 5(4), 554–68.

Colajanni, N. (1900), *Nel regno della mafia: Dai Borboni ai Sabaudi*, Palermo: Edizioni Remo Sandron.

Coleman, J. S. (1974), *Power and the Structure of Society*, New York: W. W. Norton.
  (1990), *Foundations of Social Theory*, Cambridge, MA: Harvard University Press.
  (1993), The rational reconstruction of society, *American Sociological Review*, 58(1), 1–15.

Colletti, A. (2016), *Il welfare e il suo doppio. Percorsi etnografici delle camorra del casertano*, Milan: Ledizioni LediPublishing.

Collins, R. (2004), *Interaction Rituals Chain*, Princeton, NJ: Princeton University Press.
  (2008), *Violence: A Micro-Sociological Theory*, Princeton, NJ: Princeton University Press.
  (2010), *Conflict Sociology: A Sociological Classic Updated*, New York: Academic Press.

Consiglio, A. (1959), *Camorra*, Milan: Cino del Duca.

Costas, J. and Grey, C. (2014), Bringing secrecy into the open: Towards a theorization of the social processes of organizational secrecy, *Organization Studies*, 35 (10), 1423–47.
  (2016), *Secrecy at Work: The Hidden Architecture of Organizational Life*, Stanford, CA: Stanford University Press.

Coyne, C. J. and Mathers, R. L. (2011), Rituals: An economic interpretation, *Journal of Economic Behavior & Organization*, 78, 74–84.

Crawford, S. E. S. and Ostrom, E. (1995), A grammar of institutions, *American Political Science Review*, September, 89, 3.

Cressey, D. R. (1967), The functions and structures of criminal syndicates. In *Task Force Report: Organized Crime*, Washington, DC: U.S. Government Printing Office, 25–60.
  (1969), *Theft of the Nation: The Structure and Operations of Organized Crime in America*, New York: Harper & Row.

Critchley, D. (2006), Buster, Maranzano and the Castellammare War, 1930–1931, *Global Crime*, 7(1), 43–78.

(2009), *The Origins of Organized Crime in America: The New York City Mafia, 1891–1931*, London: Routledge.

Crittle, S. (2006), *The Last Godfather: The Rise and Fall of Joey Massino*, New York: Berkley Books.

Crossan, M. M., Lane, H. W., and White, R. E. (1999), An organizational learning framework: From intuition to institution, *Academy of Management Review*, 24(3), 522–37.

Crozier, M. (1964), *The Bureaucratic Phenomenon*, Chicago: The University of Chicago Press.

Crozier, M. and Friedberg, E. (1977), *L'acteur et le système*, Paris: Éditions du Seuil.

Cutrera, A. (1900), *La Mafia e i mafiosi: origini e manifestazioni, studio di sociologia criminale*, Palermo: Alberto Reber.

Cyert, R. M. and March, J. G. (1963), *A Behavioral Theory of the Firm*, Upper Saddle River, NJ: Prentice-Hall.

Daft, R. L. (2013), *Organization Theory and Design*, 11th edn, Stamford, CT: South-Western-Cengage Learning.

Dalla Chiesa, N. (2016), *Passaggio a Nord. La colonizzazione mafiosa*, Milan: Melampo Editore.

Dalla Chiesa, N. and Panzarasa, M. (2012), *Buccinasco: La 'Ndrangheta al Nord*, Turin: Einaudi.

Dash, M. (2009), *The First Family*, New York: Ballantine Books.

Davis, F. L. (1977), *Primitive Revolutionaries of China: A Study of Secret Societies in the Late Nineteenth Century*, London-Henley: Routledge and Kegan Paul.

Deal, T. E. and Kennedy, A. (1982), *Corporate Cultures*, Reading, MA: Addison-Wesley.

De Blasio, A. (1897), *Usi e costumi dei camorristi: Storie di ieri e di oggi*, Naples: Pierro (2nd edn: Naples: Torre, 1993).

(1905), *Il tatuaggio*, Naples: Prem. Stab. Tip. G. M. Priore.

Decker, S. H. and Curry, G. D. (2002), Gangs, gang homicides, and gang loyalty: Organized crimes or disorganized criminals, *Journal of Criminal Justice*, 30, 343–52.

Decker, S. H. and van Winkle, B. (1996), *Life in the Gang*, Cambridge: Cambridge University Press.

De Gregorio, S. (1983), *I Nemici di Cutolo*, Naples: Tullio Pironti Editore.

De Lucia, M. (2015), Cosa Nostra: l'analisi, le linee evolutive, l'attuale operatività. In E. Ciconte, F. Forgione and I. Sales, eds., *Atlante delle Mafie*, vol. III. Soveria Mannelli: Rubbettino, 133–57.

Densley, J. A. (2012), Street gang recruitment: Signaling, screening, and selection, *Social Problems*, 69(3), 301–21.

(2013), *How Gangs Work: An Ethnography of Youth Violence*, London: Palgrave Macmillan.

DeStefano, A. M. (2007), *King of the Godfathers: Joseph Massino and the Fall of the Bonanno Crime Family*, New York: Kensington, Pinnacle.

Di Cagno, G. and Natoli, G. (2004), *Cosa Nostra ieri, oggi, domani*, Bari: Edizioni Dedalo.

Dick, A. R. (1995), When does organized crime pay? A transaction cost analysis, *International Review of Law and Economics*, 15, 25–45.

Dickie, J. (2004), *Cosa Nostra. A History of Sicilian Mafia*, New York: Palgrave Macmillan.

(2012) *Mafia Brotherhoods*. London: Sceptre.

Di Fiore, G. (2016), *La camorra e le sue storie: La criminalità organizzata a Napoli dalle origini alle paranze dei bimbi*, Novara: UTET.

Dill, W. R. (1958), Environment as an influence on managerial autonomy, *Administrative Science Quarterly*, 2(4), 409–43.

DiMaggio, P. J. and Powell, W. W. (1983), The iron cage revisited: Institutional isomorphism and collective rationality in organizational fields, *American Sociological Review*, 48(2), 147–60.

Di Matteo, N. and Palazzolo, S. (2015), *Collusi. Perché politici, uomini delle istituzioni e manager continuano a trattare con la mafia*, Milan: BUR.

Dino, A., ed. (2006), *Pentiti*, Rome: Donzelli.

Dino, A., (2016), *A colloquio con Gaspare Spatuzza*, Bologna: il Mulino.

Dobbin, F. and Dowd, T. (2000), The market that antitrust built: Public policy, private coercion, and railroad acquisitions, 1825–1922, *American Sociological Review*, 65(1), 635–57.

Dolgova, A. (2003), *Prestupnost': Ee organizovannost'i kriminal'noe soobshchestvo*. Moscow: Rossiiskaya Kriminalogicheskaya Assotsiatsiya.

Dore, R. (1973), *British Factory-Japanese Factory*, Berkeley: University of California Press.

Dufresne, R. L. and Offstein, E. H. (2008), On the virtues of secrets in organizations, *Journal of Management Inquiry*, 17(2), 102–6.

Dugato, M., Calderoni, F., and Berlusconi, G. (2017), Forecasting organized crime homicides: Risk terrain modeling of camorra violence in Naples, *Journal of Interpersonal Violence*, Article first published online: June 13, 1–27.

Durham, M. E. (1928), *Some Tribal Origins, Law and Customs of the Balkans*, London: George Allen & Unwin.

Durkheim, E. (1912), *Les formes élémentaires de la vie religieuse*, Paris: Presses universitaires de France.

Duverger, M. (1966), *The Idea of Politics*, London: Methuen.

Dyer, J. H. and Chu, W. (2003), The role of trustworthiness in reducing transaction costs and improving performance: Empirical evidence from the United States, Japan, and Korea, *Organization Science*, 14(1).

Easterby-Smith, M., Crossan, M., and Nicolini, D. (2000), Organizational learning. Debates past, present and future, *Journal of Management Studies*, 37(6), 783–96.

Easterby-Smith, M. and Lyles, M. (2010), *Handbook on Organizational Learning and Knowledge Management*, New York: Wiley-Blackwell.

Eilstrup-Sangiovanni, M. and Jones, C. (2008), Assessing the dangers of illicit networks, why Al-Qaida may be less threatening than we think, *International Security*, 33(2), 7–44.

Eliade, M. (1976), *Initiation, rites, sociétés secrètes*, Paris: Gallimard.

Ellickson, R. C. (1991), *Order without Law: How Neighbors Settle Disputes*, Cambridge, MA: Harvard University Press.

Elster, J. (2007), *Explaining Social Behavior*, Cambridge: Cambridge University Press.

Emery, F. and Trist, E. (1965), The causal texture of organizational environments, *Human Relations*, 18, 21–32.

Erickson, B. H. (1981), Secret societies and social structure, *Social Forces*, 60(1), 188–210.

Erikson, E. H. (1958), *Young Man Luther: A Study in Psychoanalysis and History*, New York: W. W. Norton.

Etzioni, A. (1961), *A Comparative Analysis of Complex Organizations*, Glencoe, IL: Free Press.

(1964), *Modern Organizations*, Englewood Cliffs, NJ: Prentice-Hall.

Falcone, G. and Padovani, M. (1992), *Men of Honour: The Truth about the Mafia*, New York: HarperCollins.

Fasanella, G. and Franceschini, A. (2004), *Cosa sono le BR*, Milan: RCS Libri.

Fayol, H. (1949, 1st edn: 1919), *General and Industrial Management*, London: Pitman.

Fearon, J. D. and Laitin, D. D. (1996), Explaining interethnic cooperation, *American Political Science Review*, 90, 715–35.

Feldman, M. S. (2000), Organizational routines as a source of continuous change, *Organization Science*, 11(6), 611–29.

Feldman, M. S. and Pentland, B. T. (2003), Reconceptualizing organizational routines as a source of flexibility and change, *Administrative Science Quarterly*, 48(1), 94–118.

Feldman, S. P. (1988), Secrecy, information and politics: An essay in organizational decisionmaking, *Human Relations*, 41, 73–90.

Festinger, L. (1957), *A Theory of Cognitive Dissonance*, Stanford, CA: Stanford University Press.

Finckenauer, J. O. (2000), *La Cosa Nostra in the United States*, U.S. Dept. of Justice, National Institute of Justice, International Center, United States of America: www.ncjrs.gov/App/Publications/abstract.aspx?ID=240258.

Finckenauer, J. O. and Waring, E. J. (1998), *Russian Mafia in America: Immigration, Culture and Crime*, Boston: Northeastern University Press.

Fine, G. A. (1996), Reputational entrepreneurs and the memory of incompetence: Melting supporters, partisan warriors, and images of president Harding, *American Journal of Sociology*, 5, 1159–93.

Fine, G. A. and Holyfield, L. (1996), Secrecy, trust, and dangerous leisure, generating group cohesion in voluntary organizations, *Social Psychology Quarterly*, 59(1), 22–38.

Fligstein, N., and McAdam, D. (2012), *A Theory of Fields*, New York: Oxford University Press.

Fombrun, C. (1996), *Reputation: Realizing Value from Corporate Image*, Boston: Harvard Business School Press.

(2005), Reputation. In N. Nicholson, P. G. Audia and M. M. Pillutla, eds., *Organizational Behavior*. Oxford: Blackwell, 343–5.

Forest, J. (2006), Introduction. In J. Forest, ed., *Teaching Terror: Strategic and Tactical Learning in the Terrorist World*. Lanham, MD: Rowman & Littlefield, 1–32.

Franchetti, L. (1876; 2nd edn: 1993), *Condizioni politiche ed amministrative della Sicilia*, Rome: Donzelli.

Fresolone, G. and Wagman, R. J. (1994), *Blood Oath*, New York: Simon & Schuster.

Friedberg, E. (1993), *Le pouvoir et la règle: Dynamiques de l'action organisée*, Paris: Éditions du Seuil.

Frye, T. (2002), Private protection in Russia and Poland, *American Journal of Political Science*, 46(3), 572–84.

Fukuyama, F. (1995), *Trust*, New York: Free Press.

Gabriel, Y. (2008), *Organizing Words: A Critical Thesaurus for Social and Organizations Studies*, Oxford: Oxford University Press.

Galbraith, J. R. (1973), *Designing Complex Organizations*, Reading, MA: Addison-Wesley.

Galeotti, M. (2018), *The Vory: Russia's Super Mafia*, New Haven, CT: Yale University Press.

Gambetta, D. (1988), *Trust: Making and Breaking Cooperative Relations*, Oxford: Basil Blackwell.

(1989–90), La mafia elimina la concorrenza: Ma la concorrenza può eliminare la mafia? *Meridiana*, 3(7/8), 319–36.

(1993), *The Sicilian Mafia: The Business of Private Protection*, Cambridge, MA: Harvard University Press.

(1994), La protezione mafiosa. In G. Fiandaca and S. Costantino, eds., *La mafia, le mafie. Tra vecchi e nuovi paradigmi*. Rome-Bari: Laterza, 219–31.

(2009), *Codes of the Underworld: How Criminals Communicate*, Princeton, NJ: Princeton University Press.

Gambetta, D. and Reuter, P. (1995), Conspiracy among the many: The mafia in legitimate industries. In G. Fiorentini and S. Peltzman, eds., *The Economics of the Organized Crime*. Cambridge: Cambridge University Press, 116–39.

Garfinkel, H. (1956), Conditions of successful degradation ceremonies, *American Journal of Sociology*, 61(5), 420–4.

Gennari, G. (2013), *Le fondamenta della città. Come il Nord Italia ha aperto le porte alla 'ndrangheta*, Milan: Mondadori.

Gentile, M. C., ed. (1994) *Differences That Work: Organizational Excellence through Diversity*, Boston: Harvard Business School Press.

Gentile, N. (1963), *Vita di capomafia*, Rome: Editori Riuniti.

Gephart, R. P., Jr. (1978), Status degradation and organizational succession: An ethnomethodological approach, *Administrative Science Quarterly*, 23, 553–81.

Gerlach, L. (2001), The structure of social movements: Environmental activism and its opponents. In J. Arquilla and D. Ronfeldt, eds., *Networks and Netwars: The Future of Terror, Crime, and Militancy*. Santa Monica, CA: RAND, 289–310.

Goffman, E. (1959), *The Presentation of Self in Everyday Life*, Garden City, NY: Doubleday/Anchor.

(1961), *Asylums: Essays on the Social Situation of Mental Patients and Other Inmates*, Garden City, NY: Doubleday.

(1969), *Strategic Interaction*, Philadelphia: University of Pennsylvania Press.

Goldstock, R., Marcus, M., Thacher, T. D., and Jacobs, J. B. (1990), *Corruption and Racketeering in the New York City Construction Industry: The Final Report of the New York State Organized Crime Task Force*, New York: New York University Press.

Goodman, M. (2011), What business can learn from organized crime, *Harvard Business Review*, November 27–30.

Goodwin, R. N. (1988), *Remembering America: A Voice from the Sixties*, New York: Harper & Row.

Gosch, M. A. and Hammer, R. (2013), *The Last Testament of Lucky Luciano*, New York: Enigma Books.

Gould, R. V. (2003), *Collision of Wills: How Ambiguity about Social Rank Breeds Conflicts*, Chicago: The University of Chicago Press.

Gouldner, A. W. (1954), *Patterns of Industrial Bureaucracy*, Glencoe, IL: Free Press.

(1959), Organizational analysis. In R. K. Merton, L. Broom and L. S. Cottrell, Jr., eds., *Sociology Today*. New York: Basic Books, 400–28.

Gragert, Lt. B. A. (2010), Yakuza: The warlords of Japanese organized crime, *Annual Survey of International & Comparative Law*, 4(1), 147–204.

Graham, J. (1997), Taiwan's Triads. *Asia, Inc.*, April, http://orgcrime.tripod.com/taiwansdirtybusiness.htm (last accessed on April 5, 2018).

Gratteri, N. and Nicaso, A. (2013a), *Acqua santissima*, Milan: Oscar Mondadori.
(2013b), *Dire e non dire. I dieci comandamenti della 'ndrangheta nelle parole degli affiliati*, Milano: Mondadori.

Grey, C. (2013), *Decoding Organizations: Bletchley Park, Code Breaking and Organization Studies*, Cambridge: Cambridge University Press.

Grove, A. (1996), *Only the Paranoid Survive: How to Survive the Crisis Points That Challenge Every Career*, Garden City, NY: Doubleday.

Gulati, R. and Gargiulo, M. (1999), Where do interorganizational networks come from? *American Journal of Sociology*, 104, 1439–93.

Gulick, L. and Urwick, L., eds. (1937), *Papers on the Science of Administration*, New York: Institute of Public Administration, Columbia University.

Gunaratna, R. (2002), *Inside Al Qaeda: Global Network of Terror*, New York: Columbia University Press.

Haas, J. (1972), Binging: Educational control among high steel ironworkers, *American Behavioral Scientist*, 16, 27–34.

Habyarimana, J., Macartan, H., Posner, D. N., and Weinstein, J. M. (2009), Coethnicity and trust. In K. S. Cook, M. Levi and R. Hardin, eds., *Whom Can We Trust?*. New York: Russell Sage Foundation, 42–65.

Hall, D. J. and Saias, M. A. (1980), Strategy follows structure!, *Strategic Management Journal*, 1(2), 149–63.

Hall, R. H. (1977), *Organizations – Structure and Process*, Englewood Cliffs, NJ: Prentice-Hall.

Haller, M. H. (1992), Bureaucracy and the mafia: An alternative view, *Journal of Contemporary Criminal Justice*, 8(1), 1–10.

Handel, M. J. (2003), *The Sociology of Organizations: Classic, Contemporary, and Critical Reading*, Thousands Oaks, CA: Sage.

Handy, C. (1999), *Understanding Organizations*, London: Penguin Books.

Hannan, M. T. and Freeman, J. (1977), The population ecology of organiza-tions, *American Journal of Sociology*, 82(5), 929–64.

(1984), Structural inertia and organizational change, *American Sociological Review*, 49(1), 149–64.

(1989), *Organizational Ecology*, Cambridge, MA: Harvard University Press.

Hardin, R. (2002), *Trust and Trustworthiness*, New York: Russell Sage Foundation.

Heath, C. and Staudenmayer, N. (2000), Coordination neglect: How lay theories of organizing complicate coordination in organizations, *Research in Organizational Behavior*, 22(1), 153–91.

Hechter, M. and Opp, K-D. (2001), *Social Norms*, New York: Russell Sage Foundation.

Hegghammer, T. (2012), The recruiter's dilemma: Signalling and rebel recruit-ment tactics, *Journal of Peace Research*, 50(1), 3–16.

Hess, H. (1973, 1st edn: 1970), *Mafia and Mafioso: The Structure of Power*, Lexington, MA: Lexington Books.

Hill, P. (2003a), *The Japanese Mafia, Yakuza, Law, and the State*, Oxford: Oxford University Press.

(2003b), Heisei Yakuza: Burst bubble and Bōtaihō, *Social Science Japan Journal*, 6(1), 1–18.

(2004), The changing face of the Yakuza, *Global Crime*, 6(1), 97–116.

(2014), The Japanese Yakuza. In L. Paoli, ed., *The Oxford Handbook of Organized Crime*. Oxford: Oxford University Press, 234–53.

Hirschman, A. O. (1970), *Exit, Voice, and Loyalty: Response to Decline in Firms, Organizations, and States*, Cambridge, MA: Harvard University Press.

Hobsbawm, E. (1959), *Primitive Rebels: Studies in Archaic Forms of Social Movements in the 19th and 20th Century*, New York: W. W. Norton.

Hodgson, G. M. (2008), The concept of a routine. In M. C. Becker, ed., *Handbook of Organizational Routines*. Cheltenham: Edward Elgar, 15–28.

Hooghe, L. and Marks, G. (2003), Unraveling the central State, but how? Types of multi-level governance, *IHS Political Science Series*, Wien, 87.

Hortis, C. A. (2014), *The Mob and The City: The Hidden History of How the Mafia Captured New York*, New York: Prometheus Books.

Huang, F. F. Y. and Vaughn, M. S. (1992), A descriptive analysis of Japanese organized crime: The Boryokudan from 1945 to 1988, *International Criminal Justice Review*, 2, 19–57.

Hutin, S. (1955), *Les sociétés secrètes*, Paris: Presses Universitaires de France.

Ianni, F. A. J. (1974), *The Black Mafia: Ethnic Succession in Organized Crime*, New York: Simon & Schuster.

(1976), The mafia and the web of kinship. In F. A. J. Ianni and E. Reuss-Ianni, eds., *The Crime Society: Organised Crime and Corruption in America*. New York: New American Library, 44–59.

Ianni, F. A. J. and Reuss-Ianni, E. (1972), *A Family Business: Kinship and Social Control in Organized Crime*, New York: Russell Sage Foundation.

Ino, K. (1993), *Yakuza to Nihonjin (The Yakuza and the Japanese)*, Tokyo: Gendai Shokan.

Ip, P. F. P. (1999a), *Organized Crime in Hong Kong*, Organized Crime and the 21st Century – Seminar (June, 26, 1999), Centre for Criminology,

University of Hong Kong; www.crime.hku.hk/organizecrime.htm (last accessed on April 5, 2018).

(1999b), *The Sociolinguistics of Triad Language in Hong Kong*, Unpublished Master Philosophy Thesis, University of Hong Kong.

Iwai, H. (1986), Organized crime in Japan. In R. J. Kelly, ed. *Organized Crime: A Global Perspective*. Lanham, MD: Rowman & Littlefield, 208–33.

Jacobs, D. L. (2002), *Friend of Family*, Washington, DC: Compass Press.

Jacobs, J. B. (1999), *Gotham Unbound. How New York City Was Liberated from the Grip of Organized Crime*, New York: New York University Press.

(2006), *Mobsters, Unions, and Feds: The Mafia and the American Labor Movement*, New York: New York University Press.

Jacobs, J. B. and Gouldin, L. P. (1999), Cosa Nostra: The final chapter? *Crime and Justice*, 25, 129–89.

Jacobs, J. B., Panarella, C., and Worthington, J. (1994), *Busting the Mob: The United States v. Cosa Nostra*, New York: New York University Press.

Jiang, L. and Probst, T. M. (2015), Do your employees (collectively) trust you? The importance of trust climate beyond individual trust, *Scandinavian Journal of Management*, 32, 526–35.

Jones, C. (2008), Editor's introduction (to special issue on secrecy of organizations), *Journal of Management Inquiry*, 17, 95–6.

Jordan, B. (1989), Cosmopolitical obstetrics: Some insight from training of traditional midwives, *Social Science and Medicine*, 28(9), 925–37.

Jordan, G. (1998), What drives associability at the European level? The limits of utilitarian explanations. In J. Greenwood and M. Aspinwall, eds., *Collective Action in the European Union*. London: Routledge, 31–62.

Kaplan, E. D. and Dubro, A. (2003), *Yakuza: Japan's Criminal Underworld*, London: Routledge and Kegan Paul.

Keegan, J. (1994), *The History of Warfare*, New York: Vintage.

Keiser, R. L. (1969), *The Vice Lord: Warriors of the Street*, New York: Holt, Rinehart & Winston.

Kenis, P. and Knoke, D. (2002), How organizational field networks shape inter-organizational tie-formation rates, *Academy of Management Review*, 27, 275–93.

Kenney, M. (2006), How terrorists learn. In J. Forest, ed., *Teaching Terror: Strategic and Tactical Learning in the Terrorist World*. Lanham, MD: Rowman & Littlefield, 33–51.

(2007), *From Pablo to Osama: Trafficking and Terrorist Networks, Government Bureaucracies, and Competitive Adaptation*, Philadelphia: Penn State University Press.

Kogut, B. and Walker, G. (2001), The small world of Germany and the durability of national networks, *American Sociological Review*, 66, 317–35.

Kooiman, J. (1999), Social-political governance, *Public Management*, 1(1), 67–92.

(2003), *Governing as Governance*, London: SAGE.

Kramer, R. M. (2003), The virtues of prudent trust. In R. Westwood and S. Clegg, eds., *Debating Organizations*. Malden, MA: Blackwell, 341–56.

Kramer, R. and Tyler, T., eds. (1996), *Trust in Organizations*, New York: SAGE.

Kunda, G. (1992), *Engineering Culture: Control and Commitment in a High-Tech Corporation*, Philadelphia: Temple University Press.

Kwok, S. I. (2017), *Triad Society in Hong Kong: The Hierarchical Approach and Criminal's Collaborations*, Ph.D. dissertation, City University of Hong Kong, http://lbms03.cityu.edu.hk/theses/c_ftt/phd-ss-15457829.pdf (last accessed on April 5, 2018).

Kwok, S. I. and Lo, T. W. (2013), Anti-triad legislations in Hong Kong: Issues, problems and development, *Trends in Organized Crime*, 16(1), 74–94.

La Fontaine, J. (1985), *Initiation: Ritual Drama and Secret Knowledge across the World*, New York: Penguin Books.

Landa, J. T. (1994), *Trust, Ethnicity, and Identity: Beyond the New Institutional Economics of Ethnic Trading Networks, Contract Law, and Gift-Exchange*, Ann Arbor: University of Michigan Press.

Landesco, J. (1929), *Organized Crime in Chicago*, Chicago: The University of Chicago Press.

Lange, D., Lee, P. M., and Dai, Y. (2011), Organizational reputation: A review, *Journal of Management*, 37(1), 153–84.

La Porta, R., Lopez-de-Silanes, F., and Shleifer, A. (1999), Corporate ownership around the world, *Journal of Finance*, 54(2), 471–517.

La Spina, A. (2016), *Il mondo di mezzo. Mafie e antimafie*, Bologna: il Mulino.

Lave, J. and Wenger, E. (1991), *Situated Learning: Legitimate Peripheral Participation*, Cambridge: Cambridge University Press.

Lee, K. W. (2004), *Triad Related Homicide in Hong Kong*, Ph.D. dissertation, The HKU Scholars Hub, The University of Hong Kong, http://hdl.handle.net/10722/133996 (last accessed on April 5, 2018).

Leeson, P. T. (2009), The laws of lawlessness, *The Journal of Legal Studies*, 38(2), 471–503.

(2011), *The Invisible Hook: The Hidden Economics of Pirates*, Princeton, NJ: Princeton University Press.

Leeson, P. T. and Rogers, D. B. (2012), Organizing crime, *Supreme Court Economic Review*, 20(1), 89–123.

Leeson, P. T. and Skarbek, D. B. (2010), Criminal constitutions, *Global Crime*, 11(3), 279–98.

Leonetti, P., Burnstein, S., and Graziano, C. (2012), *Mafia Prince*, Philadelphia: Running Press.

Lestingi, F. (1880), La mafia in Sicilia, *Archivio di Psichiatria e Antropologia Criminale*, 1, 291–4.

Levitt, B. and March, J. G. (1988), Organizational learning, *Annual Review of Sociology*, 14(1), 319–38.

Lipshitz, R. and Barak, D. (1995), Hindsight wisdom: Outcome knowledge and the evaluation of decisions, *Acta Psychologica*, 88(1), 105–25.

Litz, R. A. and Stewart, A. C. (2000), Where everybody knows your name: Extraorganizational clan-building as small firm strategy for home field advantage, *Journal of Small Business Strategy*, 11(1), 1–13.

Liu, T. M. (2001), *Hong Kong Triad Societies before and after 1997*, Hong Kong: Net e-Publishing.

Llewellyn, K. (1931), What price contract? An essay in perspective, *Yale Law Journal*, 40, 704–51.

Lo, T. W. (2010), Beyond social capital: Triad organized crime in Hong Kong and China, *British Journal of Criminology*, 50, 851–72.

(2012), Triadization of youth gangs in Hong Kong, *British Journal of Criminology*, 52, 556–76.

Lo, T. W. and Kwok, S. I. (2012), Traditional organized crime in the modern world: How triad societies respond to socioeconomic change. In D. Siegel and H. van de Bunt, eds., *Traditional Organized Crime in the Modern World: Responses to Socioeconomic Change (Studies of Organized Crime)*, New York: Springer, 67–89.

Lombardo, R. (2013), *Organized Crime in Chicago: Beyond the Mafia*, Champaign: University of Illinois Press.

Love, E. G. and Kraatz, M. S. (2009), Character, conformity, or the bottom line? How and why downsizing affected corporate reputation, *Academy of Management Journal*, 52, 314–35.

Luhmann, N. (1979), *Trust and Power*, New York: John Wiley & Sons.

(2000), *Organisation und Entscheidung*, Opladen: Westdeutscher Verlag.

Lukes, S. (1975), Political ritual and social integration, *Sociology*, 9, 289–308.

Lupo, S. (2008), *Quando la mafia trovò l'America. Storia di un intreccio intercontinentale, 1888–2008*, Turin: Einaudi.

(2011a), *History of Mafia*, New York: Columbia University Press.

(2011b), *Il tenebroso sodalizio: Il primo rapporto di Polizia sulla mafia siciliana*, Rome: XL Edizioni.

Maas, P. (1968), *The Valachi Papers*, New York: Bantam Books.

(1997), *Underboss: Sammy the Bull Gravano's Story of Life in the Mafia*, New York: HarperCollins.

Macharia, K. (1988), *Social Networks: Ethnicity and the Informal Sector in Nairobi*, Institute for Development Studies, working paper 463, Nairobi: University of Nairobi.

MacKenzie, N., ed. (1967), *Secret Societies*, New York: Holt, Rinehart & Winston.

Mahler, J. G. (2009), *Organizational Learning at NASA: The Challenger and Columbia Accidents*, Washington, DC: Georgetown University Press.

Maine, H. (1861), *Ancient Law*, London: Dorset Press.

Malafarina, L. (1986), *La 'Ndrangheta. Il codice segreto, la storia, i miti, i riti e i personaggi*, Reggio Calabria: Casa del Libro.

Mallory, S. L. (2012), *Understanding Organized Crime*, Burlington, MA: Jones & Bartlett Learning.

March, J. G. (1962), The business firm as a political coalition, *Journal of Politics*, 24, 662–78.

(1991), Exploration and exploitation in organizational learning, *Organization Science*, 2(1), 71–87.

(1994), *A Primer on Decision-Making: How Decisions Happen*, New York: Free Press.

March, J. G. and Olsen, J. P. (1989), *Rediscovering Institutions: The Organizational Basis of Politics*, New York: Free Press.

March, J. G., Schulz, M., and Zhou, X. (2000), *The Dynamics of Rules: Change in Written Organizational Codes*, Stanford, CA: Stanford University Press.

March, J. G. and Simon, H. A. (1958), *Organizations*, New York: John Wiley & Sons.

Markham, V. (1972), *Planning the Corporate Reputation*, London: George Allen & Unwin.

Marmo, M. (2011), *Il coltello e il mercato. La Camorra prima e dopo l'Unità d'Italia*, Naples and Rome: L'ancora del Mediterraneo.

Martens, T. F. (2017), *From Cosa Nostra to Crime, Inc.: The Task Force Report and Fifty Years of War*, paper presented at the Annual Meeting of the American Society of Criminology, Philadelphia, November 15–18.

Martocchia, S., Tenti, V., and Calderoni, F. (2014), Infiltrare gli appalti: i casi di studio. In S. Caneppele, ed., *Le mafie dentro gli appalti. Casi di studio e modelli preventivi*. Milan: Franco Angeli, 36–162.

Massari, M. (1998), *La Sacra Corona Unita. Potere e segreto*, Rome-Bari: Laterza. (2013), Società segreta. In M. Mareso and L. Pepino, eds., *Dizionario enciclopedico di mafie e antimafia*. Turin: Edizioni Gruppo Abele, 464–72.

Mastriani, F. (1889–90), *La malavita* (2nd edn, 2016), Naples: Guida Editori.

Mayntz, R. (2004), *Organizational Forms of Terrorism. Hierarchy, Network, or a Type Sui Generis?*, Cologne: Max Planck Institute for the Study of Societies, MPIfG discussion paper, 04/4.

Mayo, E. (1945), *The Social Problems of an Industrial Civilization*, Boston: Graduate School of Business Administration, Harvard University.

Mazzitelli, A. L. (2011), *Mexican Cartels Influence in Central America*, Western Hemisphere Security Analysis Center, paper 45, http://digitalcommons.fiu.edu/whemsac/45 (last accessed on April 5, 2018).

McEvily, B., Perrone, V., and Zaheer, A. (2003), Trust as an organizing principle, *Organization Science*, 14, 91–103.

McKenna, J. J. (1996), Organised crime in the Royal Colony of Hong Kong, *Journal of Contemporary Criminal Justice*, 12(4), 316–28.

Mendelsohn, B. (2016), *The Al-Qaeda Franchise: The Expansion of Al-Qaeda and Its Consequences*, New York: Oxford University Press.

Merton, R. K. (1936), The unanticipated consequences of purposive social action, *American Sociological Review*, 1(6), 894–904. (1968), *Social Theory and Social Structure*, New York: Free Press.

Meyer, J. W. and Rowan, B. (1977), Institutionalized organizations: Formal structure as myth and ceremony, *American Journal of Sociology*, 83(2), 340–463.

Meyer, J. W., Scott, W. R., Strang, D., and Creighton, A. (1988), Bureaucratization without centralization: Changes in the organizational system of American public education, 1940–1980. In G. L. Zucker, ed., *Institutional Patterns and Organizations*. Cambridge, MA: Ballinger, 139–68.

Michels, R. (1911), *Zur Soziologie des Parteiwesens in der modernen Demokratie. Untersuchungen über die oligarchischen Tendenzen des Gruppenlebens*. Translated as *Political Parties: A Sociological Study of the Oligarchical Tendencies of Modern Democracy* (1962), New York: Crowell-Collier.

Milgrom, P. and Roberts, J. (1986), Price and advertising signals of product quality, *Journal of Political Economy*, 94, 796–821.

Miller, G. J. (1992), *Managerial Dilemmas: The Political Economy of Hierarchy*, Cambridge: Cambridge University Press.

Mintzberg, H. (1983), *Structure in Fives: Designing Effective Organizations*, Englewood Cliffs, NJ: Prentice-Hall.

Mizruchi, M. S. and Yoo, M. (2005), Interorganizational power and dependence. In J. A. C. Baum, ed., *Companion to Organizations*, Oxford: Blackwell, 599–620.

Möllering, G. (2006), *Trust: Reason, Routine, Reflexivity*, Oxford: Elsevier.

Monnier, M. (1862), *La Camorra. Notizie storiche raccolte e documentate*, Florence: Barbera.

Moore, J. F. (1993), Predator and prey: A new ecology of competition, *Harvard Business Review*, May/June, 75–86.

   (1996), *The Death of Competition: Leadership & Strategy in the Age of Business Ecosystems*, New York: HarperBusiness.

Moore, M. H. (1977), *Buy and Bust*, Lexington, MA: Lexington Books.

Moretti, M. (1994), *Brigate Rosse: Una storia italiana*, Milan: Anabasi.

Morgan, G. (1986), *Images of Organization*, Beverly Hills, CA: SAGE.

Morgan, W. P. (1960), *Triad Societies in Hong Kong*, Hong Kong: The Government Printer.

Moro, F. N. and Catino, M. (2016), La protezione mafiosa nei mercati legali. Un framework analitico ed evidenze empiriche in Lombardia, *Stato & Mercato*, 3, 311–52.

Moro, F. N., Petrella, A., and Sberna, S. (2016), The politics of mafia violence: Explaining variation in mafia killings in Southern Italy (1983–2008), *Terrorism and Political Violence*, 28, 90–113.

Morosini, P. (2009), *Il Gotha di Cosa Nostra*, Soveria Mannelli: Rubbettino.

Morselli, C. (2009), *Inside Criminal Networks*, Montreal: Springer.

Morselli, C., Giguère, C., and Petit, K. (2007), The efficiency/security trade-off in criminal networks, *Social Networks*, 29, 143–53.

Mosse, G. L. (1974), *The Nationalization of the Masses: Political Symbolism and Mass Movement in Germany from Napoleonic Wars through the Third Reich*, New York: Howard Fertig.

Murphy, P. (2016), *True Crime Japan: Thieves, Rascals, Killers and Dope Heads: True Stories from a Japanese Courtroom*, Singapore: Tuttle.

Mutti, A. (2006), Sfiducia, *Rassegna Italiana di Sociologia*, 2, 199–223.

   (2007), Reputazione, *Rassegna Italiana di Sociologia*, 4, 601–22.

Naìm, M. (2005), *Illicit: How Smugglers, Traffickers, and Copycats Are Hijacking the Global Economy*, Garden City, NY: Doubleday.

National Police Agency (NPA) (2017), *Heisei 29-nen kamihanki ni okeru soshiki hanzai no jōsei* (The situation of organized crime in the first half of 2017). Retrieved from www.npa.go.jp/sosikihanzai/kikakubunseki/sotaikikaku01/h28 .sotaijyousei.pdf (last accessed on April 5, 2018).

Natoli, L. (1971; 1st edn: 1909–10), *I Beati Paoli*, Palermo: Flaccovio Editore.

Nee, V. and Opper, S. (2012), *Capitalism from Below: Markets and Institutional Change in China*, Cambridge, MA: Harvard University Press.

Nee, V., Opper, S., and Holm, H. (2018), Learning to trust: From relational exchange to generalized trust. *Organization Science*, 29(5), 969–86.

Nelson, R. R. and Winter, S. G. (1982), *An Evolutionary Theory of Economic Change*, Cambridge, MA: Belknap Press of Harvard University Press.

Nohria, N. and Eccles, R. G., eds. (1992), *Networks and Organizations. Structure, Form and Action*, Boston: Harvard Business School Press.

Normann, R. (1977), *Management for Growth*, Chichester: John Wiley & Sons.

North, D. C. (1990), *Institution, Institutional Change and Economic Performance*, Cambridge: Cambridge University Press.

Obstfeld, M., Shambaugh, J. C., and Taylor, A. M. (2004), *The Trilemma in History: Tradeoffs among Exchange Rates, Monetary Policies, and Capital Mobility*, NBER working paper No. 10396, issued in March, www.nber.org/papers/w10396 (last accessed on April 5, 2018).

Ocasio, W. (2005), Organizational power and dependence. In J. A. C. Baum, ed., *Companion to Organizations*, Oxford: Blackwell, 363–85.

Okhuysen, G. A. and Bechky, B. A. (2009), Coordination in organizations: An integrative perspective, *The Academy of Management Annals*, 3(1), 463–502.

OSPA Stajano, C., ed. (2010), *Mafia: L'atto d'accusa dei giudici di Palermo*, Rome: Editori Riuniti (contains sections from OSPA 1985, *Ordinanza Sentenza della Corte di Assise di Palermo contro Abbate Giovanni+706*, Palermo, 08.11.1985, 40 vols.).

Ouchi, W. G. (1980), Markets, bureaucracies, and clans, *Administrative Science Quarterly*, 25(1), 129–41.

  (1981), *Theory Z*, Reading, MA: Addison-Wesley.

Padilla, F. (1992), *The Gang as an America Enterprise*, New Brunswick, NJ: Rutgers University Press.

Palazzolo, S. and Prestipino, M. (2007), *Il codice Provenzano*, Bari: Laterza.

Panebianco, A. (1982), *Modelli di partito*, Bologna: il Mulino.

Paoli, L. (2003), *Mafia Brotherhoods: Organized Crime, Italian Style*, Oxford: Oxford University Press.

  (2004), Italian organised crime: Mafia associations and criminal enterprises, *Global Crime*, 6(1), 19–31.

Paoli, L., Greenfield, V., and Reuter, P. (2009), *The World Heroin Market: Can Supply Be Cut?* New York: Oxford University Press.

Papachristos, A. V. (2009), Murder by structure: Dominance relations and the social structure of gang homicide, *American Journal of Sociology*, 115, 74–128.

Parker, G. R. (2004), *Self-Policing in Politics: The Political Economy of Reputational Controls on Politicians*, Princeton, NJ: Princeton University Press.

Parker, M. (2012), *Alternative Business: Outlaws, Crime and Culture*, London: Routledge.

  (2016), Secret societies: Intimations of organization, *Organization Studies*, 37(1), 99–113.

Parsons, T. (1956), Suggestions for a sociological approach to the theory of organizations, *Administrative Science Quarterly*, 1, 63–85.

Pentland, B. T. and Feldman, M. S. (2005), Organizational routines as a unit of analysis, *Industrial and Corporate Change*, 14(5), 793–815.

  (2008), Designing routines: On the folly of designing artifacts, while hoping for patterns of action, *Information and Organization*, 18(4), 235–50.

Perrone, N. (2009), *L'inventore del trasformismo. Liborio Romano, strumento di Cavour per la conquista di Napoli*, Soveria Mannelli: Rubbettino.

Perrow, C. (1986), *Complex Organizations: A Critical Essay*, New York: Random House.

(2007), *The Next Catastrophe: Reducing Our Vulnerabilities to Natural, Industrial, and Terrorist Disasters*, Princeton, NJ: Princeton University Press.

Petrillo, A. (2013), *Dentro le BR-PCC*, Rome: Laurus Robuffo.

Pezzino, P. (1990), *Una certa reciprocità di favori. Mafia e modernizzazione violenta nella Sicilia postunitaria*, Milan: Franco Angeli.

Pfeffer, J. (1981), *Power in Organizations*, Marshfield, MA: Pitman.

Pfeffer, J. and Salancik, G. R. (1978), *The External Control of Organizations: In a Resource Dependence Perspective*, New York: Harper & Row.

Pignatone, G. and Prestipino, M. (2013), Cosa Nostra e 'Ndrangheta: due modelli criminali. In E. Ciconte, F. Forgione and I. Sales, eds., *Atlante delle Mafie*, vol. II, Soveria Mannelli: Rubbettino, 207–49.

Pistone, J. (2004), *The Way of the Wiseguy*, Philadelphia: Running Press.

Pistone, J. and Brandt, C. (2007), *Donnie Brasco: Unfinished Business*, Philadelphia: Running Press.

Pistone, J. and Woodley, R. (1987), *Donnie Brasco: A True Story by FBI Agent Joseph D. Pistone*, New York: Signet.

Pitrè, G. (1889), *Usi, costumi, credenze e pregiudizi del popolo siciliano*, Palermo: Libreria Pedone Lauriel.

Pizzini-Gambetta, V. and Hamill, H. (2011), *Shady Advertising: Recruitment among Rebels and Mobsters*, 6th ECPR (European Consortium for Political Research) General Conference, Reyjkavik, August 25–27.

Podolny, J. and Page, K. L. (1998), Network forms of organization, *Annual Review of Sociology*, 24(1), 57–76.

Polanyi, M. (1962), *Personal Knowledge*, Chicago: The University of Chicago Press.

Porter, M. E. (1996), What is strategy, *Harvard Business Review*, November–December 61–78.

Posner, E. A. (2000), Law and social norms: The case of tax compliance, *Virginia Law Review*, 86(8), 1781–819.

Potter, D. V. (2000), Scale matters, *Across the Board*, July–August, 36–9.

Potter, G. W. (1994), *Criminal Organizations: Vice, Racketeering, and Politics in an American City*, Prospect Heights, IL: Waveland.

Powell, W. W. (1990), Neither market nor hierarchy: Network forms of organizations. In B. M. Staw and L. L. Cummings, eds., *Research in Organizational Behaviour*, Greenwich, CT: JAI Press, 295–336.

Powell, W. W., White, D. R., Koput, K. W., and Owen-Smith, J. (2005), Network dynamics and field evolution: The growth of interorganizational collaboration in the life sciences, *American Journal of Sociology*, 110, 1132–205.

Pugh, D. S., Hickson, D. J., Hinings, C. R., and Turner, C. (1968), Dimensions of organizational structure, *Administrative Science Quarterly*, 13, 65–105.

Putnam, R. D. (1993), *Making Democracy Work: Civic Traditions in Modern Italy*, Princeton, NJ: Princeton University Press.

Raab, S. (2016), *Five Families: The Rise, Decline and Resurgence of America's Most Powerful Mafia Empires*, New York: St. Martin's Press.

Rankin, A. (2012a), 21st-Century Yakuza: Recent trends in organized crime in Japan, Part 1, *The Asia-Pacific Journal*, 10, (7)2, February 13, http://apjjf.org/2012/10/7/Andrew-Rankin/3688/article.html (last accessed on April 5, 2018).

(2012b), Recent Trends in Organized Crime in Japan: Yakuza vs. the Police, & Foreign Crime Gangs, Part 2, *The Asia-Pacific Journal*, 10,(7)1, February 20, http://apjjf.org/2012/10/7/Andrew-Rankin/3692/article.html (last accessed on April 5, 2018).

Reavill, G. (2013), *Mafia Summit*, New York: St. Martin's Press.

Reed, M. I. (2001), Organization, trust and control: A realist analysis, *Organization Studies*, 22(2), 201–28.

Reilly, E. F. Jr. (2014), Criminalizing Yakuza membership: A comparative study of the anti-Boryokudan law, *Washington University Global Studies Law Review*, 13(4), 801–29.

Reno, W. (1995), *Corruption and State Politics in Sierra Leone*, Cambridge: Cambridge University Press.

Repetto, T. (2004), *American Mafia: A History of Its Rise to Power*, New York: Holt.

Reuter, P. (1983), *Disorganized Crime: The Economics of the Visible Hand*, Cambridge, MA: MIT Press.

(1985a), *The Organization of Illegal Markets: An Economic Analysis*, Washington, DC: U.S. Department of Justice, National Institute of Justice, Reprints of the collection of the University of Michigan Library.

(1985b), Racketeers as cartel organizers. In H. E. Alexander and G. E. Caiden, eds., *The Politics and Economics of Organized Crime*. Lexington, MA: D. C. Heath, 49–65.

(1987), *Racketeering in Legitimate Industries: A Study in the Economics of Intimidation*, Santa Monica, CA: RAND Corporation.

(1995), The decline of the American mafia, *The Public Interest*, Summer, 89–99.

(2009), Systemic violence in drug markets, *Crime, Law and Social Change*, 52(3), 275–89.

(2014), Drug markets and organized crime. In L. Paoli, ed., *The Oxford Handbook of Organized Crime*. Oxford: Oxford University Press, 359–80.

Ries, J., ed. (1986), *Les rites d'initiation*, Louvain-la-Neuve: Centre d'Histoire des Religions.

Ritti, R. and Funkhouser, G. R. (1987), *The Ropes to Skip and the Ropes to Know*, New York: John Wiley & Sons.

Roberts, B., Hanson, G., Cornwell, D., and Borger, S. (2010), *An Analysis of Migrant Smuggling Costs along the Southwest Border*, Washington DC: U.S. Department of Homeland Security, Office of Immigration Statistics, working paper.

Roberts, P. W. and Dowling, G. R. (2002), Corporate reputation and sustained superior financial performance, *Strategic Management Journal*, 23, 1077–93.

Rodrik, D. (2011), *The Globalization Paradox*, New York: W. W. Norton.

Roethlisberger, F. J. and Dickson, W. J. (1939), *Management and the Worker*, Cambridge, MA: Harvard University Press.

Rohen, T. P. (1973), Spiritual education in a Japanese bank, *American Anthropologist*, 75, 1542–62.

Romano, L. (1873, 2nd edn: 1992), *Memorie politiche*, Milan: Giuffré.

Romano, S. (1918, 2nd edn: 1951), *L'ordinamento giuridico*, Florence: Sansoni.

Ron, N., Lipshitz, R., and Popper, M. (2006), How organizations learn: Post-flight reviews in an F-16 Fighter squadron, *Organization Studies*, 27(8), 1069–89.

Roosevelt, T. R. (1991), *Beyond Race and Gender: Unleashing the Power of Your Total Work Force by Managing Diversity*, New York: American Management Association.

Rousseau, D. M., Sitkin, S. B., Burt, R. S., and Camerer, C. (1998), Special topic forum on trust in and between organizations, *Academy of Management Review*, 23(3), 393–404.

Sales, I. (1988), *La Camorra, le Camorre*, Rome: Editori Riuniti.

Sanchez-Jankowski, M. (1991), *Islands in the Street: Gangs and American Urban Society*, Berkeley: University of California Press.

Santino, U. (2017), *La mafia dimenticata. La criminalità organizzata in Sicilia dall'Unità d'Italia ai primi del Novecento. Le inchieste, i processi. Un documento storico*, Milano: Melampo.

Santoro, M., ed. (2015), *Riconoscere le mafie. Cosa sono, come funzionano, come si muovono*, Bologna: il Mulino.

Savona, E. U. (2012), Italian mafias' asymmetries. In D. Siegel and H. van de Bunt, eds., *Traditional Organized Crime in the Modern World*. New York: Springer, 3–25.

Savona, E. U., Calderoni, F., Campedelli, G. M., Comunale, T., Ferrarini, M., and Meneghini, C. (2018), *Recruitment into Mafias: Criminal Careers of Mafia Members and Mafia Bosses*, Transcrime, www.projectproton.eu (last accessed on April 5, 2018).

Sberna, S. (2014), *Conceptualizing Organized Crime: A Transaction Cost Approach to Make-or-Buy Decisions and Corruption*, European University Institute, working paper, Deliverable WP1, ANTICORRP Project, European Commission, FP7 Grant n. 290529.

Scanni, M. and Oliva, R. H. (2006), *'O Sistema*, Milan: Rizzoli.

Scharpf, F. W. (1997), *Games Real Actors Play: Actor-Centered Institutionalism in Policy Research*, Boulder, CO: Westview Press.

Schelling, T. (1966), *Arms and Influence*, New Haven, CT: Yale University Press.
   (1967), *Appendix D – Economic Analysis and Organized Crime, Task Force Report on Organized Crime*, Washington, DC: GPO, President's Commission on Crime and the Administration of Justice.
   (1971), What is the business of organized crime? *Journal of Public Law*, 20 (1), 71–84.

Schneider, J. C. and Schneider, P. T. (1976), *Culture and Political Economy in Western Sicily*, New York: Academy Press.

Schulz, M. (2001), The uncertain relevance of newness: Organizational learning and knowledge flows, *Academy of Management Journal*, 44(4), 661–82.

Schulz, M. and Beck, N. (2002), *Organizational Rules and Rule Histories. A Review of Current Research on Rule-Based Models of Organizational Learning*, paper presented at the Academy of Management Meeting, Denver, August.

Sciarrone, R. (2009), *Mafie vecchie, mafie nuove: Radicamento ed espansione*, Rome: Donzelli.

Sciarrone, R. (Fondazione Res), ed., (2014), *Mafie del Nord. Strategie criminali e contesti locali*, Rome: Donzelli.

Scott, C. (2013), *Anonymous Agencies, Backstreet Businesses, and Covert Collectives: Rethinking Organizations in the 21st Century*, Stanford, CA: Stanford University Press.

Scott, R. W. and Davis, G. F. (2007), *Organization and Organizing: Rational, Natural, and Open System Perspectives*, Upper Saddle River, NJ: Pearson Education.

Selznick, P. (1948), Foundations of the theory of organization, *American Sociological Review*, 13(1), 25–35.

Sergi, A. (2016), A qualitative reading of the ecological (dis)organisation of criminal associations: The case of the Famiglia Basilischi in Italy, *Trends in Organized Crime*, 19(2), 149–74.

Sergi, A. and Lavorgna, A. (2016), *'Ndrangheta: The Glocal Dimensions of the Most Powerful Italian Mafia*, London: Palgrave Macmillan.

Serio, J. D. (2008), *Investigating Russian Mafia*, Durham, NC: Carolina Academic Press.

Serio, J. D. and Razinkin, V. (1995), Thieves professing the Code: The traditional role of *Vory v Zakone* in Russia's criminal world and adaptations to a new social reality, *Journal of Low Intensity Conflict and Law Enforcement*, 4(1), 72–88.

Shapiro, J. N. (2013), *The Terrorist's Dilemma: Managing Violent Covert Organizations*, Princeton, NJ: Princeton University Press.

Shelley, L. (2004), Contemporary Russian organised crime: Embedded in Russian society. In C. Fijnaut and L. Paoli, eds., *Organised Crime in Europe: Patterns and Policies in the European Union and Beyond*. Dordrecht: Springer, 563–84.

(2016), Crime and Corruption. In S. K. Wegren, ed., *Putin's Russia: Past Imperfect, Future Uncertain*. Lanham, MD: Rowman & Littlefield, 193–213.

Shortland, A. and Varese, F. (2014), The protector's choice: An application of protection theory to Somali piracy, *British Journal of Criminology*, 54, 741–64.

Siegel, D. (2012), *Vory v Zakone*: Russian organized crime. In D. Siegel and H. van de Bunt, eds., *Traditional Organized Crime in the Modern World: Responses to Socioeconomic Change*, New York: Springer, 27–47.

Siehl, C. and Martin, J. (1990), Organizational culture: A key to financial performance? In B. Schneider, ed., *Organizational Climate and Culture*, San Francisco: Jossey-Bass, 228–63.

Simmel, G. (1906), The sociology of secrecy and of secret societies, *American Journal of Sociology*, 11(4), 441–98.

Simon, H. A. (1947), *Administrative Behavior*, New York: MacMillan.

(1957), *Models of Man: Social and Rational*, New York: John Wiley & Sons.

Simon, H. A., Smithburg, D. W., and Thompson, V. A. (1950), *Public Administration*, New York: Knopf.

Sinn, E. (1989), *Power and Charity: The Early History of the Tung Wah Hospital*, Hong Kong: Oxford University Press.

Sinno, A. H. (2010), *Organizations at War in Afghanistan and Beyond*, Ithaca, NY: Cornell University Press.

Sjöstrand, S. E. (1985), *Samhallsorganisation: En ansats till en institutionell ekonomisk mikroteori*, Lund, Sweden: Doxa.

Skarbek, D. B. (2011), Governance and prison gangs, *American Political Science Review*, 105(4), 702–16.

    (2012), Prison gangs, norms, and organizations, *Journal of Economic Behavior & Organization*, 82(1): 96–109.

    (2014), *The Social Order of the Underworld: How Prison Gangs Govern the American Penal System*, New York: Oxford University Press.

Skarbek, D. B. and Wang, P. (2015), Criminal rituals, *Global Crime*, 16(4), 288–305.

Slade, G. (2013), *Reorganizing Crime: Mafia and Anti-Mafia in Post-Soviet Georgia*, Oxford: Oxford University Press.

Smith, D. C. Jr. (1975), *The Mafia Mystique*, New York: Basic Books.

Smith, D. C. Jr. (1980), Paragons, pariahs, and pirates: A spectrum-based theory of enterprise, *Crime & Delinquency*, 26(3), 358–86.

    (1994), Illicit enterprise: An organized crime paradigm for the Nineties. In R. J. Kelly, K.-L. Chin and R. Schatzberg, eds., *Handbook of Organized Crime in the United States*, Westport, CT: Greenwood, 121–50.

Smith, E. L. and Cooper, A. (2013), *Homicide in the U.S. Known to Law Enforcement, 2011*, US Department of Justice, Office of Justice Programs, Bureau of Justice Statistics (NCJ, 243035), www.bjs.gov/content/pub/pdf/hus11.pdf (last accessed on April 5, 2018).

Soudijn, M. and Reuter, P. (2013), Managing potential conflict in illegal markets: An exploratory study of cocaine smuggling in the Netherlands. In F. Trautmann, B. Kilmer, P. Turnbull, eds., *Further Insights into Aspects of the Illicit EU Drugs Market*, Luxembourg: Publications Office of the European Union, Part II, Report 2, 345–59.

Southerland, M. D. and Potter, G. W. (1993), Applying organization theory to organized crime, *Journal of Contemporary Criminal Justice*, 9, 251–67.

Spence, A. M. (1974), *Market Signalling: Informational Transfer in Hiring and Related Screening Processes*, Cambridge, MA: Harvard University Press.

Squires, C. (2002), Rethinking the black public sphere: An alternative vocabulary for multiple spheres, *Communication Theory*, 12(4), 446–68.

Stark, H. (1981), *The Yakuza: Japanese Crime Incorporated*, Ph.D. dissertation, University of Michigan, Department of Anthropology.

Stephenson, S. (2015), *Gangs of Russia*, Ithaca, NY: Cornell University Press.

Stohl, C. and Stohl, M. (2011), Secret agencies: The communicative constitution of a clandestine organization, *Organization Studies*, 32(9), 1197–2015.

Suchman, M. C. (1995), Managing legitimacy: Strategic and institutional approaches, *Academy of Management Review*, 20, 571–610.

Sukharenko, A. (2016), Русская мафия не канула в Лету (*Russian mafia is not sunk into oblivion*), Московская правда (*Moskovskaya Pravda*), 25.03.2016, http://a.mospravda.ru/crime/article/russkaya_mafiya_ne_kanula_v_letu/ (last accessed on April 5, 2018).

Superchi, E. (2018), *Criminal Leaders' Behaviour: Exploring Criminal Capital of 'Ndrangheta Bosses Involved in Different Activities*, Ph.D. dissertation, Università Cattolica del Sacro Cuore (Catholic University of Milan), XXX ciclo, a.a. 2016/17, Milano, http://hdl.handle.net/10280/38238.

Sutton, J. and Dobbin, F. (1996), The two faces of governance: Responses to legal uncertainty in American firms, 1955–1985, *American Sociological Review*, 61(5), 794–811.

Sutton, J., Dobbin, F., Meyer, J., and Scott, W. R. (1994), The legalization of the workplace, *American Journal of Sociology*, 99(1), 944–71.

Tadelis, S. and Williamson, O. E. (2013), Transaction cost economics. In R. Gibbons and J. Roberts, eds., *The Handbook of Organizational Economics*, Princeton, NJ: Princeton University Press, 159–89.

Tat-wing, P. Y. (2011), Triads. *UNAFEI (Asia and Far East Institute for the Prevention of Crime and the Treatment of Offenders)*, 116th International Training Course, Resource material series 58, 27–38.

Taylor, J. R. and Robichaud, D. (2004), Finding the organization in the communication, discourse as action and sensemaking, *Organization*, 11(3), 395–413.

Ter Haar, B. J. (1998), *The Ritual and Mythology of the Chinese Triads: Creating an Identity*, Leiden: E. J. Brill.

Thomas, D. and Ely, R. (1996), Making differences matter: A new paradigm for managing diversity, *Harvard Business Review*, 5, 79–90.

Thompson, J. D. (1967), *Organizations in Action*, New York: McGraw-Hill.

Thompson, V. A. (1961), Hierarchy, specialization, and organizational conflict, *Administrative Science Quarterly*, 5(4), 485–521.

Tolbert, P. S. and Hall, H. R. (2009), *Organizations: Structures, Processes, and Outcomes*, 10th edn, Upper Saddle River, NJ: Pearson Prentice-Hall.

Touraine, A. (1973), *La production de la société*, Paris: Éditions du Seuil.

Transcrime (2013), *Progetto PON Sicurezza 2007–2013: Gli investimenti delle mafie*, Rapporto Linea 1, Milano: Ministero dell'Interno, www.transcrime.it/pubblicazioni/progetto-pon-sicurezza-2007-2013/ (last accessed on April 5, 2018).

Trujillo, H. R. and Jackson, B. A. (2006), Organizational learning and terrorist groups. In J. Forest, ed., *Teaching Terror: Strategic and Tactical Learning in the Terrorist World*. Lanham, MD: Rowman & Littlefield, 52–68.

Trumper, J. B., Nicaso, A., Maddalon, M., and Gratteri, N. (2014), *Malelingue. Vecchi e nuovi codici delle mafie*, Cosenza: Luigi Pellegrini Editore.

Truzzolillo, F. (2013), Criminale e Gran Criminale. La struttura unitaria e verticistica della 'ndrangheta delle origini, *Meridiana*, 77(2), 203–32.

Ullmann-Margalit, E. (1977), *The Emergence of Norms*, Oxford: Oxford University Press.

UNODC–United Nations Office on Drugs and Crime (2002), *Results of a Pilot Survey of Forty Selected Organized Criminal Groups in Sixteen Countries*, Wien: United Nations Office on Drugs and Crime.

Uzzi, B. (1997), Social structure and competition in interfirm networks: The paradox of embeddedness, *Administrative Science Quarterly*, 42, 35–67.

van Doorn, J. A. (1966), Conflict in formal organization. In A. V. S. de Reuck and J. Knight, eds., *Conflict in Society*, Boston: Little, Brown, 111–33.

van de Ven, A. H., Delbecq, A. L., and Koenig, R. (1976), Determinants of coordination modes within organizations, *American Sociological Review*, 41(2), 322–38.

van de Ven, A. H. and Ferry, D. L. (1980), *Measuring and Assessing Organizations*, New York: John Wiley & Sons.

van Gennep, A. (1960, 1st edn: 1909), *The Rites of Passage*, Chicago: University of Chicago Press.

Varese, F. (2001), *The Russian Mafia*, Oxford: Oxford University Press.

(2006), The secret history of Japanese cinema: The Yakuza movies, *Global Crime*, 7(1), 105–24.

(2010), General introduction. What is organized crime? In F. Varese, ed., *Organized Crime*, London and New York: Routledge, 1–33.

(2011), *Mafias on the Move: How Organized Crime Conquers New Territories*, Princeton, NJ: Princeton University Press.

(2014), Protection and extortion. In L. Paoli, ed., *The Oxford Handbook of Organized Crime*, Oxford: Oxford University Press, 343–58.

(2017), *Mafia Life*, London: Profile Books.

Varon, J. P. (2004), *Bringing the War Home: The Weather Underground, the Red Army Faction, and Revolutionary Violence in the Sixties and Seventies*, Berkeley, CA: University of California Press.

Vaughan, D. (1996), *The Challenger Launch Decision: Risky Technology, Culture, and Deviance at NASA*, Chicago: University of Chicago Press.

Volkov, V. (2002), *Violent Entrepreneurs: The Use of the Force in the Making of Russian Capitalism*, Ithaca, NY: Cornell University Press.

von Hayek, F. A. (1973), *Law, Legislation and Liberty*. Vol. I: *Rules and Order*, Chicago: The University of Chicago Press.

von Lampe, K. (2009), Human capital and social capital in criminal networks: Introduction to the special issue on the 7th Blankensee Colloquium, *Trends in Organized Crime*, 12(2), 93–100.

(2016), *Organized Crime: Analyzing Illegal Activities, Criminal Structures, and Extra-Legal Governance*, London: SAGE.

von Lampe, K. and Johansen, P. O. (2004), Organized crime and trust: On the conceptualization and empirical relevance of trust in the context of criminal networks, *Global Crime*, 6(2), 159–84.

Wainwright, T. (2016), *Narco-Nomics: How to Run a Drug Cartel*, New York: Public Affairs.

Wasen, K. (2015), *Innovation Management in Robot Society*, London: Routledge, Routledge Studies in Technology, Work and Organizations.

Weber, M. (1904), Die Protestantische Ethik und der Geist des Kapitalismus, *Archiv fur Sozialwissenschaft und Sozialpolitik*, 20–21.

(1922), *Wirtschaft und Gesellschaft*, Tübingen: Mohr.

(1993, 1st edn: 1922), *The Sociology of Religion*, Boston: Beacon Press.

Weichbrodt, J. and Grote, G. (2010), *Rules and Routines in Organizations: A Review and Extension*, paper presented at the Fourth International Conference in Organizational Routines, Nice, June 11–12.

Weick, K. E. (1995), *Sensemaking in Organizations*, Thousands Oaks, CA: Sage.

Weick, K. E. and Sutcliffe, K. M. (2007), *Managing the Unexpected: Assuring High Performance in an Age of Complexity*, San Francisco: Jossey-Bass.

Weiner, M. (2013), *The Rule of the Clan*, New York: Farrar, Straus & Giroux.

Weinstein, J. M. (2005), Resources and the information problem in rebel recruitment, *Journal of Conflict Resolution*, 49(4), 598–624.

(2007), *Inside Rebellion: The Politics of Insurgent Violence*, Cambridge, MA: Cambridge University Press.

Wildes, H. (1948), Underground Politics in Post-War Japan, *The American Political Science Review*, 42(6), 1149–62.

Williamson, O. E. (1970), *Corporate Control and Business Behavior: Managerial Objectives in a Theory of the Firm*, Englewood Cliffs, NJ: Prentice-Hall.

(1975), *Markets and Hierarchies: Analysis and Antitrust Implications*, New York: Free Press.

(1985), *The Economic Institutions of Capitalism*, New York: Free Press.

(1996), *The Mechanisms of Governance*, New York: Oxford University Press.

(2007), *Transaction Cost Economics: An Introduction*, Discussion paper 2007–3, www.economics-ejournal.org/economics/discussionpapers.

Willmott, H. (1993), Strength is ignorance, slavery is freedom: Managing culture in modern organizations, *Journal of Management Studies*, 30(4), 515–52.

Wilson, J. Q. (1989), *Bureaucracy: What Government Agencies Do and Why They Do It*, New York: Basic Books.

Winter, S. G. (1987), Knowledge and competence as strategic assets. In D. J. Teece, ed., *The Competitive Challenge: Strategies for Industrial Innovation and Renewal*, Cambridge, MA: Ballinger, 159–84.

Wong, P. T. P. and Weiner, B. (1981), When people ask "why." Questions, and the heuristics of attributional search, *Journal of Personality and Social Psychology*, 40(4), 650–63.

Woodward, J. (1958), *Management and Technology*, London: H.M. Stationery Off.

(1965), *Industrial Organization: Theory and Practice*, Oxford: Oxford University Press.

Xia, M. (2008), Organizational formations of organised crime in China: Perspectives from the state, markets, and networks, *Journal of Contemporary China*, 17(54), 1–23.

Yablonsky, L. (1962), *The Violent Gang*, Baltimore: Penguin Books.

Zagari, A. (1992), *Ammazzare stanca, Autobiografia di uno 'ndranghetista pentito*, Cosenza: Edizioni Periferia.

Zahavi, A. and Zahavi, A. (1997), *The Handicap Principle: A Missing Piece of Darwin's Puzzle*, Oxford: Oxford University Press.

Zaheer, A. and Soda, G. (2009), Network evolution: The origins of structural holes, *Administrative Science Quarterly*, 54, 1–31.

Zakay, D., Ellis, E., and Shevalsky, M. (1998), *Do Managers Learn from Experience? The Negative Outcome Bias*, Tel Aviv: Tel Aviv University.

Zand, D. E. (1972), Trust and managerial problem solving, *Administrative Science Quarterly*, 17(2).

Zeigler, H. A. (1970), *Sam the Plumber*, New York: Signet.

Zerubavel, E. (2006), *The Elephant in the Room: Silence and Denial in Everyday Life, Zerubavel*. Oxford: Oxford University Press.

Zhou, X. (1993), The dynamics of organizational rules, *American Journal of Sociology*, 98,(5), 1134–66.

Zuckerman, E. W. (2010), Speaking with One Voice: A "Stanford School" Approach to Organizational Hierarchy, in *Research in the Sociology of Organizations*, 28 (Stanford's Organization Theory Renaissance, 1970–2000), 289–307.

Index